1

My Love Mix-Up!

Art by **Aruko**
Story by **Wataru Hinekure**

Contents

THIS IS A SLIGHTLY
SILLY LOVE STORY
ABOUT SOME
GOOD, EAGER
HIGH SCHOOL KIDS.

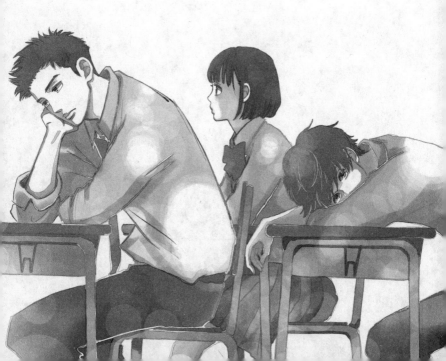

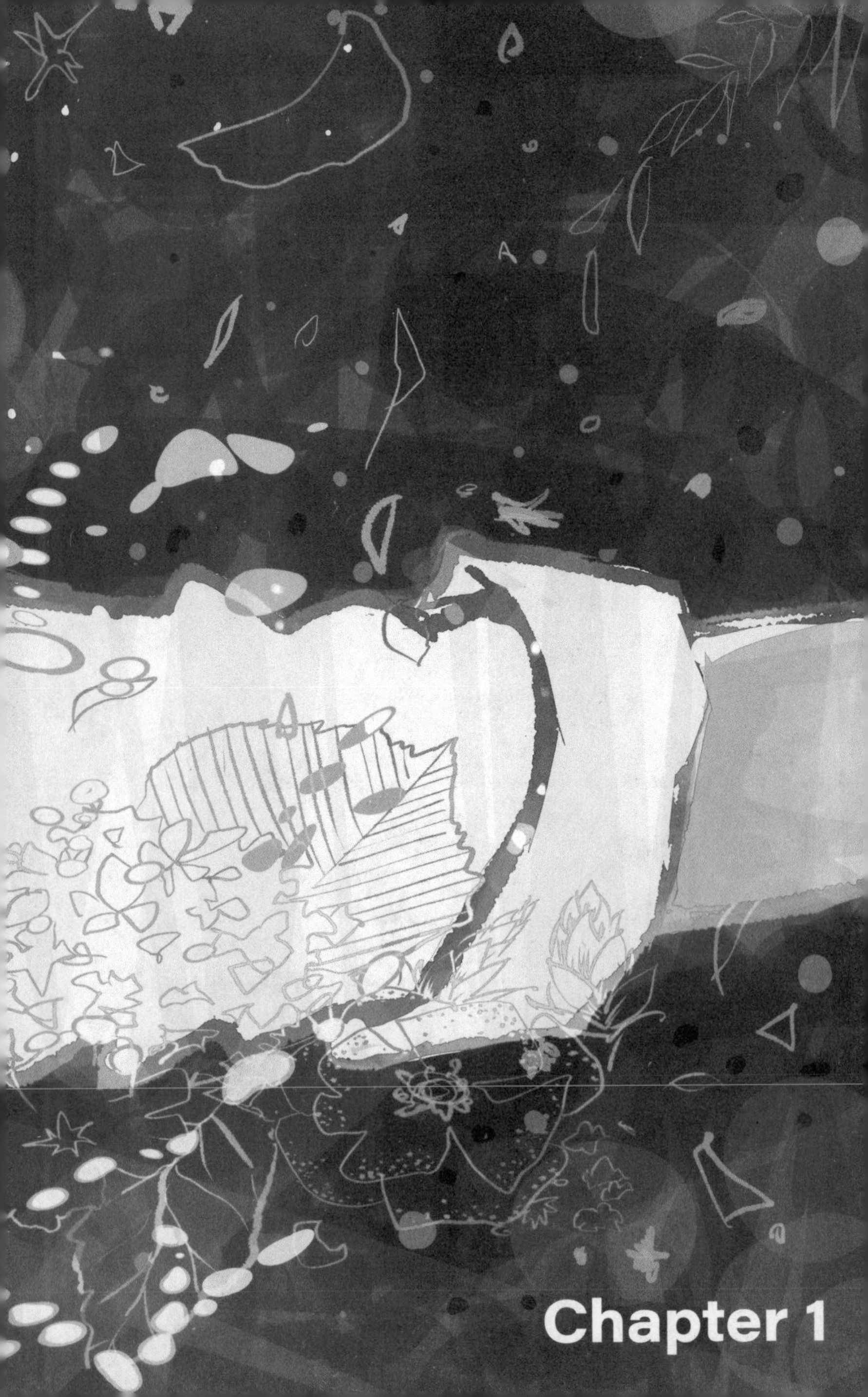

Chapter 1

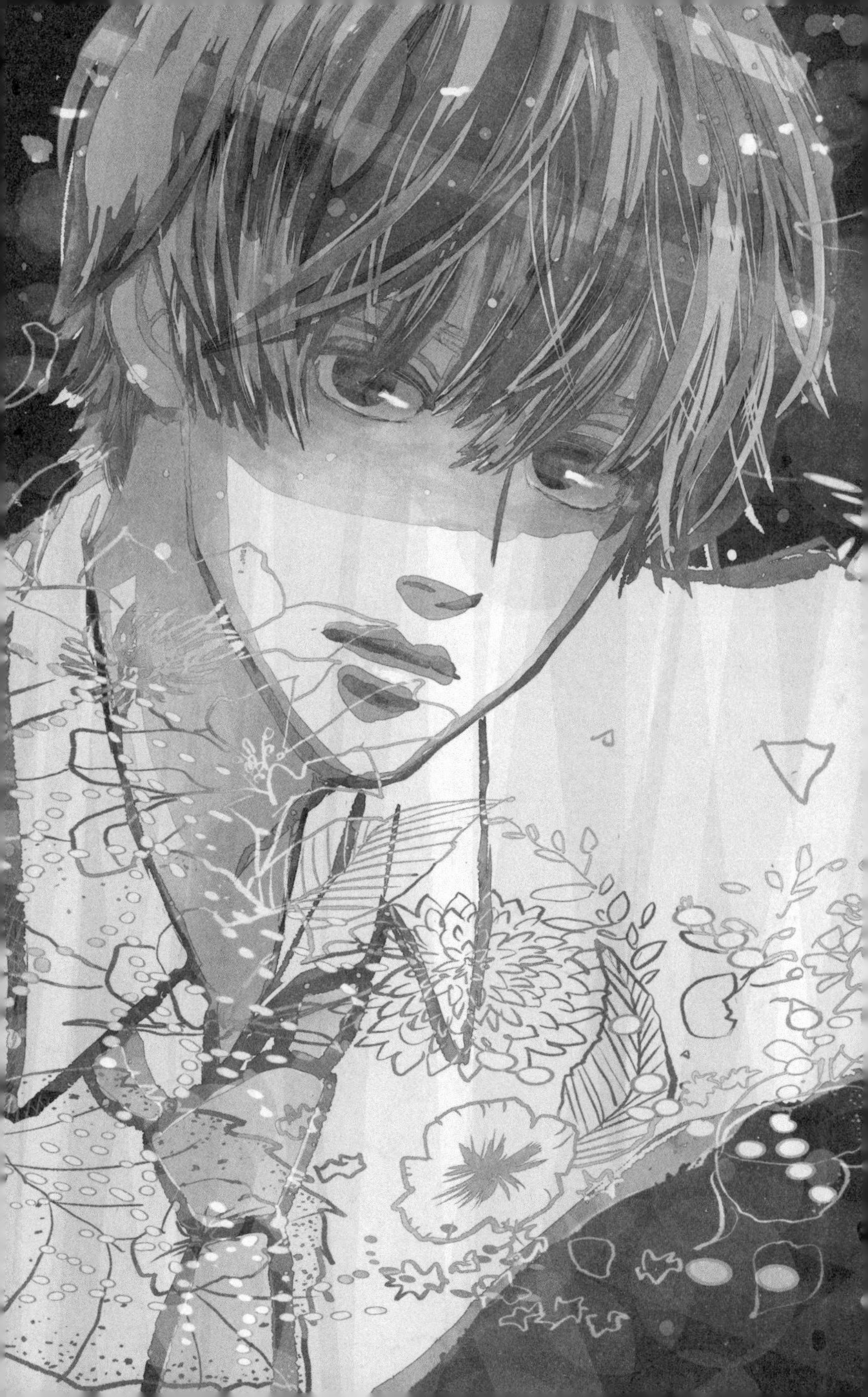

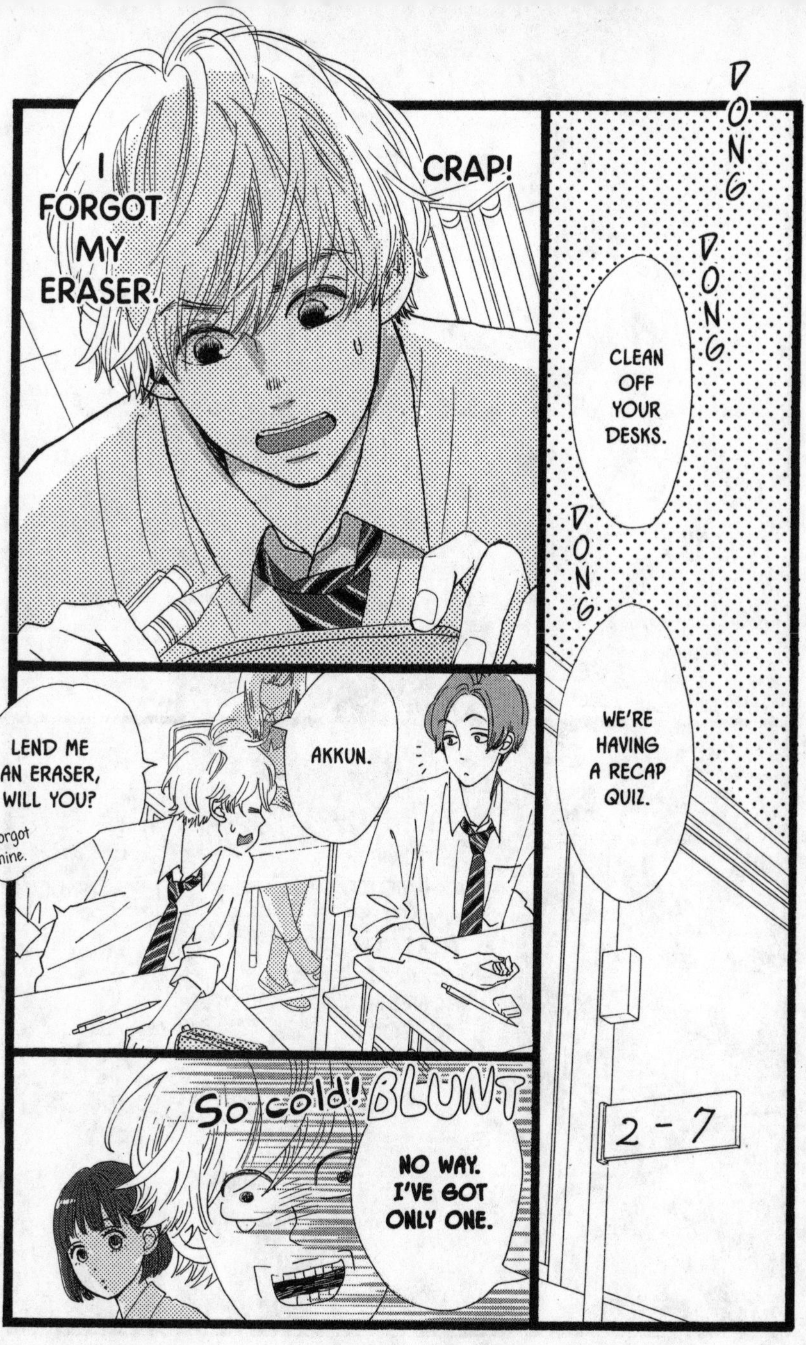
DONG
DONG DONG
CLEAN OFF YOUR DESKS.
DONG
WE'RE HAVING A RECAP QUIZ.
2-7
CRAP!
I FORGOT MY ERASER.
AKKUN.
LEND ME AN ERASER, WILL YOU?
I forgot mine.
NO WAY. I'VE GOT ONLY ONE.
BLUNT
So cold!

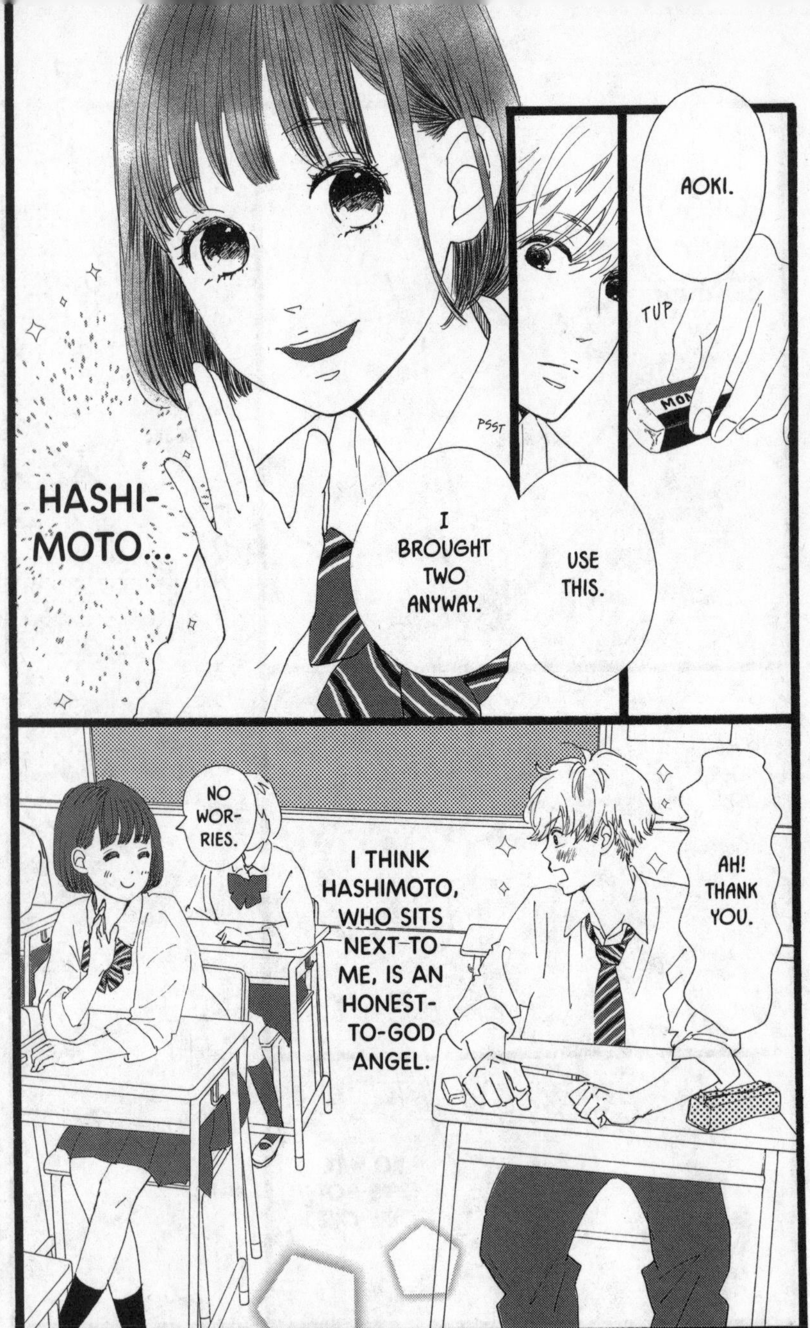
AOKI.
TUP
PSST
USE THIS.
I BROUGHT TWO ANYWAY.
HASHI-MOTO...
AH! THANK YOU.
I THINK HASHIMOTO, WHO SITS NEXT TO ME, IS AN HONEST-TO-GOD ANGEL.
NO WORRIES.

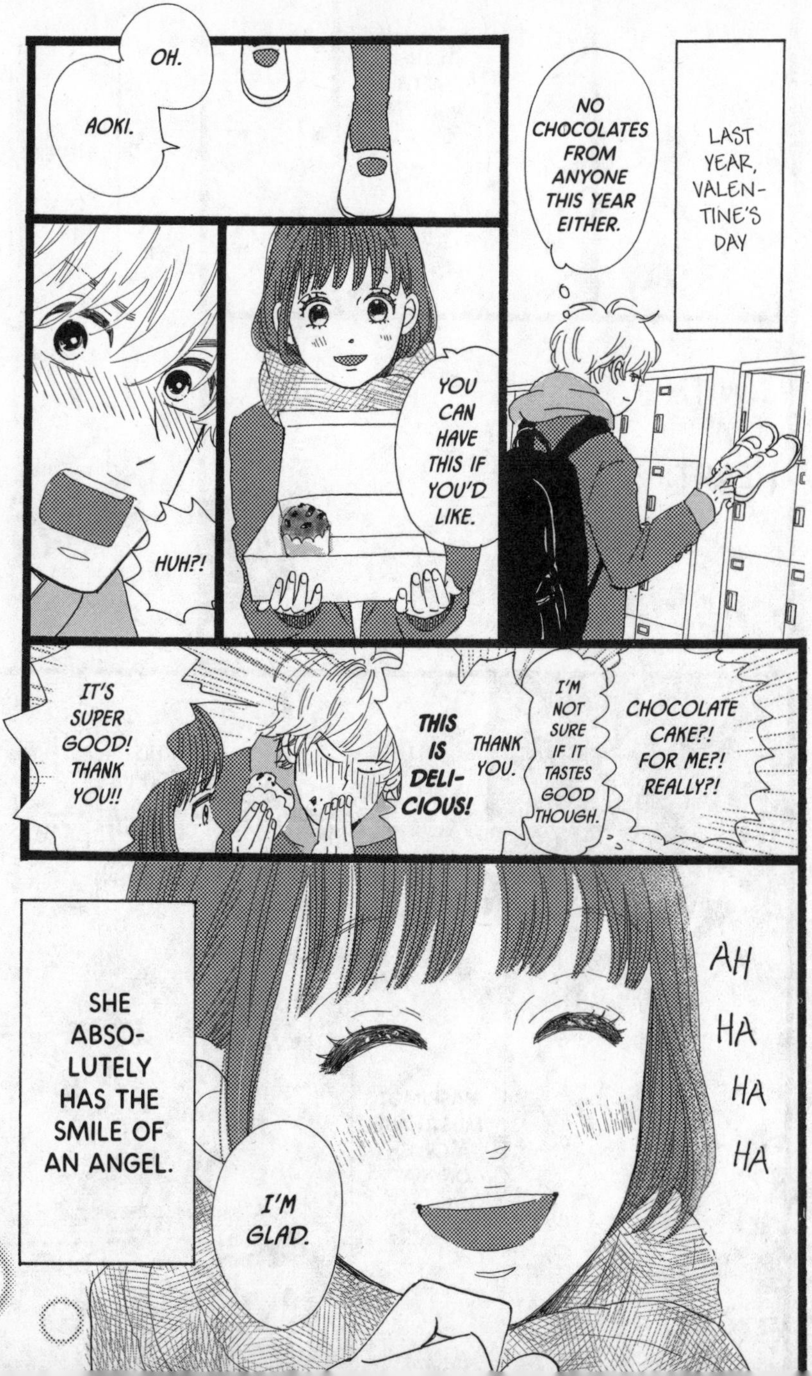
LAST YEAR, VALEN-TINE'S DAY
NO CHOCOLATES FROM ANYONE THIS YEAR EITHER.
OH.
AOKI.
YOU CAN HAVE THIS IF YOU'D LIKE.
HUH?!
CHOCOLATE CAKE?! FOR ME?! REALLY?!
I'M NOT SURE IF IT TASTES GOOD THOUGH.
THANK YOU.
THIS IS DELI-CIOUS!
IT'S SUPER GOOD! THANK YOU!!
AH HA HA HA
I'M GLAD.
SHE ABSO-LUTELY HAS THE SMILE OF AN ANGEL.

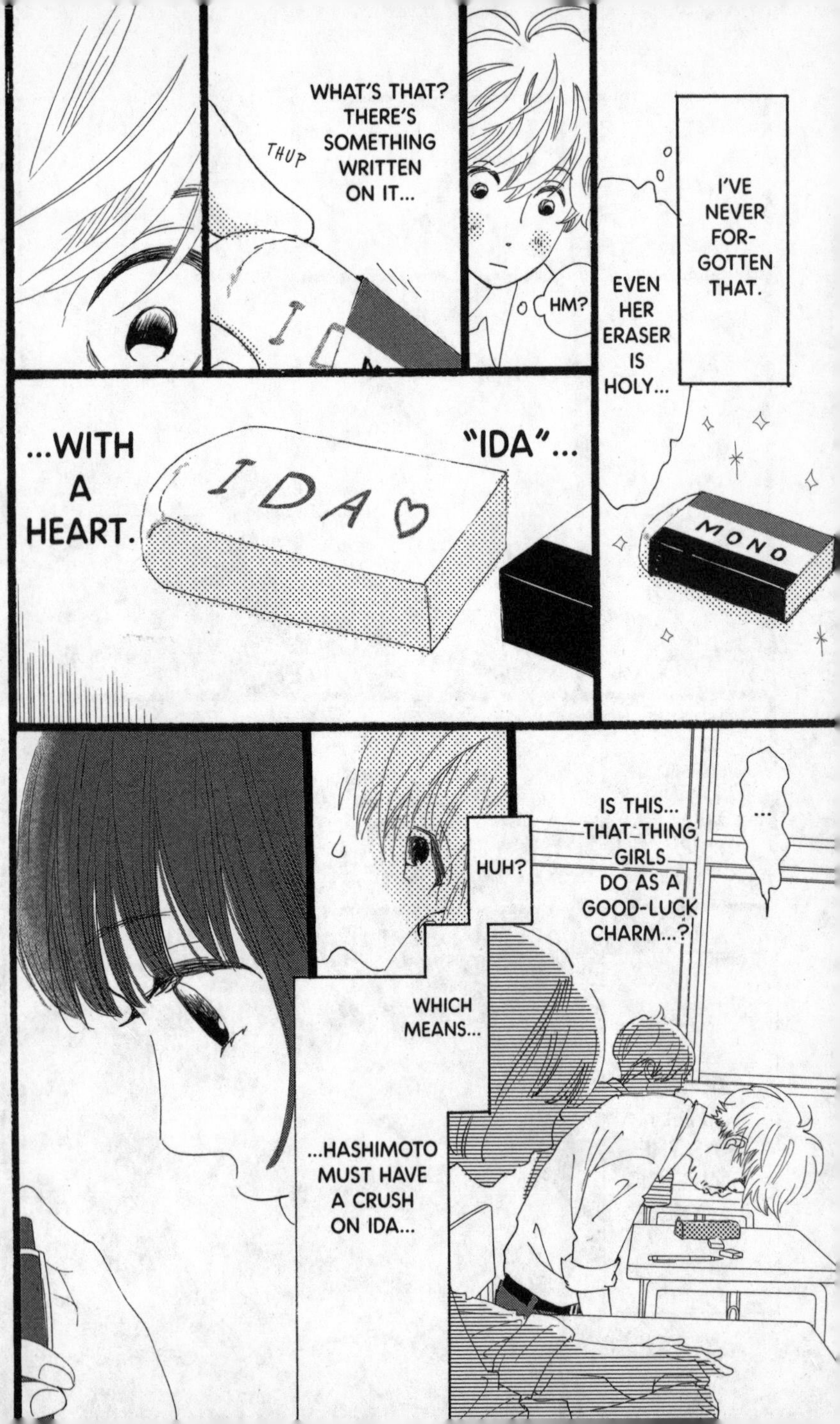
I'VE NEVER FOR- GOTTEN THAT.
EVEN HER ERASER IS HOLY...
MONO
HM?
WHAT'S THAT? THERE'S SOMETHING WRITTEN ON IT...
THUP
"IDA"...
...WITH A HEART.
IDA
...
IS THIS... THAT THING GIRLS DO AS A GOOD-LUCK CHARM...?
HUH?
WHICH MEANS...
...HASHIMOTO MUST HAVE A CRUSH ON IDA...

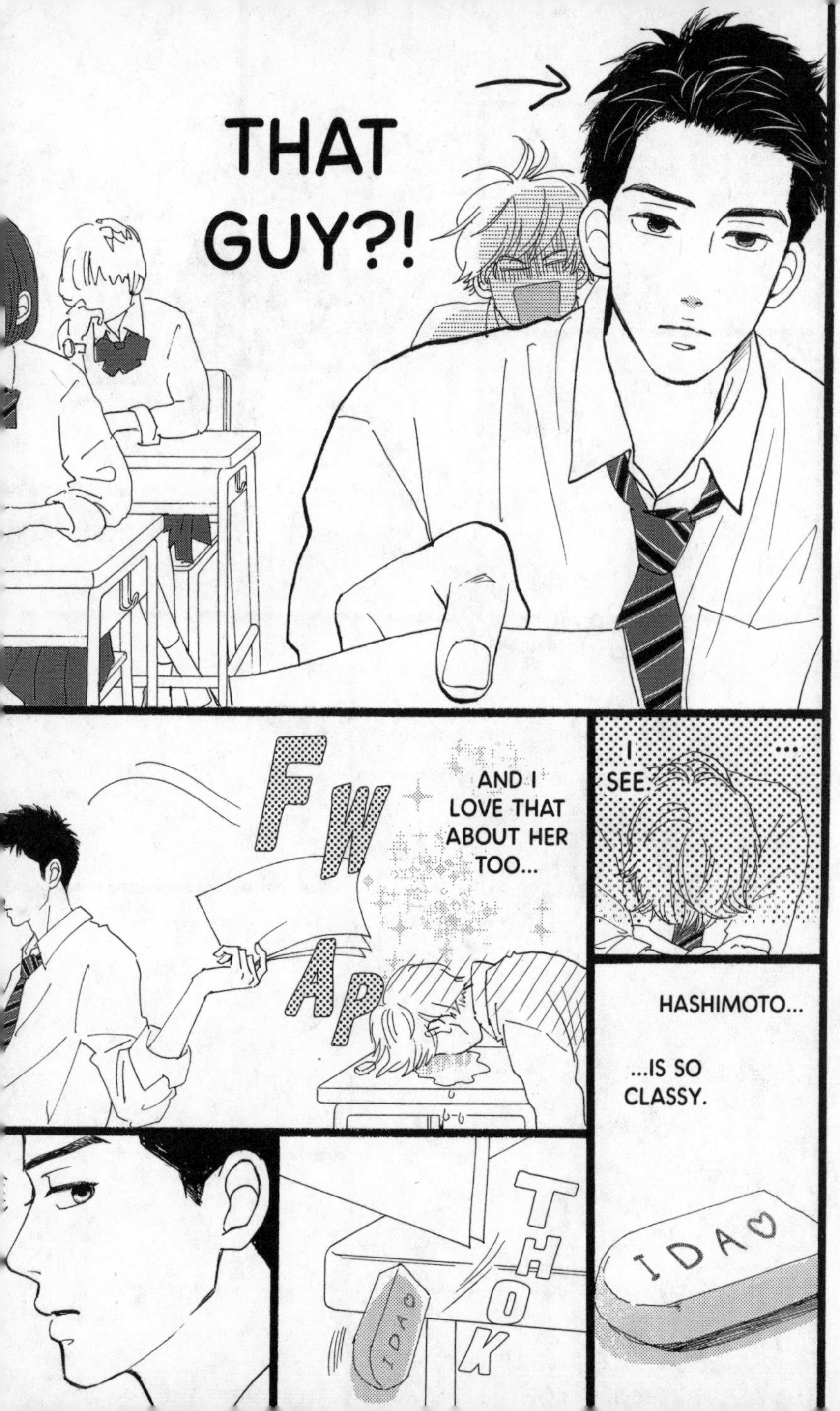
THAT GUY?!
I SEE.
...
HASHIMOTO...
...IS SO CLASSY.
AND I LOVE THAT ABOUT HER TOO...
FWAP
IDA♡
THOK
IDA

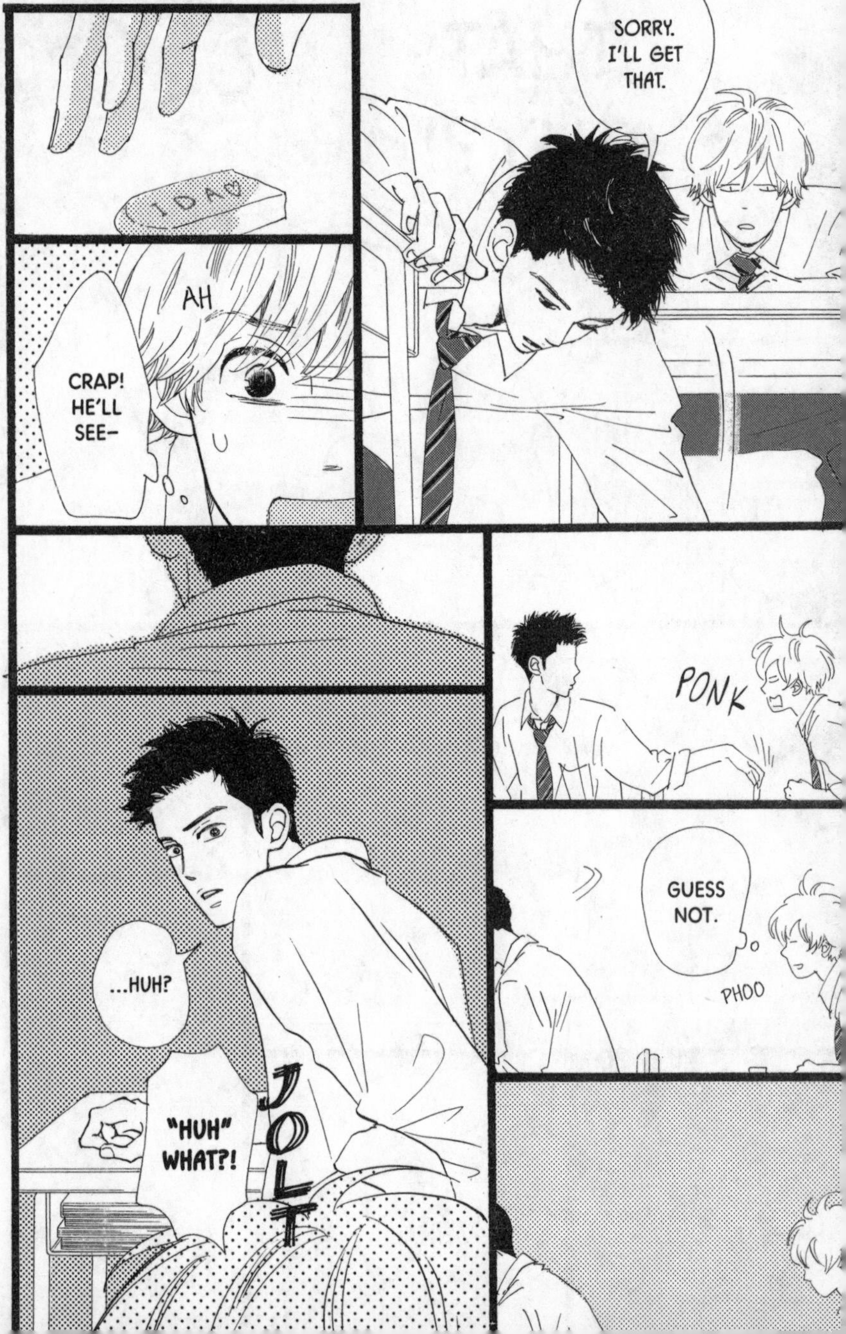
SORRY. I'LL GET THAT.
AH
CRAP! HE'LL SEE-
PONK
GUESS NOT.
PHOO
...HUH?
"HUH" WHAT?!
JOLT

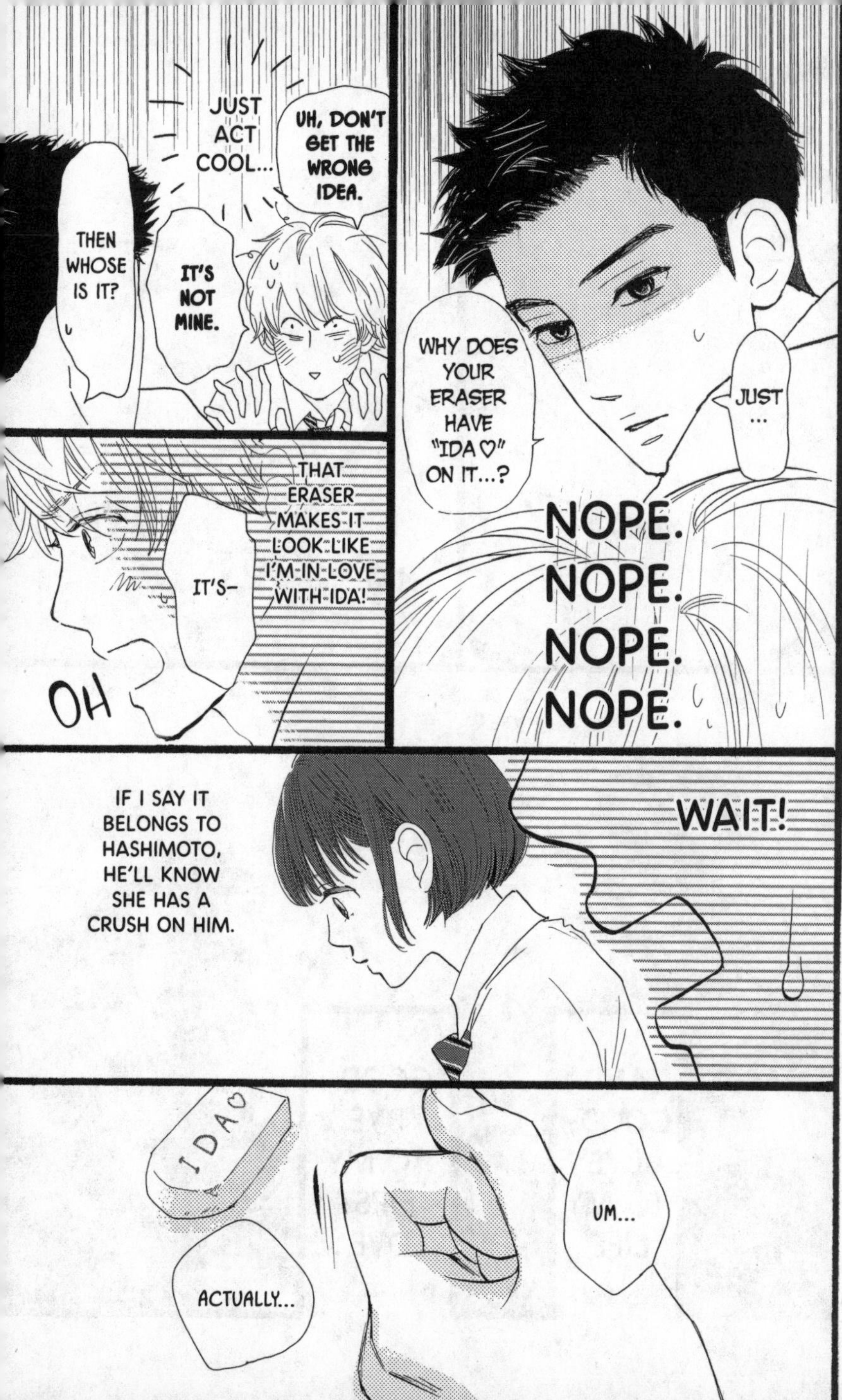
WHY DOES YOUR ERASER HAVE "IDA♡" ON IT...?
JUST...
NOPE. NOPE. NOPE. NOPE.
UH, DON'T GET THE WRONG IDEA.
JUST ACT COOL...
IT'S NOT MINE.
THEN WHOSE IS IT?
THAT ERASER MAKES IT LOOK LIKE I'M IN LOVE WITH IDA!
IT'S—
OH
WAIT!
IF I SAY IT BELONGS TO HASHIMOTO, HE'LL KNOW SHE HAS A CRUSH ON HIM.
UM...
IDA♡
ACTUALLY...

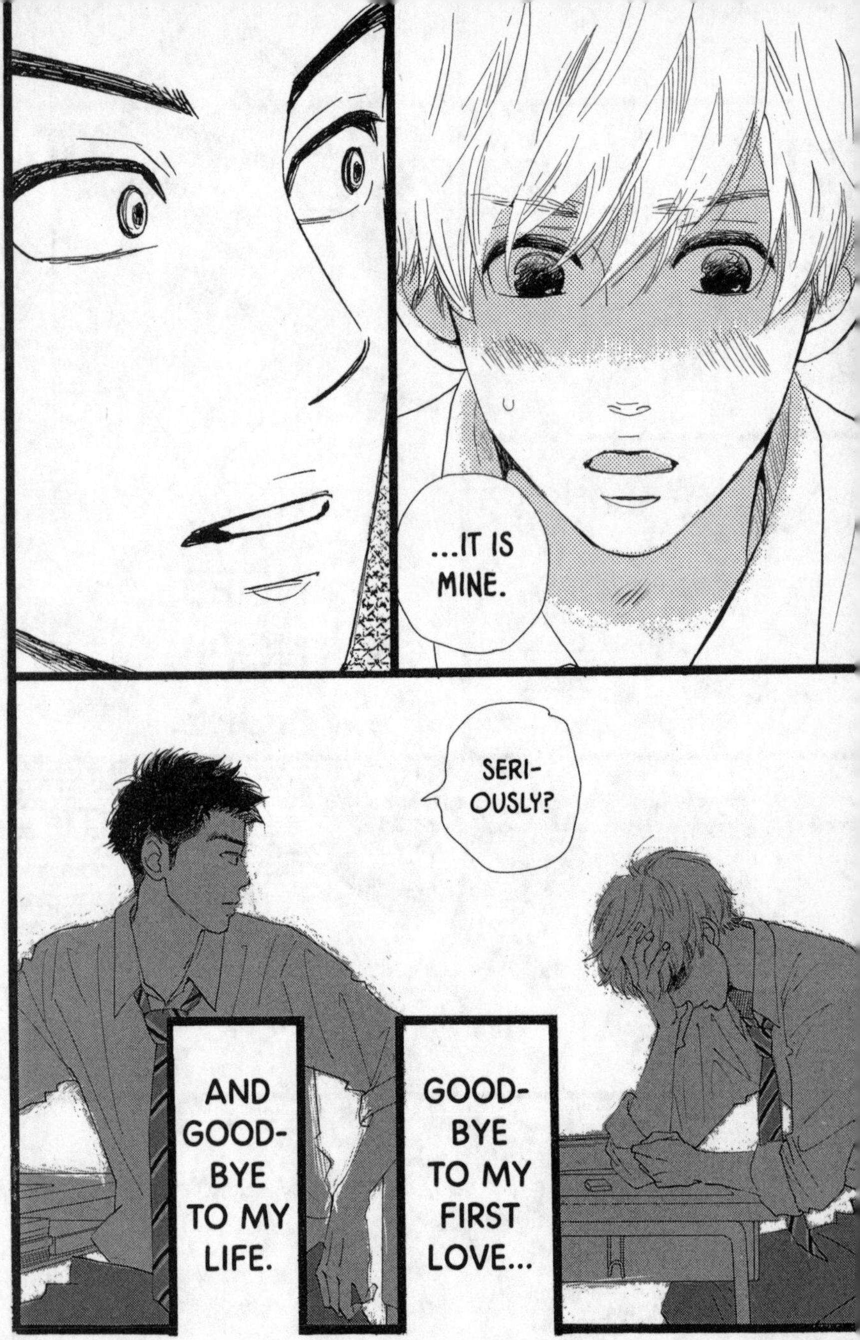
...IT IS MINE.
SERI-OUSLY?
GOOD-BYE TO MY FIRST LOVE...
AND GOOD-BYE TO MY LIFE.

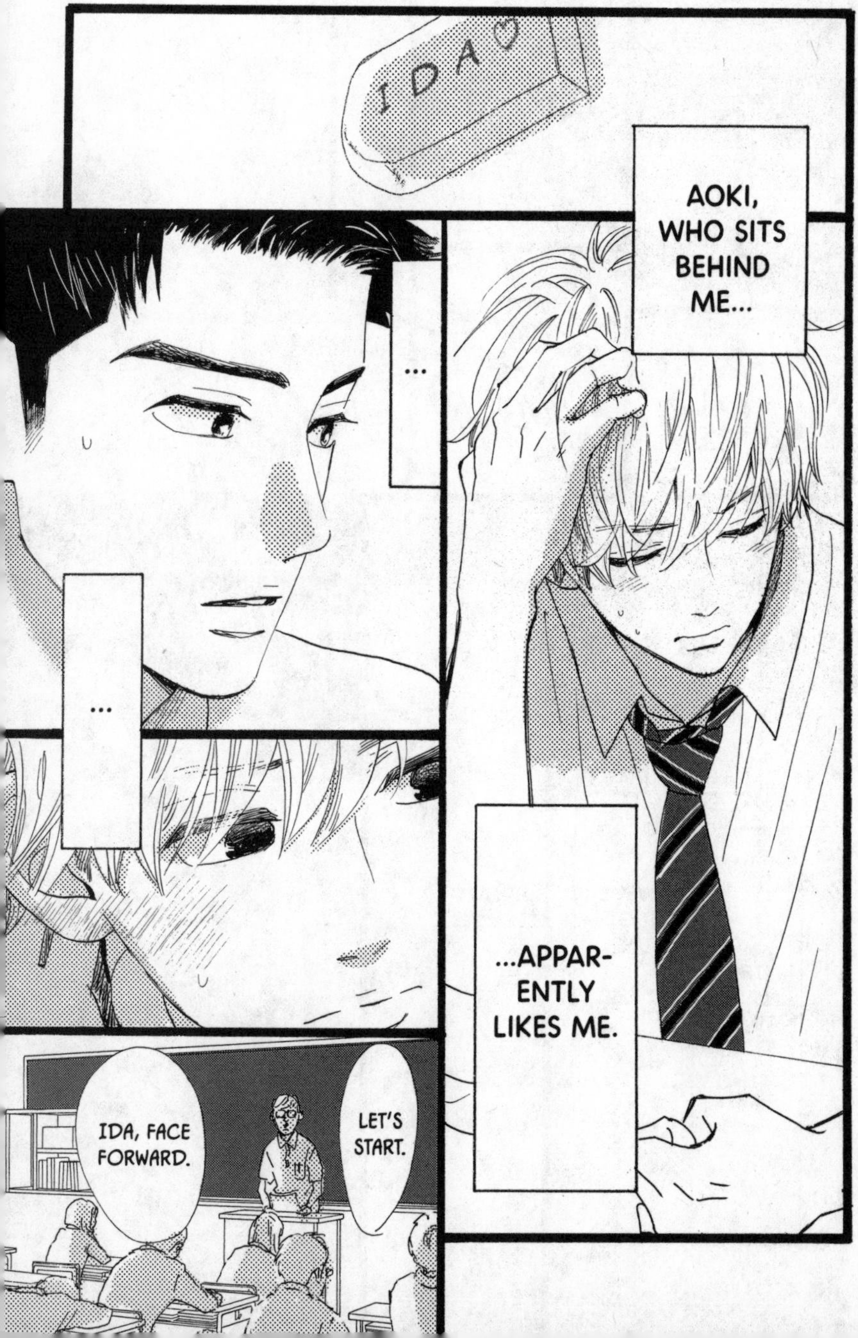
IDA♡
AOKI, WHO SITS BEHIND ME...
...APPARENTLY LIKES ME.
...
...
LET'S START.
IDA, FACE FORWARD.

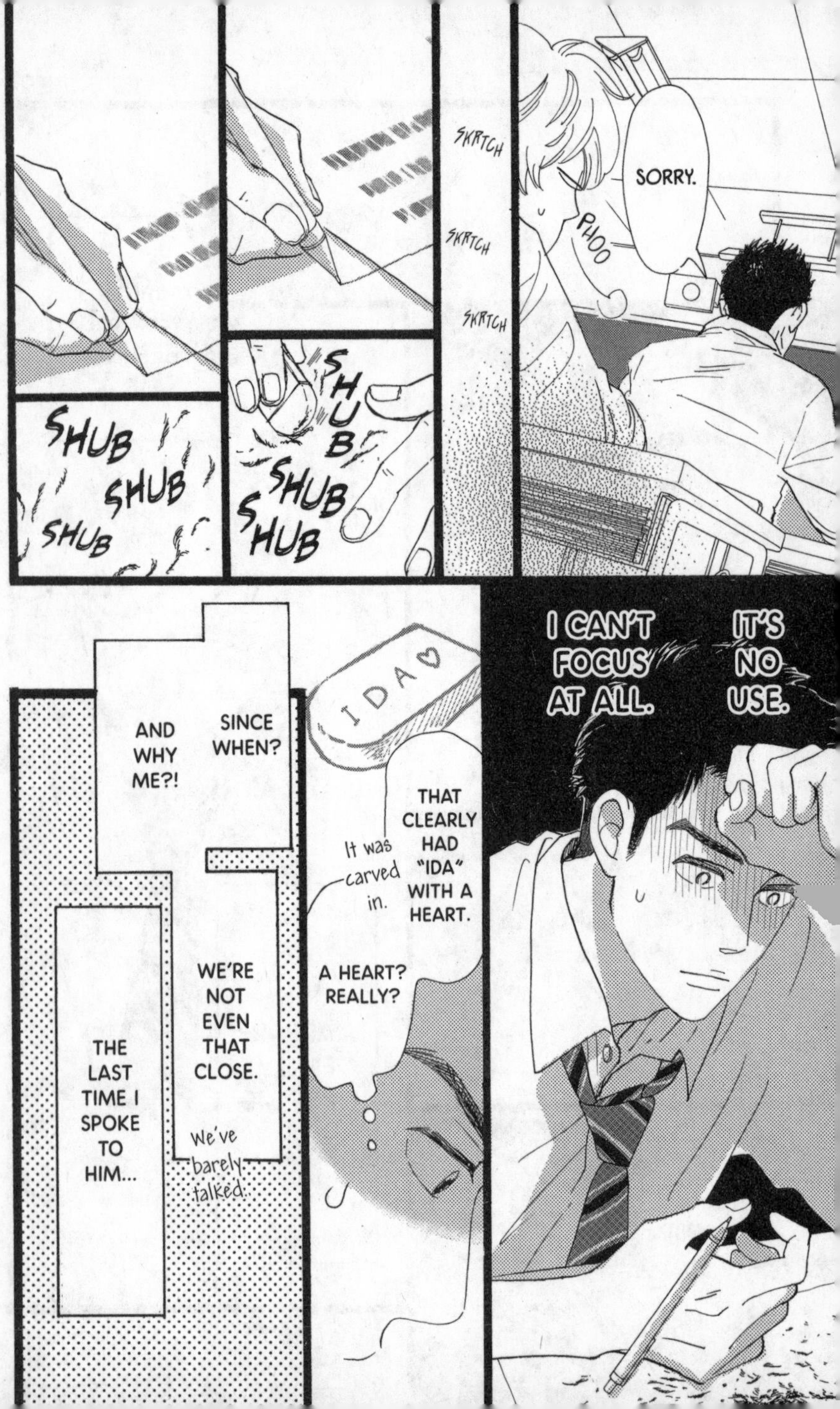
SORRY.
PHOO
SKRTCH
SKRTCH
SKRTCH
SHUB
SHUB
SHUB
SHUB
SHUB
SHUB
SHUB
IT'S NO USE.
I CAN'T FOCUS AT ALL.
IDA♡
THAT CLEARLY HAD "IDA" WITH A HEART.
It was carved in.
A HEART? REALLY?
SINCE WHEN?
AND WHY ME?!
WE'RE NOT EVEN THAT CLOSE.
We've barely talked.
THE LAST TIME I SPOKE TO HIM...

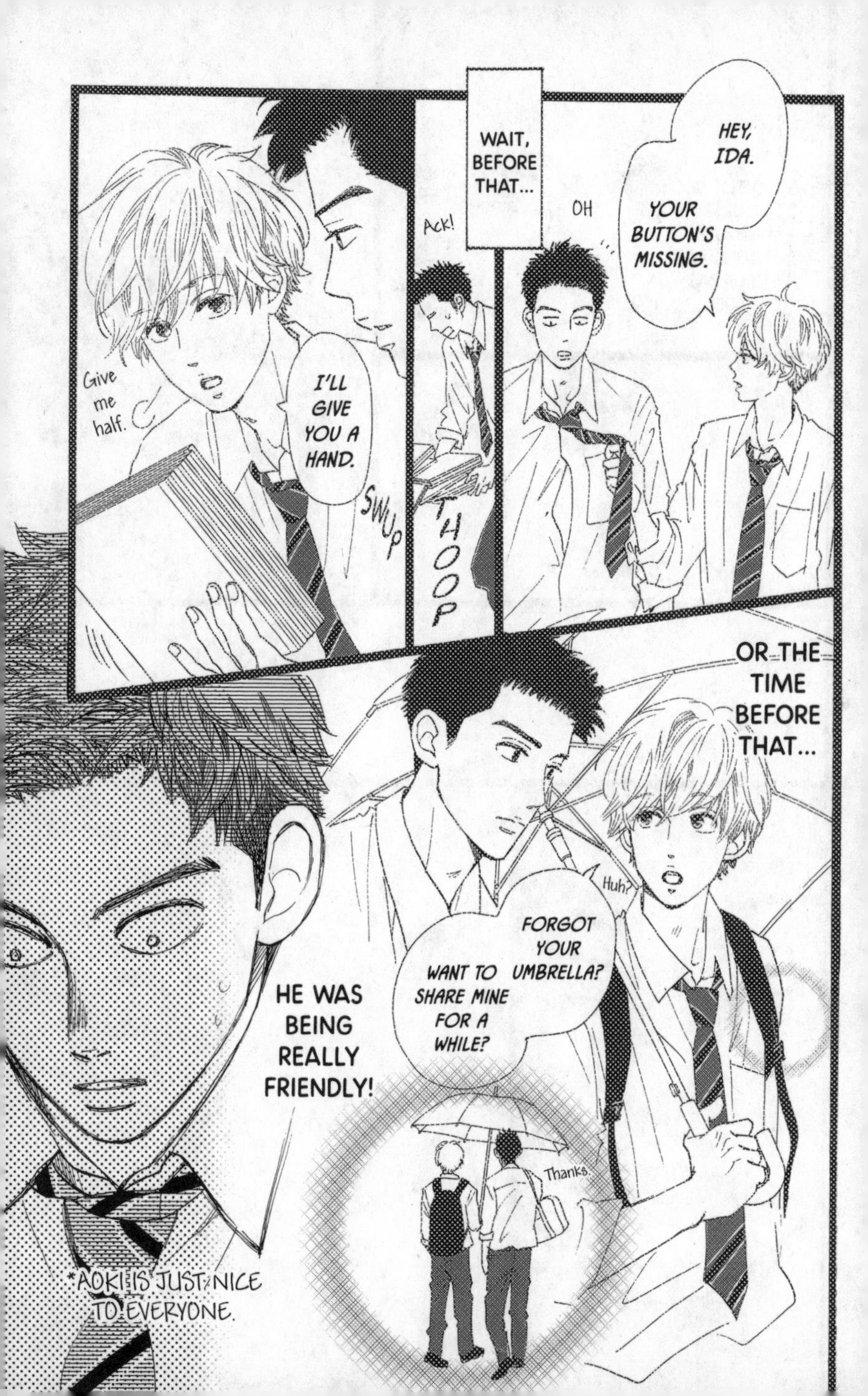
WAIT, BEFORE THAT...
HEY, IDA.
YOUR BUTTON'S MISSING.
OH
Ack!
THOOP
I'LL GIVE YOU A HAND.
SWUP
Give me half.
OR THE TIME BEFORE THAT...
Huh?
FORGOT YOUR UMBRELLA?
WANT TO SHARE MINE FOR A WHILE?
Thanks.
HE WAS BEING REALLY FRIENDLY!
*AOKI IS JUST NICE TO EVERYONE.

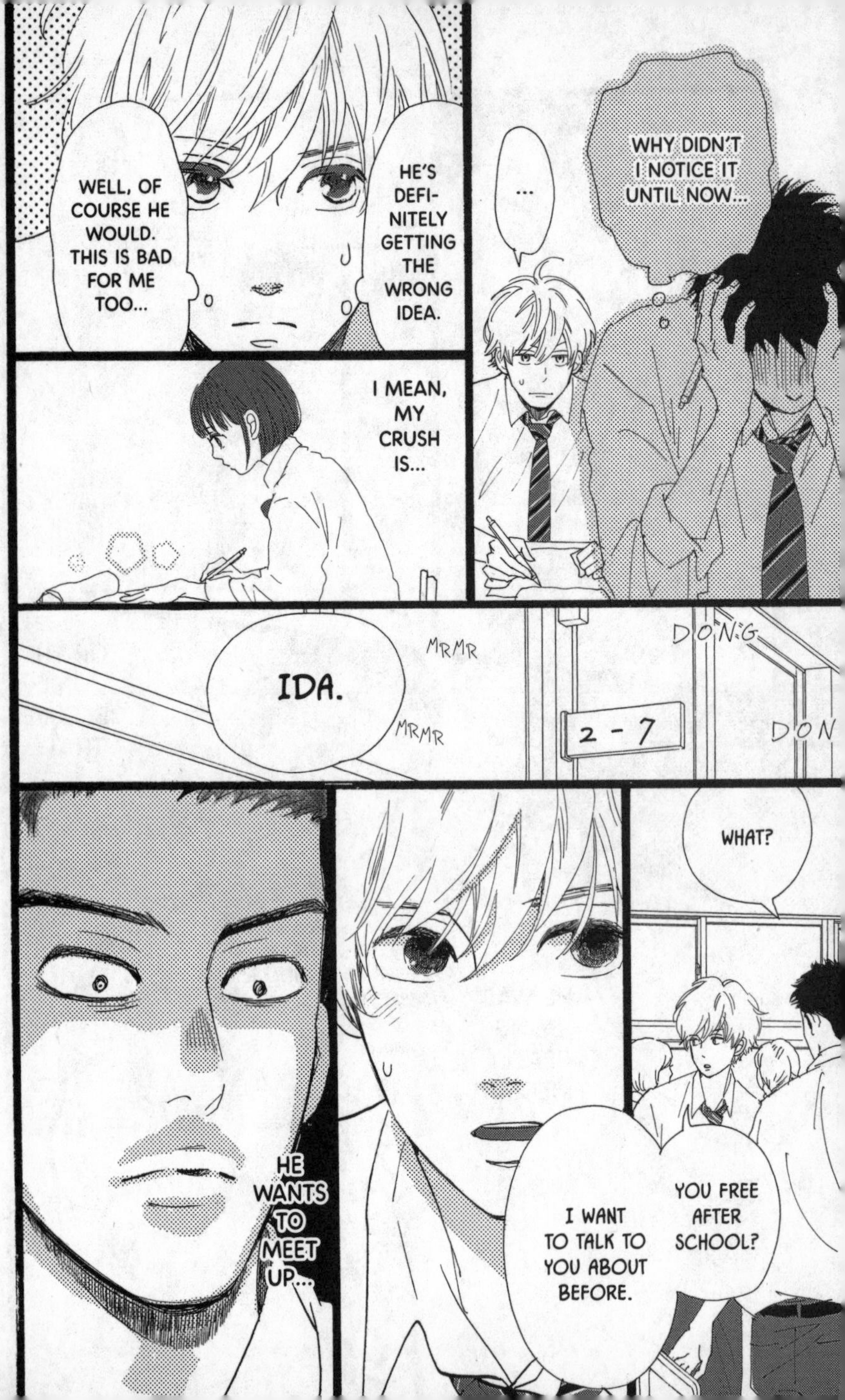
WHY DIDN'T I NOTICE IT UNTIL NOW...
...
HE'S DEFI-NITELY GETTING THE WRONG IDEA.
WELL, OF COURSE HE WOULD. THIS IS BAD FOR ME TOO...
I MEAN, MY CRUSH IS...
DONG
DON
MRMR
IDA.
MRMR
WHAT?
YOU FREE AFTER SCHOOL?
I WANT TO TALK TO YOU ABOUT BEFORE.
HE WANTS TO MEET UP...

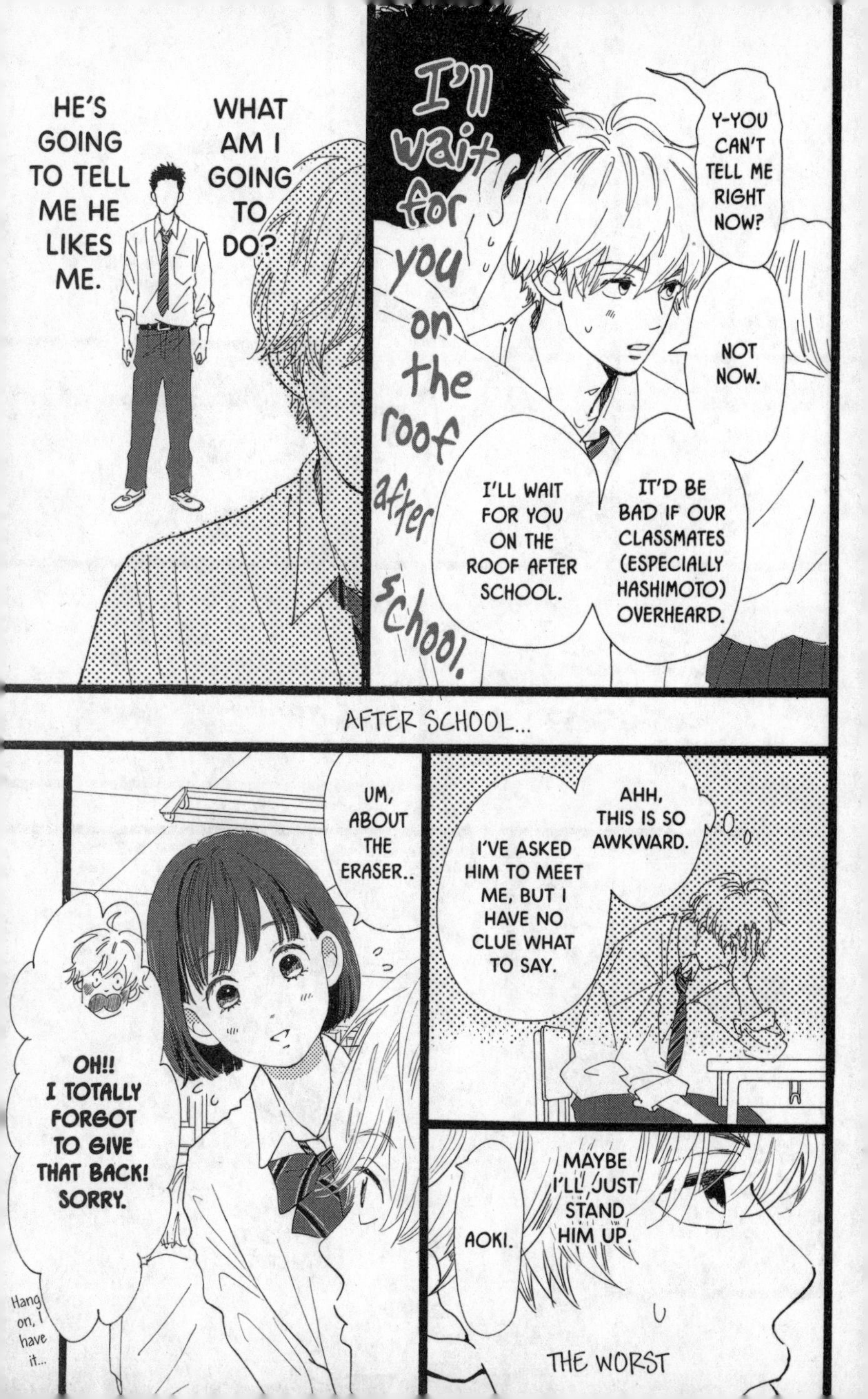
Y-YOU CAN'T TELL ME RIGHT NOW?
NOT NOW.
IT'D BE BAD IF OUR CLASSMATES (ESPECIALLY HASHIMOTO) OVERHEARD.
I'LL WAIT FOR YOU ON THE ROOF AFTER SCHOOL.
I'll wait for you on the roof after school.
WHAT AM I GOING TO DO?
HE'S GOING TO TELL ME HE LIKES ME.
AFTER SCHOOL...
AHH, THIS IS SO AWKWARD.
I'VE ASKED HIM TO MEET ME, BUT I HAVE NO CLUE WHAT TO SAY.
MAYBE I'LL JUST STAND HIM UP.
AOKI.
THE WORST
UM, ABOUT THE ERASER..
OH!! I TOTALLY FORGOT TO GIVE THAT BACK! SORRY.
Hang on, I have it...

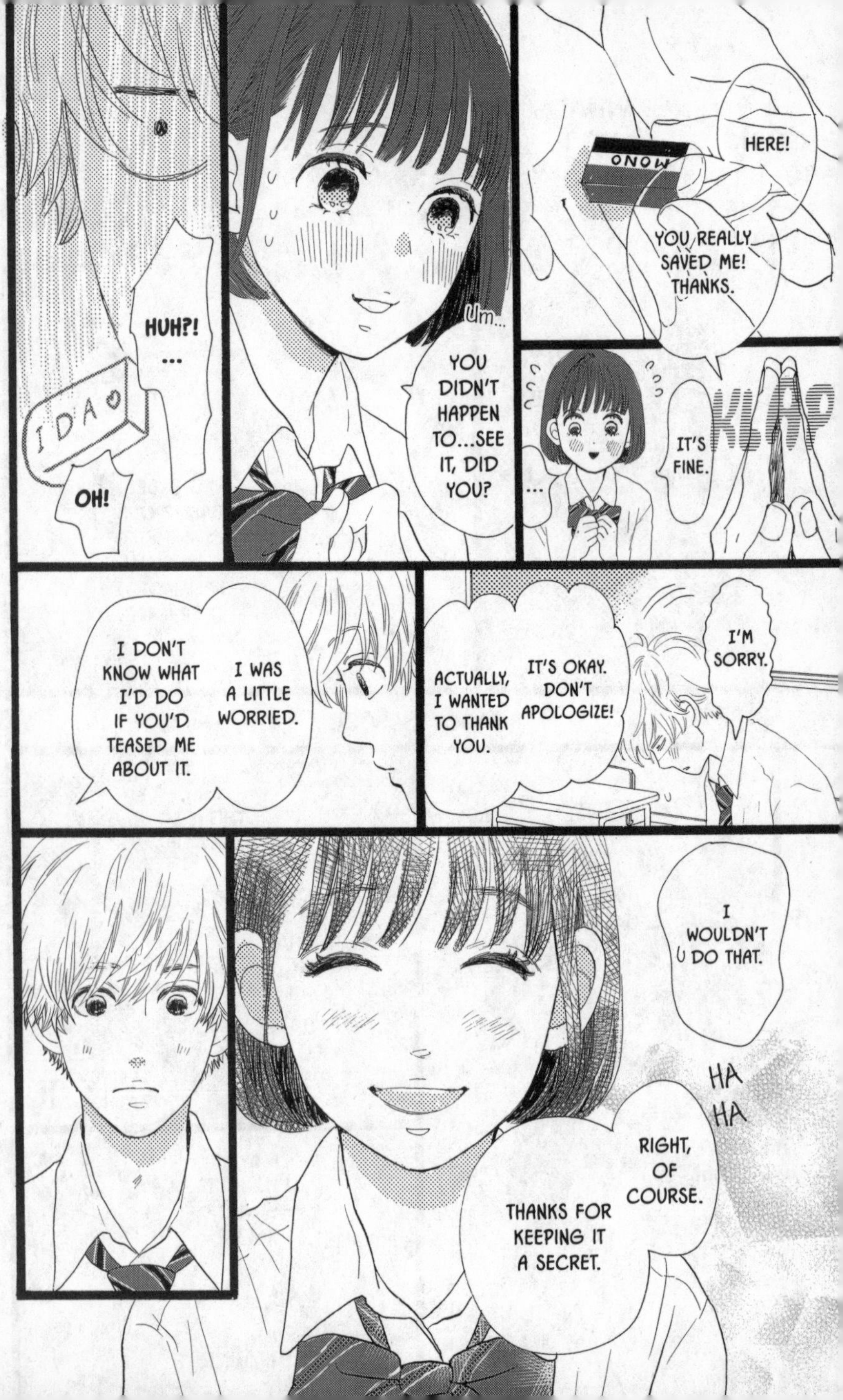
HERE!
YOU REALLY SAVED ME! THANKS.
KLAP
IT'S FINE.
...
Um...
YOU DIDN'T HAPPEN TO...SEE IT, DID YOU?
HUH?! ...
IDA
OH!
I'M SORRY.
IT'S OKAY. DON'T APOLOGIZE!
ACTUALLY, I WANTED TO THANK YOU.
I WAS A LITTLE WORRIED.
I DON'T KNOW WHAT I'D DO IF YOU'D TEASED ME ABOUT IT.
I WOULDN'T DO THAT.
HA HA
RIGHT, OF COURSE.
THANKS FOR KEEPING IT A SECRET.

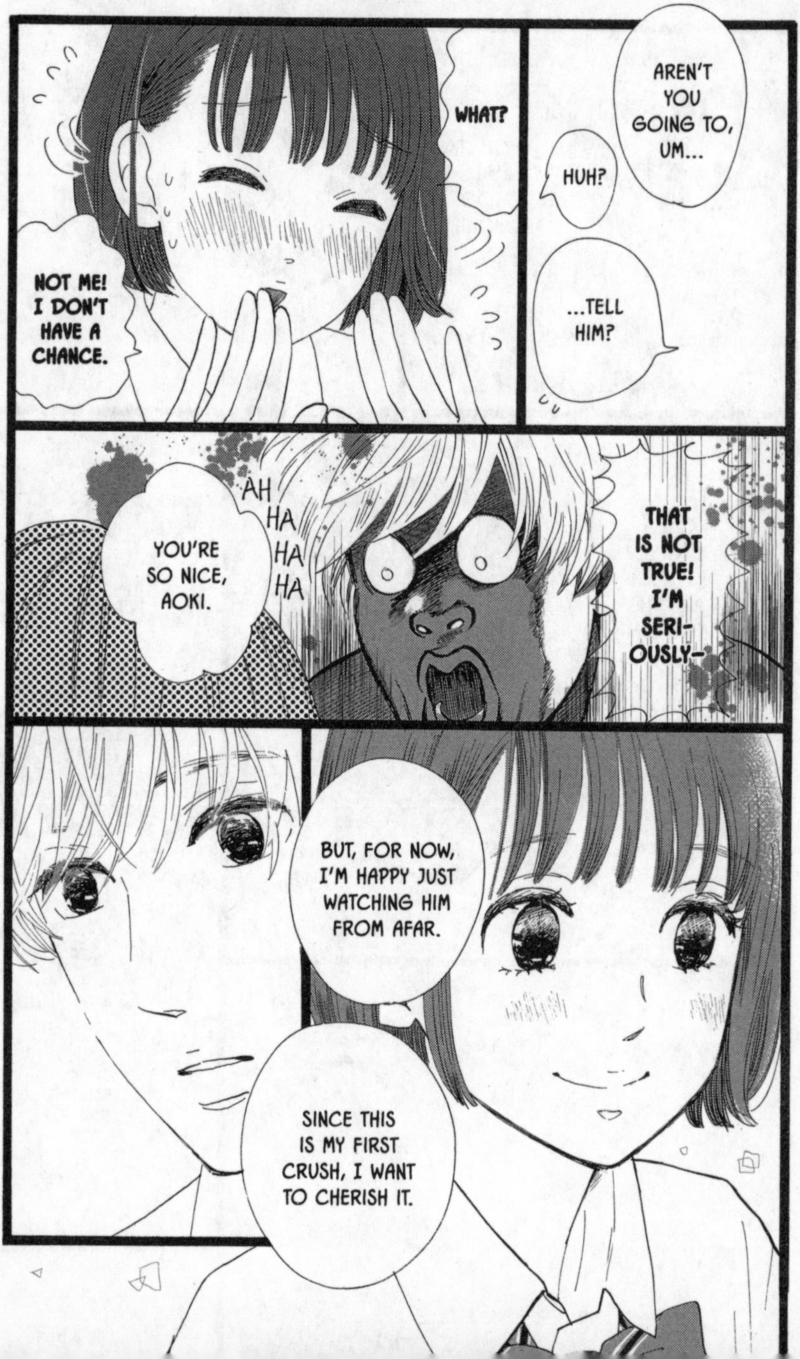
AREN'T YOU GOING TO, UM...
HUH?
...TELL HIM?
WHAT?
NOT ME! I DON'T HAVE A CHANCE.
THAT IS NOT TRUE! I'M SERI-OUSLY—
AH HA HA HA
YOU'RE SO NICE, AOKI.
BUT, FOR NOW, I'M HAPPY JUST WATCHING HIM FROM AFAR.
SINCE THIS IS MY FIRST CRUSH, I WANT TO CHERISH IT.

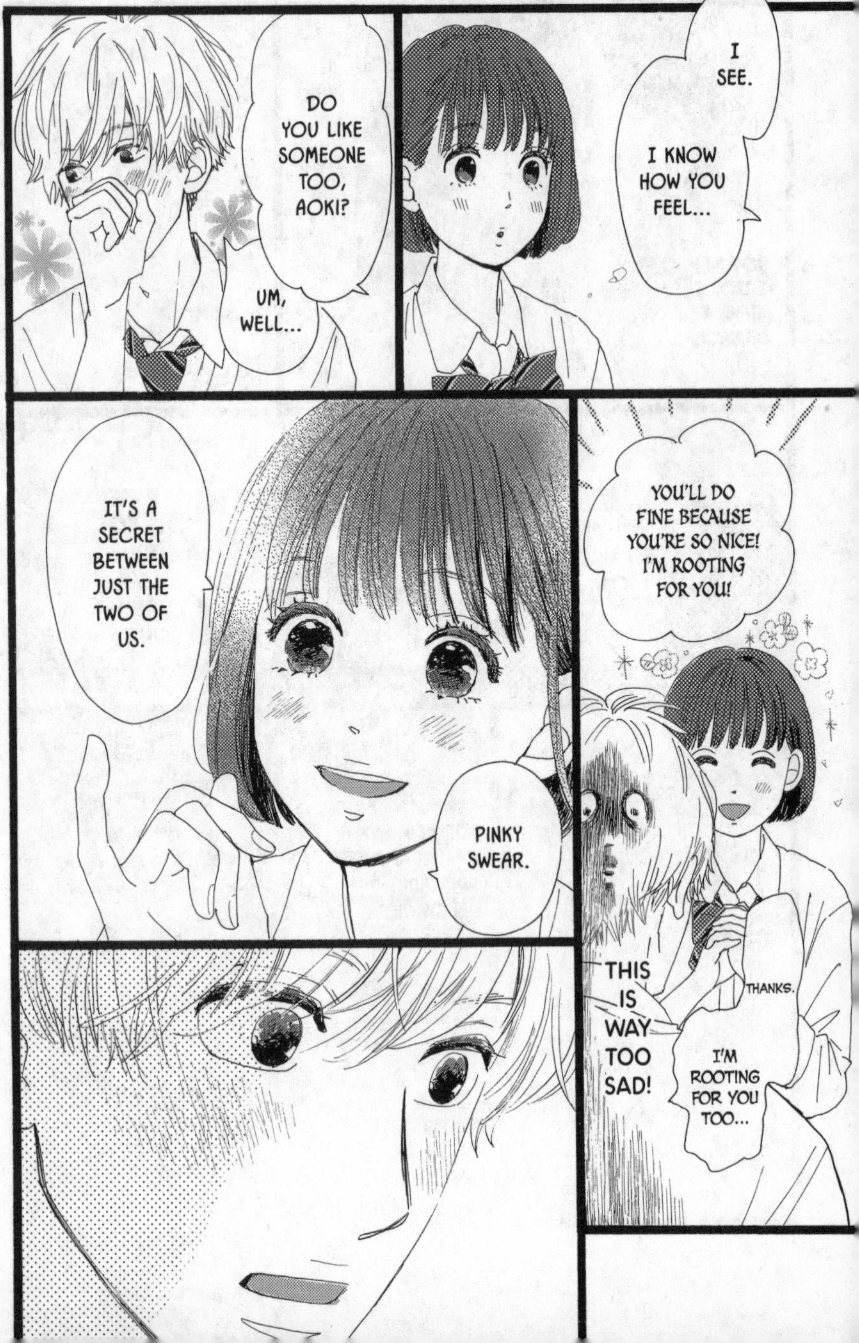
I SEE.
I KNOW HOW YOU FEEL...
DO YOU LIKE SOMEONE TOO, AOKI?
UM, WELL...
YOU'LL DO FINE BECAUSE YOU'RE SO NICE! I'M ROOTING FOR YOU!
THANKS.
I'M ROOTING FOR YOU TOO...
THIS IS WAY TOO SAD!
IT'S A SECRET BETWEEN JUST THE TWO OF US.
PINKY SWEAR.

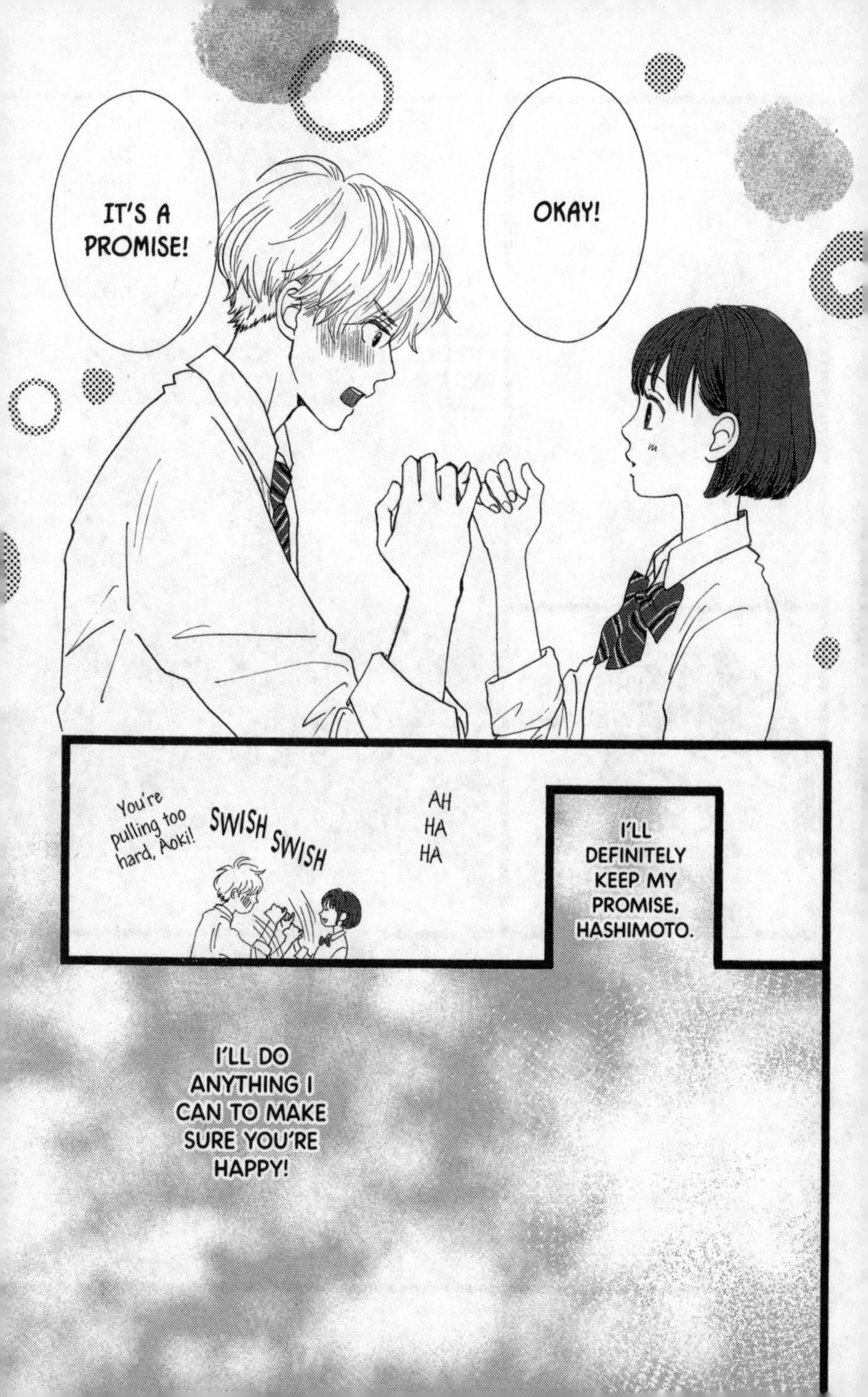
IT'S A PROMISE!
OKAY!
I'LL DEFINITELY KEEP MY PROMISE, HASHIMOTO.
AH HA HA
SWISH SWISH
You're pulling too hard, Aoki!
I'LL DO ANYTHING I CAN TO MAKE SURE YOU'RE HAPPY!

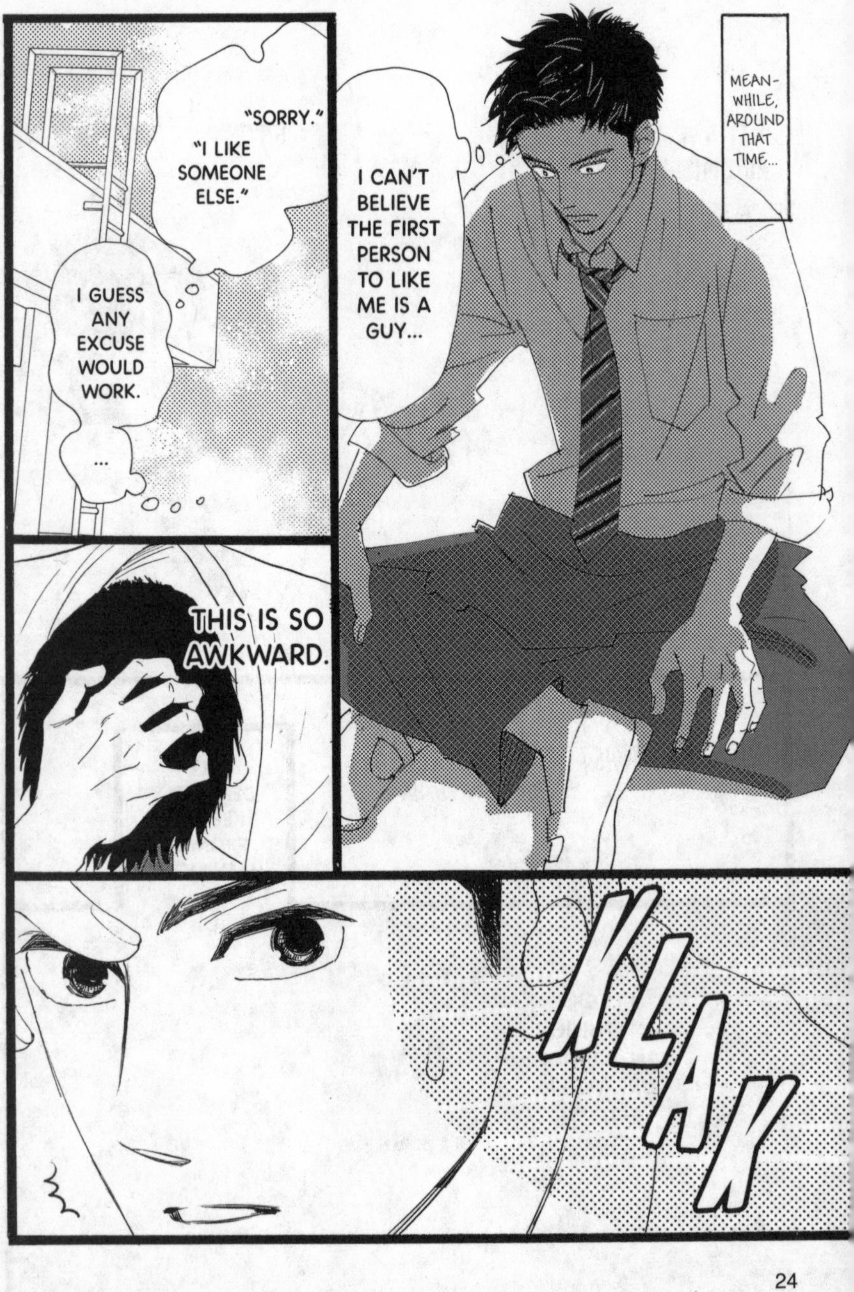
MEAN-WHILE, AROUND THAT TIME...
I CAN'T BELIEVE THE FIRST PERSON TO LIKE ME IS A GUY...
"SORRY."
"I LIKE SOMEONE ELSE."
I GUESS ANY EXCUSE WOULD WORK.
...
THIS IS SO AWKWARD.
KLAK

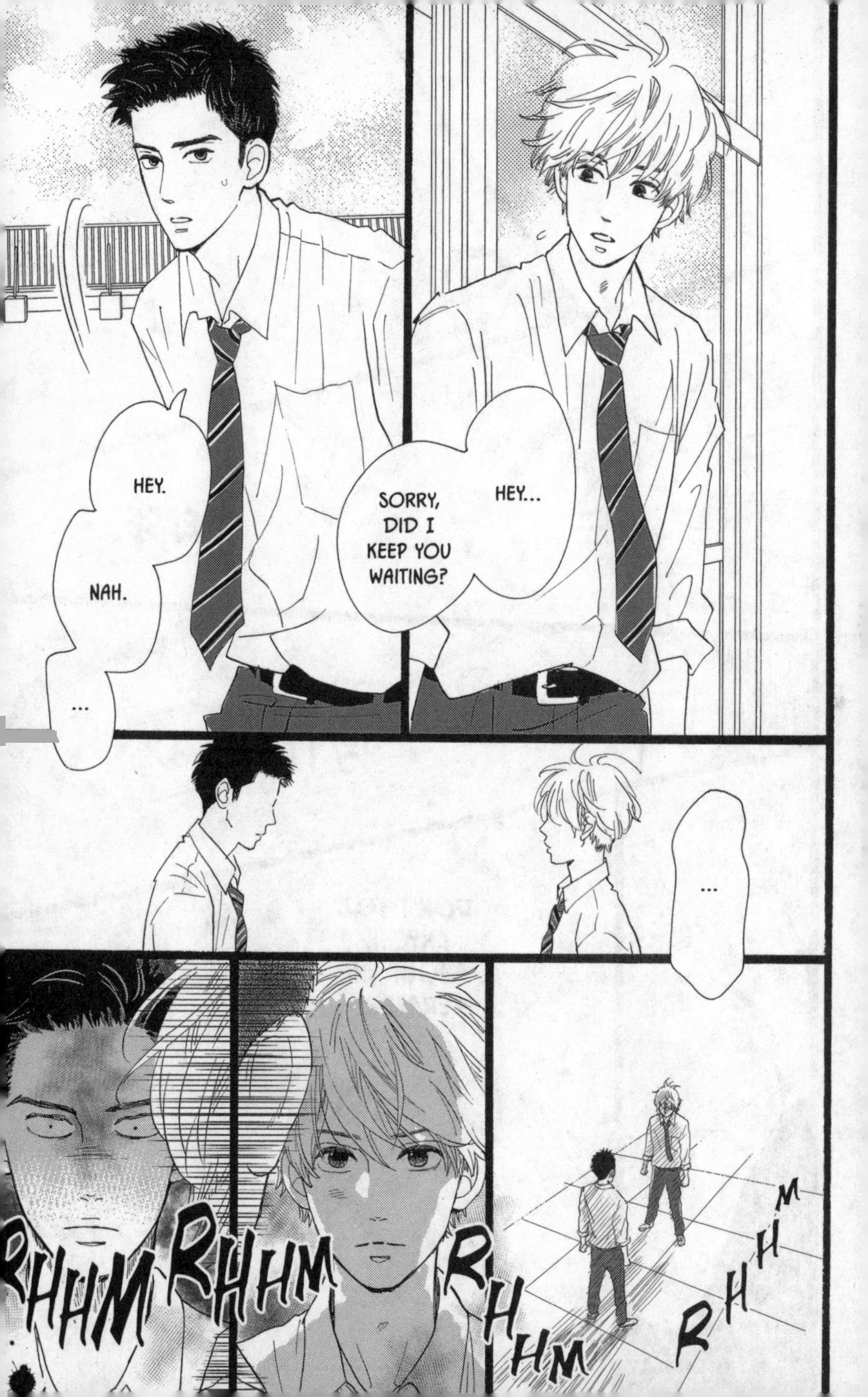
HEY...
SORRY, DID I KEEP YOU WAITING?
HEY.
NAH.
...
...
RHHM
RHHM
RHHM
RHHM

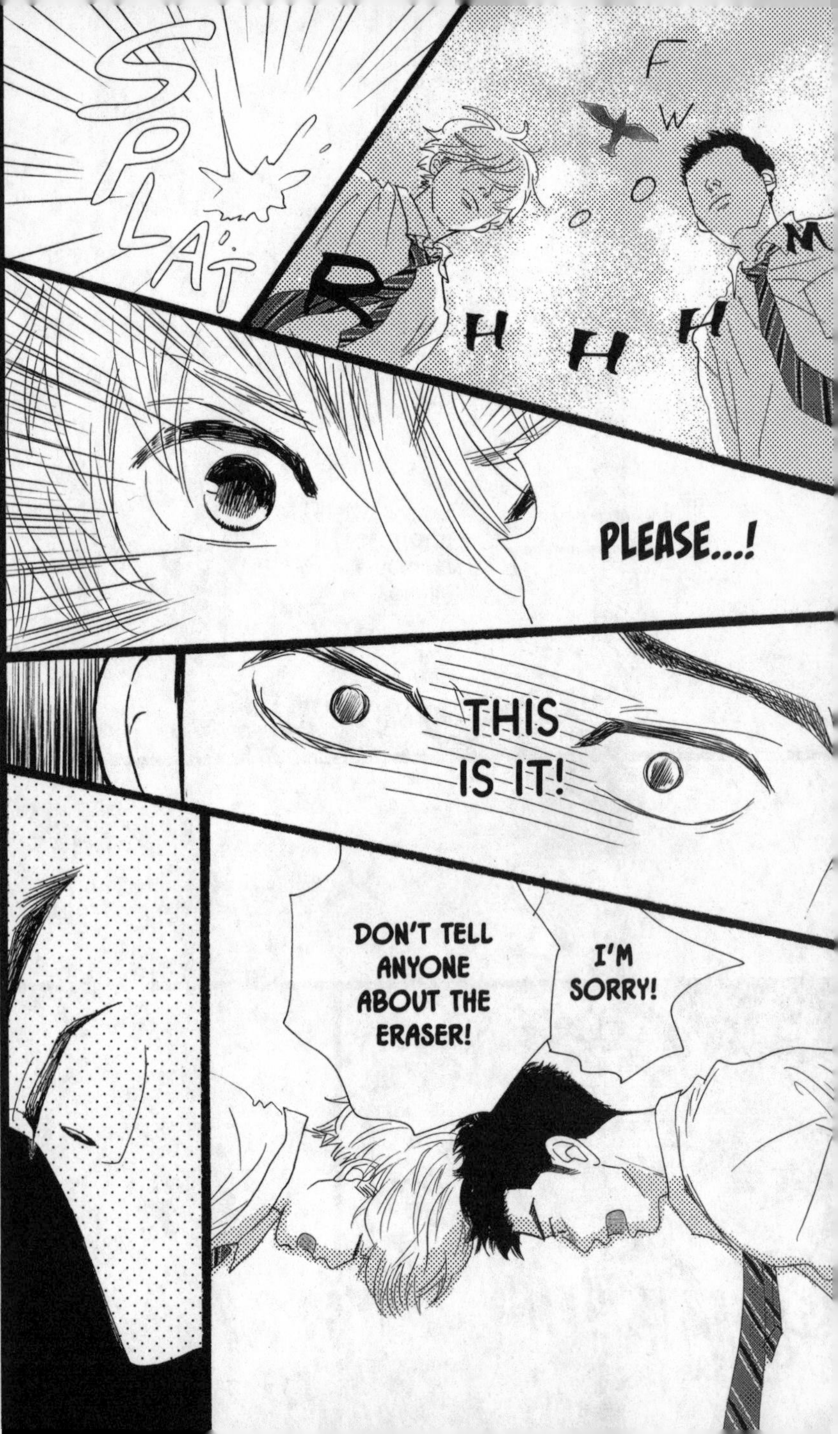
FWOOM
RHHH
SPLAT
PLEASE...!
THIS IS IT!
I'M SORRY!
DON'T TELL ANYONE ABOUT THE ERASER!

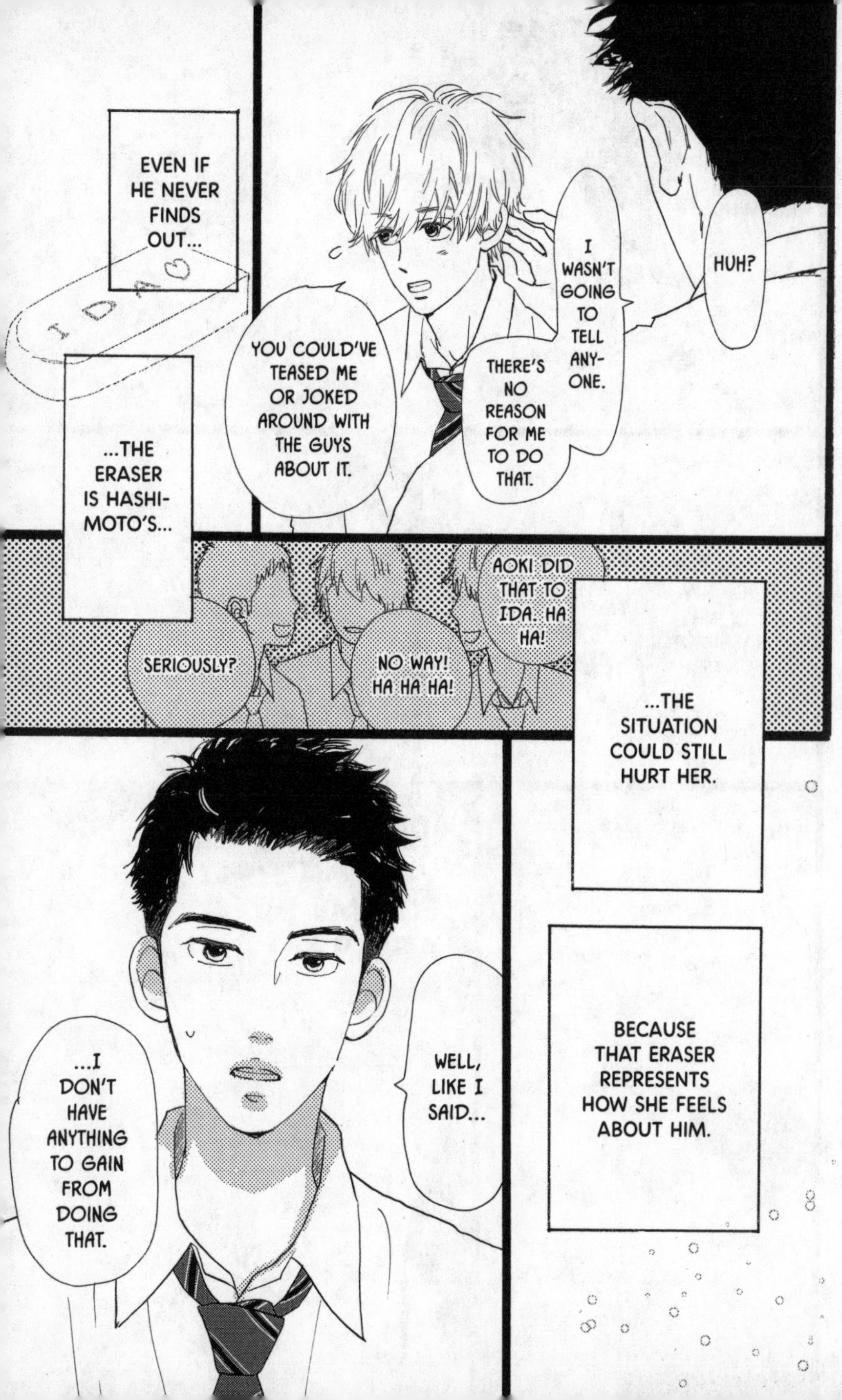
HUH?
I WASN'T GOING TO TELL ANYONE.
THERE'S NO REASON FOR ME TO DO THAT.
YOU COULD'VE TEASED ME OR JOKED AROUND WITH THE GUYS ABOUT IT.
EVEN IF HE NEVER FINDS OUT...
...THE ERASER IS HASHIMOTO'S...
...THE SITUATION COULD STILL HURT HER.
AOKI DID THAT TO IDA. HA HA!
NO WAY! HA HA HA!
SERIOUSLY?
BECAUSE THAT ERASER REPRESENTS HOW SHE FEELS ABOUT HIM.
WELL, LIKE I SAID...
...I DON'T HAVE ANYTHING TO GAIN FROM DOING THAT.

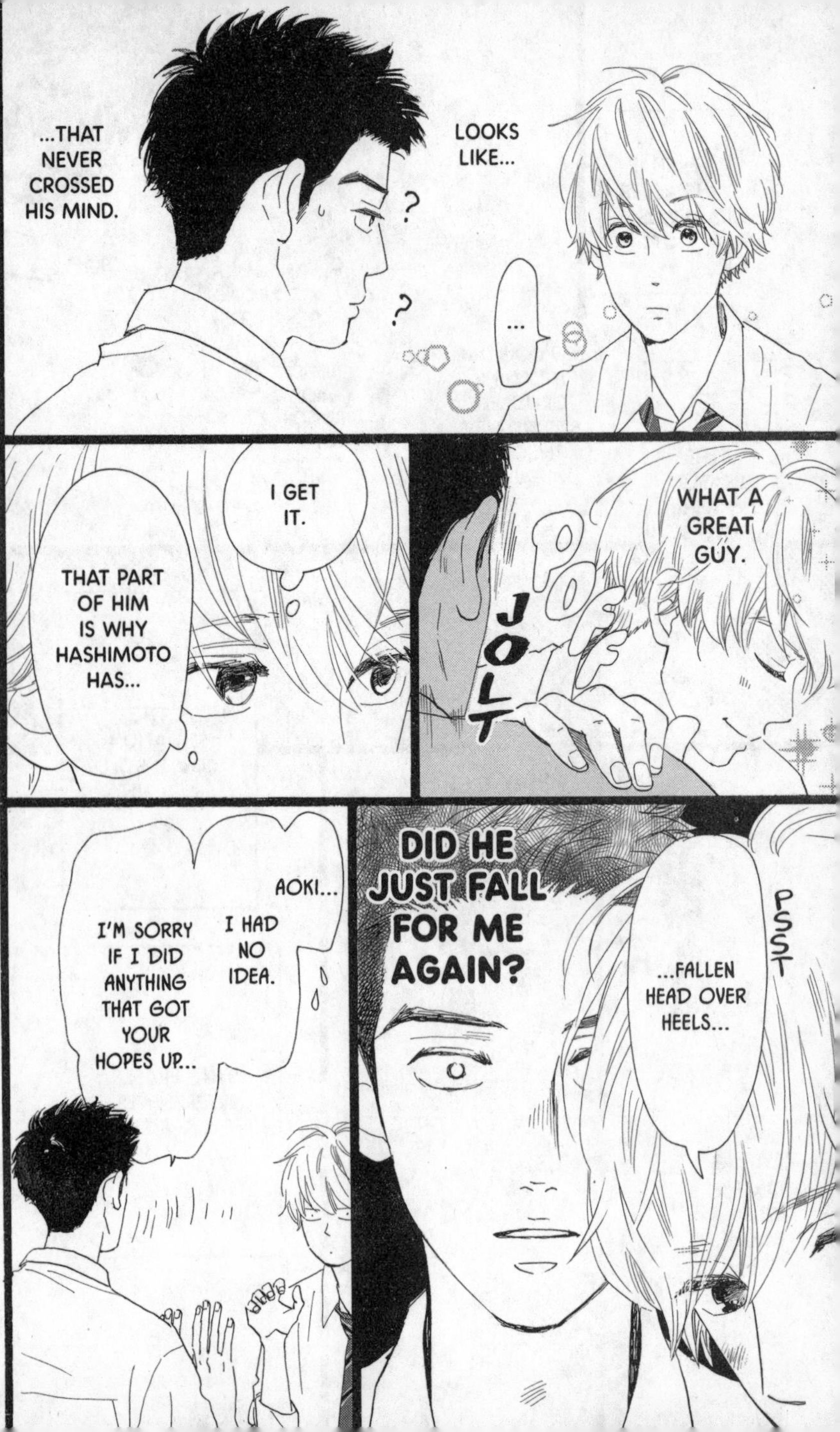
LOOKS LIKE...
...
...THAT NEVER CROSSED HIS MIND.
WHAT A GREAT GUY.
POP
JOLT
I GET IT.
THAT PART OF HIM IS WHY HASHIMOTO HAS...
...FALLEN HEAD OVER HEELS...
PSST
DID HE JUST FALL FOR ME AGAIN?
AOKI...
I HAD NO IDEA.
I'M SORRY IF I DID ANYTHING THAT GOT YOUR HOPES UP...

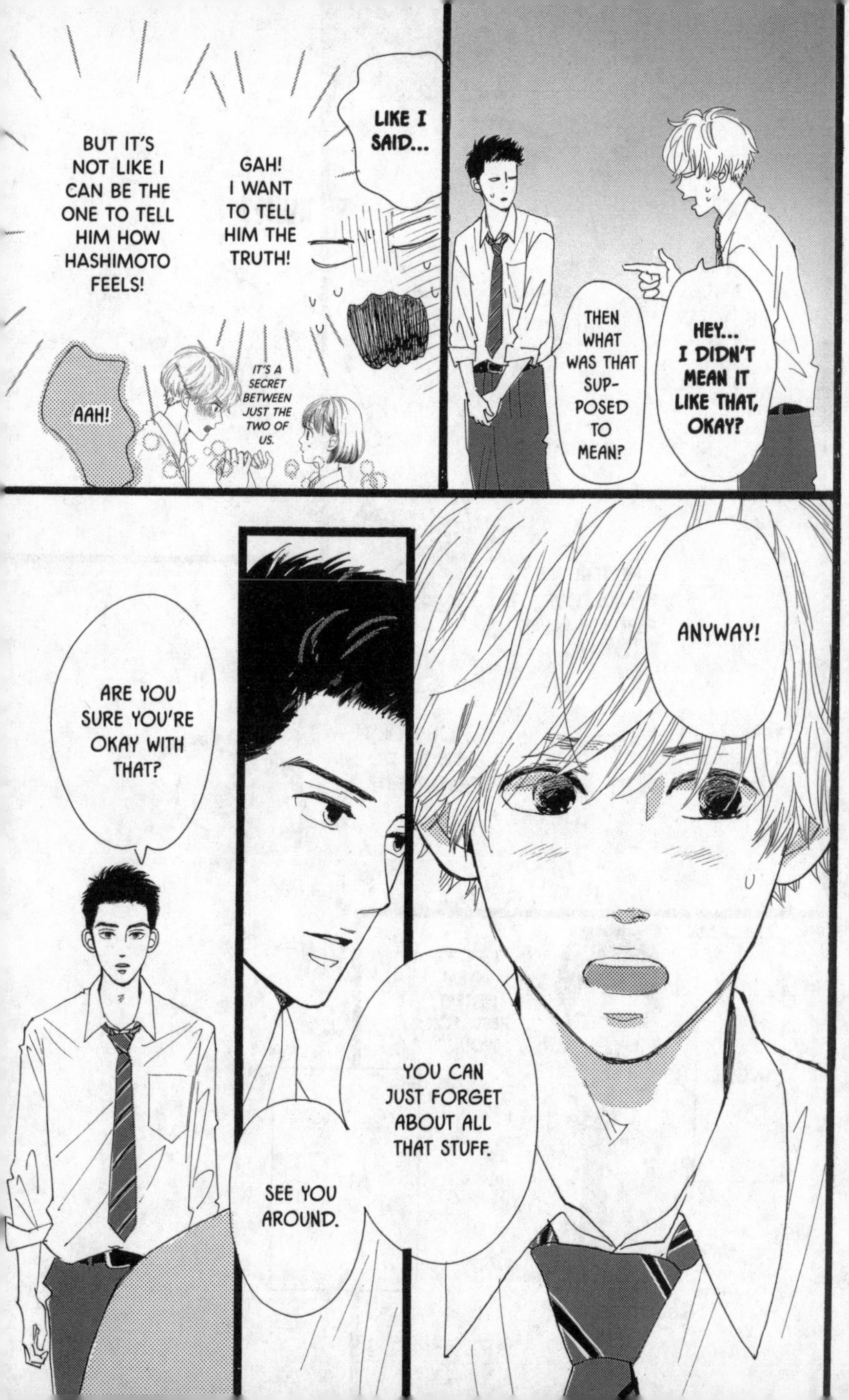
HEY... I DIDN'T MEAN IT LIKE THAT, OKAY?
THEN WHAT WAS THAT SUP-POSED TO MEAN?
LIKE I SAID...
GAH! I WANT TO TELL HIM THE TRUTH!
BUT IT'S NOT LIKE I CAN BE THE ONE TO TELL HIM HOW HASHIMOTO FEELS!
IT'S A SECRET BETWEEN JUST THE TWO OF US.
AAH!
ANYWAY!
YOU CAN JUST FORGET ABOUT ALL THAT STUFF.
SEE YOU AROUND.
ARE YOU SURE YOU'RE OKAY WITH THAT?

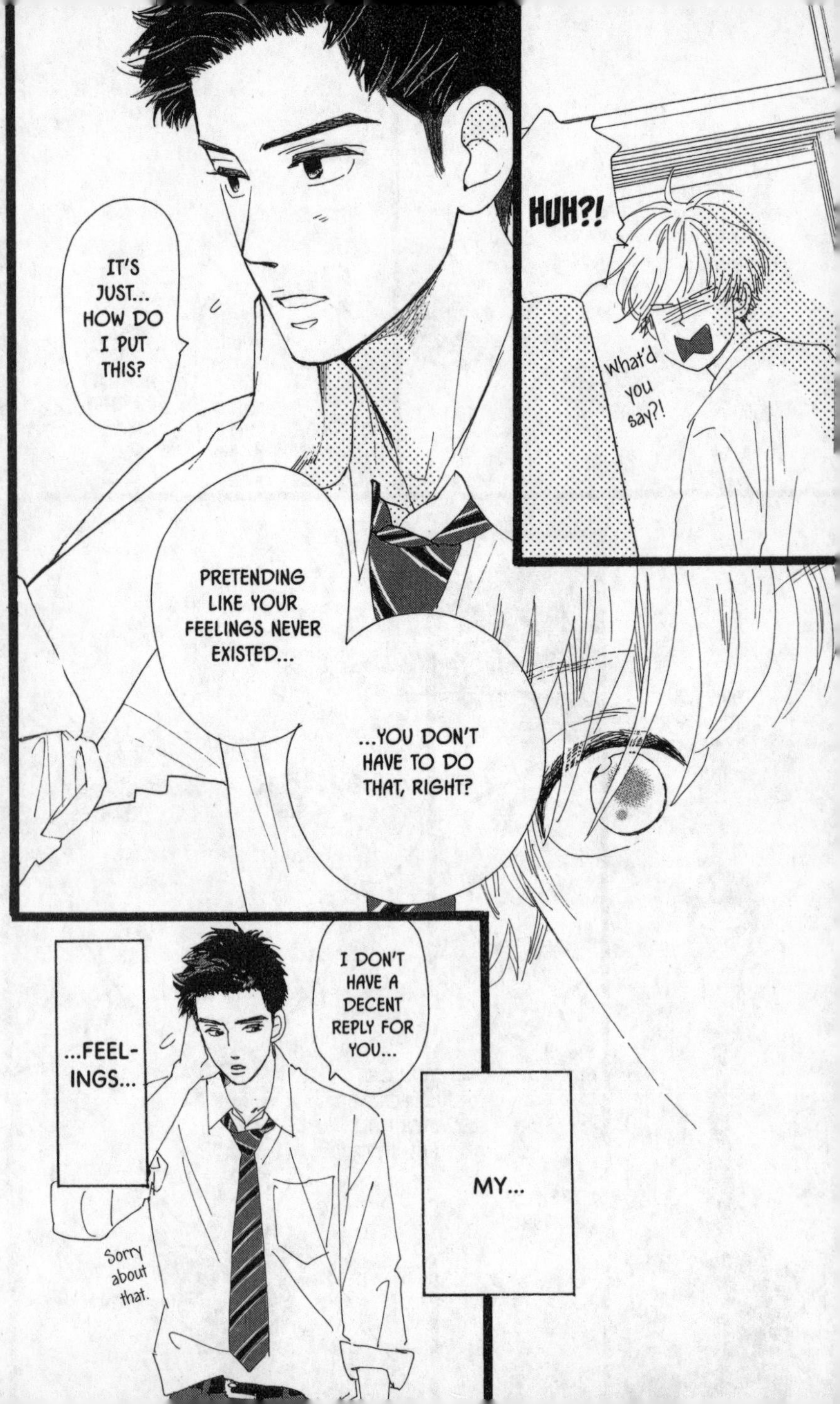
HUH?!
What'd you say?!
IT'S JUST... HOW DO I PUT THIS?
PRETENDING LIKE YOUR FEELINGS NEVER EXISTED...
...YOU DON'T HAVE TO DO THAT, RIGHT?
I DON'T HAVE A DECENT REPLY FOR YOU...
...FEEL-INGS...
Sorry about that.
MY...

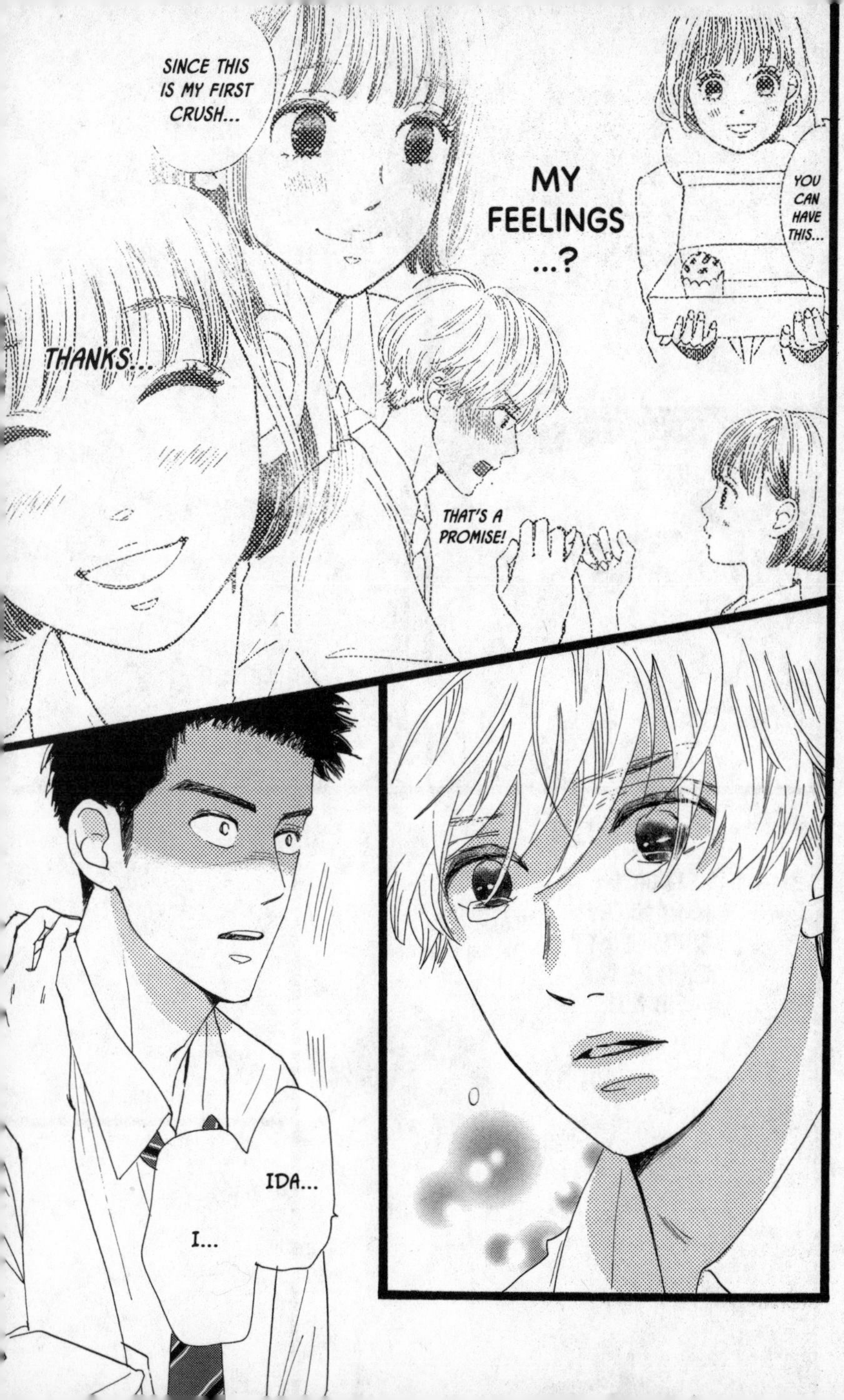
YOU CAN HAVE THIS...
MY FEELINGS ...?
SINCE THIS IS MY FIRST CRUSH...
THAT'S A PROMISE!
THANKS...
IDA...
I...

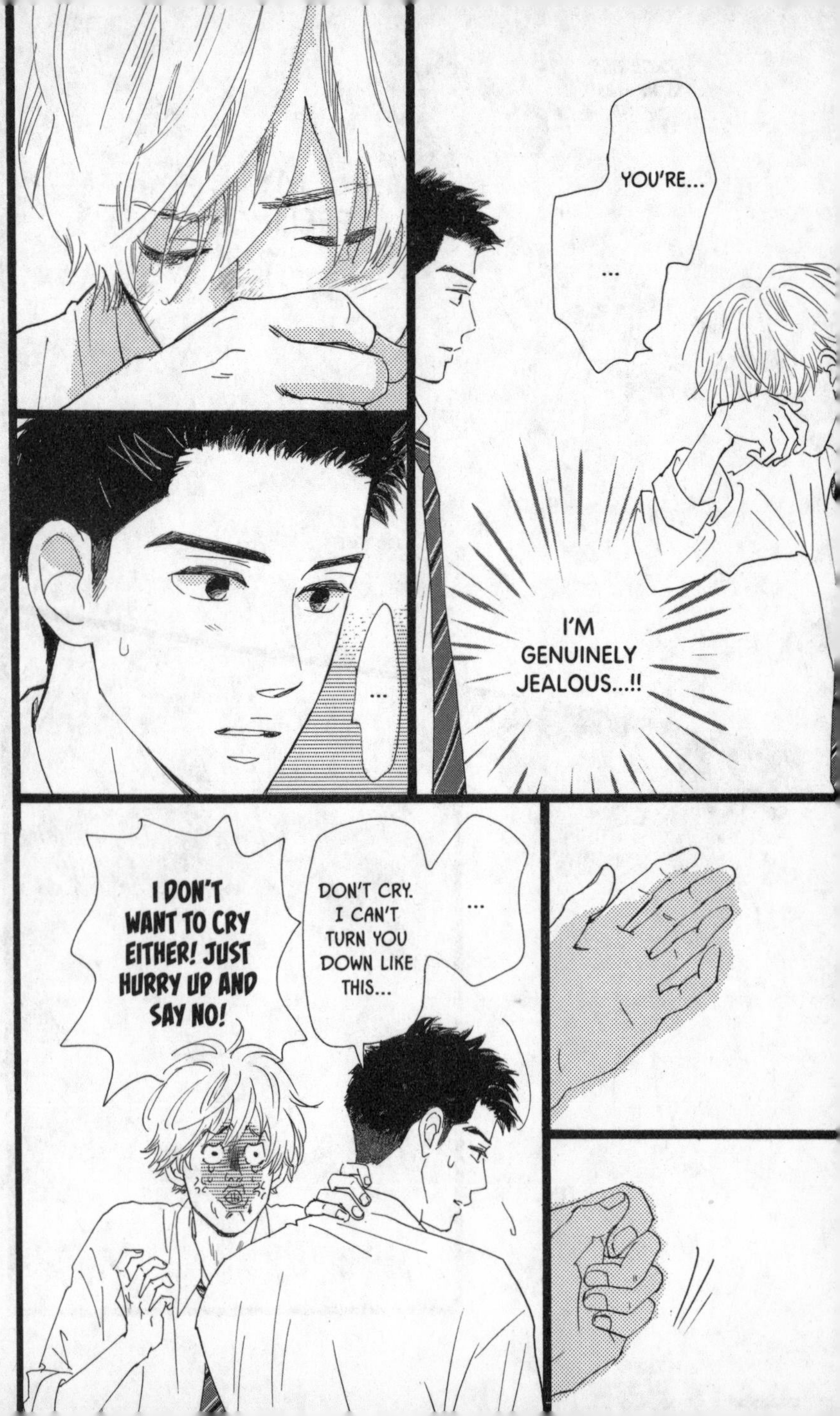

YOU'RE...
...
I'M GENUINELY JEALOUS...!!
...
...
DON'T CRY. I CAN'T TURN YOU DOWN LIKE THIS...
I DON'T WANT TO CRY EITHER! JUST HURRY UP AND SAY NO!

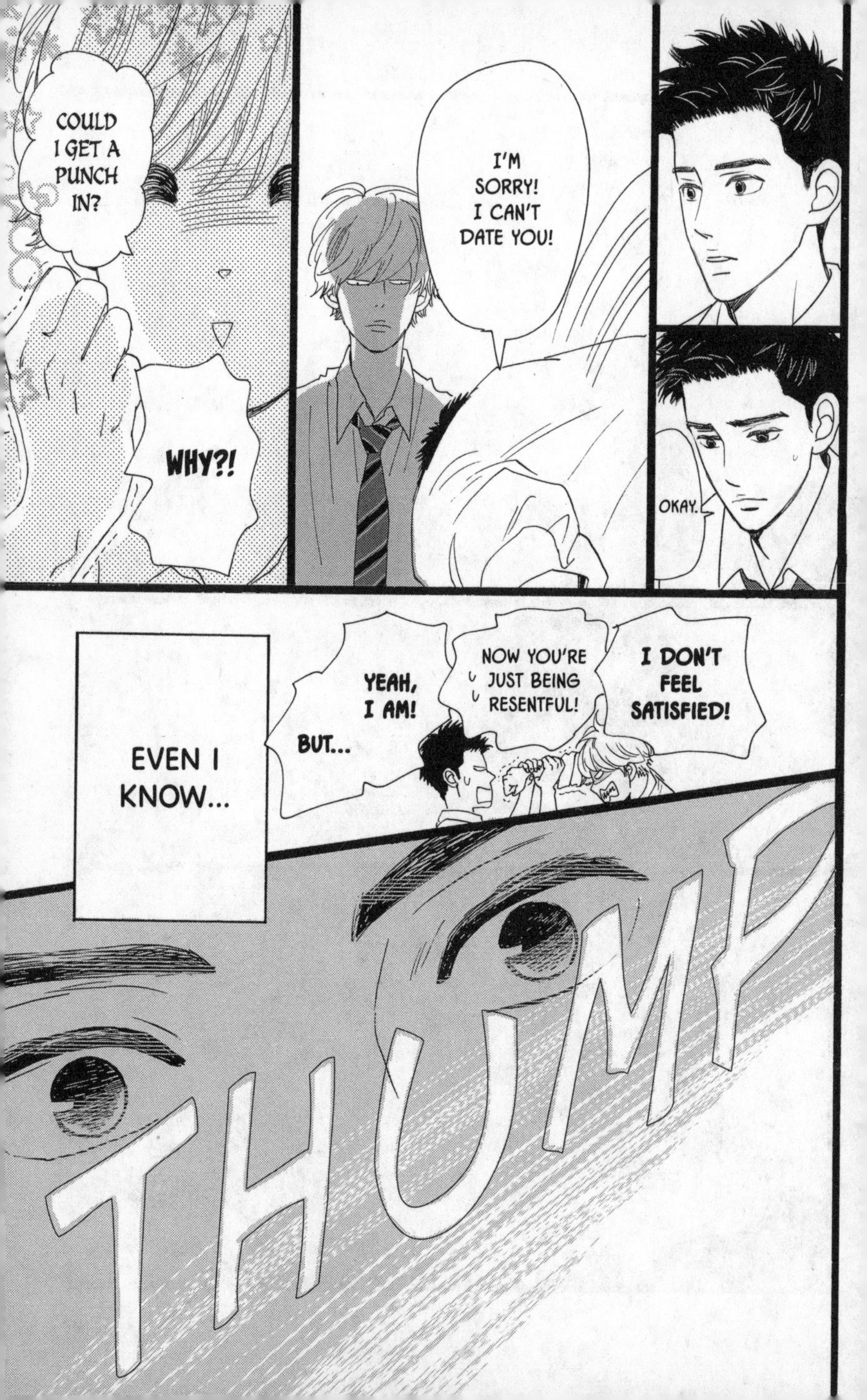
OKAY.
I'M SORRY! I CAN'T DATE YOU!
COULD I GET A PUNCH IN?
WHY?!
I DON'T FEEL SATISFIED!
NOW YOU'RE JUST BEING RESENTFUL!
YEAH, I AM!
BUT...
EVEN I KNOW...
THUMP

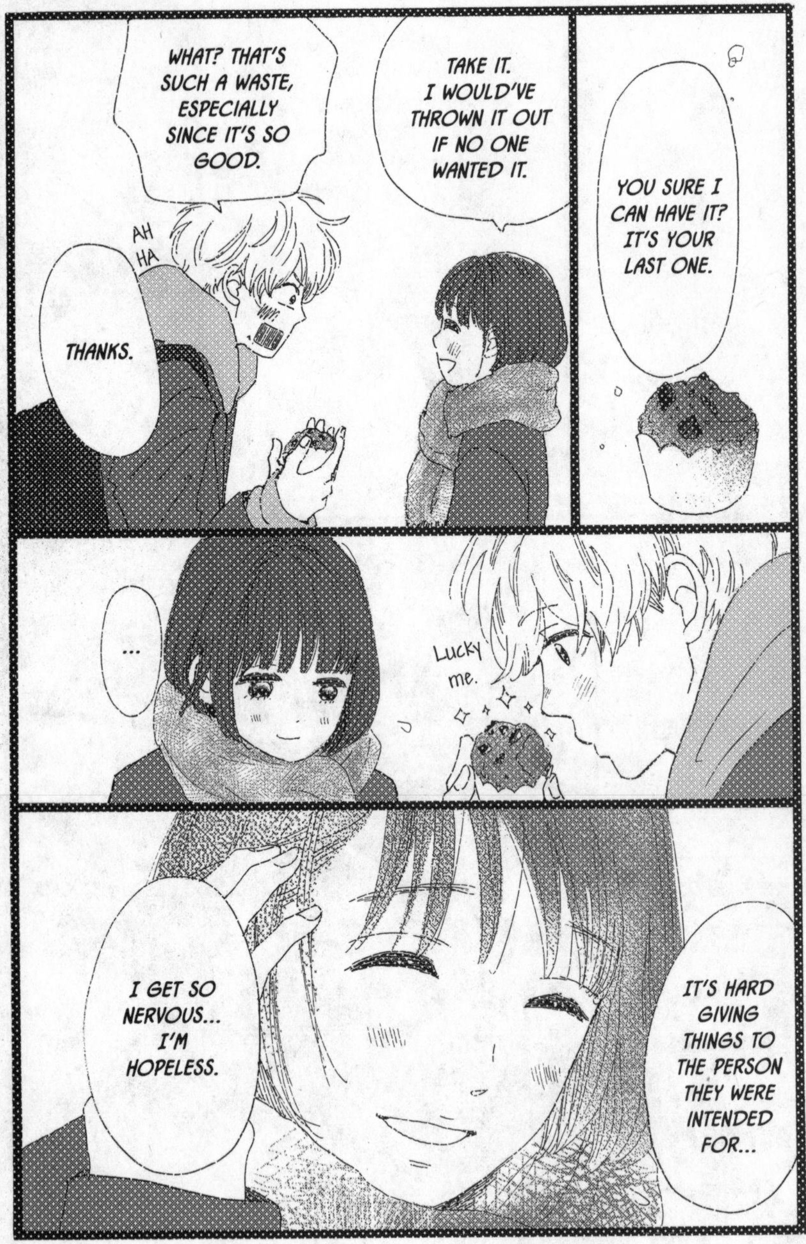
YOU SURE I CAN HAVE IT? IT'S YOUR LAST ONE.
TAKE IT. I WOULD'VE THROWN IT OUT IF NO ONE WANTED IT.
WHAT? THAT'S SUCH A WASTE, ESPECIALLY SINCE IT'S SO GOOD.
AH HA
THANKS.
Lucky me.
...
IT'S HARD GIVING THINGS TO THE PERSON THEY WERE INTENDED FOR...
I GET SO NERVOUS... I'M HOPELESS.

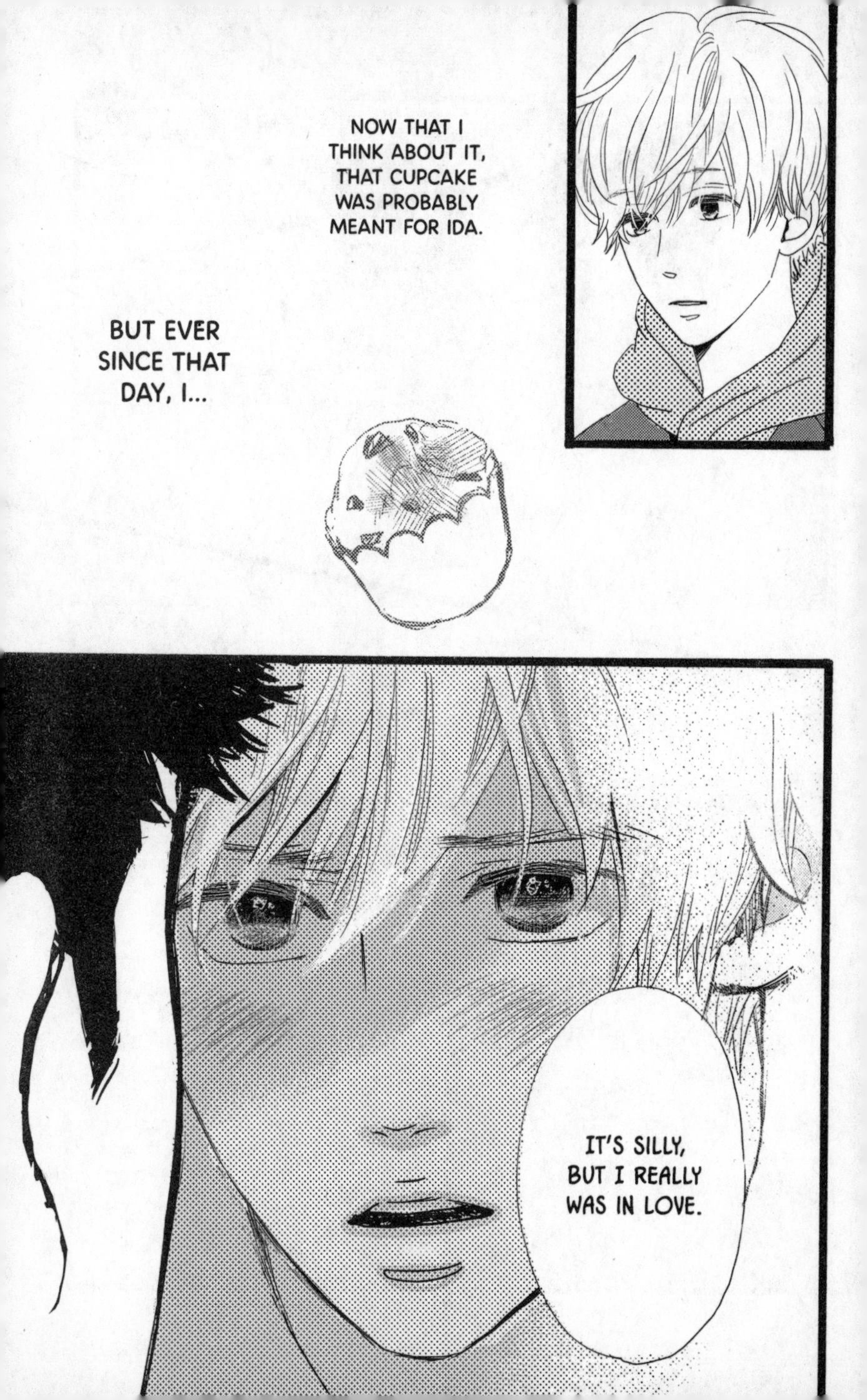
NOW THAT I THINK ABOUT IT, THAT CUPCAKE WAS PROBABLY MEANT FOR IDA.
BUT EVER SINCE THAT DAY, I...
IT'S SILLY, BUT I REALLY WAS IN LOVE.

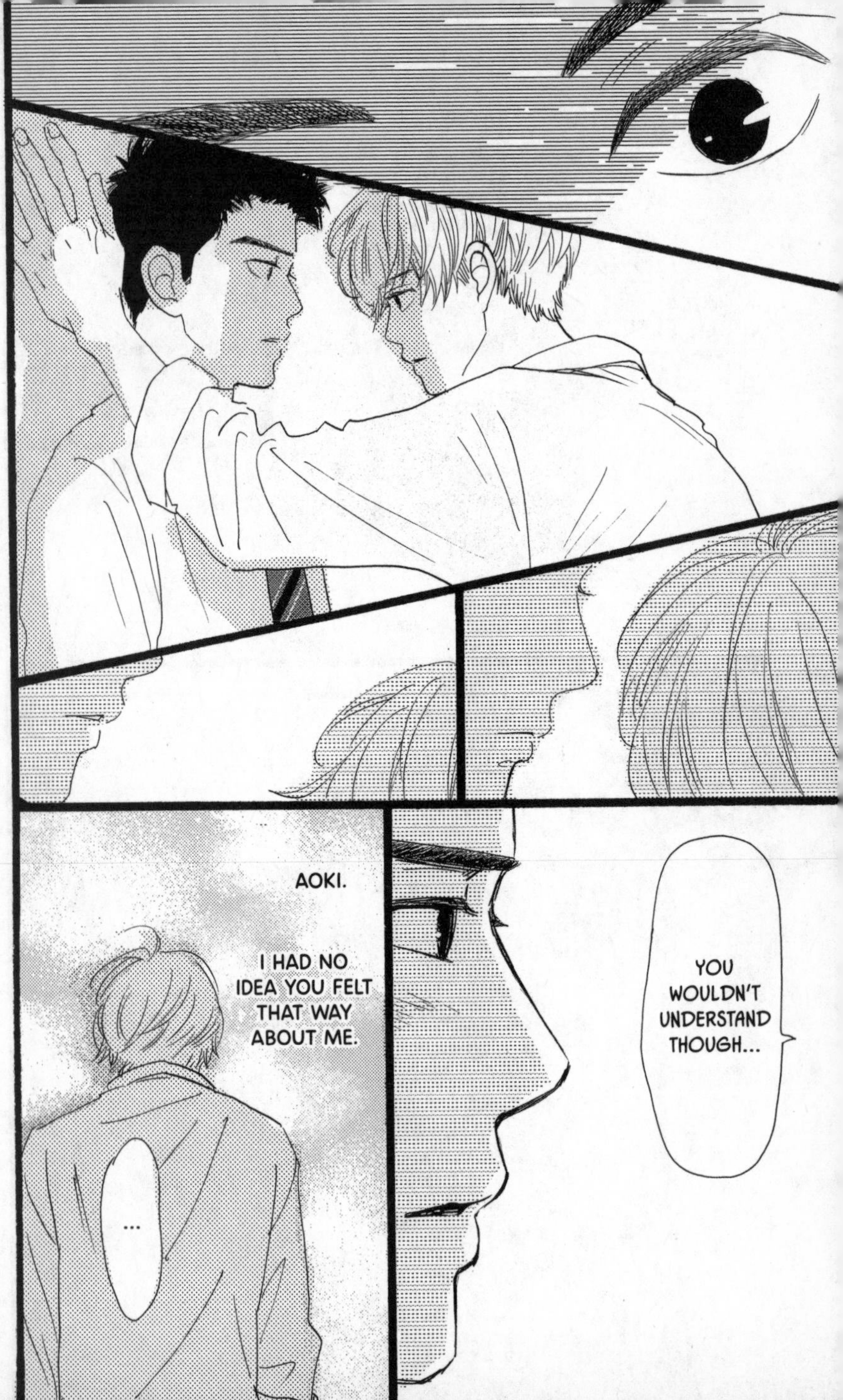
YOU WOULDN'T UNDERSTAND THOUGH...
AOKI.
I HAD NO IDEA YOU FELT THAT WAY ABOUT ME.
...

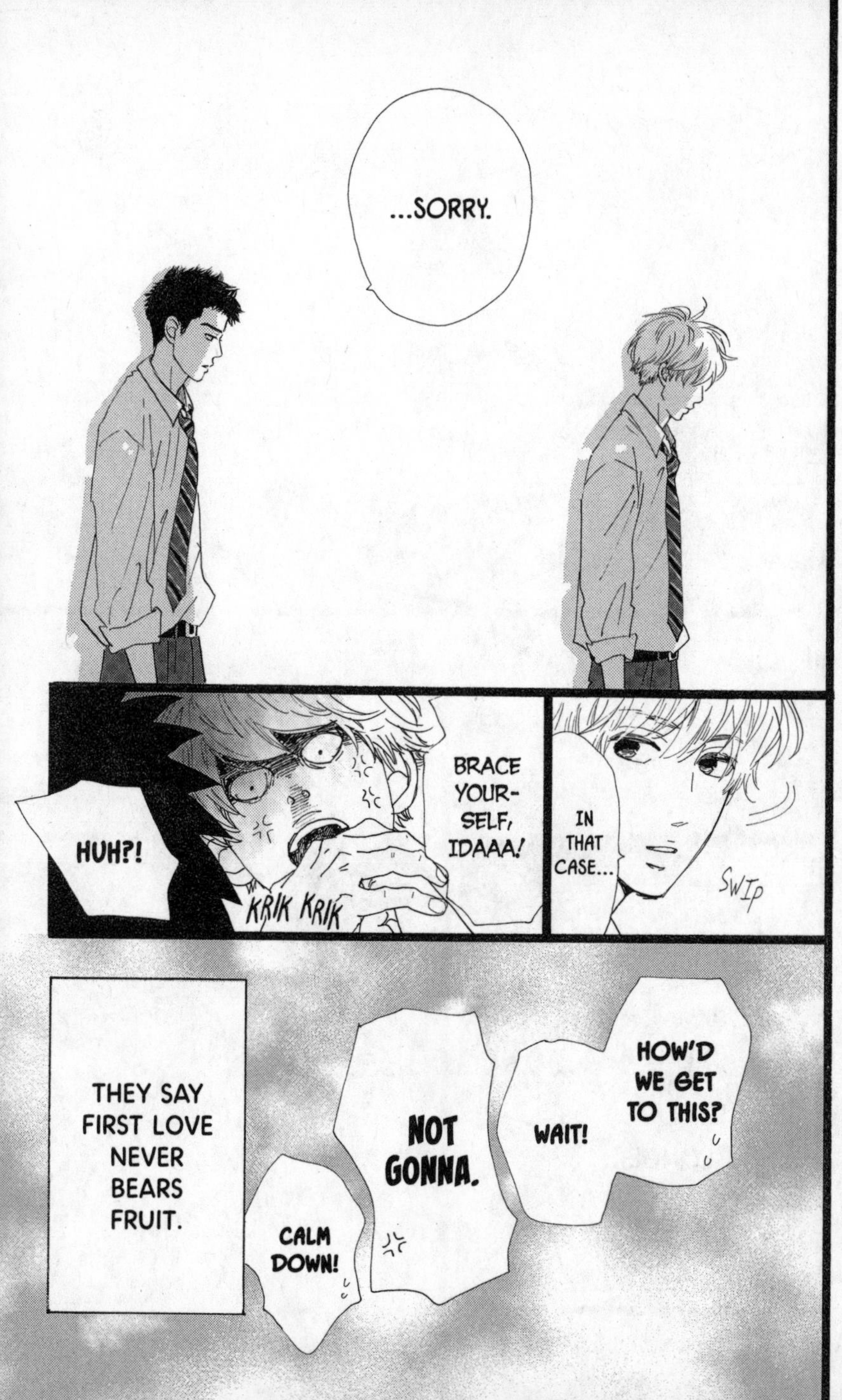
...SORRY.
IN THAT CASE...
SWIP
BRACE YOURSELF, IDAAA!
HUH?!
KRIK KRIK
HOW'D WE GET TO THIS?
WAIT!
NOT GONNA.
CALM DOWN!
THEY SAY FIRST LOVE NEVER BEARS FRUIT.

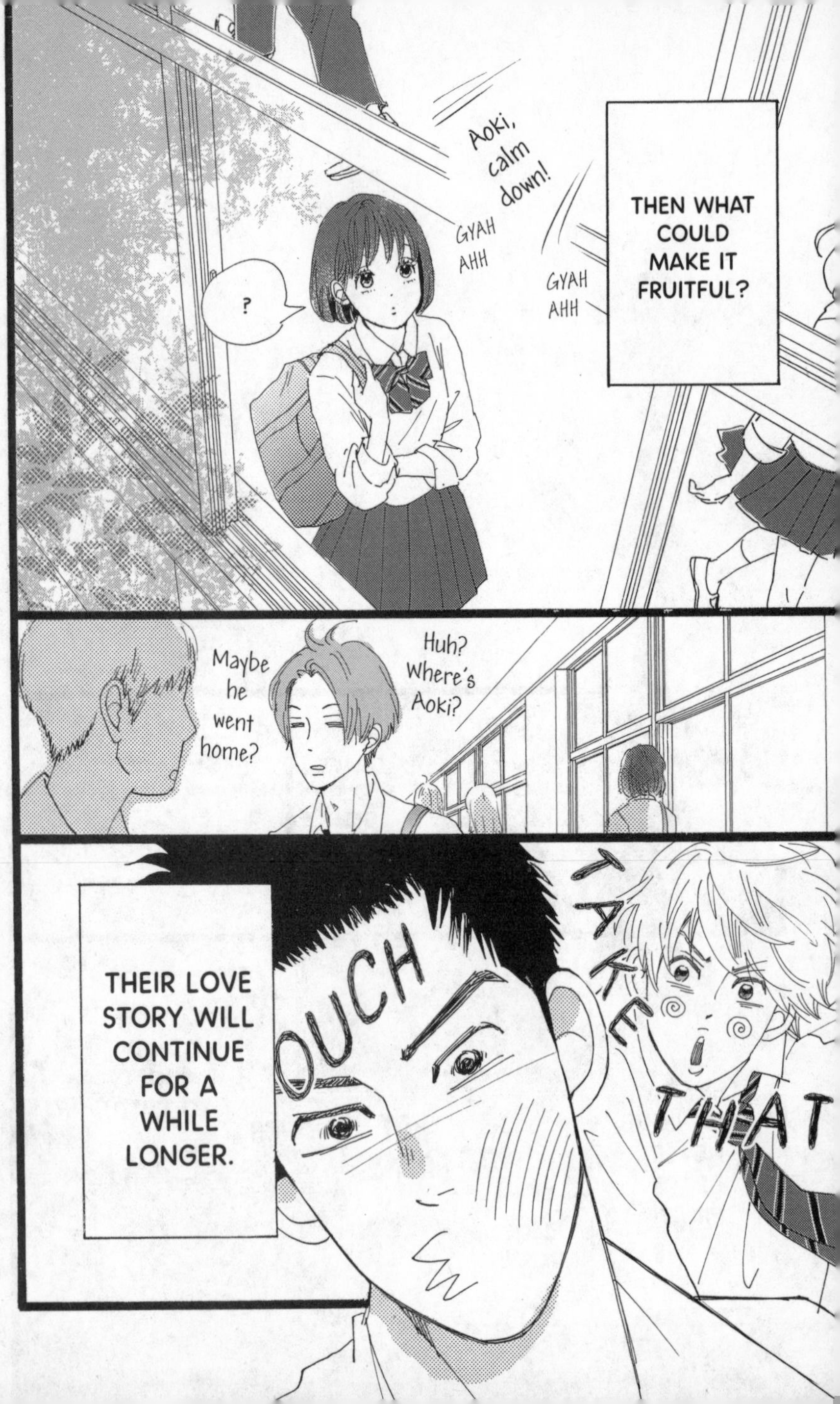
THEN WHAT COULD MAKE IT FRUITFUL?
GYAH AHH
Aoki, calm down!
GYAH AHH
?
Huh? Where's Aoki?
Maybe he went home?
TAKE THAT
OUCH
THEIR LOVE STORY WILL CONTINUE FOR A WHILE LONGER.

Chapter 2

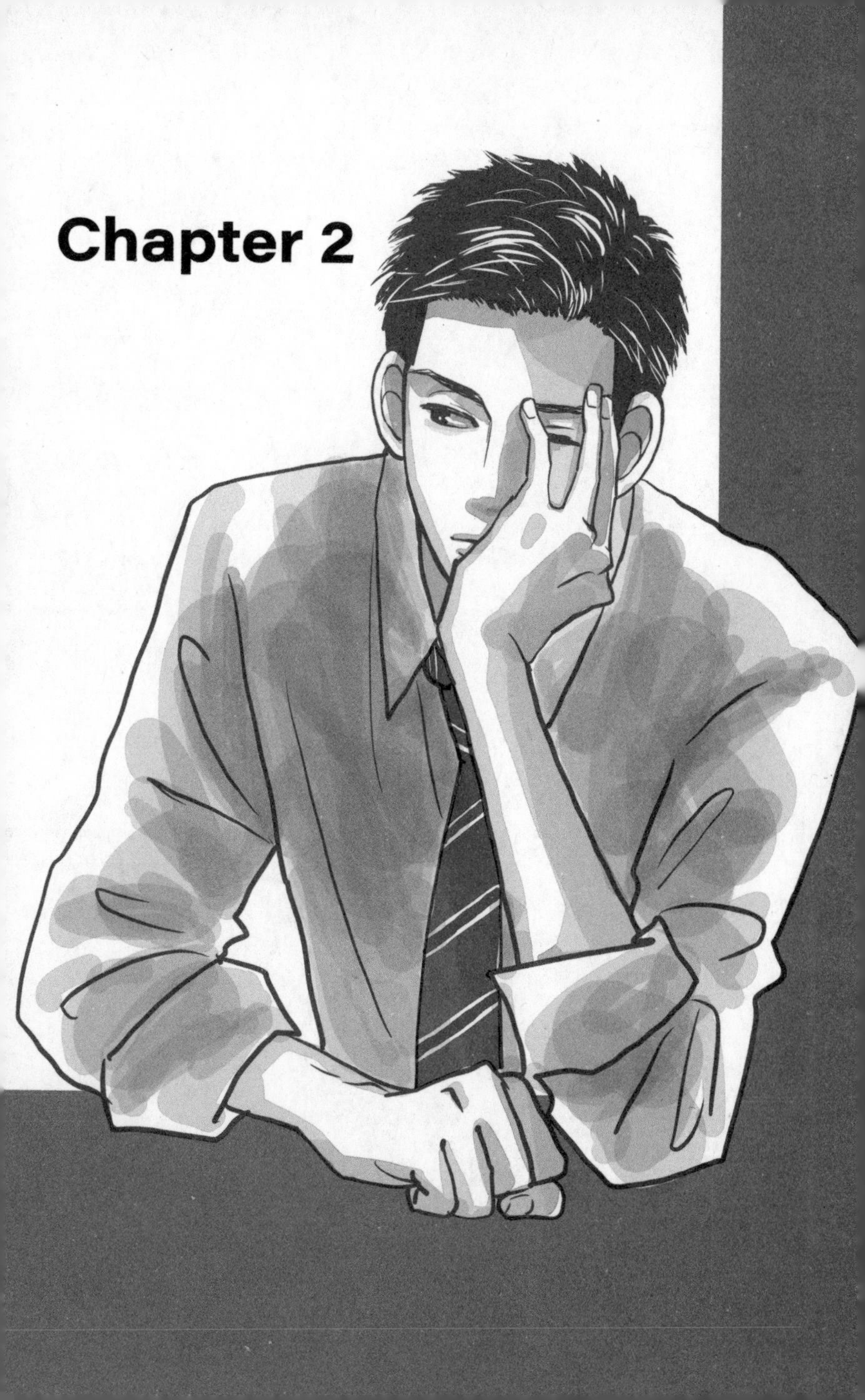

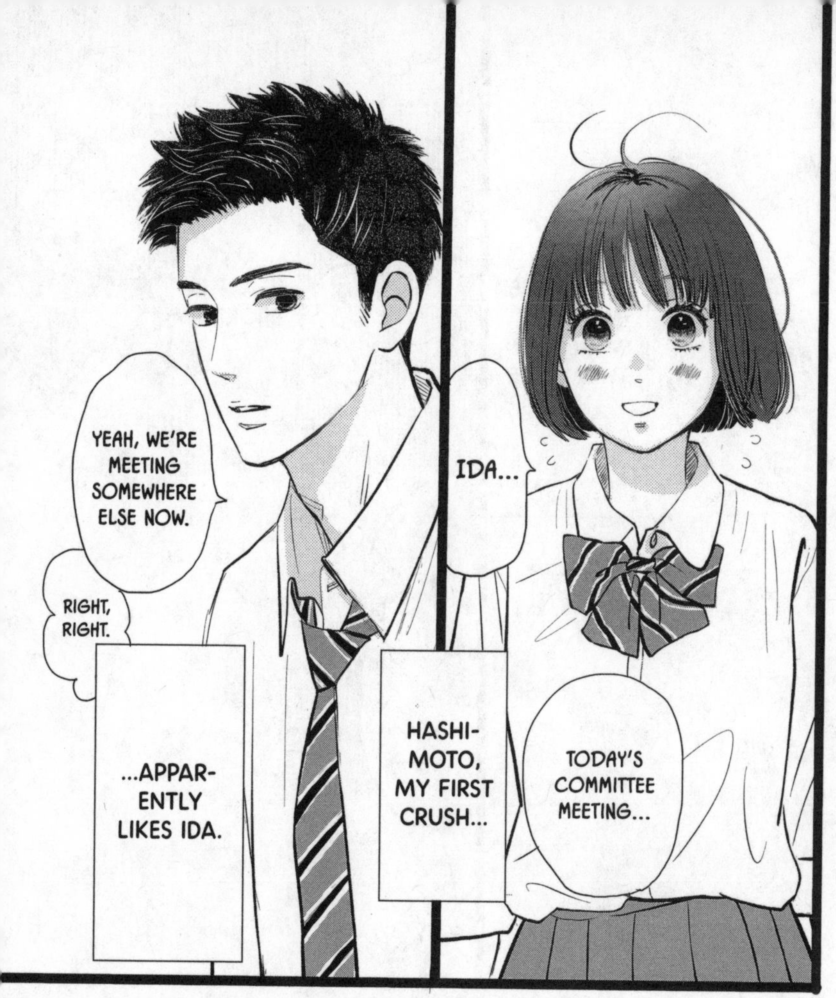
IDA...
TODAY'S COMMITTEE MEETING...
HASHI-MOTO, MY FIRST CRUSH...
YEAH, WE'RE MEETING SOMEWHERE ELSE NOW.
RIGHT, RIGHT.
...APPAR-ENTLY LIKES IDA.

My Love Mix-Up!

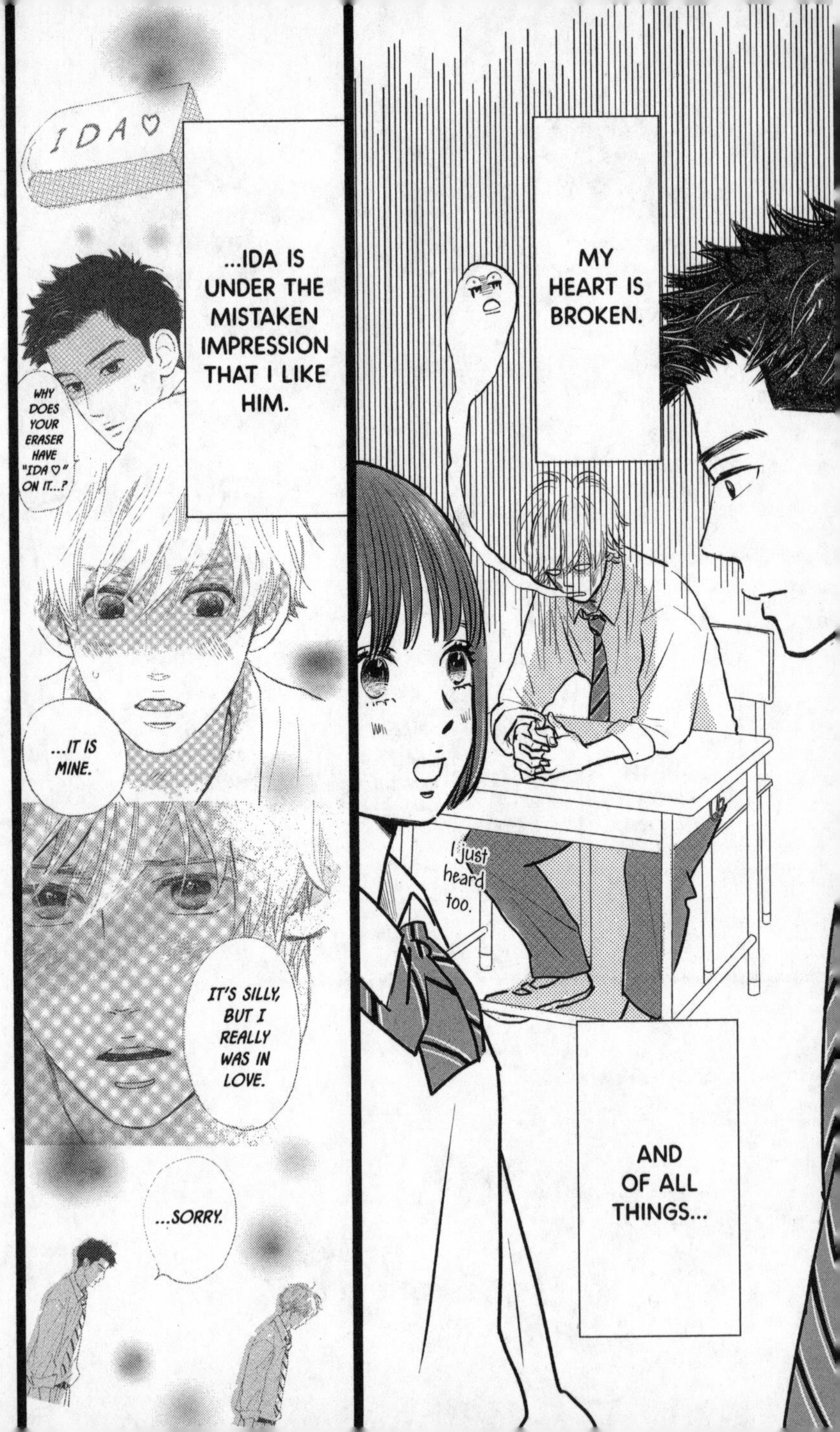
MY HEART IS BROKEN.
I just heard too.
AND OF ALL THINGS...
IDA ♡
...IDA IS UNDER THE MISTAKEN IMPRESSION THAT I LIKE HIM.
WHY DOES YOUR ERASER HAVE "IDA ♡" ON IT...?
...IT IS MINE.
IT'S SILLY, BUT I REALLY WAS IN LOVE.
...SORRY.

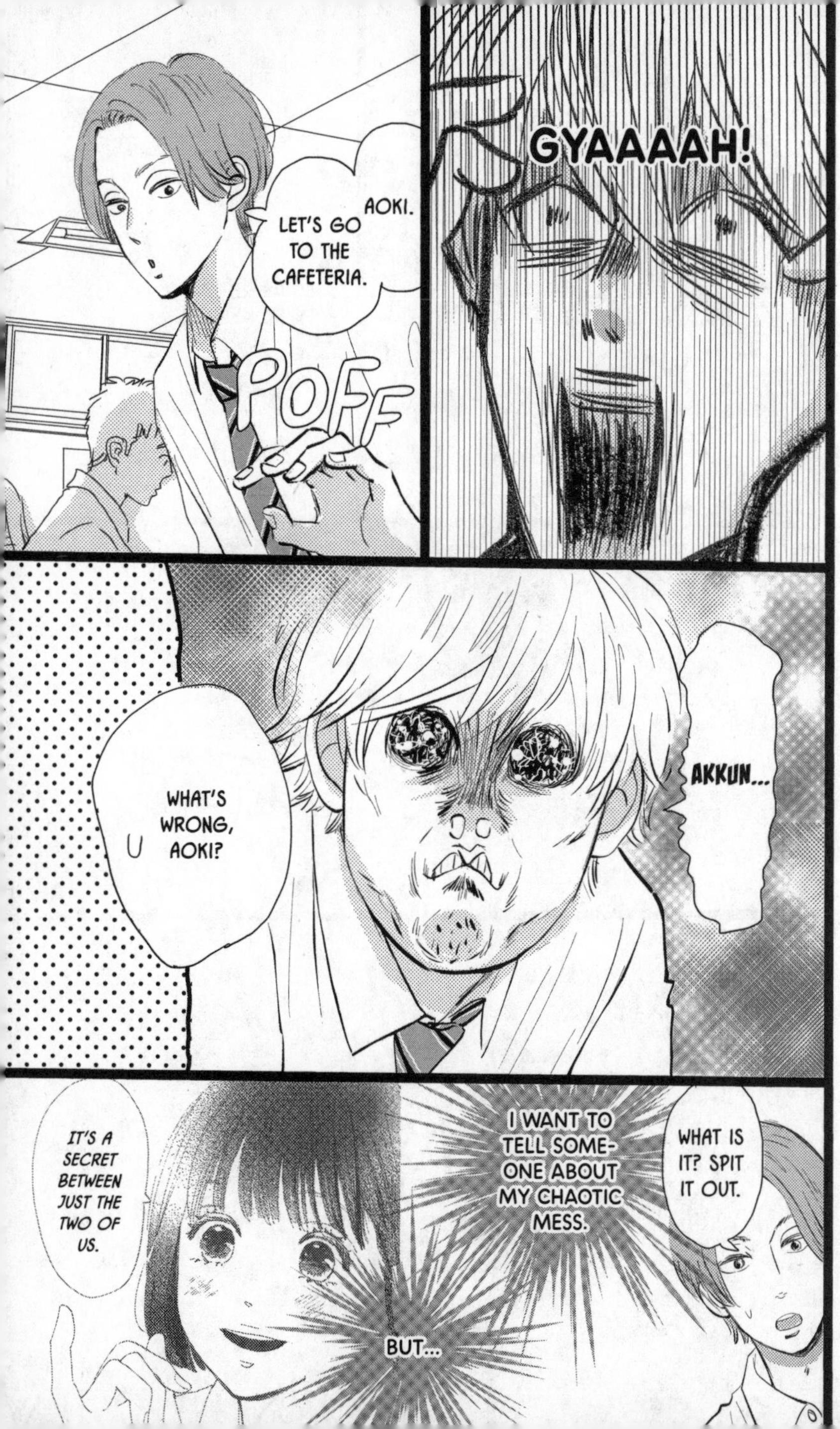
GYAAAAH!
AOKI. LET'S GO TO THE CAFETERIA.
POFF
AKKUN...
WHAT'S WRONG, AOKI?
WHAT IS IT? SPIT IT OUT.
I WANT TO TELL SOME-ONE ABOUT MY CHAOTIC MESS.
BUT...
IT'S A SECRET BETWEEN JUST THE TWO OF US.

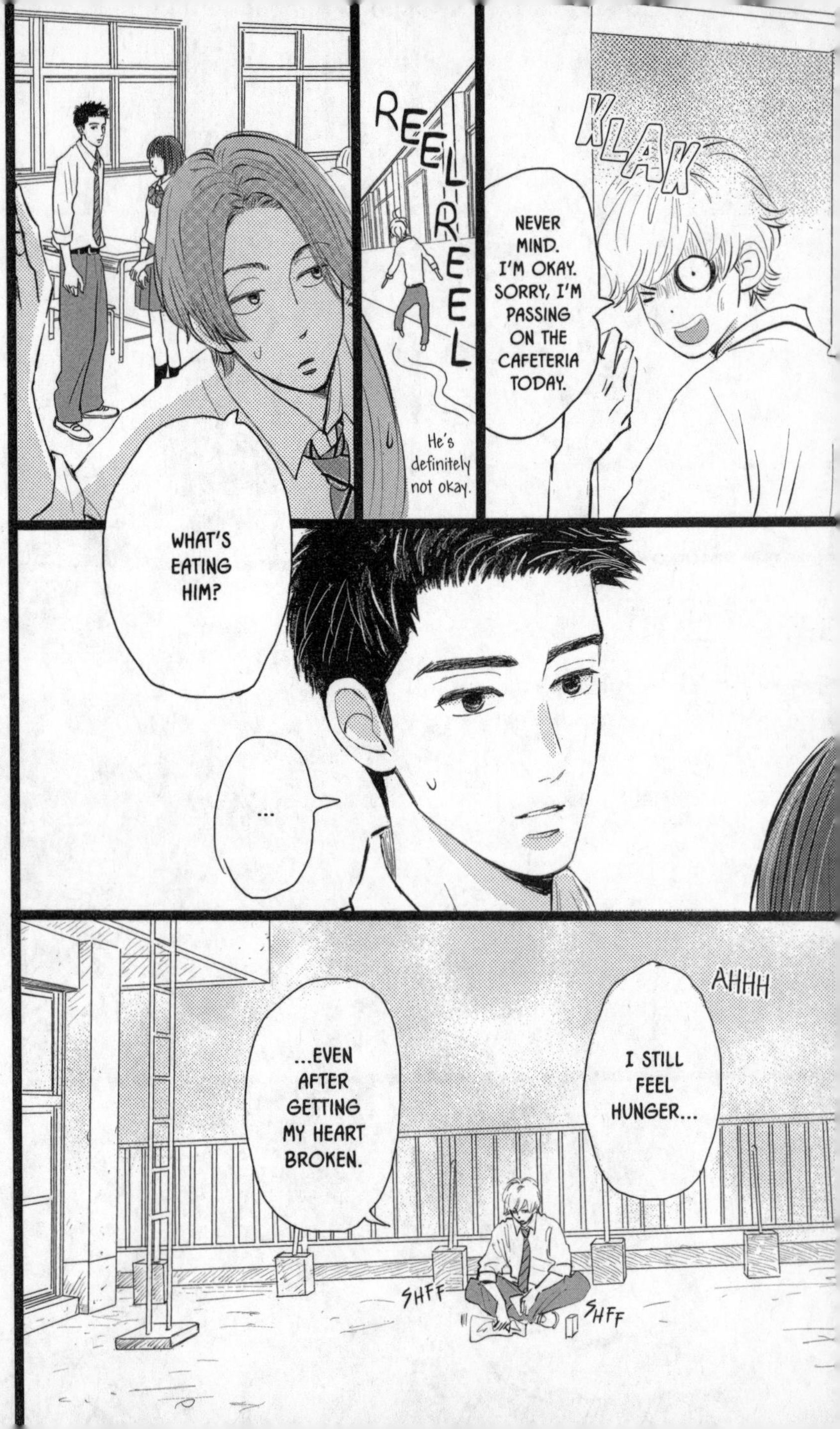
KLAK
NEVER MIND. I'M OKAY. SORRY, I'M PASSING ON THE CAFETERIA TODAY.
REELREEL
He's definitely not okay.
WHAT'S EATING HIM?
...
AHHH
I STILL FEEL HUNGER...
...EVEN AFTER GETTING MY HEART BROKEN.
SHFF
SHFF

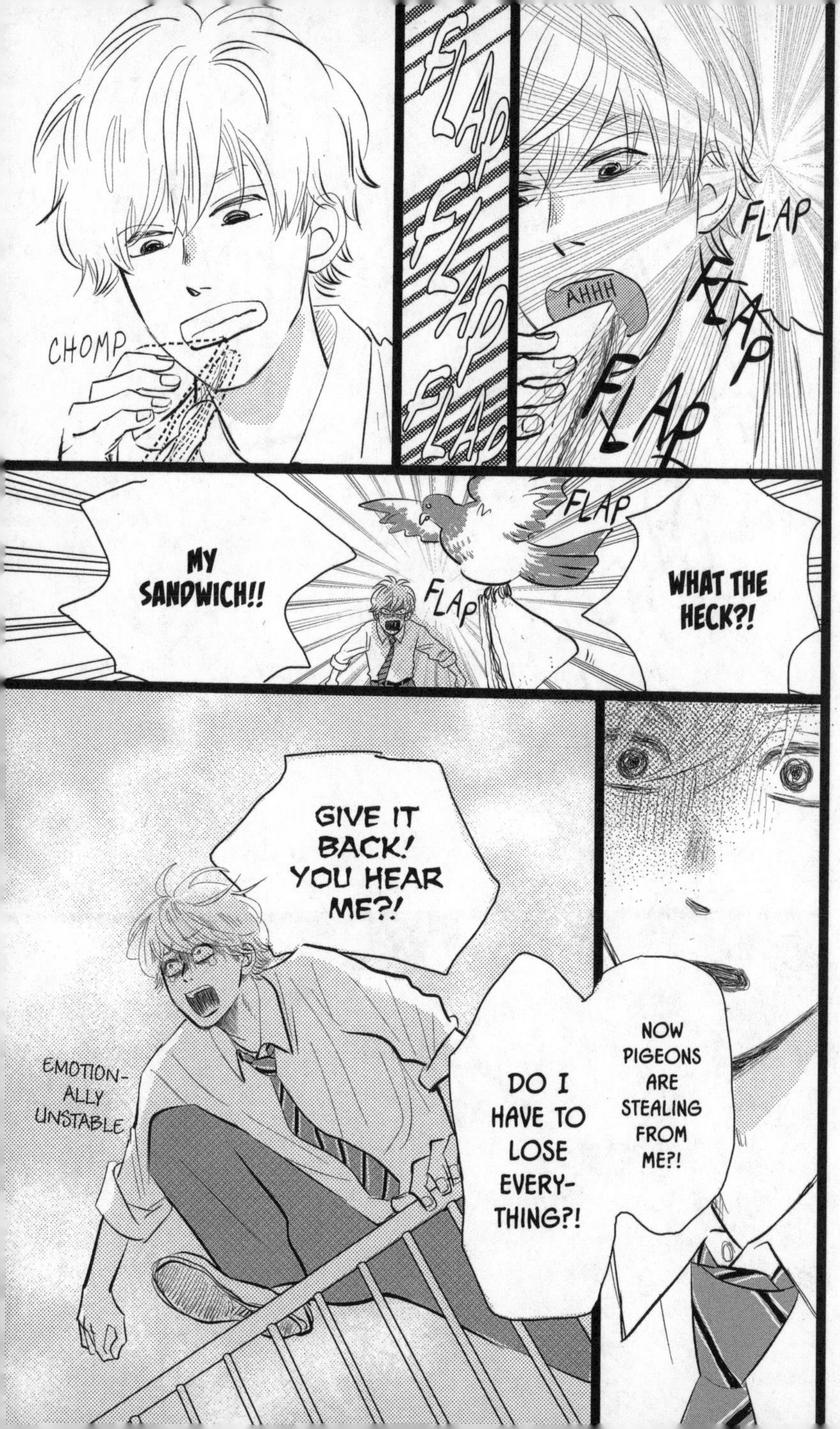
FLAP
FLAP
FLAP
FLAP
AHHH
FLAP
FLAP
FLAP
FLAP
CHOMP
WHAT THE HECK?!
FLAP
FLAP
MY SANDWICH!!
NOW PIGEONS ARE STEALING FROM ME?!
DO I HAVE TO LOSE EVERYTHING?!
GIVE IT BACK! YOU HEAR ME?!
EMOTIONALLY UNSTABLE

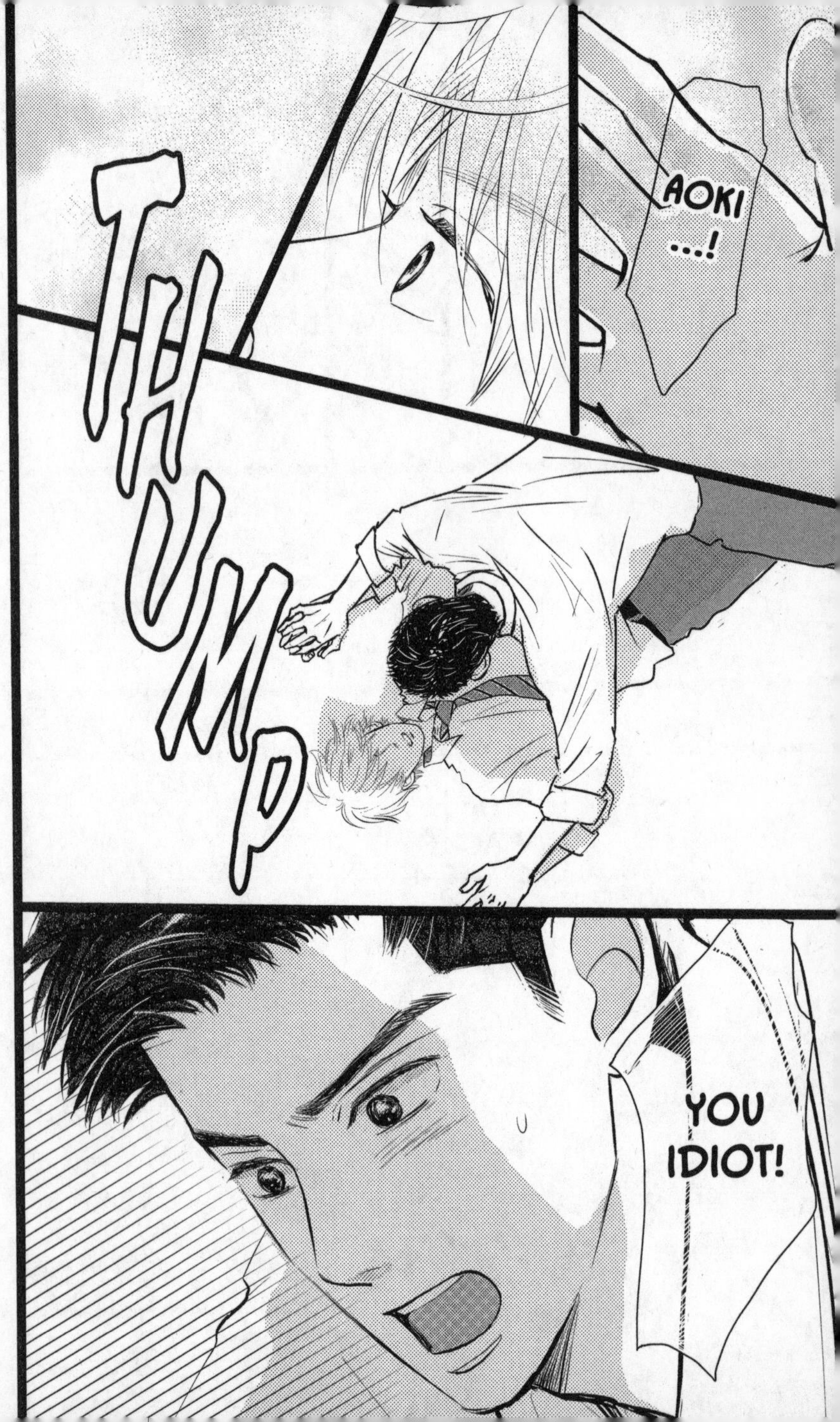
AOKI ...!
THUMP
YOU IDIOT!

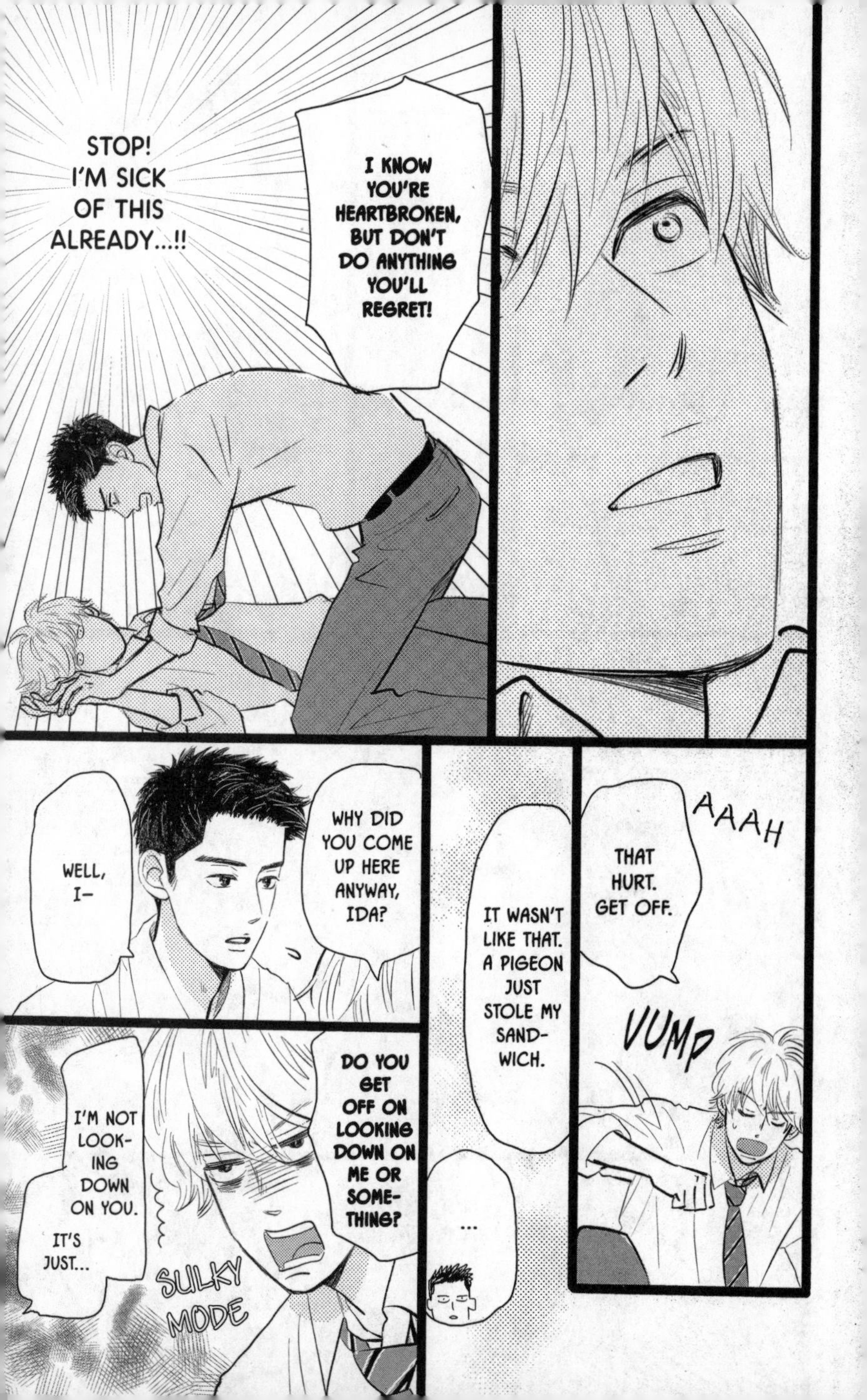

I KNOW YOU'RE HEARTBROKEN, BUT DON'T DO ANYTHING YOU'LL REGRET!
STOP! I'M SICK OF THIS ALREADY...!!
AAAH
THAT HURT. GET OFF.
VUMP
IT WASN'T LIKE THAT. A PIGEON JUST STOLE MY SAND-WICH.
...
WHY DID YOU COME UP HERE ANYWAY, IDA?
WELL, I–
DO YOU GET OFF ON LOOKING DOWN ON ME OR SOME-THING?
I'M NOT LOOK-ING DOWN ON YOU.
IT'S JUST...
SULKY MODE

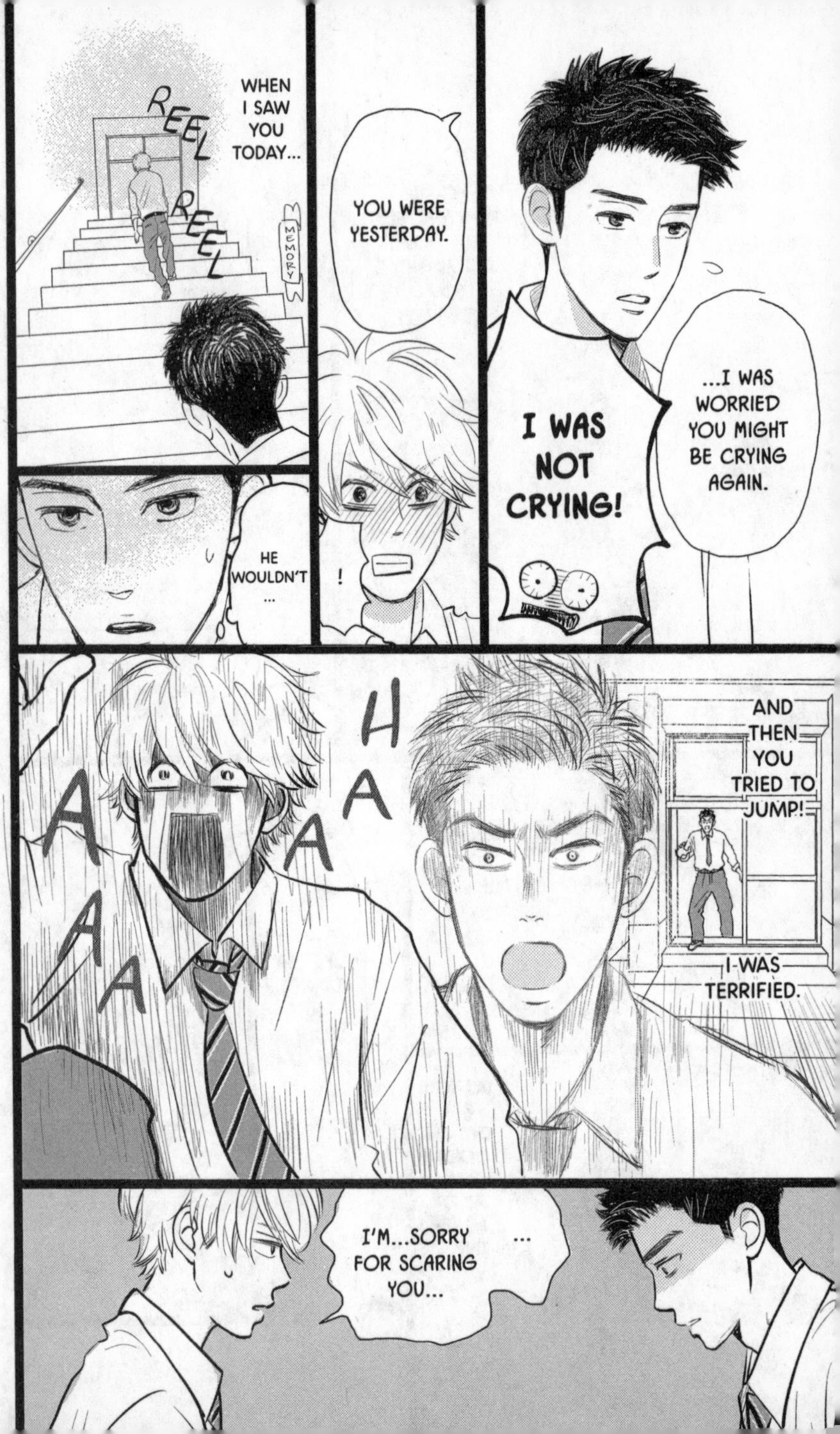
...I WAS WORRIED YOU MIGHT BE CRYING AGAIN.
I WAS NOT CRYING!
YOU WERE YESTERDAY.
!
WHEN I SAW YOU TODAY...
REEL REEL
MEMORY
HE WOULDN'T ...
AND THEN YOU TRIED TO JUMP!
I WAS TERRIFIED.
HAAAAAAA
...
I'M...SORRY FOR SCARING YOU...

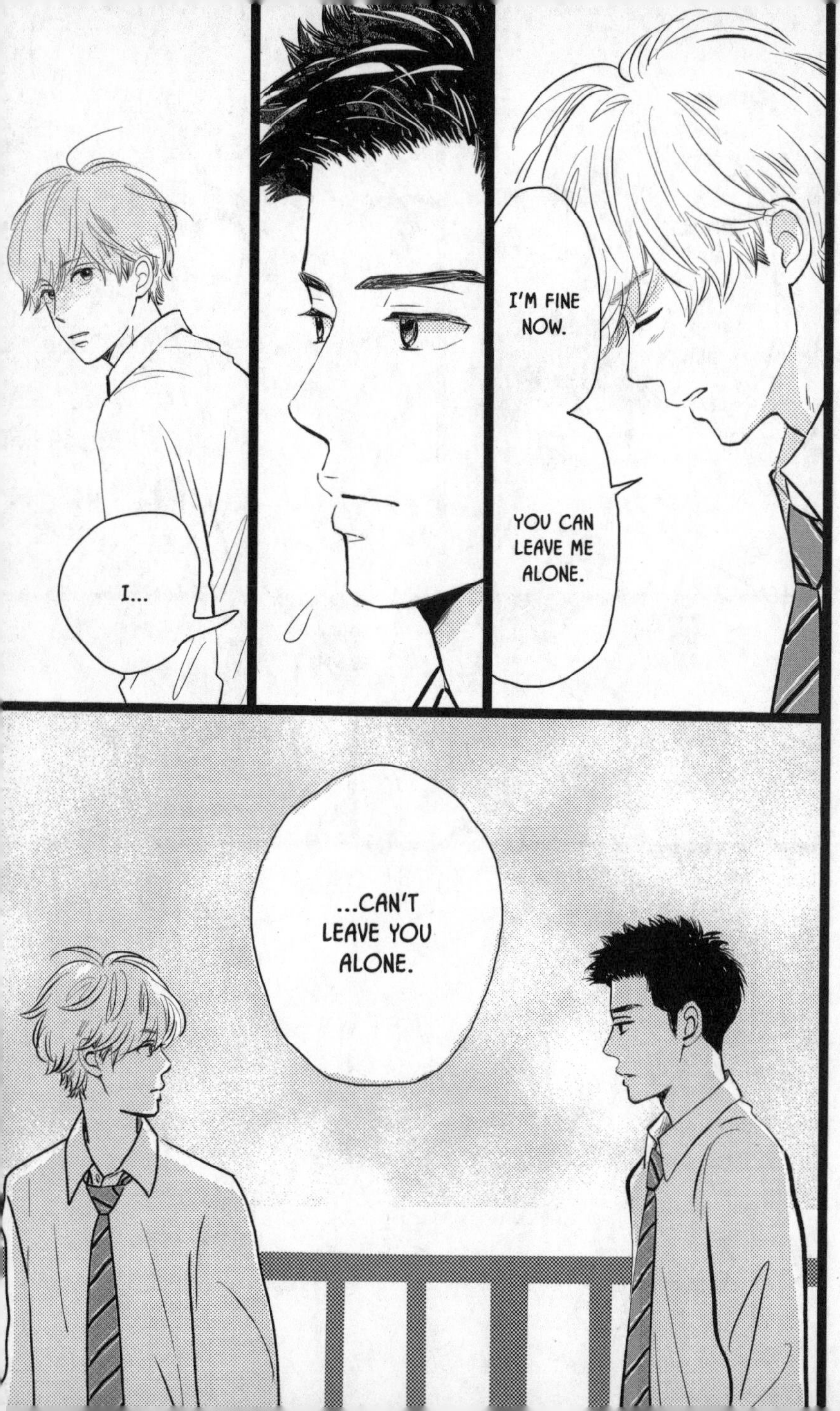
I'M FINE NOW.
YOU CAN LEAVE ME ALONE.
I...
...CAN'T LEAVE YOU ALONE.

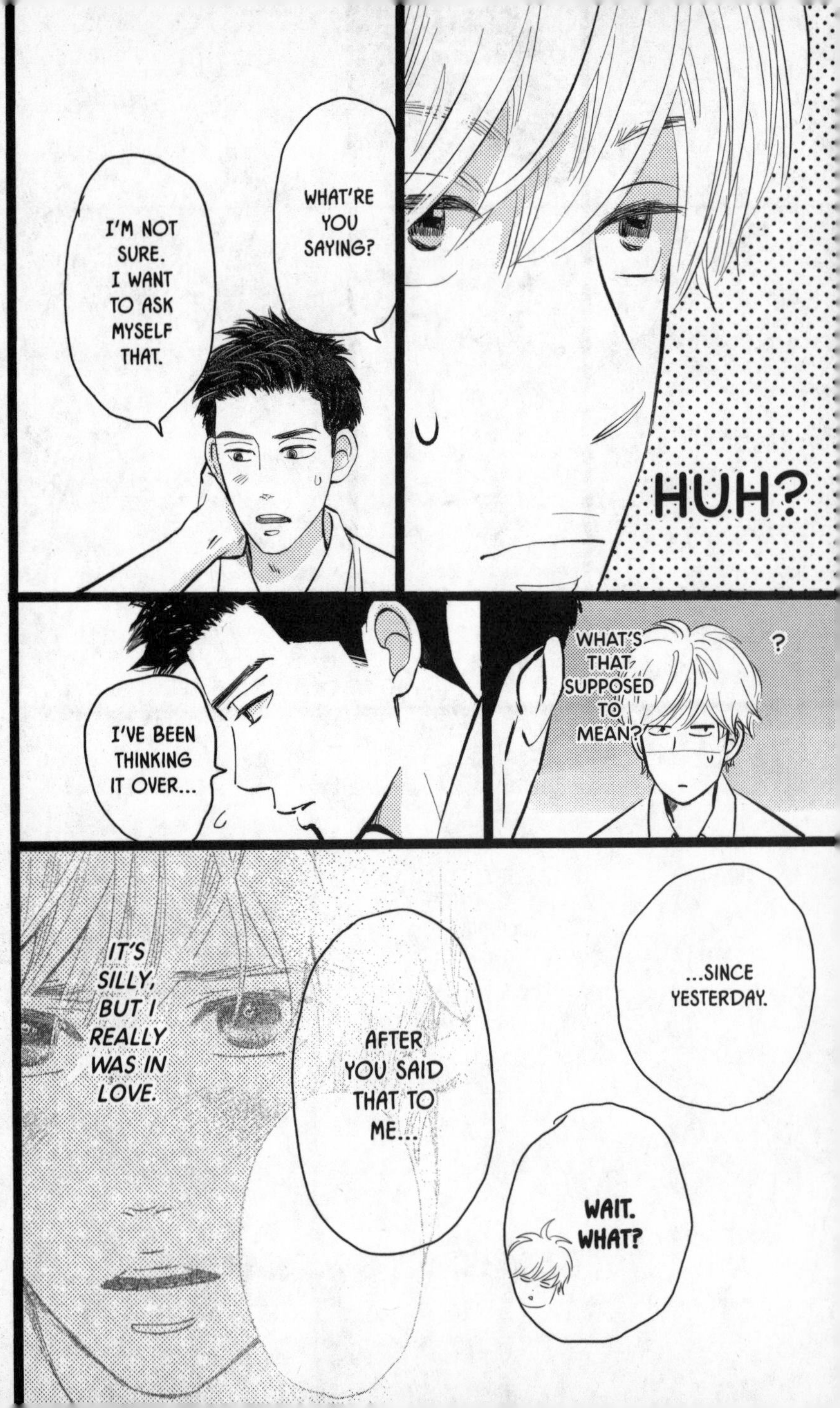
HUH?
WHAT'RE YOU SAYING?
I'M NOT SURE. I WANT TO ASK MYSELF THAT.
WHAT'S THAT SUPPOSED TO MEAN?
?
I'VE BEEN THINKING IT OVER...
...SINCE YESTERDAY.
AFTER YOU SAID THAT TO ME...
IT'S SILLY, BUT I REALLY WAS IN LOVE.
WAIT. WHAT?

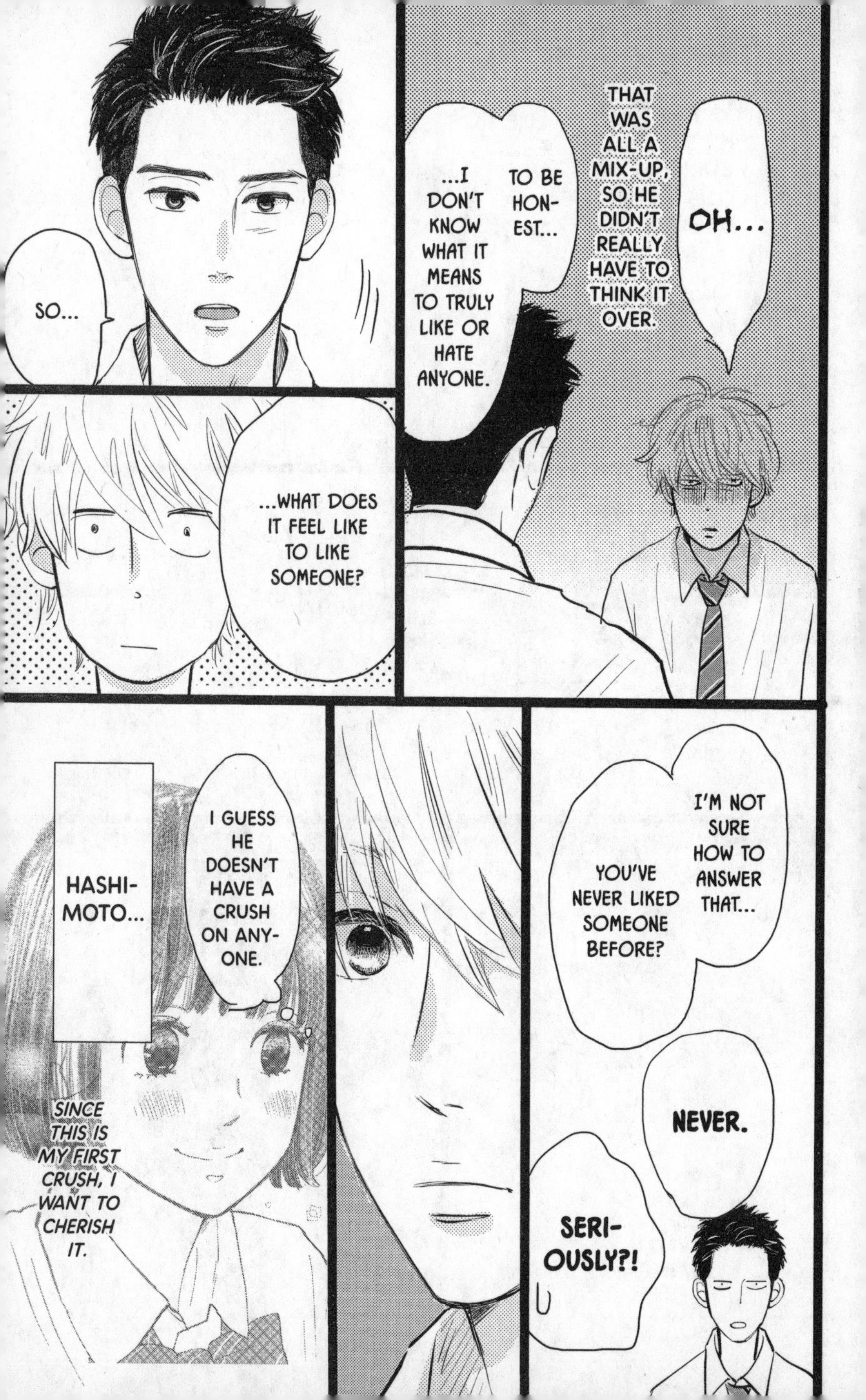
OH...
THAT WAS ALL A MIX-UP, SO HE DIDN'T REALLY HAVE TO THINK IT OVER.
TO BE HON-EST...
...I DON'T KNOW WHAT IT MEANS TO TRULY LIKE OR HATE ANYONE.
SO...
...WHAT DOES IT FEEL LIKE TO LIKE SOMEONE?
I'M NOT SURE HOW TO ANSWER THAT...
YOU'VE NEVER LIKED SOMEONE BEFORE?
NEVER.
SERI-OUSLY?!
I GUESS HE DOESN'T HAVE A CRUSH ON ANY-ONE.
HASHI-MOTO...
SINCE THIS IS MY FIRST CRUSH, I WANT TO CHERISH IT.

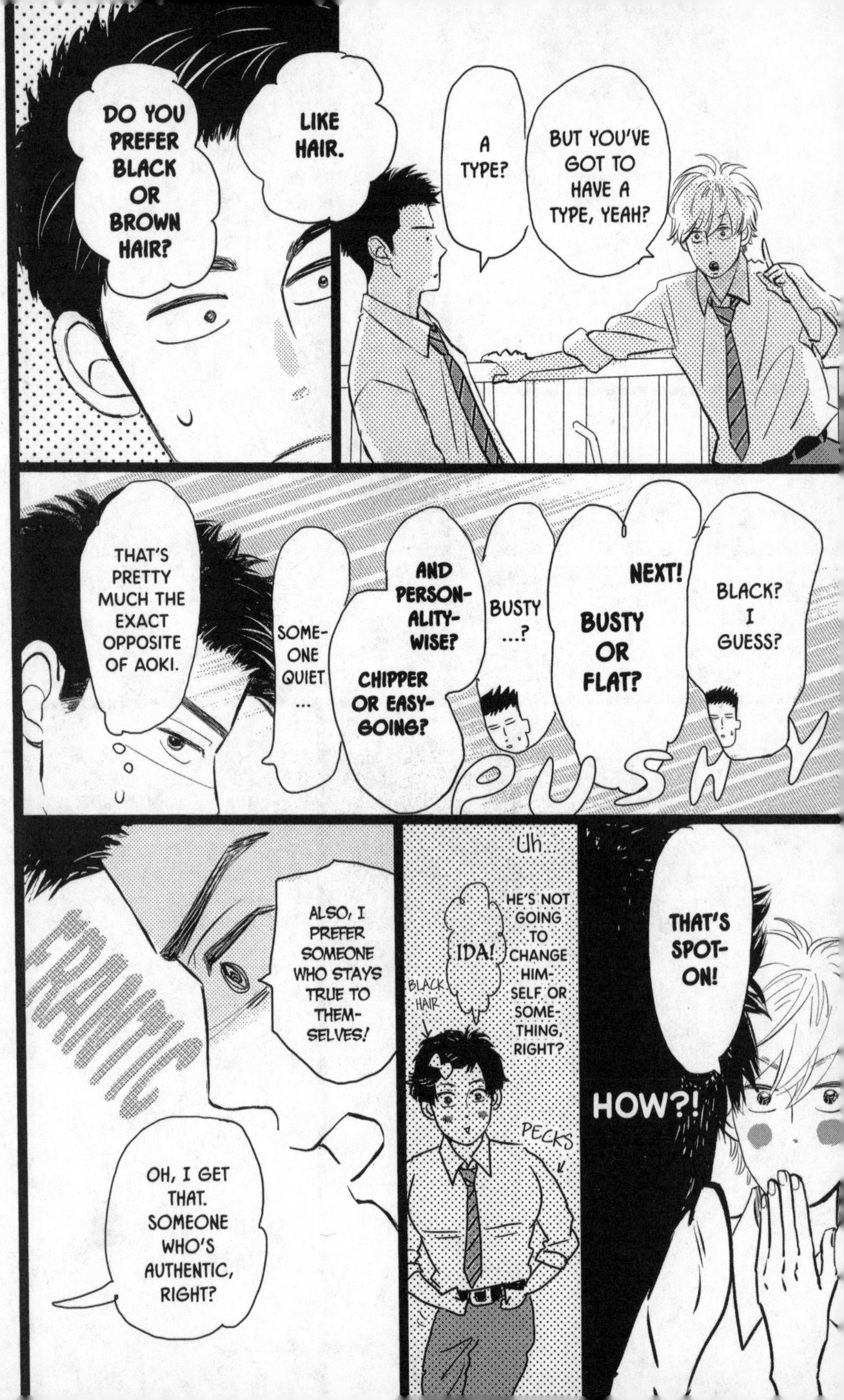
BUT YOU'VE GOT TO HAVE A TYPE, YEAH?
A TYPE?
LIKE HAIR.
DO YOU PREFER BLACK OR BROWN HAIR?
BLACK? I GUESS?
NEXT!
BUSTY OR FLAT?
BUSTY ...?
AND PERSONALITY-WISE?
CHIPPER OR EASY-GOING?
SOME-ONE QUIET ...
PUSH
THAT'S PRETTY MUCH THE EXACT OPPOSITE OF AOKI.
THAT'S SPOT-ON!
HOW?!
Uh
HE'S NOT GOING TO CHANGE HIMSELF OR SOMETHING, RIGHT?
IDA!
BLACK HAIR
PECKS
FRANTIC
ALSO, I PREFER SOMEONE WHO STAYS TRUE TO THEMSELVES!
OH, I GET THAT. SOMEONE WHO'S AUTHENTIC, RIGHT?

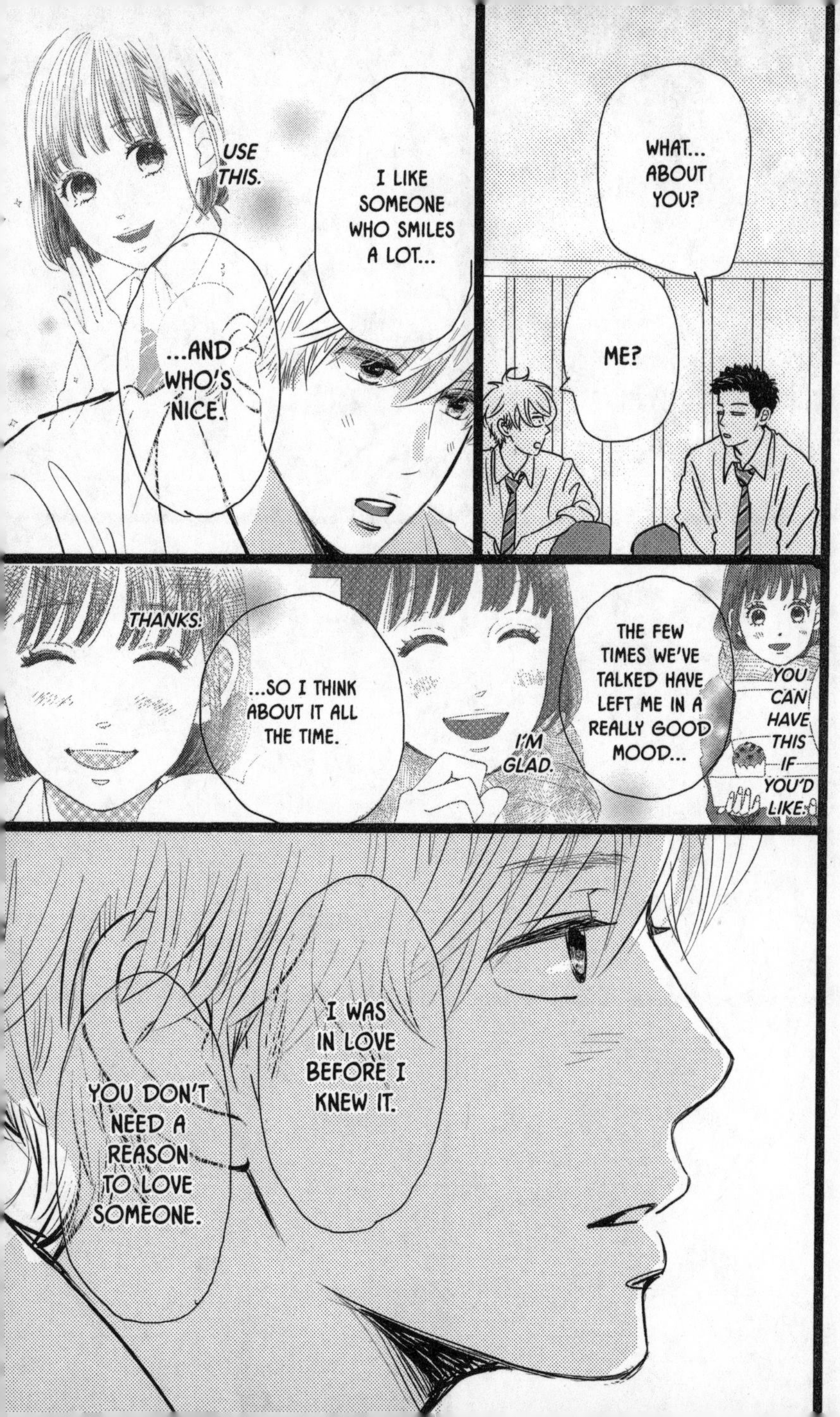
WHAT... ABOUT YOU?
ME?
I LIKE SOMEONE WHO SMILES A LOT...
USE THIS.
...AND WHO'S NICE.
YOU CAN HAVE THIS IF YOU'D LIKE.
THE FEW TIMES WE'VE TALKED HAVE LEFT ME IN A REALLY GOOD MOOD...
I'M GLAD.
...SO I THINK ABOUT IT ALL THE TIME.
THANKS.
I WAS IN LOVE BEFORE I KNEW IT.
YOU DON'T NEED A REASON TO LOVE SOMEONE.

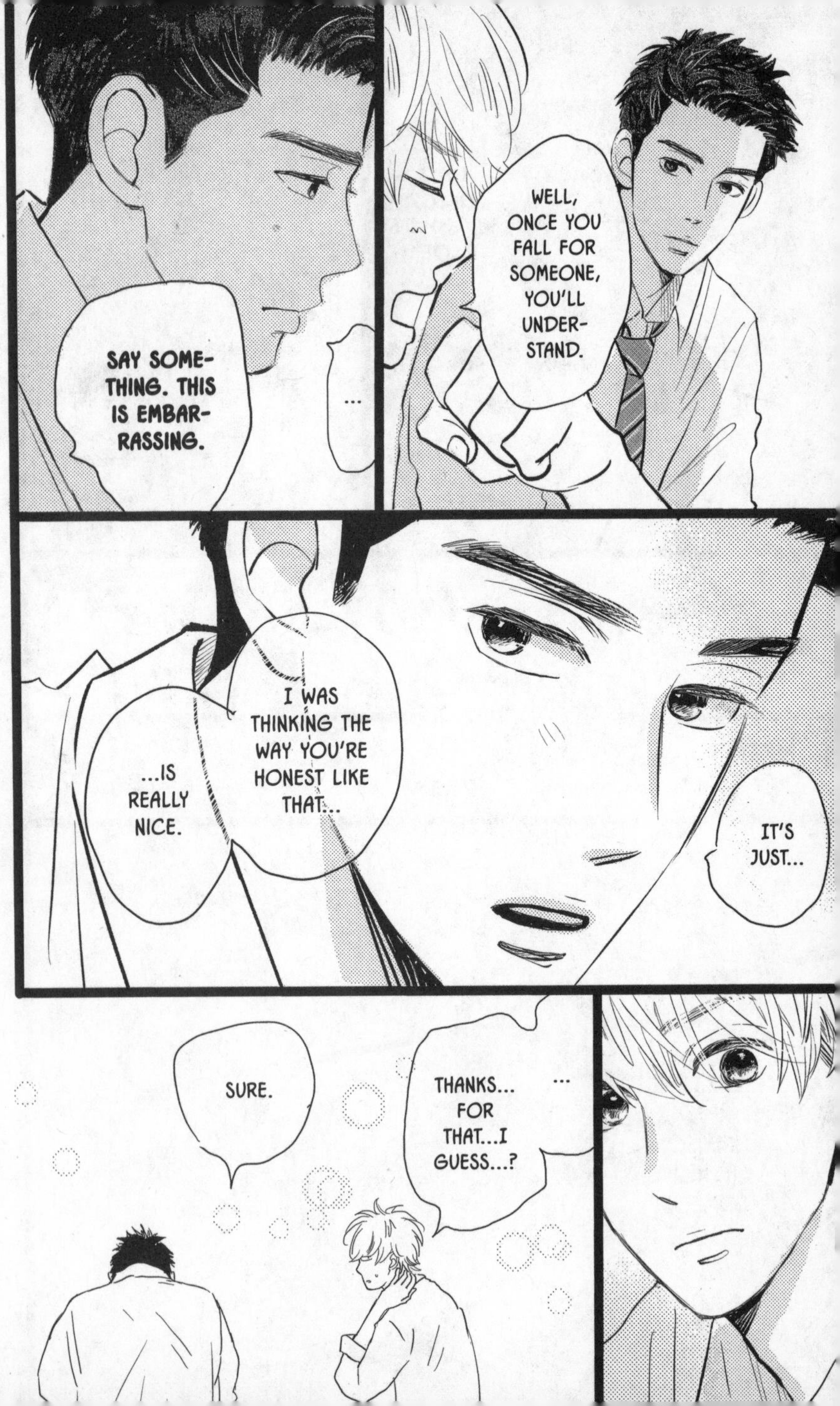
WELL, ONCE YOU FALL FOR SOMEONE, YOU'LL UNDER-STAND.
...
SAY SOME-THING. THIS IS EMBAR-RASSING.
IT'S JUST...
I WAS THINKING THE WAY YOU'RE HONEST LIKE THAT...
...IS REALLY NICE.
...
THANKS... FOR THAT...I GUESS...?
SURE.

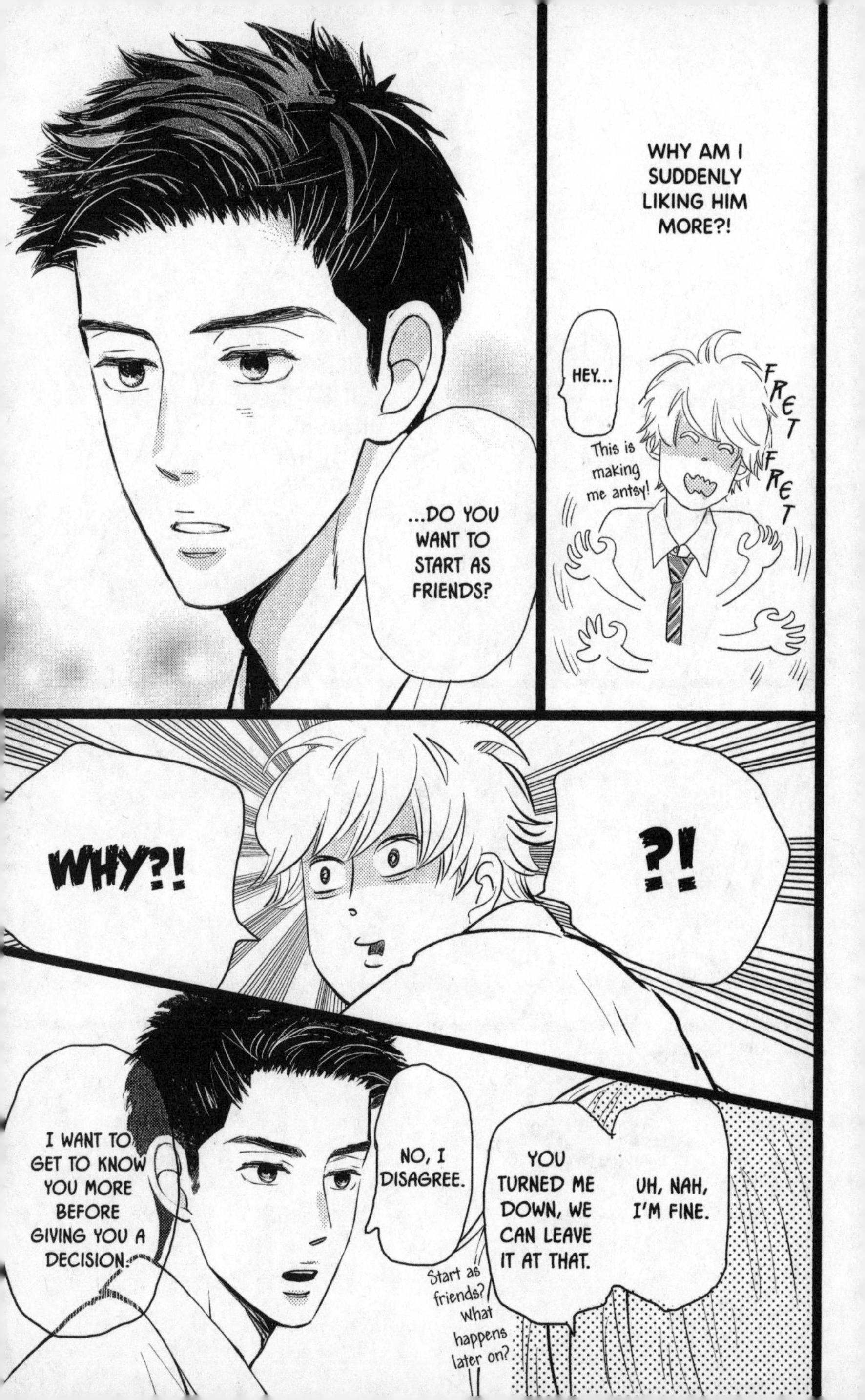
WHY AM I SUDDENLY LIKING HIM MORE?!
HEY...
This is making me antsy!
FRET FRET
...DO YOU WANT TO START AS FRIENDS?
?!
WHY?!
UH, NAH, I'M FINE.
YOU TURNED ME DOWN, WE CAN LEAVE IT AT THAT.
Start as friends? What happens later on?
NO, I DISAGREE.
I WANT TO GET TO KNOW YOU MORE BEFORE GIVING YOU A DECISION.

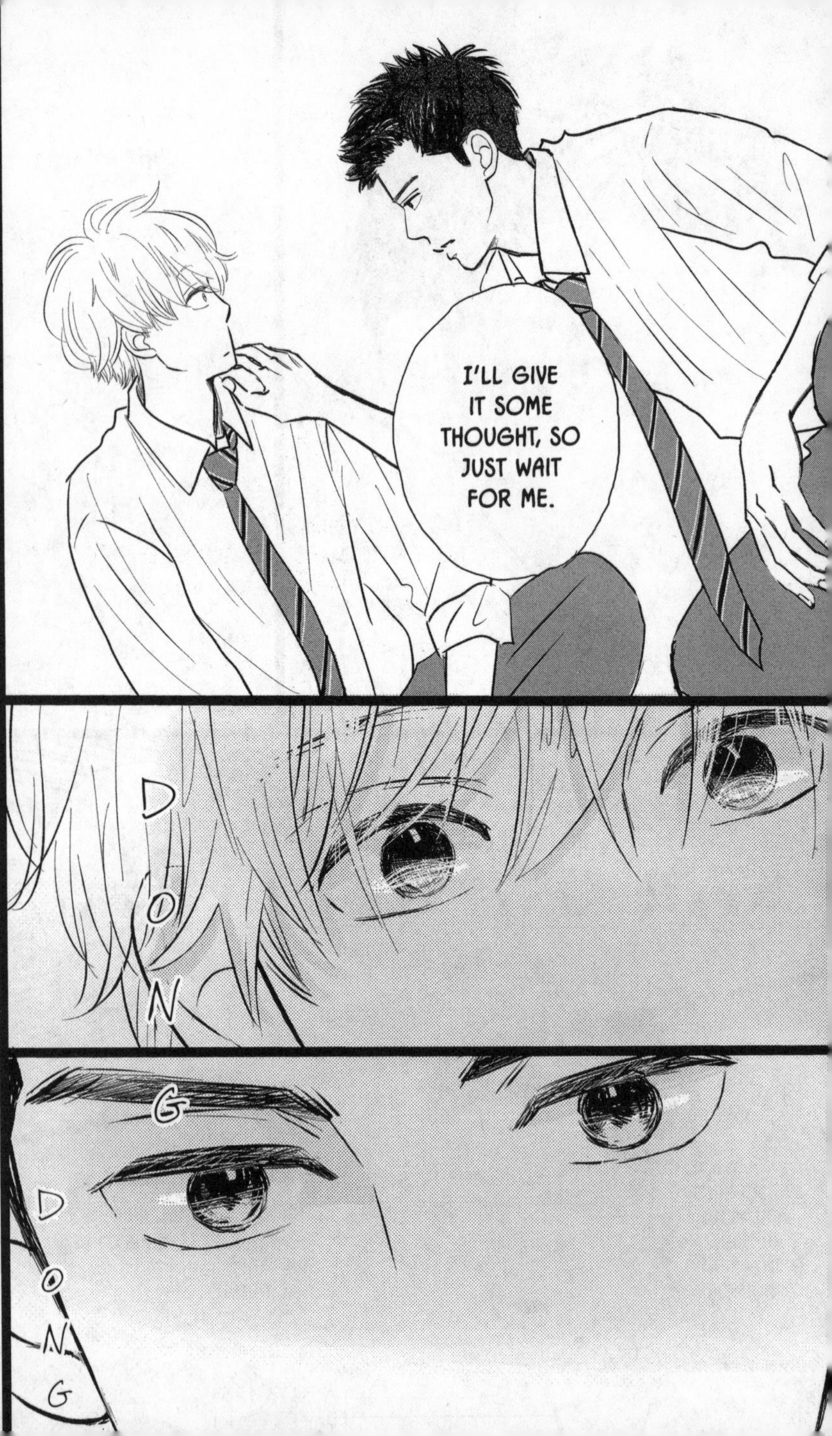
I'LL GIVE IT SOME THOUGHT, SO JUST WAIT FOR ME.
DONG
DONG

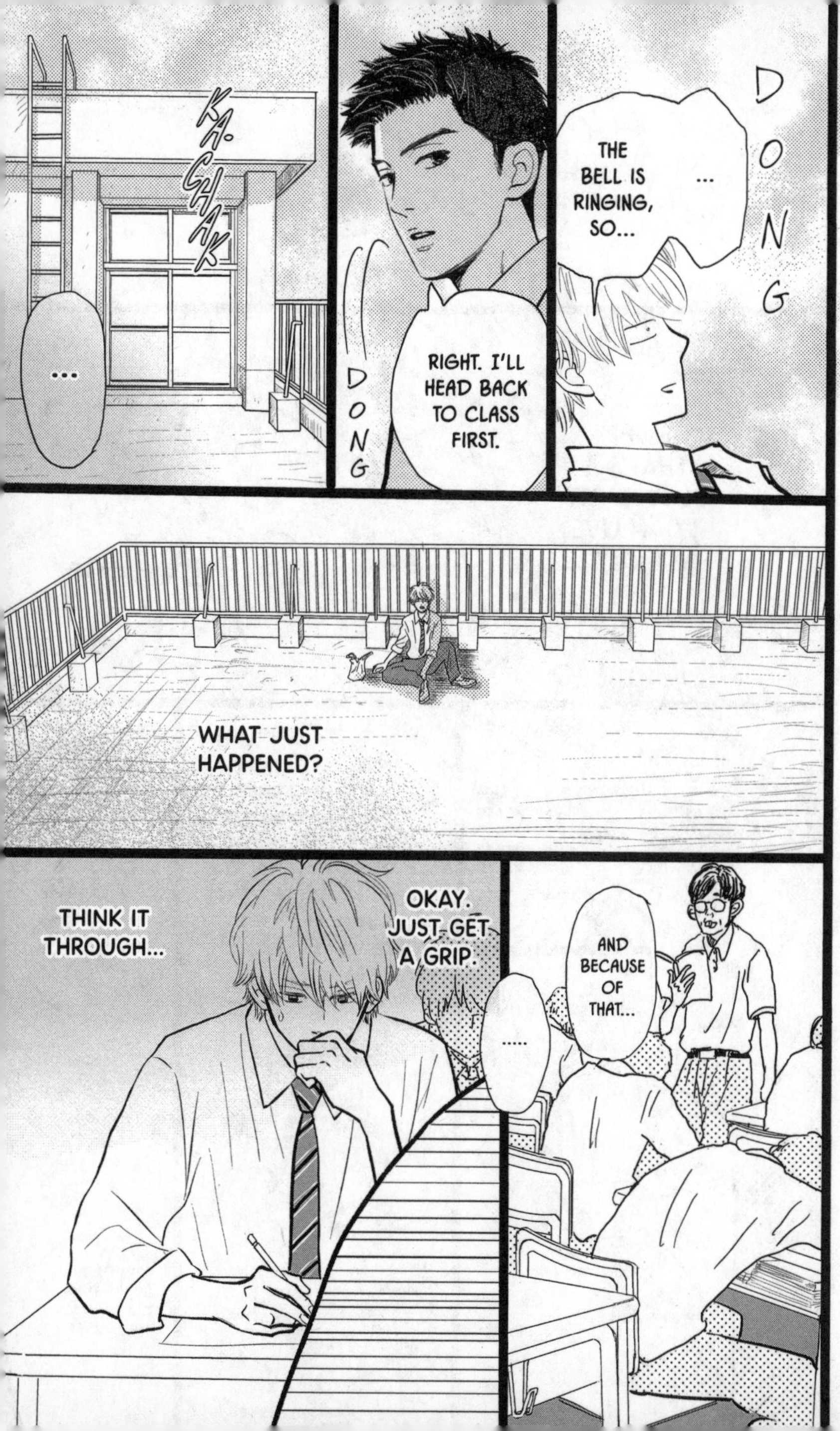
DONG
...
THE BELL IS RINGING, SO...
RIGHT. I'LL HEAD BACK TO CLASS FIRST.
DONG
KA-CHAK
...
WHAT JUST HAPPENED?
AND BECAUSE OF THAT...
.....
OKAY. JUST GET A GRIP.
THINK IT THROUGH...

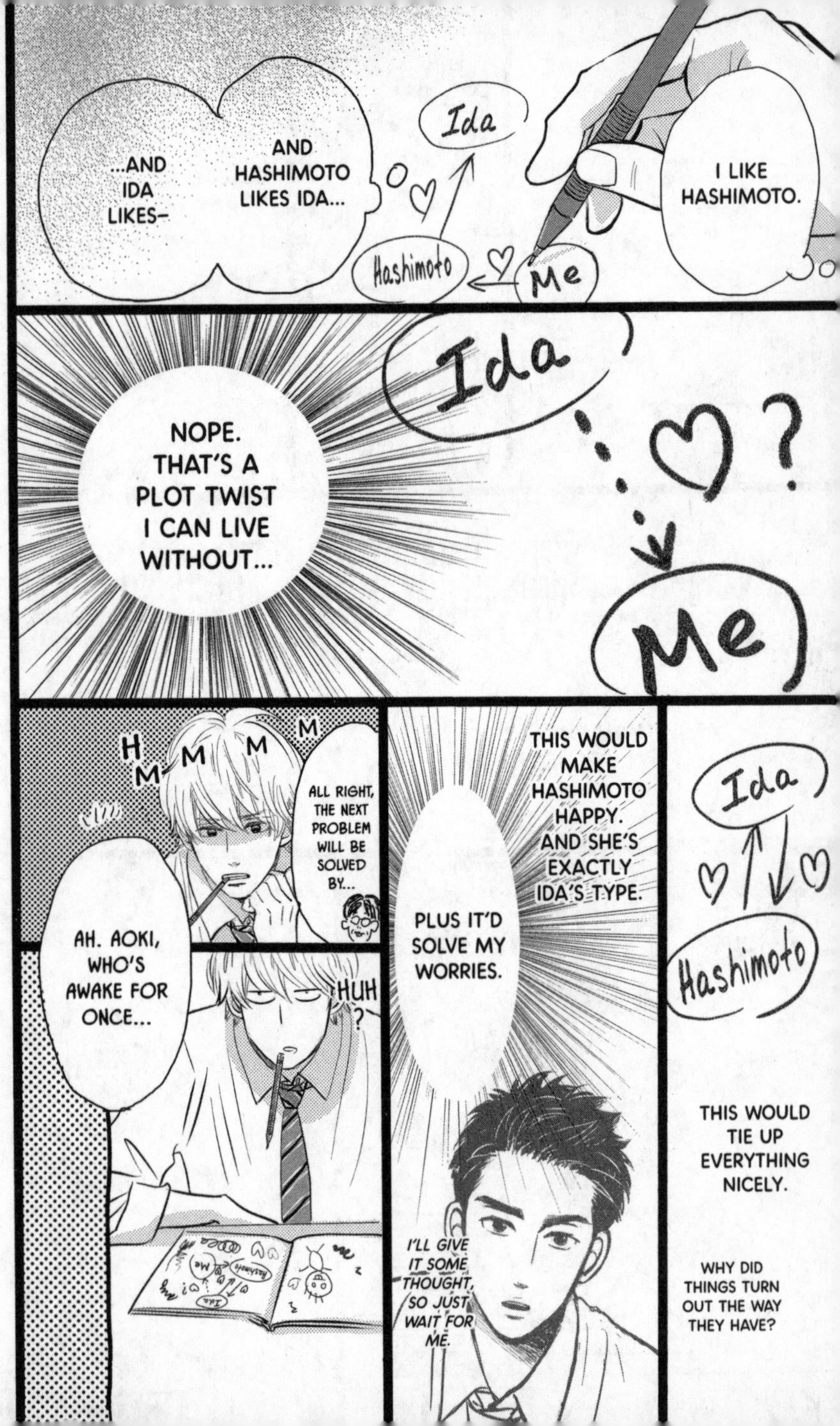
I LIKE HASHIMOTO.
Me
Hashimoto
Ida
AND HASHIMOTO LIKES IDA...
...AND IDA LIKES–
Ida
?
Me
NOPE. THAT'S A PLOT TWIST I CAN LIVE WITHOUT...
Ida
Hashimoto
THIS WOULD TIE UP EVERYTHING NICELY.
WHY DID THINGS TURN OUT THE WAY THEY HAVE?
THIS WOULD MAKE HASHIMOTO HAPPY. AND SHE'S EXACTLY IDA'S TYPE.
PLUS IT'D SOLVE MY WORRIES.
I'LL GIVE IT SOME THOUGHT, SO JUST WAIT FOR ME.
HMMMMM
ALL RIGHT, THE NEXT PROBLEM WILL BE SOLVED BY...
AH. AOKI, WHO'S AWAKE FOR ONCE...
HUH?

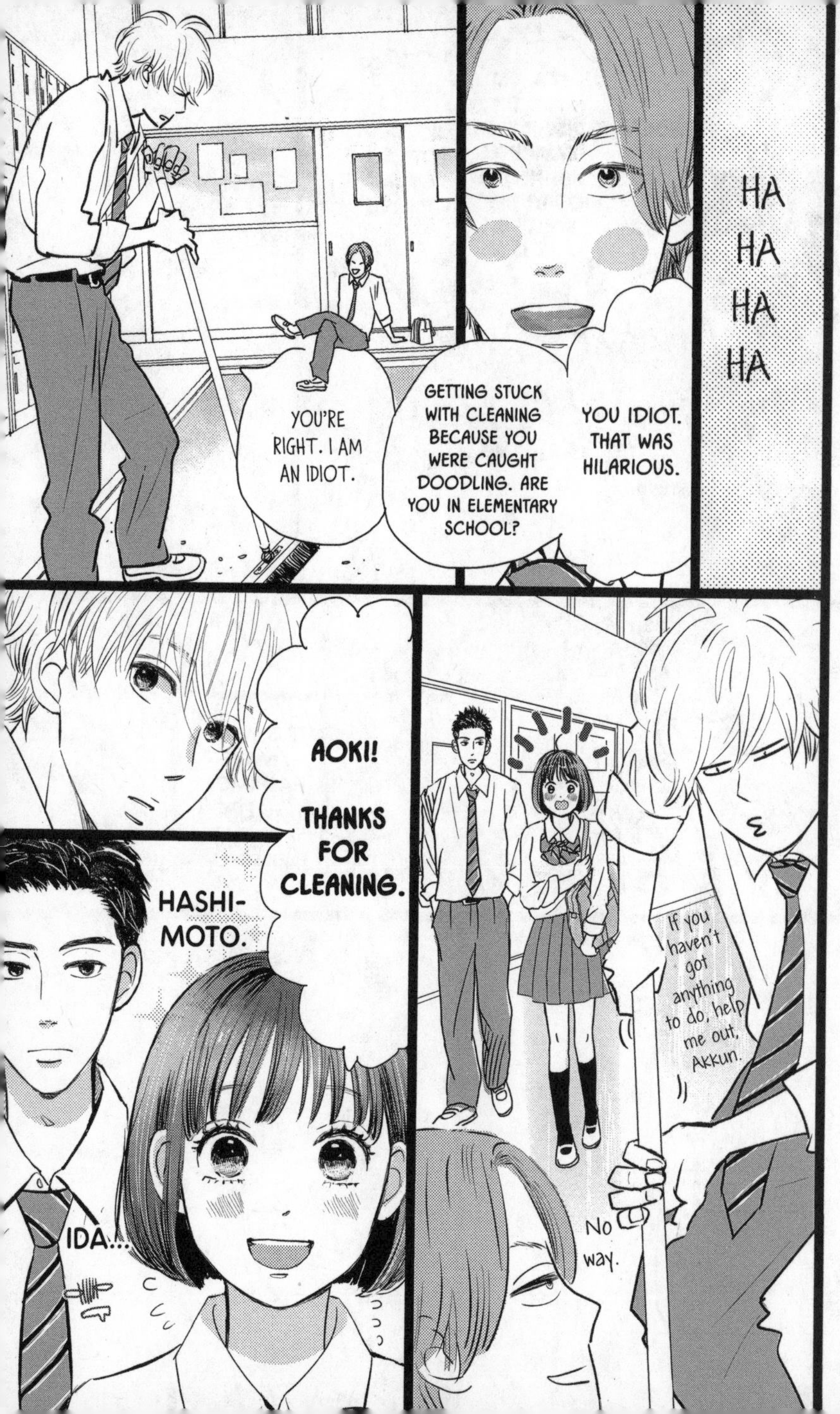
HA HA HA HA
YOU IDIOT. THAT WAS HILARIOUS.
GETTING STUCK WITH CLEANING BECAUSE YOU WERE CAUGHT DOODLING. ARE YOU IN ELEMENTARY SCHOOL?
YOU'RE RIGHT. I AM AN IDIOT.
If you haven't got anything to do, help me out, Akkun.
No way.
AOKI!
THANKS FOR CLEANING.
HASHI-MOTO.
IDA...

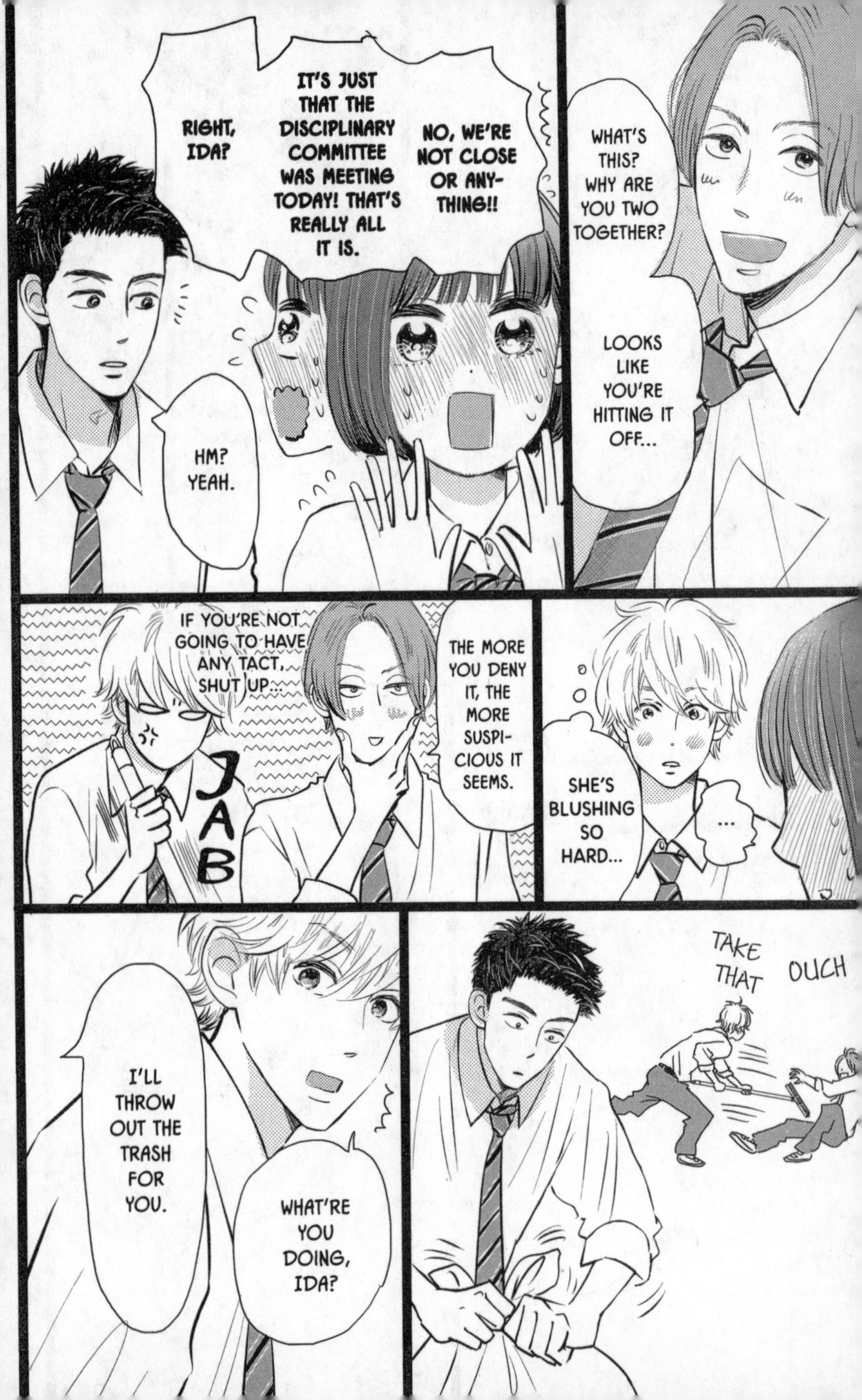

WHAT'S THIS? WHY ARE YOU TWO TOGETHER?
LOOKS LIKE YOU'RE HITTING IT OFF...
NO, WE'RE NOT CLOSE OR ANY-THING!!
IT'S JUST THAT THE DISCIPLINARY COMMITTEE WAS MEETING TODAY! THAT'S REALLY ALL IT IS.
RIGHT, IDA?
HM? YEAH.
SHE'S BLUSHING SO HARD...
...
THE MORE YOU DENY IT, THE MORE SUSPICIOUS IT SEEMS.
IF YOU'RE NOT GOING TO HAVE ANY TACT, SHUT UP...
JAB
OUCH
TAKE THAT
WHAT'RE YOU DOING, IDA?
I'LL THROW OUT THE TRASH FOR YOU.

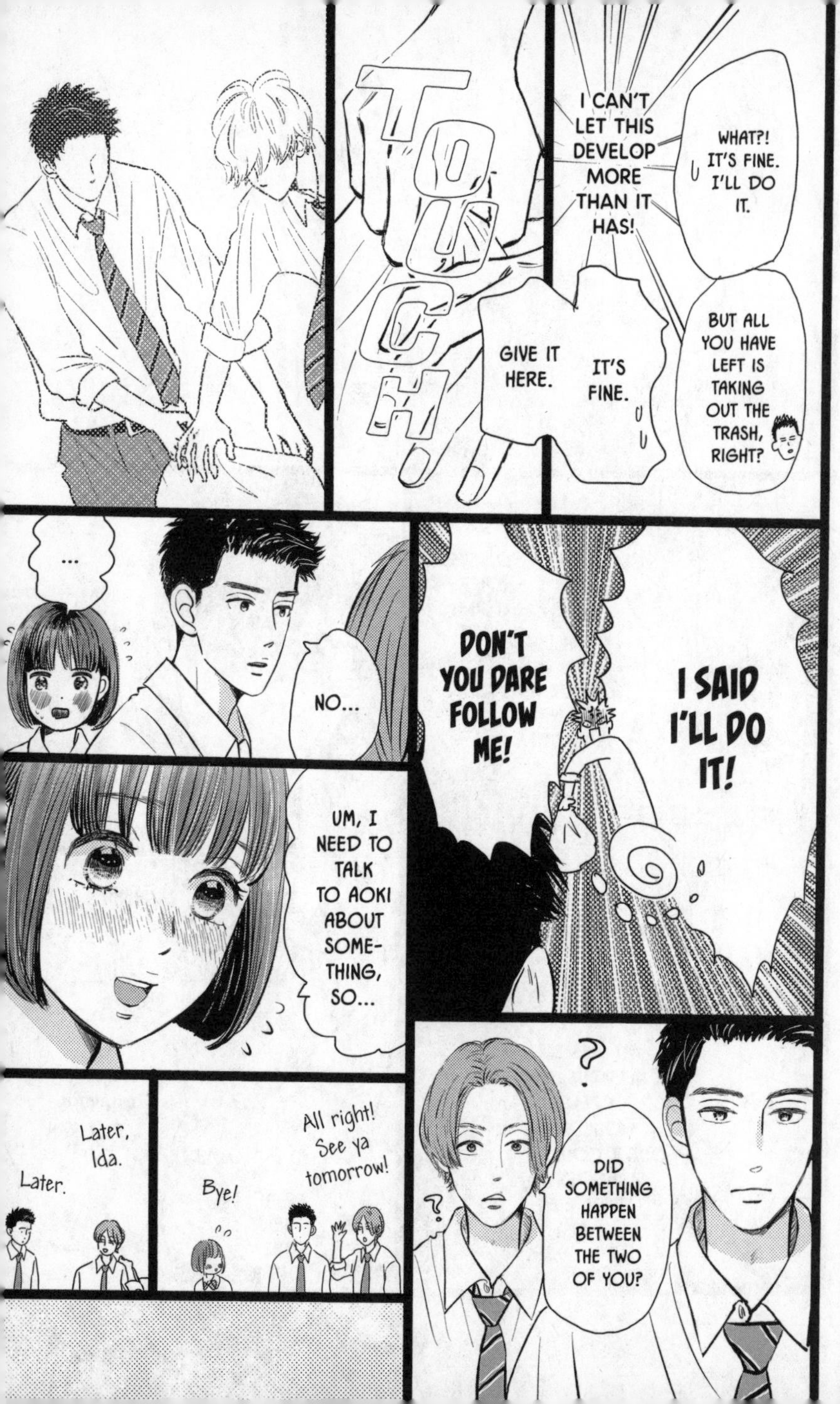

WHAT?! IT'S FINE. I'LL DO IT.
I CAN'T LET THIS DEVELOP MORE THAN IT HAS!
BUT ALL YOU HAVE LEFT IS TAKING OUT THE TRASH, RIGHT?
IT'S FINE.
GIVE IT HERE.
TOUCH
I SAID I'LL DO IT!
DON'T YOU DARE FOLLOW ME!
NO...
...
UM, I NEED TO TALK TO AOKI ABOUT SOME-THING, SO...
All right! See ya tomorrow!
Bye!
Later, Ida.
Later.
?
DID SOMETHING HAPPEN BETWEEN THE TWO OF YOU?
?

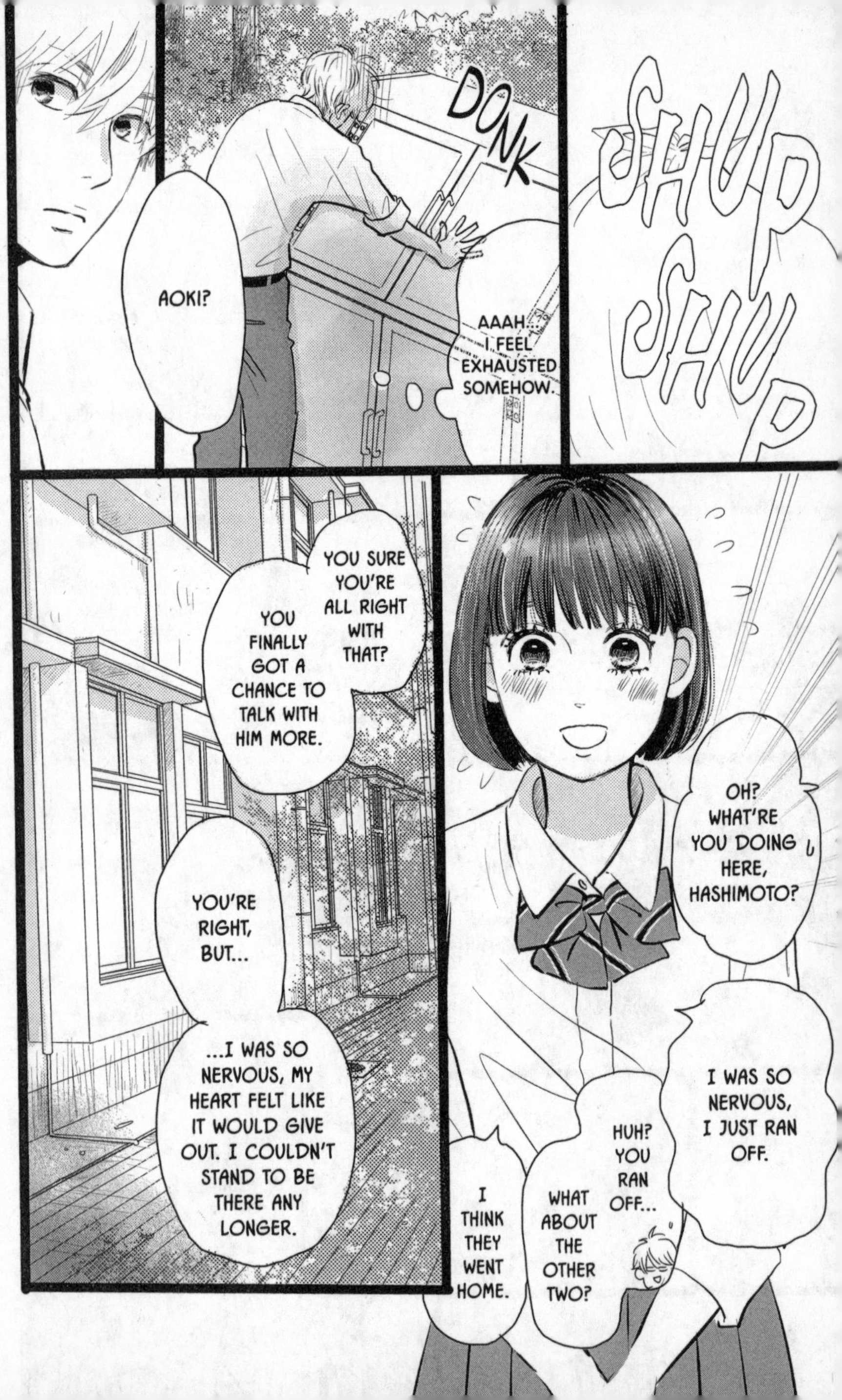
SHUP SHUP SHUP
DONK
AAAH... I FEEL EXHAUSTED SOMEHOW.
AOKI?
OH? WHAT'RE YOU DOING HERE, HASHIMOTO?
I WAS SO NERVOUS, I JUST RAN OFF.
HUH? YOU RAN OFF...
WHAT ABOUT THE OTHER TWO?
I THINK THEY WENT HOME.
YOU SURE YOU'RE ALL RIGHT WITH THAT?
YOU FINALLY GOT A CHANCE TO TALK WITH HIM MORE.
YOU'RE RIGHT, BUT...
...I WAS SO NERVOUS, MY HEART FELT LIKE IT WOULD GIVE OUT. I COULDN'T STAND TO BE THERE ANY LONGER.

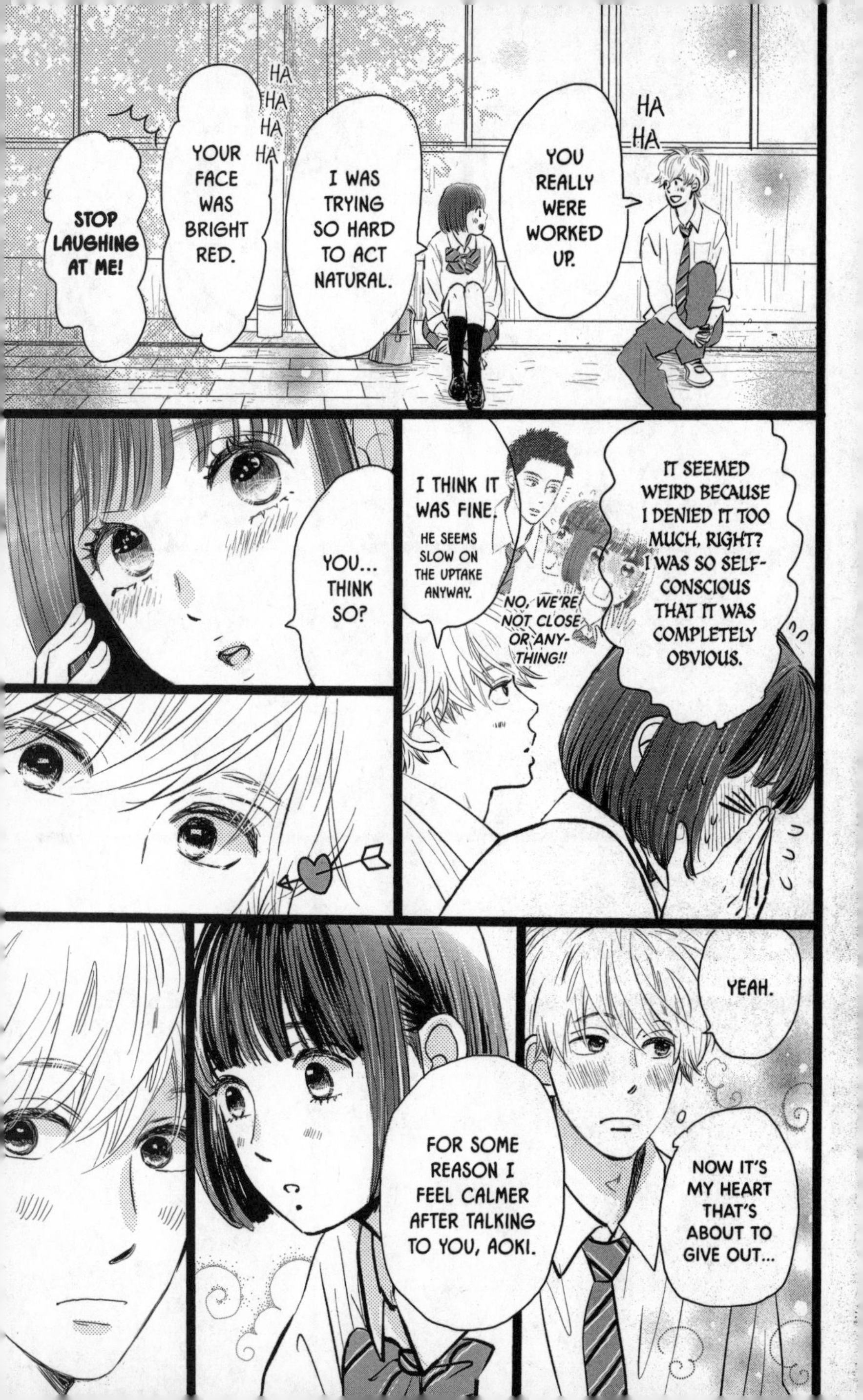
HA HA
YOU REALLY WERE WORKED UP.
I WAS TRYING SO HARD TO ACT NATURAL.
HA HA HA HA
YOUR FACE WAS BRIGHT RED.
STOP LAUGHING AT ME!
IT SEEMED WEIRD BECAUSE I DENIED IT TOO MUCH, RIGHT? I WAS SO SELF-CONSCIOUS THAT IT WAS COMPLETELY OBVIOUS.
NO, WE'RE NOT CLOSE OR ANY-THING!!
I THINK IT WAS FINE.
HE SEEMS SLOW ON THE UPTAKE ANYWAY.
YOU... THINK SO?
FOR SOME REASON I FEEL CALMER AFTER TALKING TO YOU, AOKI.
YEAH.
NOW IT'S MY HEART THAT'S ABOUT TO GIVE OUT...

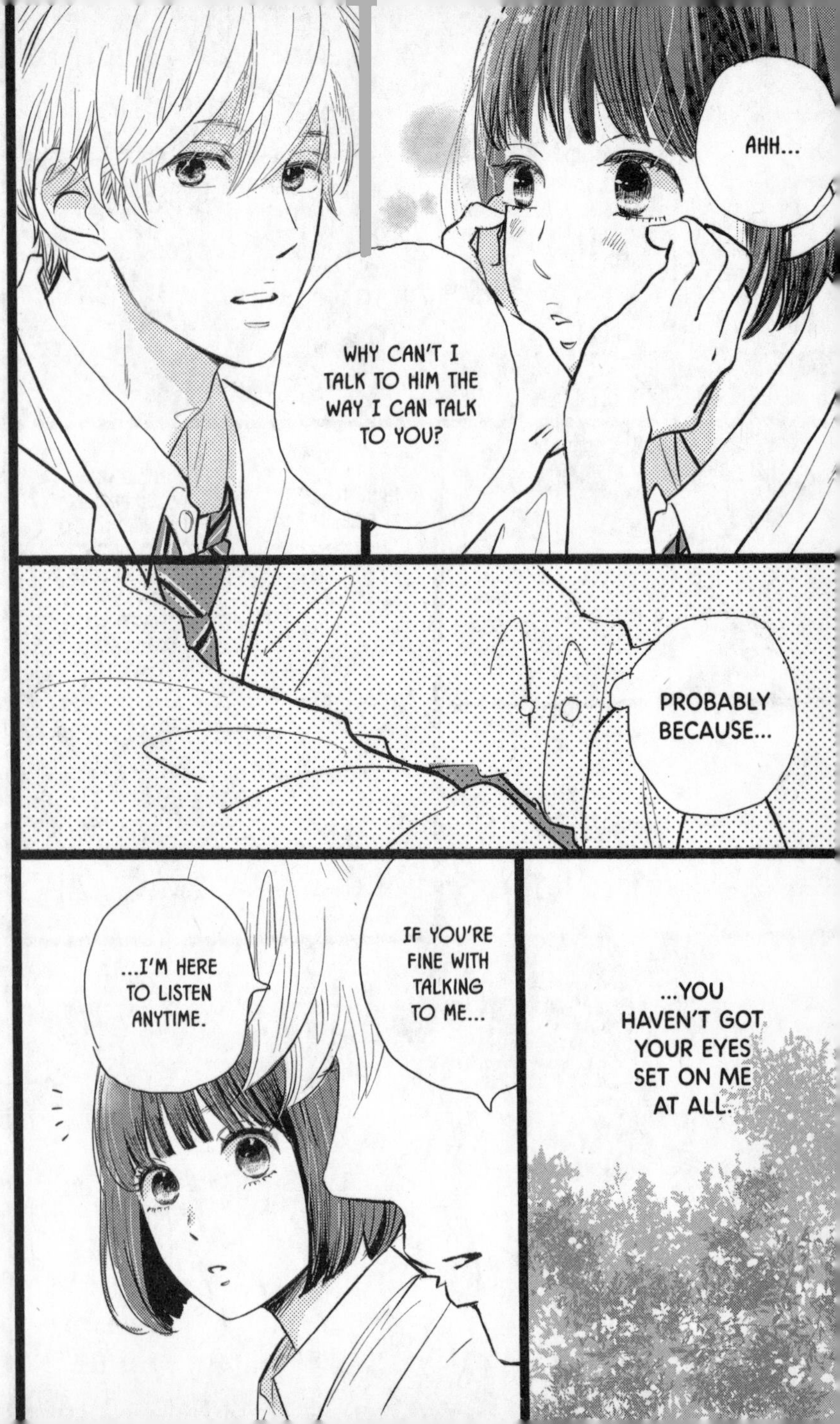
AHH...
WHY CAN'T I TALK TO HIM THE WAY I CAN TALK TO YOU?
PROBABLY BECAUSE...
...YOU HAVEN'T GOT YOUR EYES SET ON ME AT ALL.
IF YOU'RE FINE WITH TALKING TO ME...
...I'M HERE TO LISTEN ANYTIME.

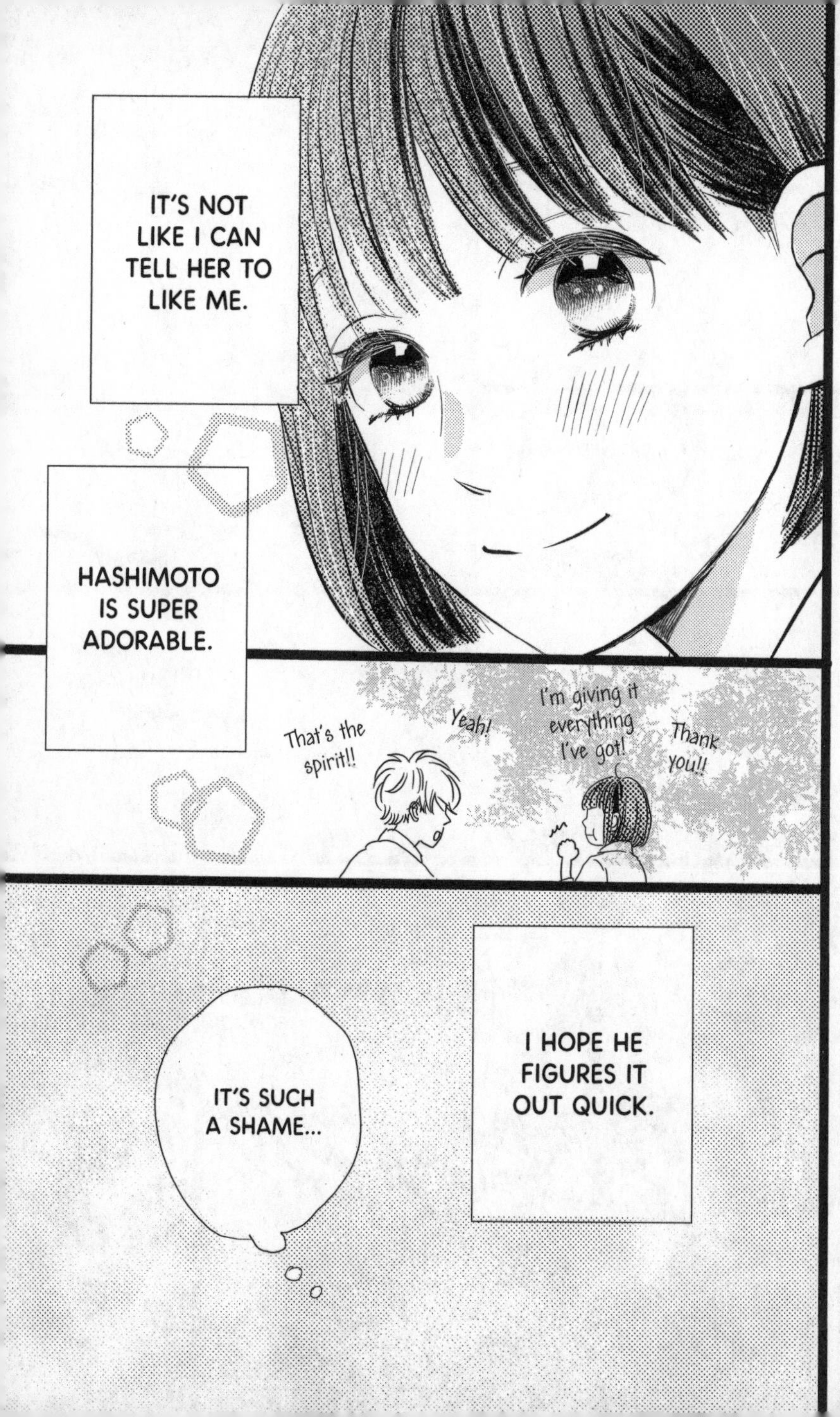
IT'S NOT LIKE I CAN TELL HER TO LIKE ME.
HASHIMOTO IS SUPER ADORABLE.
Thank you!!
I'm giving it everything I've got!
Yeah!
That's the spirit!!
I HOPE HE FIGURES IT OUT QUICK.
IT'S SUCH A SHAME...

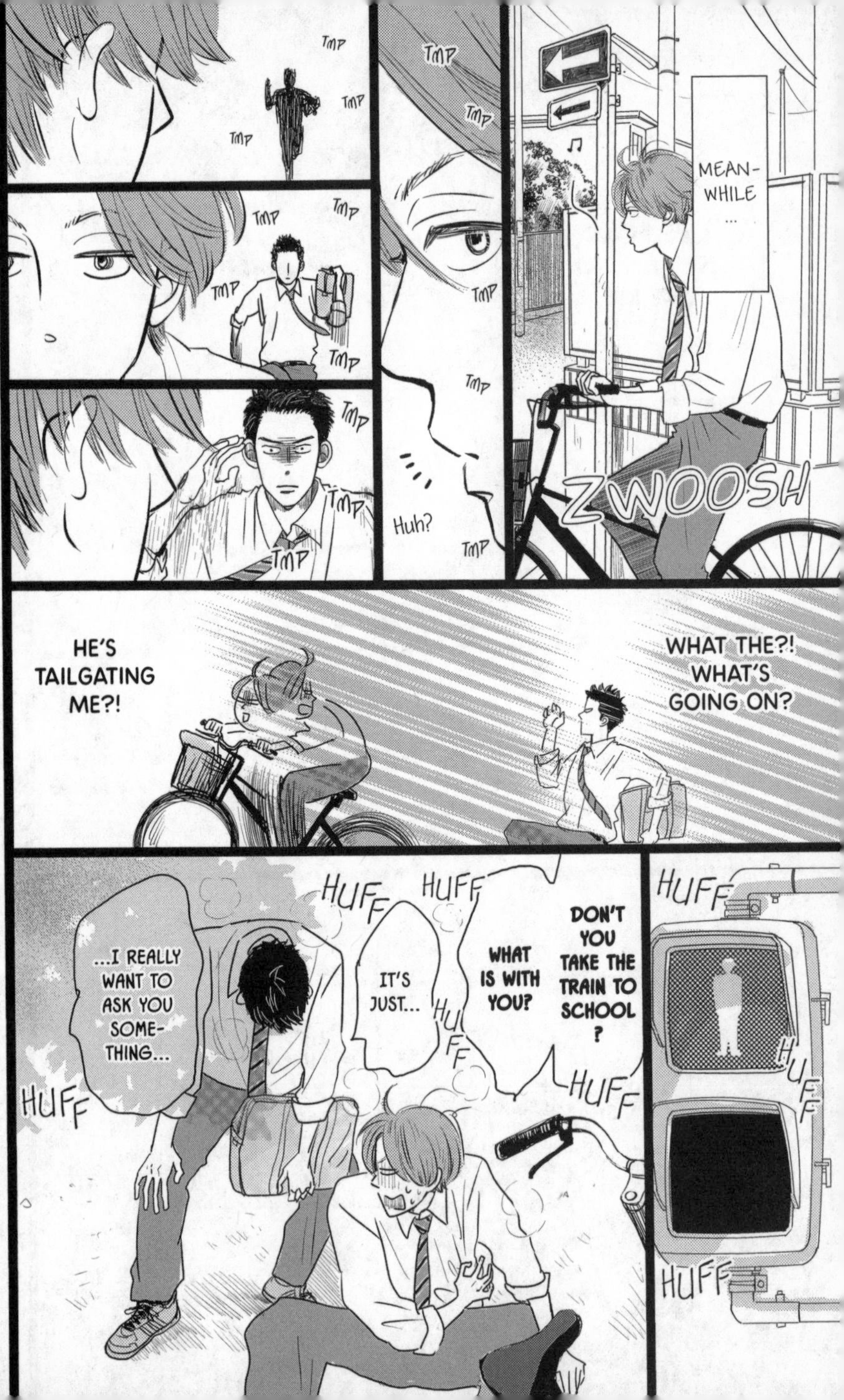
MEAN-WHILE ...
♪
ZWOOSH
TMP
TMP
TMP
TMP
...
Huh?
TMP
TMP
TMP
TMP
TMP
TMP
TMP
TMP
TMP
TMP
TMP
WHAT THE?! WHAT'S GOING ON?
HE'S TAILGATING ME?!
HUFF
HUFF
HUFF
DON'T YOU TAKE THE TRAIN TO SCHOOL?
WHAT IS WITH YOU?
HUFF
HUFF
IT'S JUST...
HUFF
HUFF
...I REALLY WANT TO ASK YOU SOME-THING...
HUFF

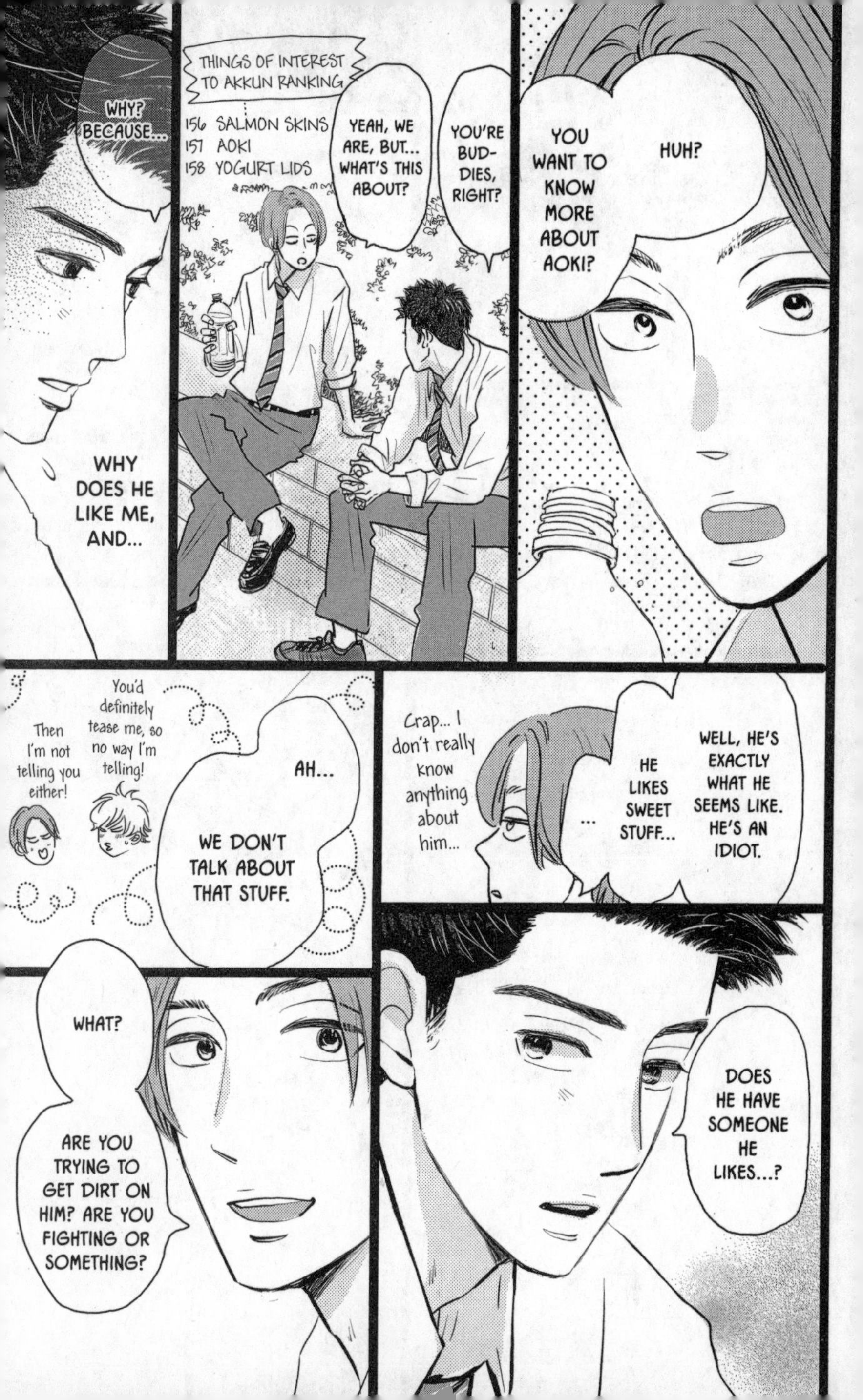
HUH?
YOU WANT TO KNOW MORE ABOUT AOKI?
YOU'RE BUDDIES, RIGHT?
YEAH, WE ARE, BUT... WHAT'S THIS ABOUT?
THINGS OF INTEREST TO AKKUN RANKING
156 SALMON SKINS
157 AOKI
158 YOGURT LIDS
WHY? BECAUSE...
WHY DOES HE LIKE ME, AND...
WELL, HE'S EXACTLY WHAT HE SEEMS LIKE. HE'S AN IDIOT.
HE LIKES SWEET STUFF...
...
Crap... I don't really know anything about him...
AH...
WE DON'T TALK ABOUT THAT STUFF.
You'd definitely tease me, so no way I'm telling!
Then I'm not telling you either!
DOES HE HAVE SOMEONE HE LIKES...?
WHAT?
ARE YOU TRYING TO GET DIRT ON HIM? ARE YOU FIGHTING OR SOMETHING?

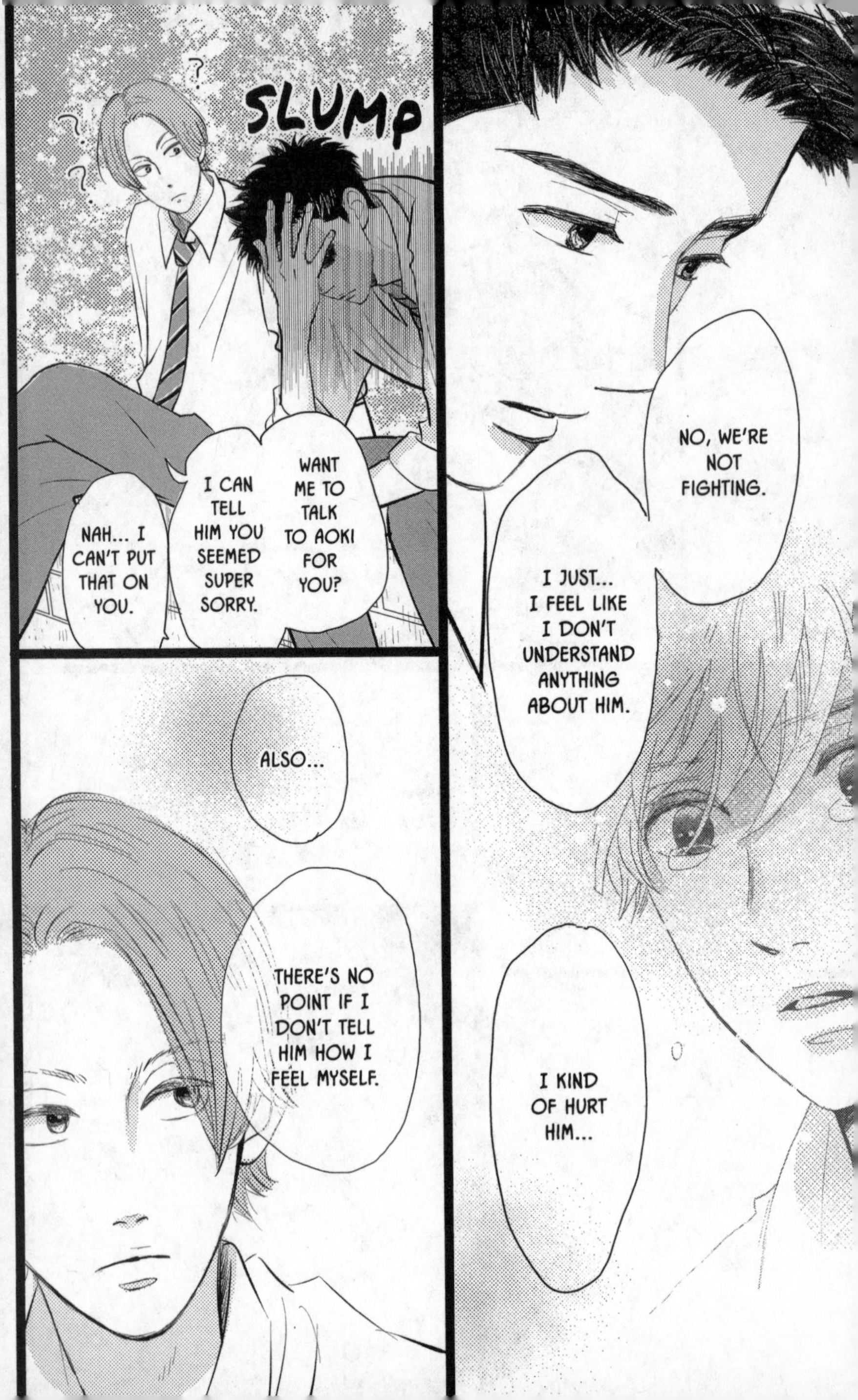
NO, WE'RE NOT FIGHTING.
I JUST... I FEEL LIKE I DON'T UNDERSTAND ANYTHING ABOUT HIM.
I KIND OF HURT HIM...
SLUMP
WANT ME TO TALK TO AOKI FOR YOU?
I CAN TELL HIM YOU SEEMED SUPER SORRY.
NAH... I CAN'T PUT THAT ON YOU.
ALSO...
THERE'S NO POINT IF I DON'T TELL HIM HOW I FEEL MYSELF.

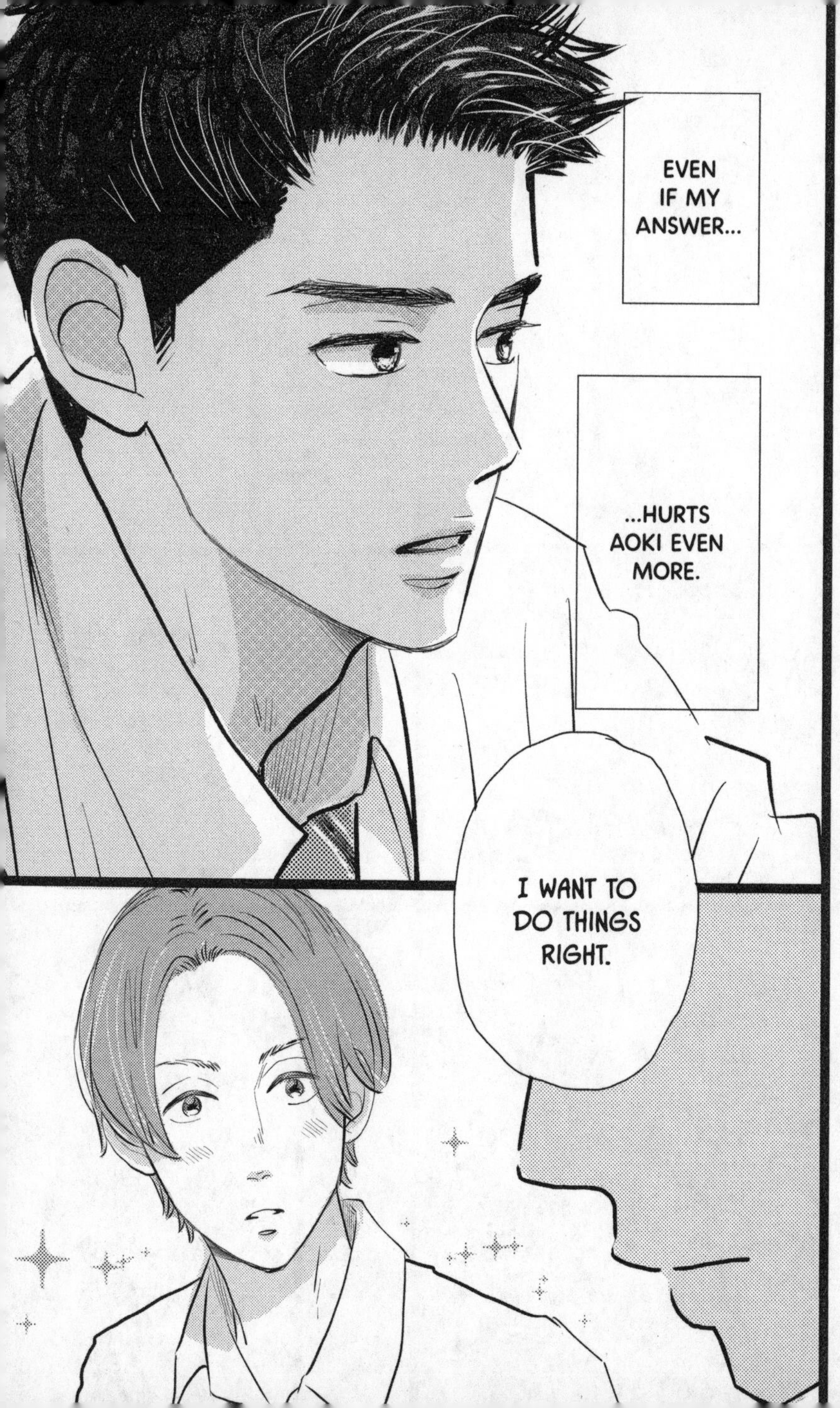
EVEN IF MY ANSWER...
...HURTS AOKI EVEN MORE.
I WANT TO DO THINGS RIGHT.

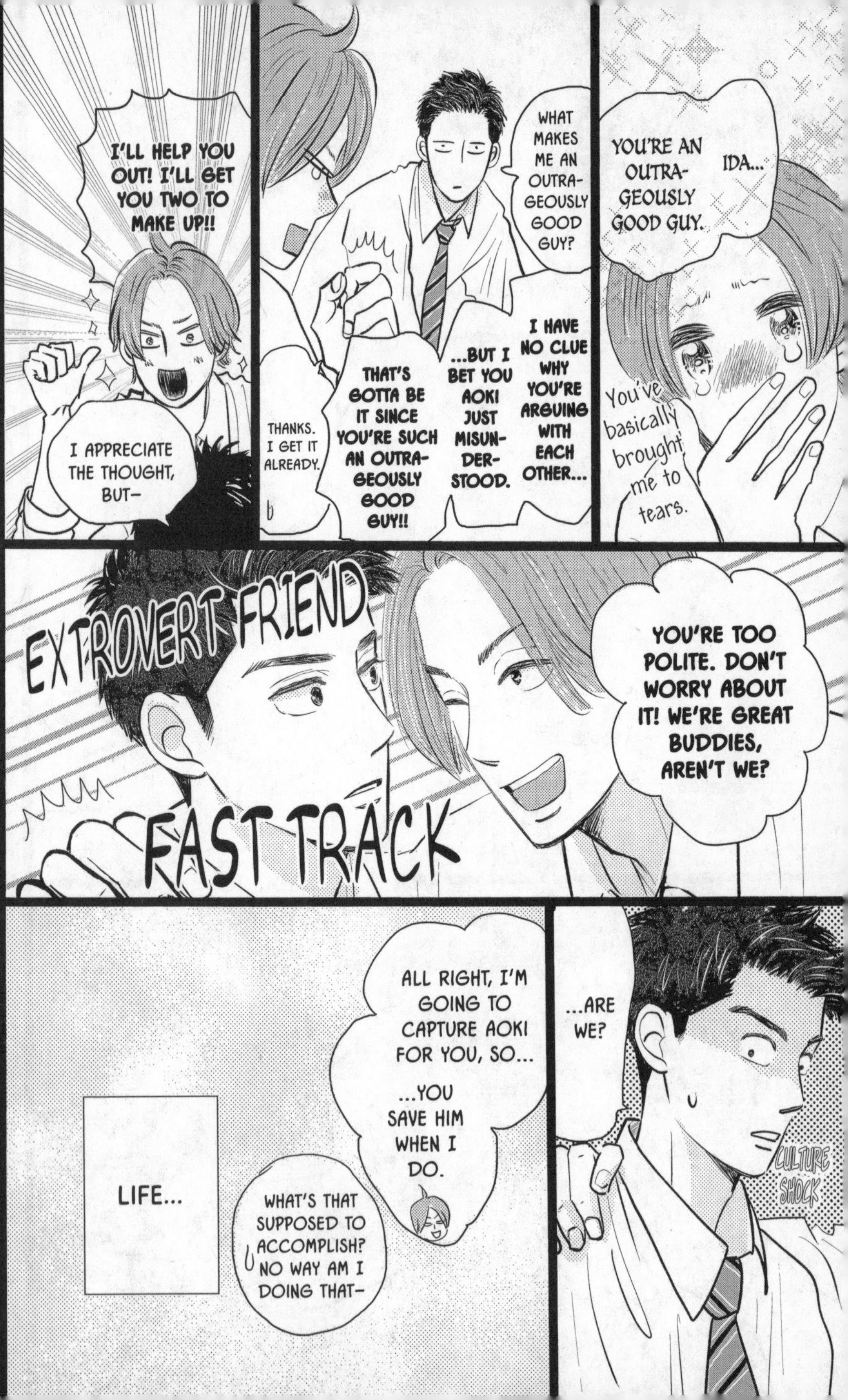
IDA...
YOU'RE AN OUTRAGEOUSLY GOOD GUY.
You've basically brought me to tears.
WHAT MAKES ME AN OUTRAGEOUSLY GOOD GUY?
I HAVE NO CLUE WHY YOU'RE ARGUING WITH EACH OTHER...
...BUT I BET YOU AOKI JUST MISUNDERSTOOD.
THAT'S GOTTA BE IT SINCE YOU'RE SUCH AN OUTRAGEOUSLY GOOD GUY!!
THANKS. I GET IT ALREADY.
I'LL HELP YOU OUT! I'LL GET YOU TWO TO MAKE UP!!
I APPRECIATE THE THOUGHT, BUT—
YOU'RE TOO POLITE. DON'T WORRY ABOUT IT! WE'RE GREAT BUDDIES, AREN'T WE?
EXTROVERT FRIEND
FAST TRACK
...ARE WE?
CULTURE SHOCK
ALL RIGHT, I'M GOING TO CAPTURE AOKI FOR YOU, SO...
...YOU SAVE HIM WHEN I DO.
WHAT'S THAT SUPPOSED TO ACCOMPLISH? NO WAY AM I DOING THAT—
LIFE...

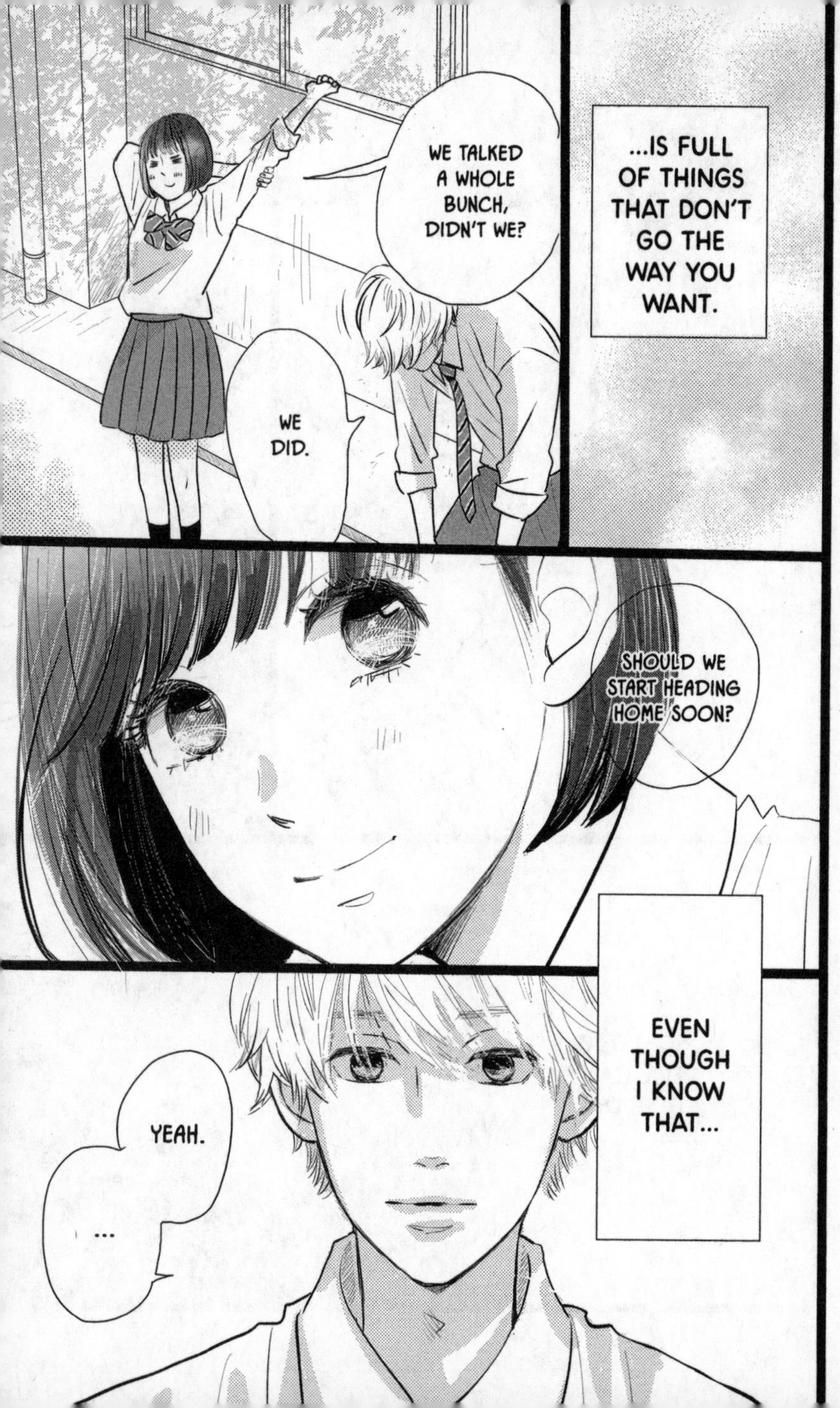
...IS FULL OF THINGS THAT DON'T GO THE WAY YOU WANT.
WE TALKED A WHOLE BUNCH, DIDN'T WE?
WE DID.
SHOULD WE START HEADING HOME SOON?
EVEN THOUGH I KNOW THAT...
YEAH.
...

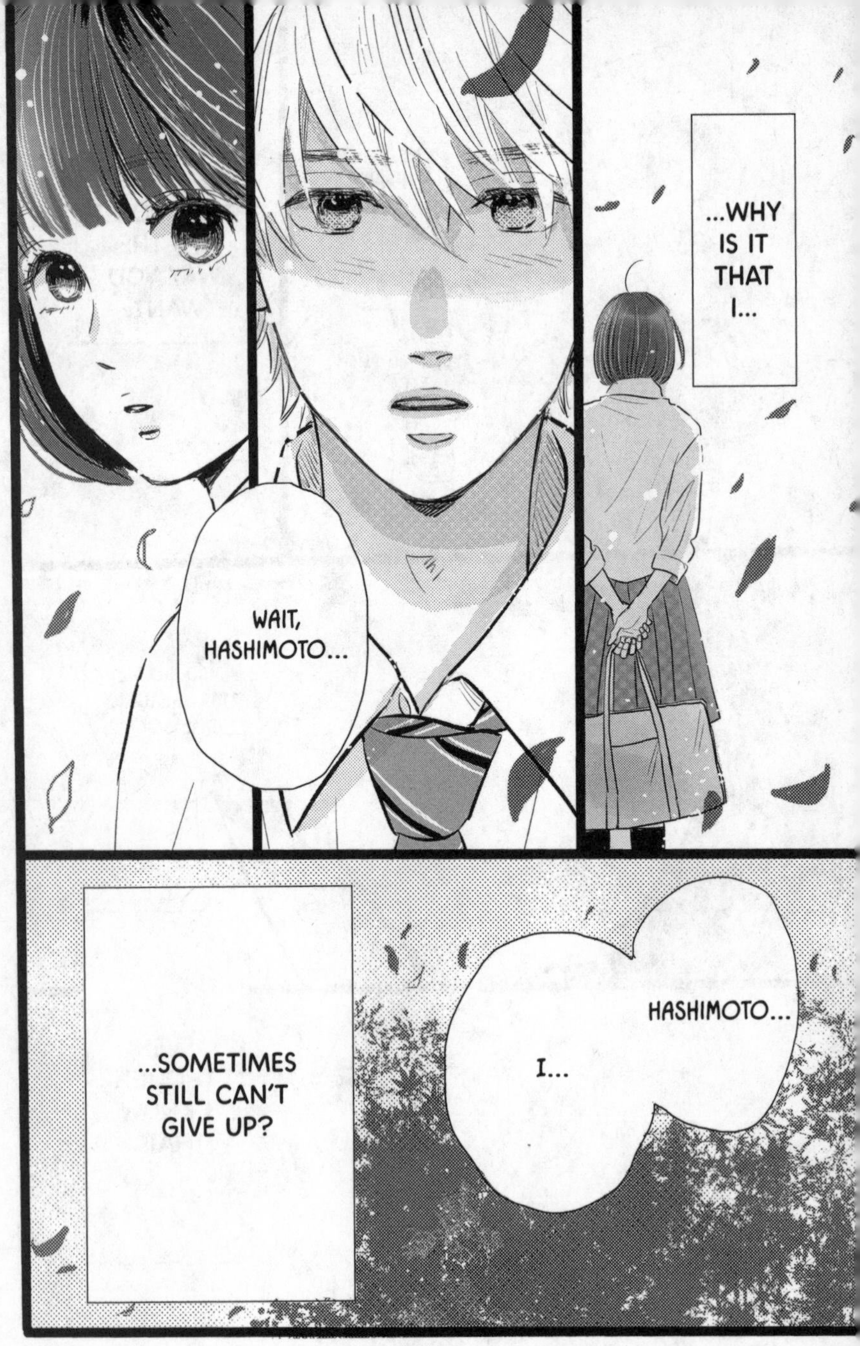
...WHY IS IT THAT I...
WAIT, HASHIMOTO...
HASHIMOTO... I...
...SOMETIMES STILL CAN'T GIVE UP?

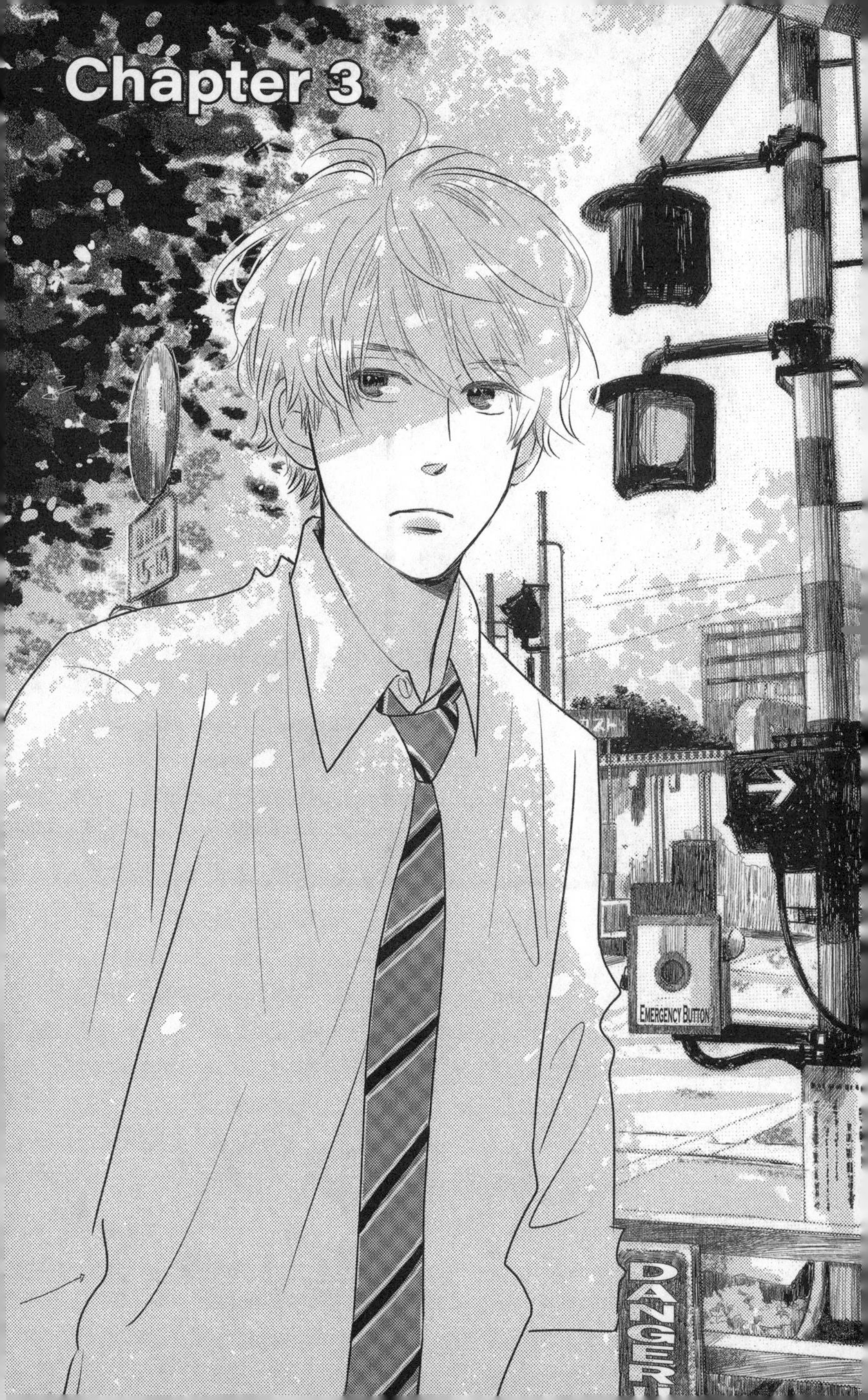
Chapter 3
EMERGENCY BUTTON
DANGER

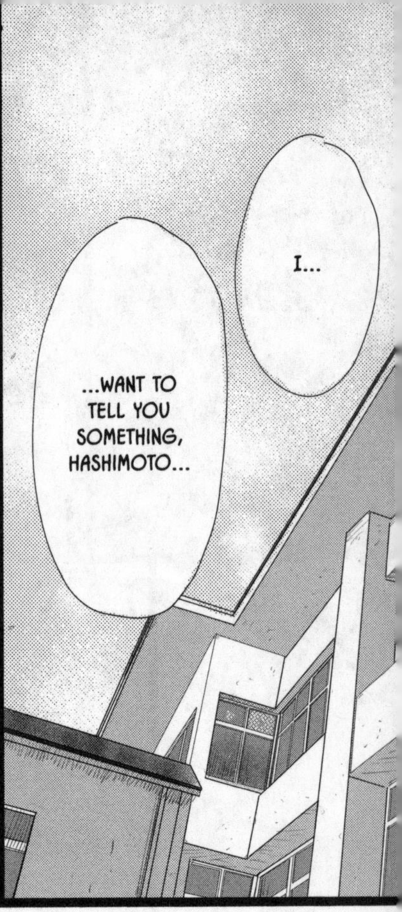
I...
...WANT TO TELL YOU SOMETHING, HASHIMOTO...

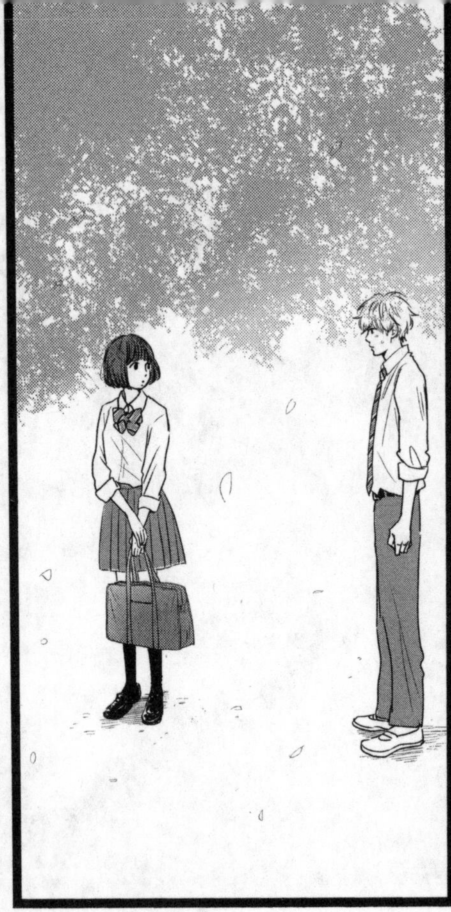

My Love Mix-Up!

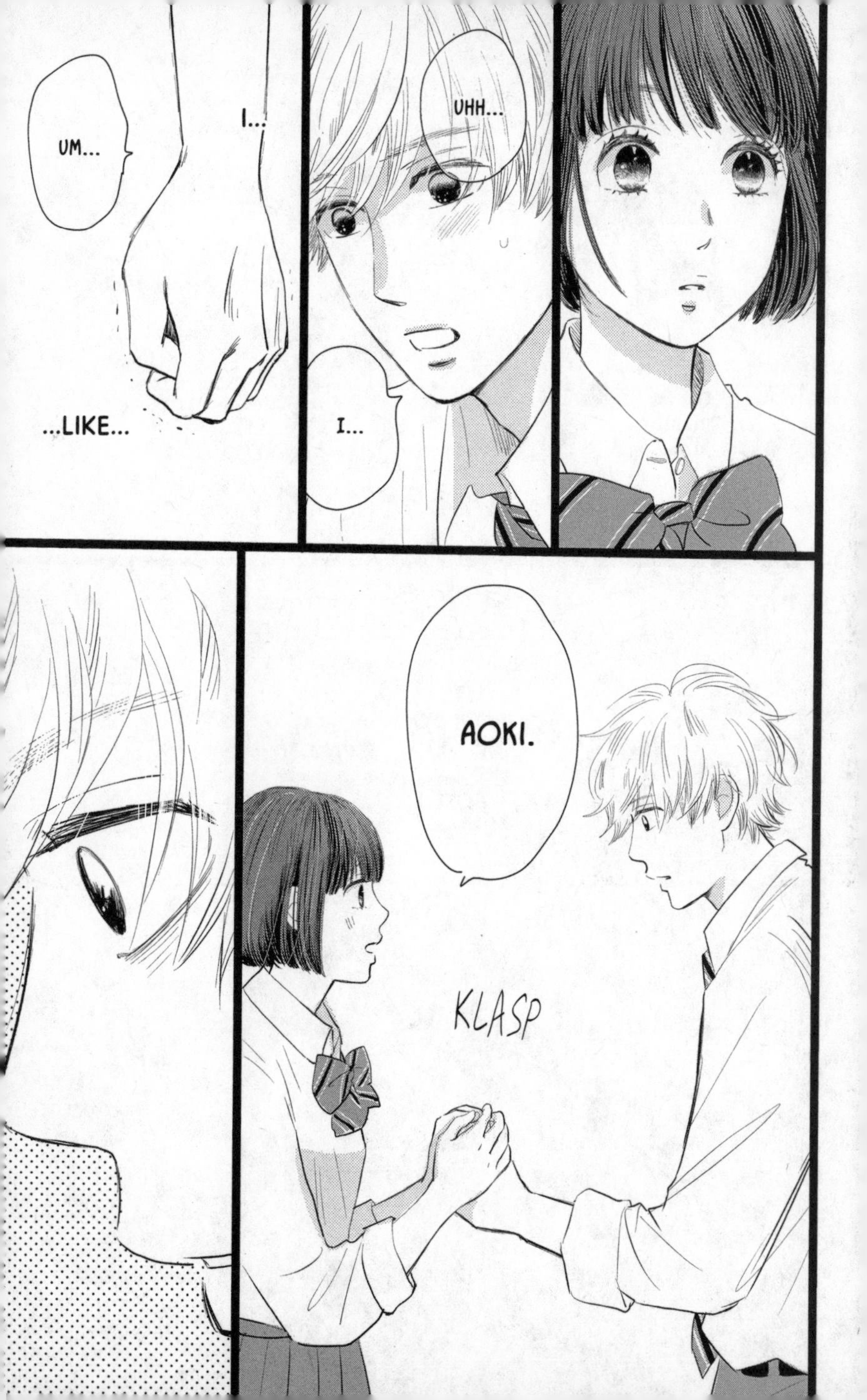
UHH...
I...
I...
UM...
...LIKE...
AOKI.
KLASP

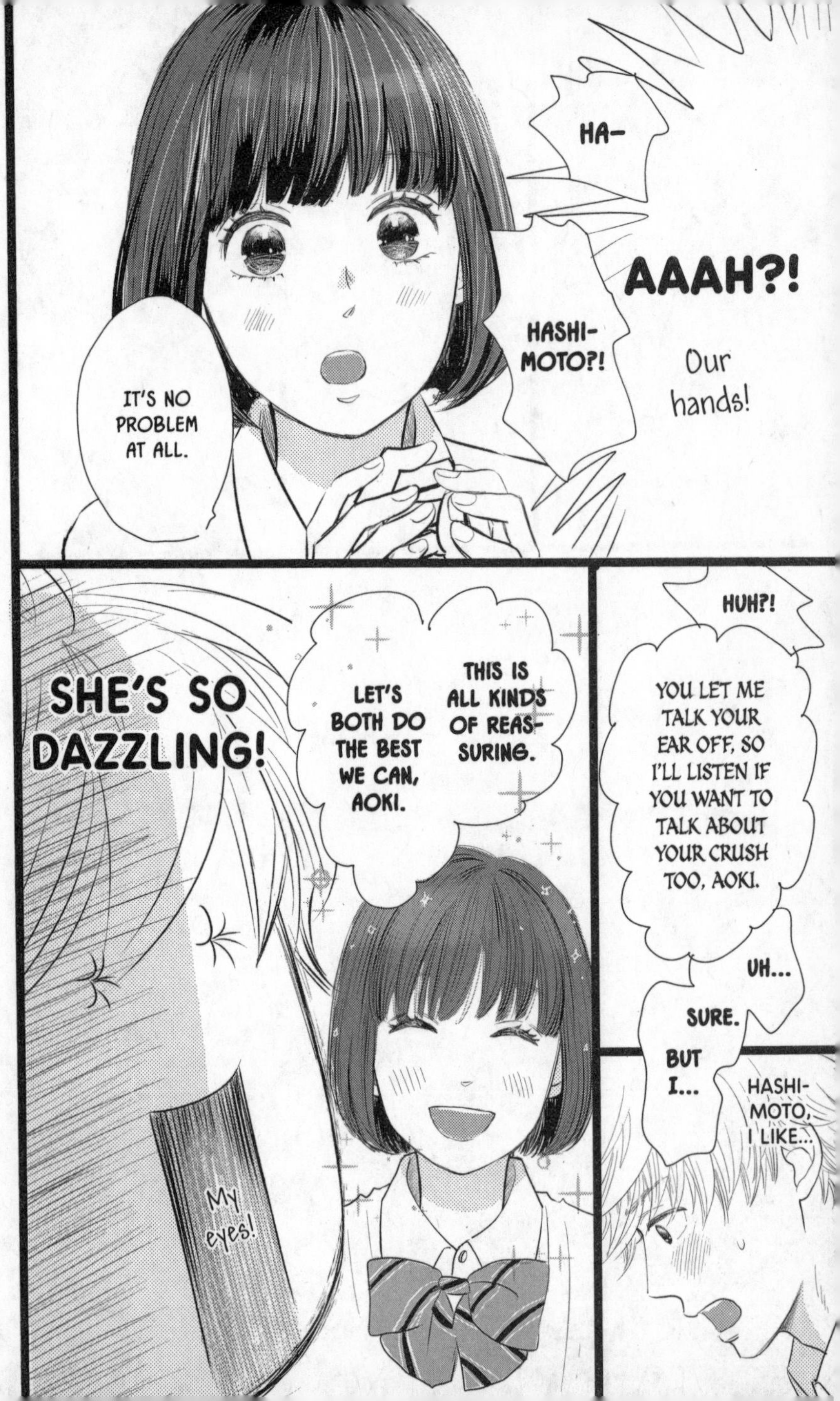
HA-
AAAH?!
HASHIMOTO?!
Our hands!
IT'S NO PROBLEM AT ALL.
HUH?!
YOU LET ME TALK YOUR EAR OFF, SO I'LL LISTEN IF YOU WANT TO TALK ABOUT YOUR CRUSH TOO, AOKI.
UH... SURE.
BUT I...
HASHIMOTO, I LIKE...
THIS IS ALL KINDS OF REASSURING.
LET'S BOTH DO THE BEST WE CAN, AOKI.
SHE'S SO DAZZLING!
My eyes!

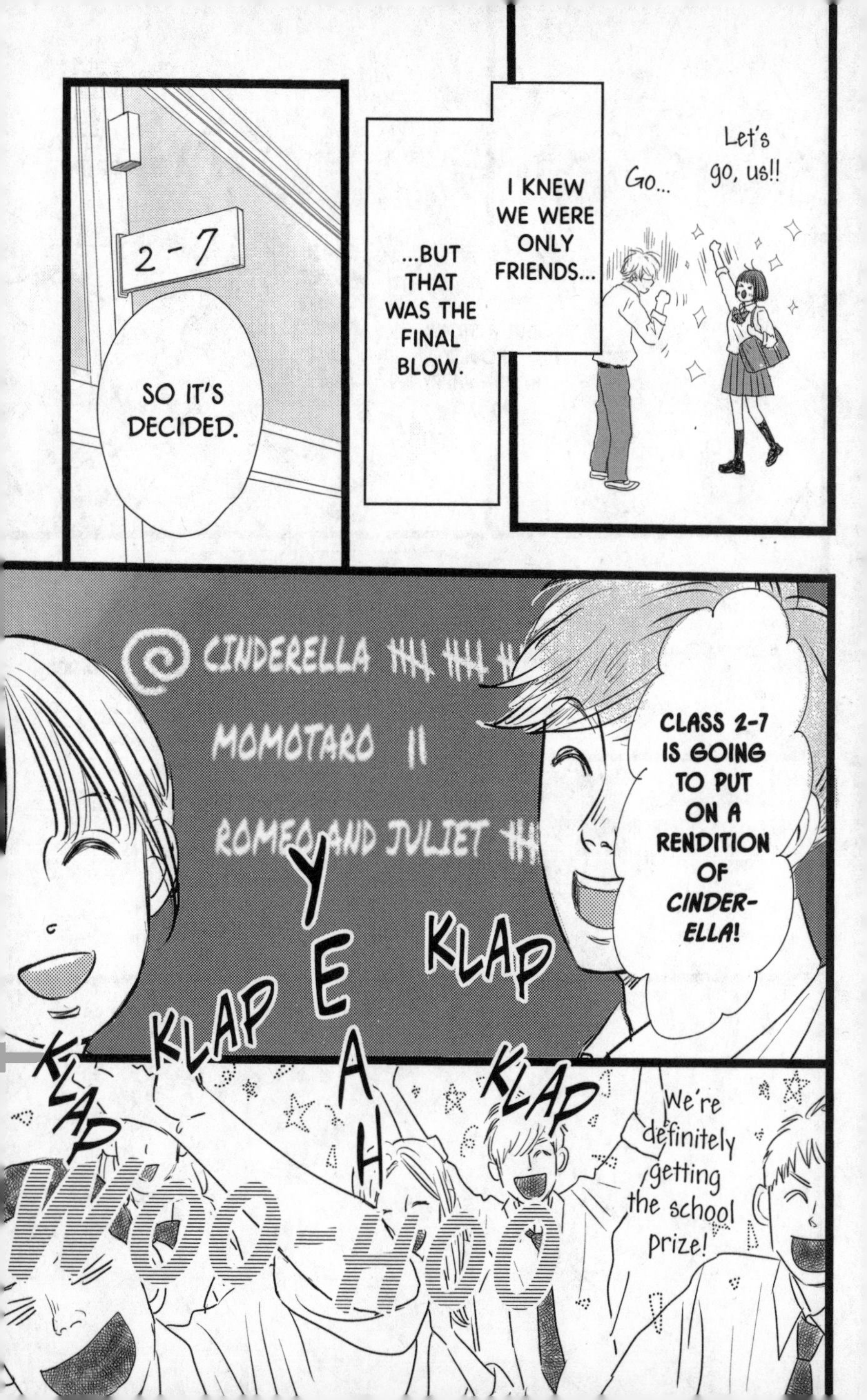
Let's go, us!!
Go...
I KNEW WE WERE ONLY FRIENDS...
...BUT THAT WAS THE FINAL BLOW.
2-7
SO IT'S DECIDED.
CLASS 2-7 IS GOING TO PUT ON A RENDITION OF CINDERELLA!
CINDERELLA
MOMOTARO
ROMEO AND JULIET
KLAP
KLAP
YEAH
KLAP
KLAP
We're definitely getting the school prize!
WOO-HOO

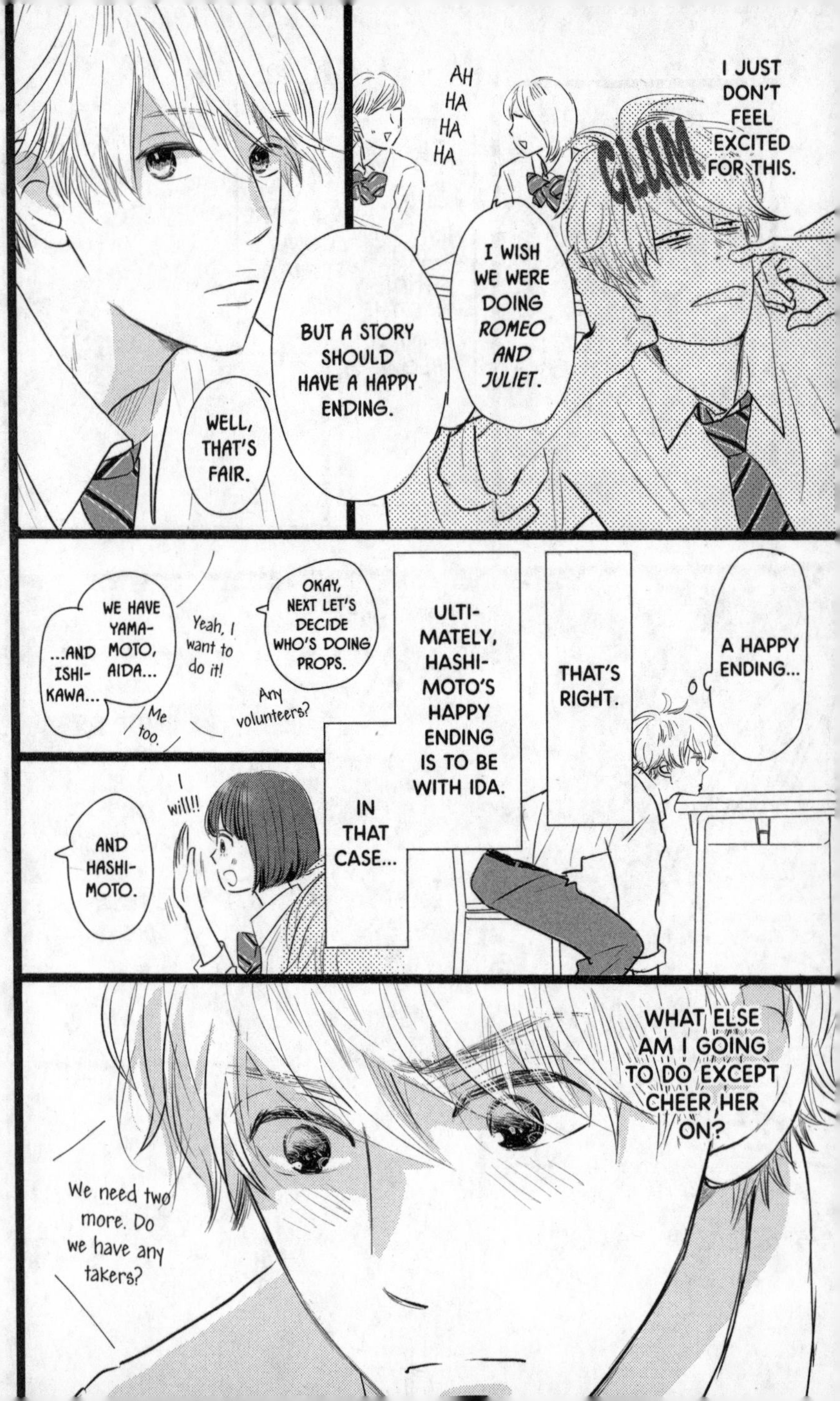
I JUST DON'T FEEL EXCITED FOR THIS.
GLUM
AH HA HA HA
I WISH WE WERE DOING *ROMEO AND JULIET*.
BUT A STORY SHOULD HAVE A HAPPY ENDING.
WELL, THAT'S FAIR.
A HAPPY ENDING...
THAT'S RIGHT.
ULTIMATELY, HASHIMOTO'S HAPPY ENDING IS TO BE WITH IDA.
OKAY, NEXT LET'S DECIDE WHO'S DOING PROPS.
Any volunteers?
Yeah, I want to do it!
Me too.
WE HAVE YAMAMOTO, AIDA...
...AND ISHIKAWA...
IN THAT CASE...
I will!!
AND HASHIMOTO.
WHAT ELSE AM I GOING TO DO EXCEPT CHEER HER ON?
We need two more. Do we have any takers?

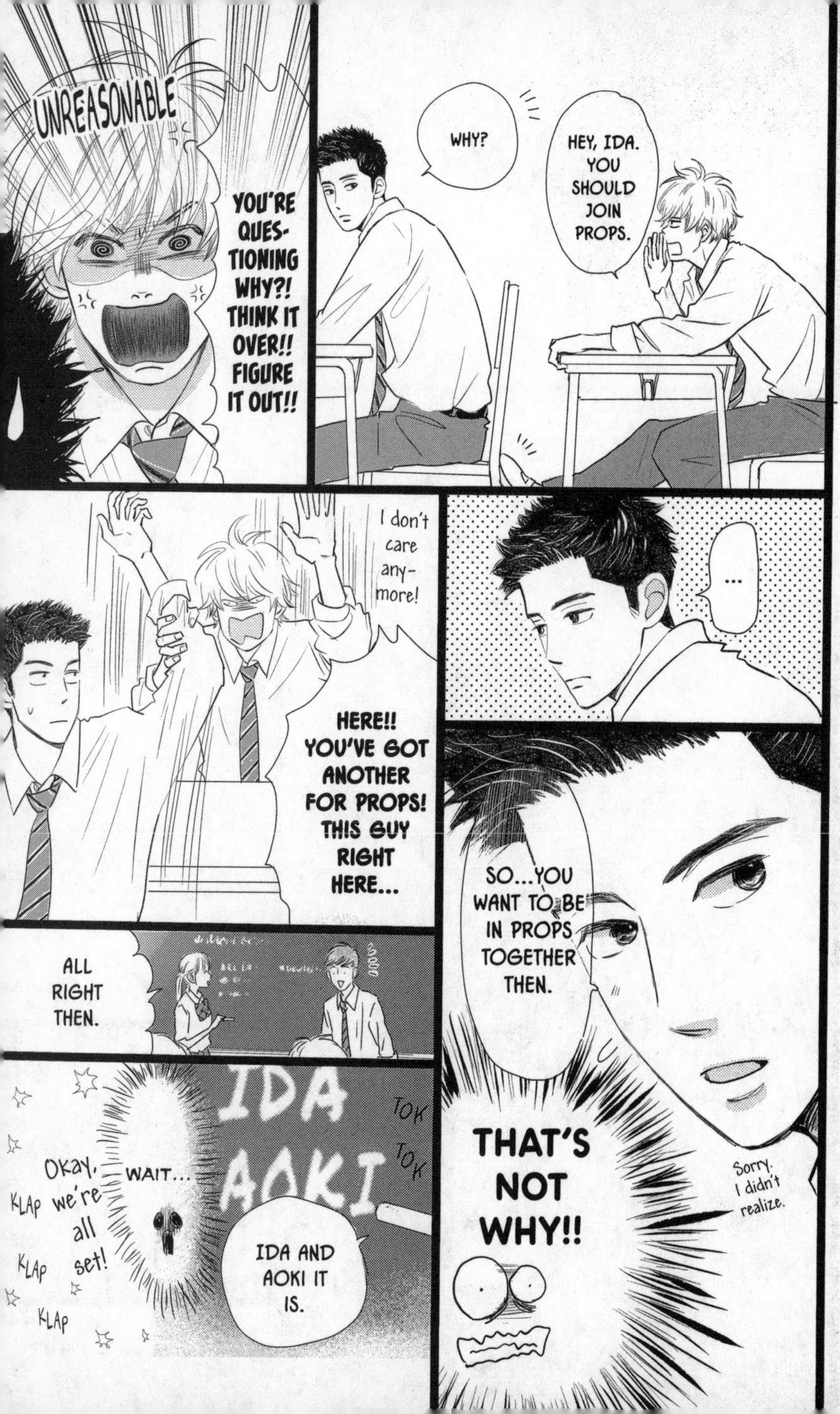
HEY, IDA. YOU SHOULD JOIN PROPS.
WHY?
UNREASONABLE
YOU'RE QUES-TIONING WHY?! THINK IT OVER!! FIGURE IT OUT!!
...
SO...YOU WANT TO BE IN PROPS TOGETHER THEN.
THAT'S NOT WHY!!
Sorry. I didn't realize.
I don't care any-more!
HERE!! YOU'VE GOT ANOTHER FOR PROPS! THIS GUY RIGHT HERE...
ALL RIGHT THEN.
IDA
AOKI
TOK TOK
IDA AND AOKI IT IS.
WAIT...
Okay, we're all set!
KLAP KLAP KLAP

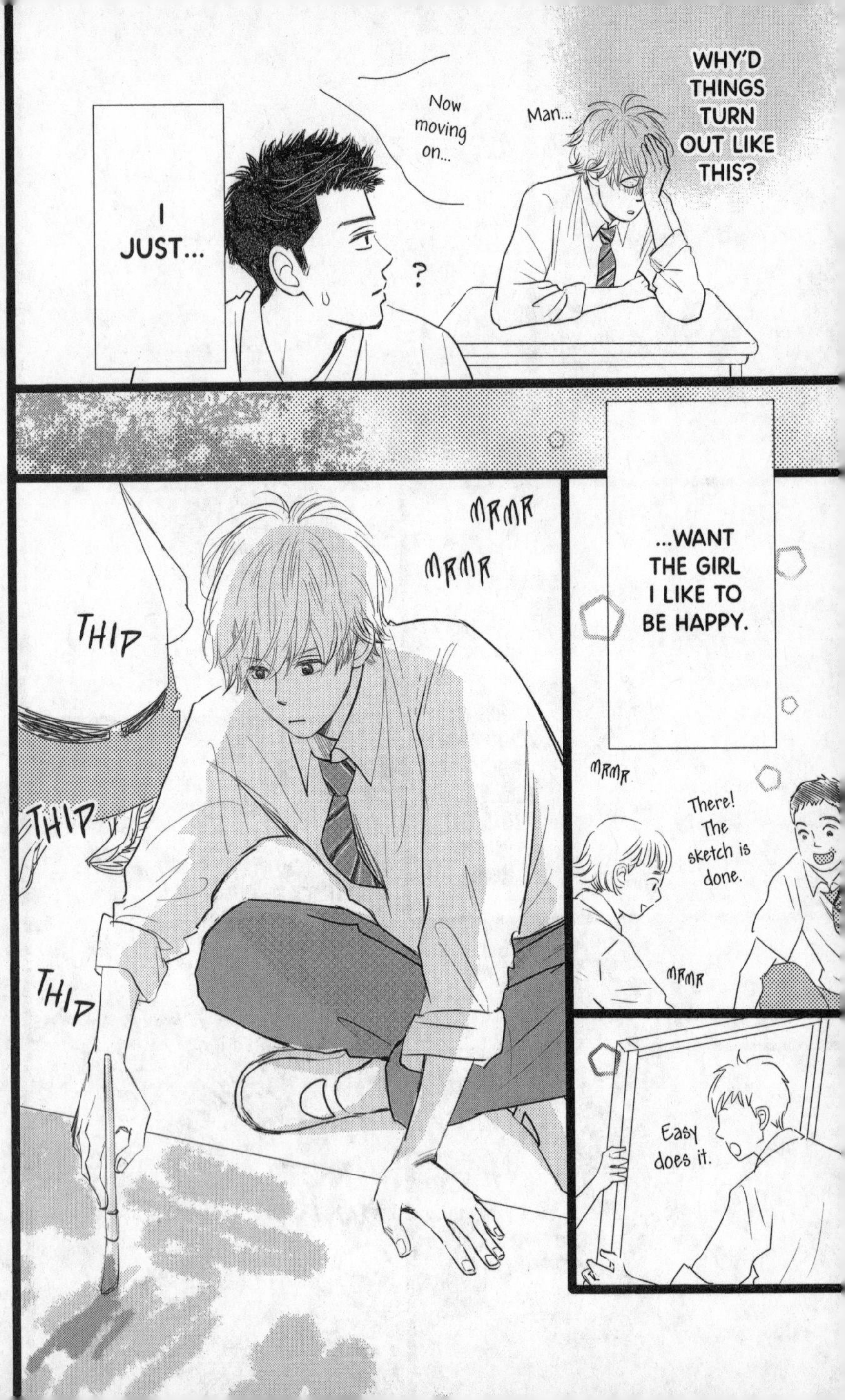
WHY'D THINGS TURN OUT LIKE THIS?
Man...
Now moving on...
?
I JUST...
...WANT THE GIRL I LIKE TO BE HAPPY.
MRMR
There! The sketch is done.
MRMR
Easy does it.
MRMR
MRMR
THIP
THIP
THIP

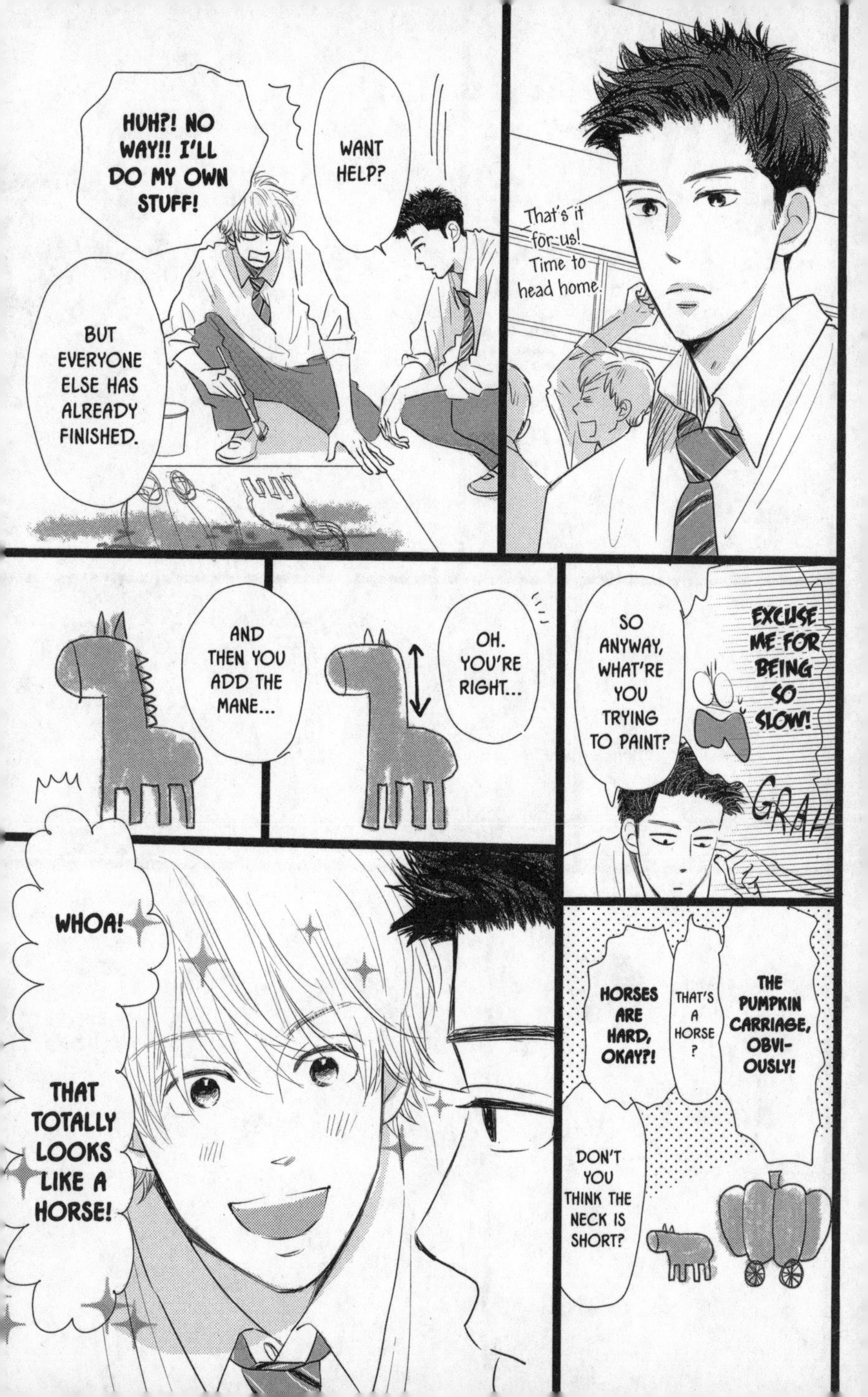
That's it for us! Time to head home!
WANT HELP?
HUH?! NO WAY!! I'LL DO MY OWN STUFF!
BUT EVERYONE ELSE HAS ALREADY FINISHED.
EXCUSE ME FOR BEING SO SLOW!
SO ANYWAY, WHAT'RE YOU TRYING TO PAINT?
GRAH
THE PUMPKIN CARRIAGE, OBVI-OUSLY!
THAT'S A HORSE?
HORSES ARE HARD, OKAY?!
DON'T YOU THINK THE NECK IS SHORT?
OH. YOU'RE RIGHT...
AND THEN YOU ADD THE MANE...
WHOA!
THAT TOTALLY LOOKS LIKE A HORSE!

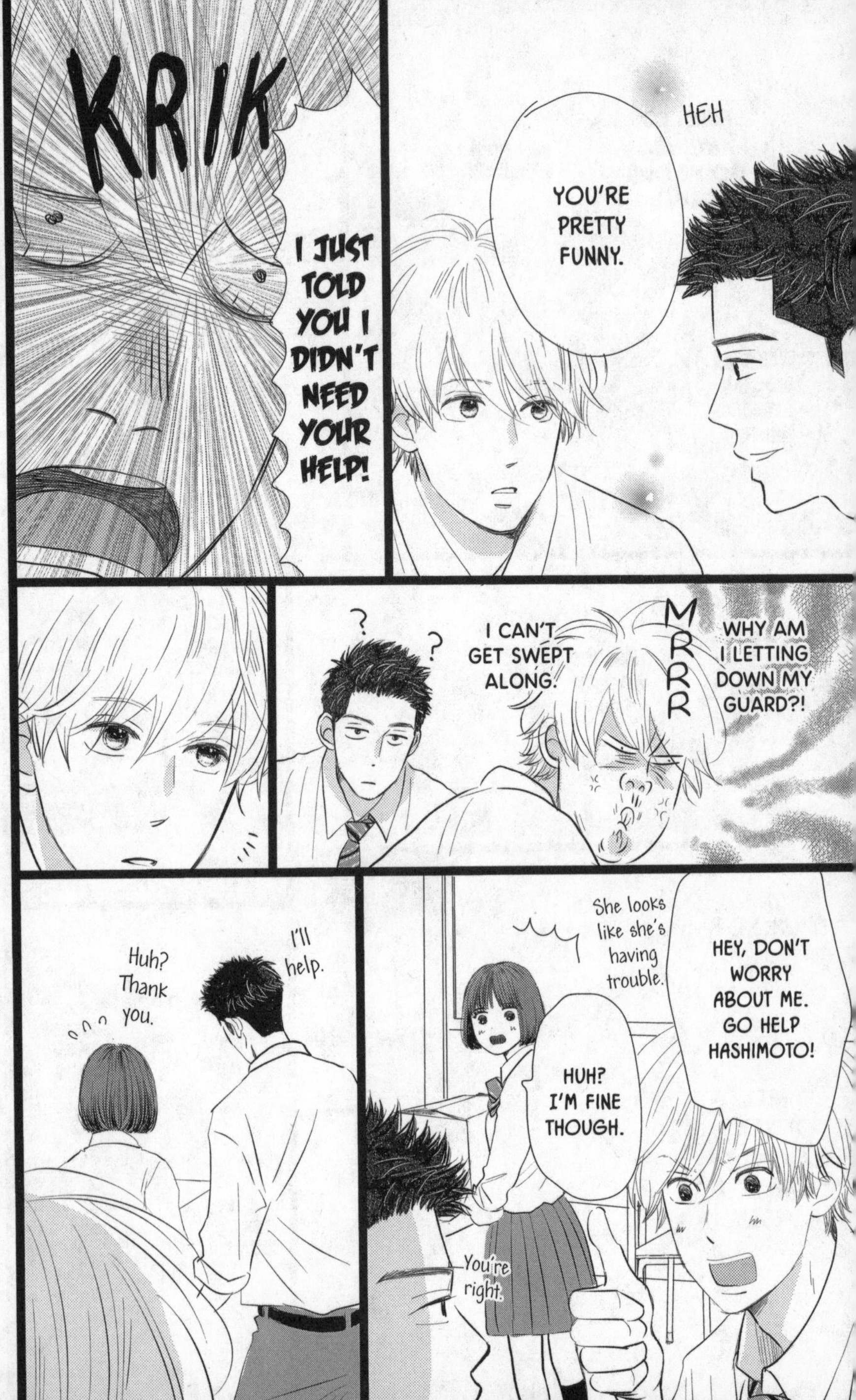
HEH
YOU'RE PRETTY FUNNY.
KRIK
I JUST TOLD YOU I DIDN'T NEED YOUR HELP!
WHY AM I LETTING DOWN MY GUARD?!
MRRR
I CAN'T GET SWEPT ALONG.
HEY, DON'T WORRY ABOUT ME. GO HELP HASHIMOTO!
She looks like she's having trouble.
HUH? I'M FINE THOUGH.
You're right.
I'll help.
Huh? Thank you.

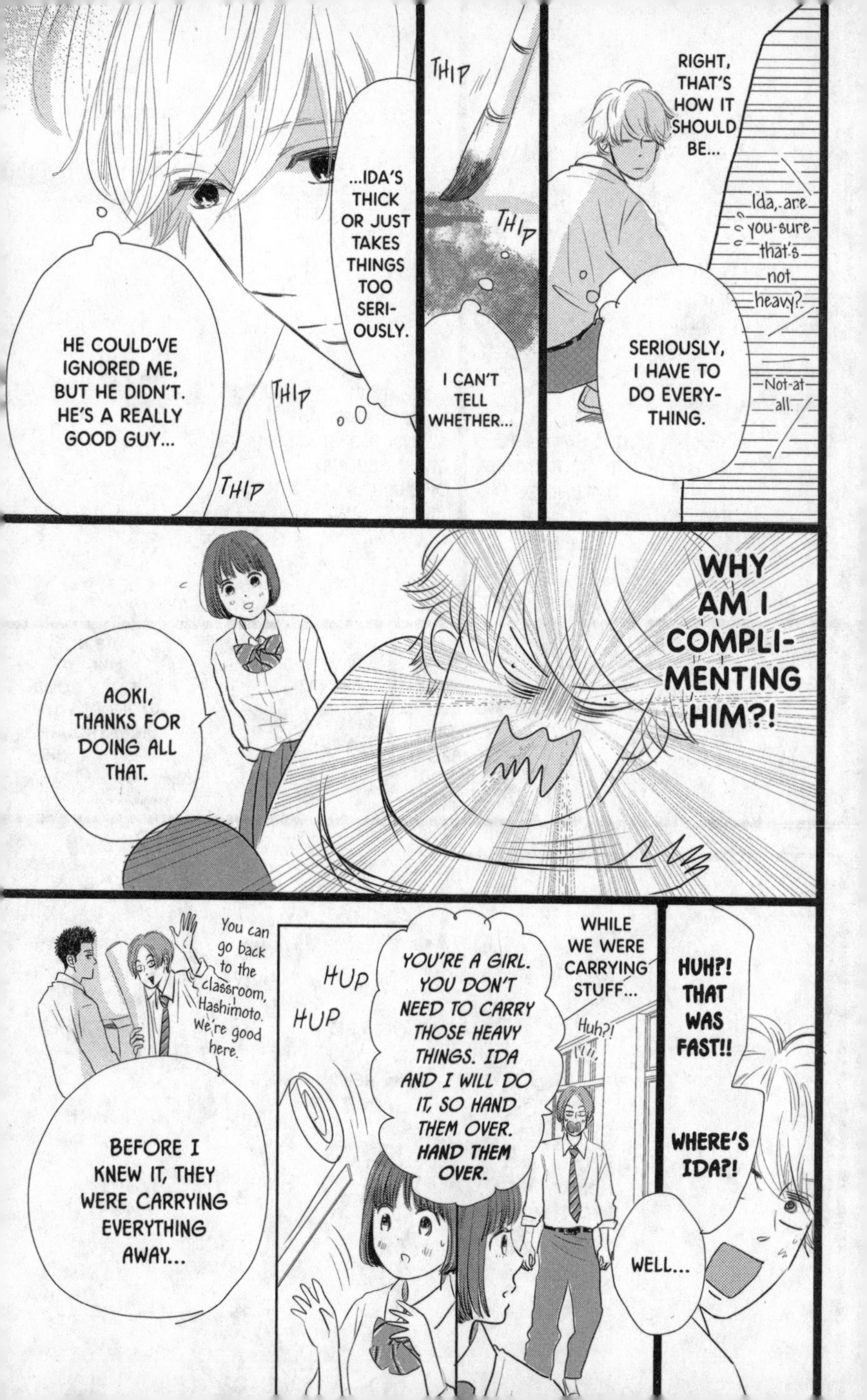
RIGHT, THAT'S HOW IT SHOULD BE...
Ida, are you sure that's not heavy?
Not at all.
SERIOUSLY, I HAVE TO DO EVERYTHING.
THIP
THIP
I CAN'T TELL WHETHER...
...IDA'S THICK OR JUST TAKES THINGS TOO SERIOUSLY.
THIP
THIP
HE COULD'VE IGNORED ME, BUT HE DIDN'T. HE'S A REALLY GOOD GUY...
WHY AM I COMPLIMENTING HIM?!
AOKI, THANKS FOR DOING ALL THAT.
HUH?! THAT WAS FAST!!
WHERE'S IDA?!
WELL...
WHILE WE WERE CARRYING STUFF...
Huh?!
YOU'RE A GIRL. YOU DON'T NEED TO CARRY THOSE HEAVY THINGS. IDA AND I WILL DO IT, SO HAND THEM OVER. HAND THEM OVER.
HUP
HUP
You can go back to the classroom, Hashimoto. We're good here.
BEFORE I KNEW IT, THEY WERE CARRYING EVERYTHING AWAY...

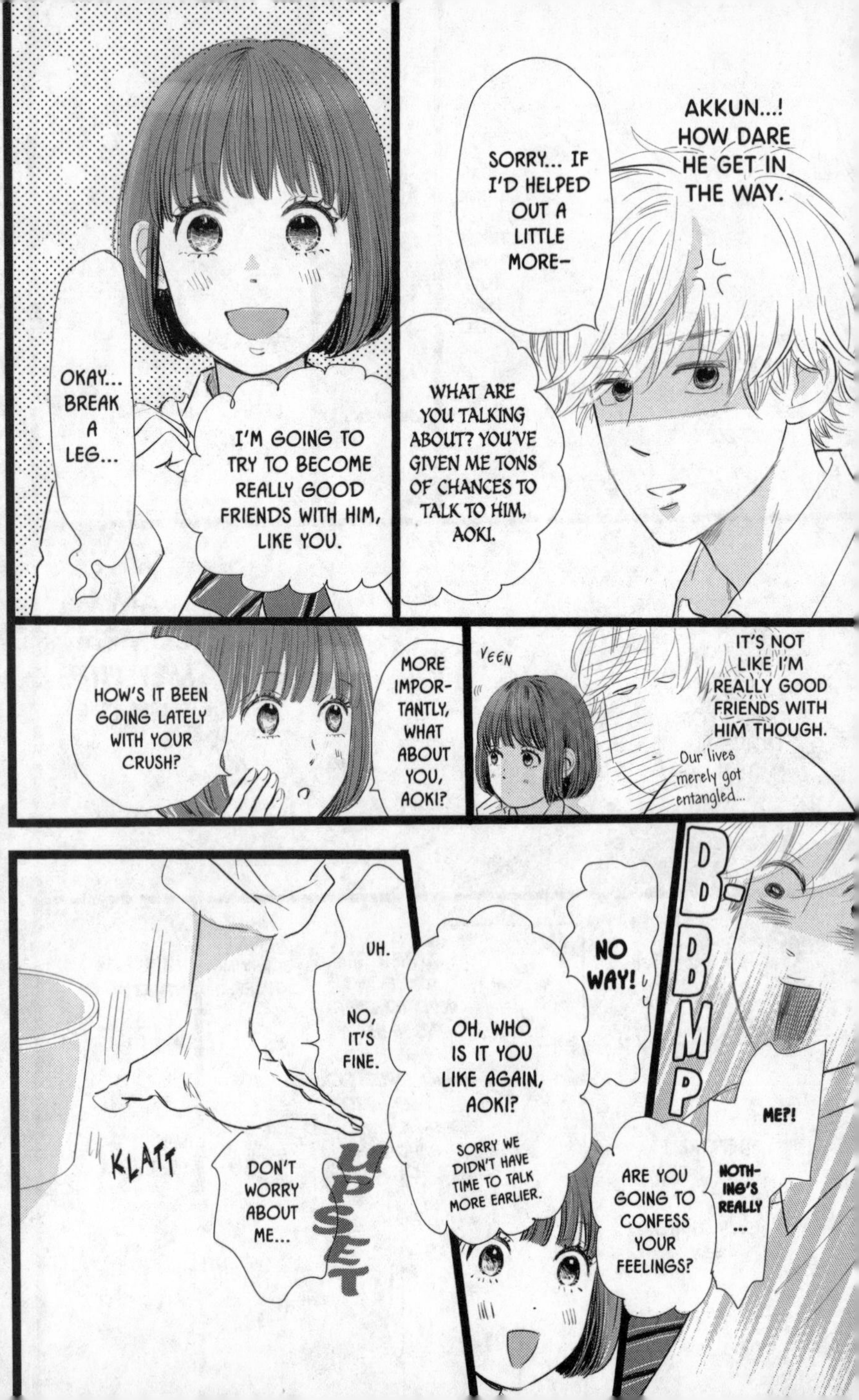
AKKUN...! HOW DARE HE GET IN THE WAY.
SORRY... IF I'D HELPED OUT A LITTLE MORE–
WHAT ARE YOU TALKING ABOUT? YOU'VE GIVEN ME TONS OF CHANCES TO TALK TO HIM, AOKI.
I'M GOING TO TRY TO BECOME REALLY GOOD FRIENDS WITH HIM, LIKE YOU.
OKAY... BREAK A LEG...
IT'S NOT LIKE I'M REALLY GOOD FRIENDS WITH HIM THOUGH.
VEEN
Our lives merely got entangled...
MORE IMPORTANTLY, WHAT ABOUT YOU, AOKI?
HOW'S IT BEEN GOING LATELY WITH YOUR CRUSH?
B-BMP
ME?!
NOTHING'S REALLY...
NO WAY!
OH, WHO IS IT YOU LIKE AGAIN, AOKI?
ARE YOU GOING TO CONFESS YOUR FEELINGS?
SORRY WE DIDN'T HAVE TIME TO TALK MORE EARLIER.
UH.
NO, IT'S FINE.
UPSET
DON'T WORRY ABOUT ME...
KLATT

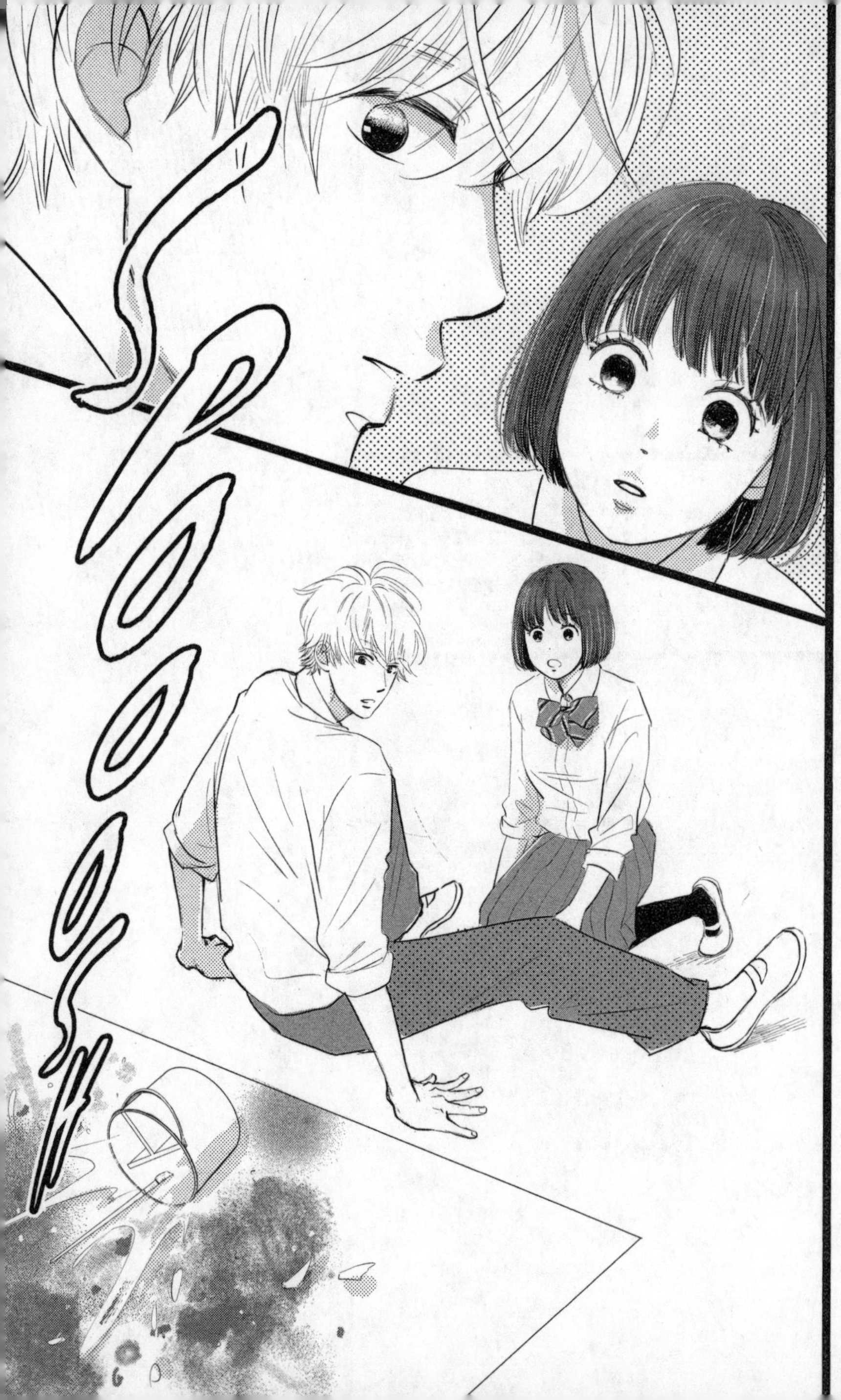
Sploosh

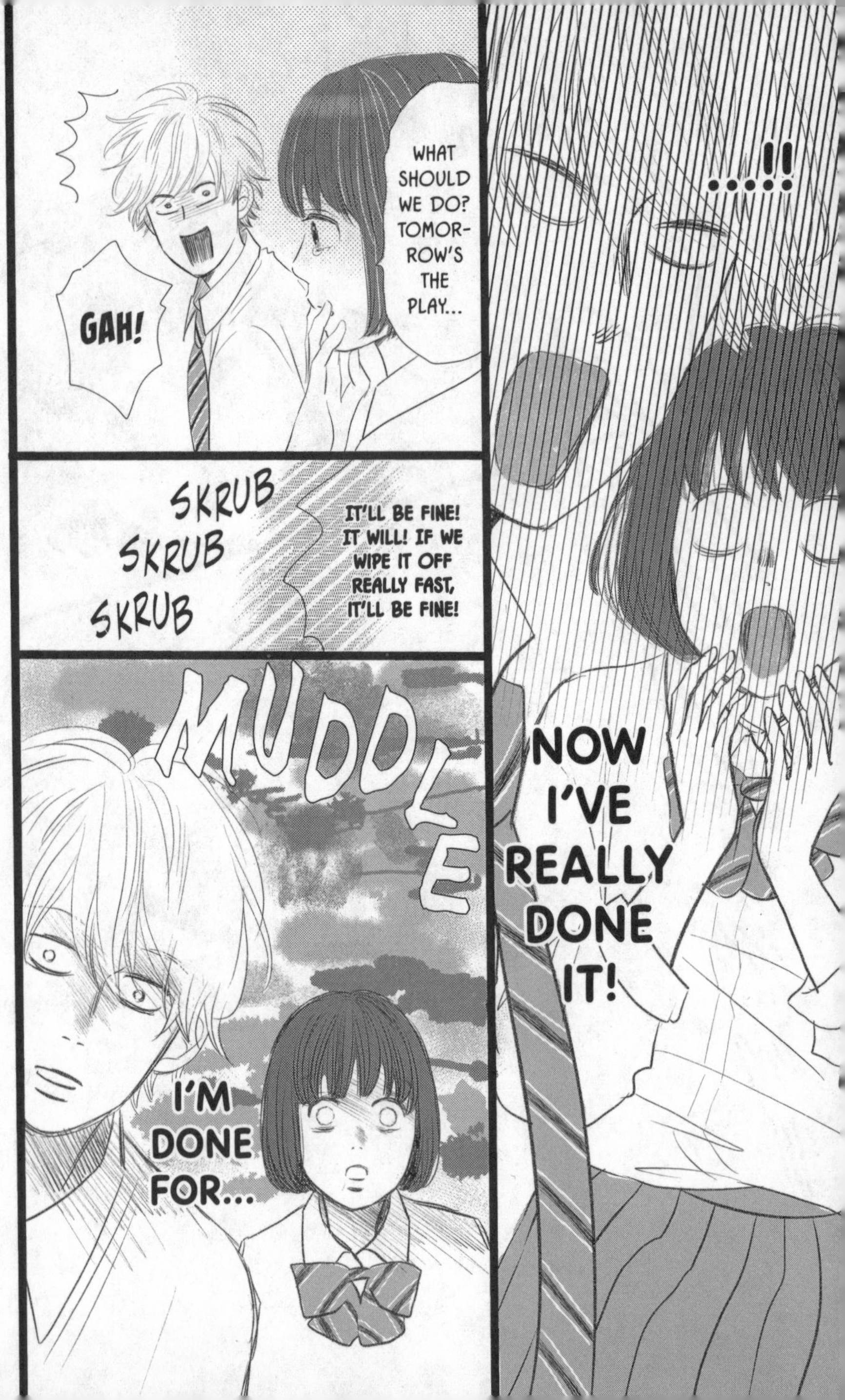
...!!
NOW I'VE REALLY DONE IT!
WHAT SHOULD WE DO? TOMORROW'S THE PLAY...
GAH!
IT'LL BE FINE! IT WILL! IF WE WIPE IT OFF REALLY FAST, IT'LL BE FINE!
SKRUB SKRUB SKRUB
MUDDLE
I'M DONE FOR...

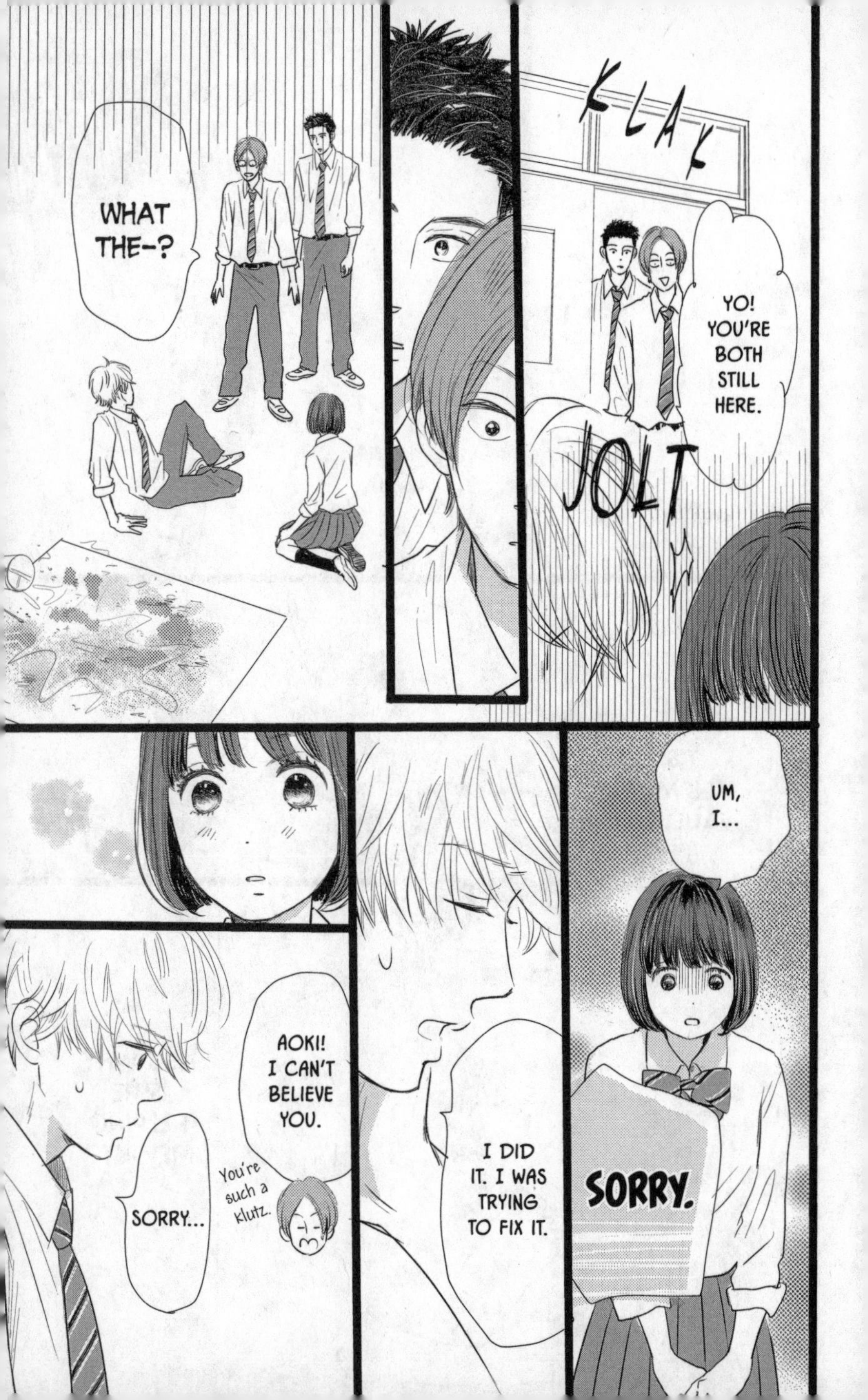
KLAK
YO! YOU'RE BOTH STILL HERE.
JOLT
WHAT THE-?
UM, I...
SORRY.
I DID IT. I WAS TRYING TO FIX IT.
AOKI! I CAN'T BELIEVE YOU.
You're such a klutz.
SORRY...

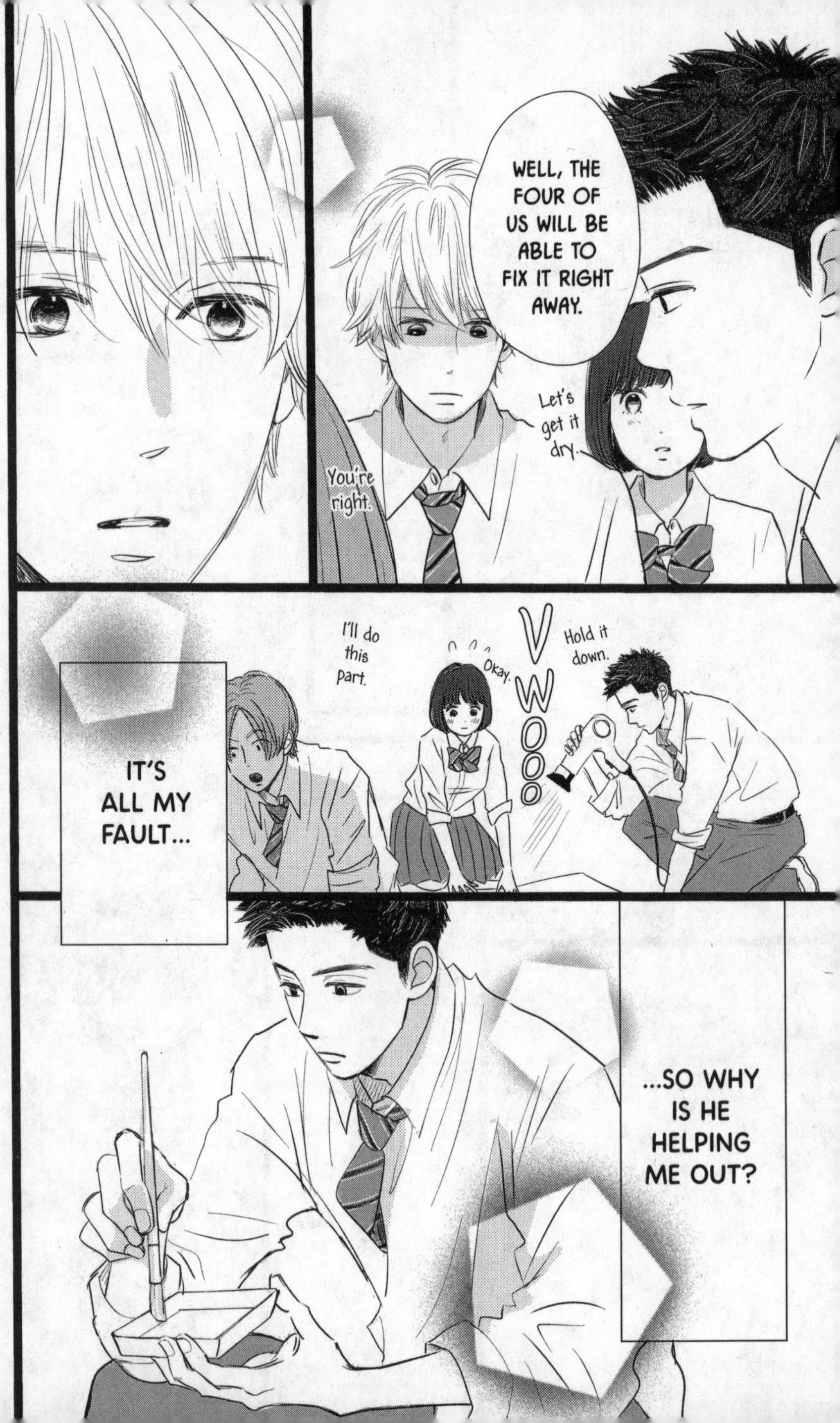
WELL, THE FOUR OF US WILL BE ABLE TO FIX IT RIGHT AWAY.
Let's get it dry.
You're right.
Hold it down.
VWOOO
Okay.
I'll do this part.
IT'S ALL MY FAULT...
...SO WHY IS HE HELPING ME OUT?

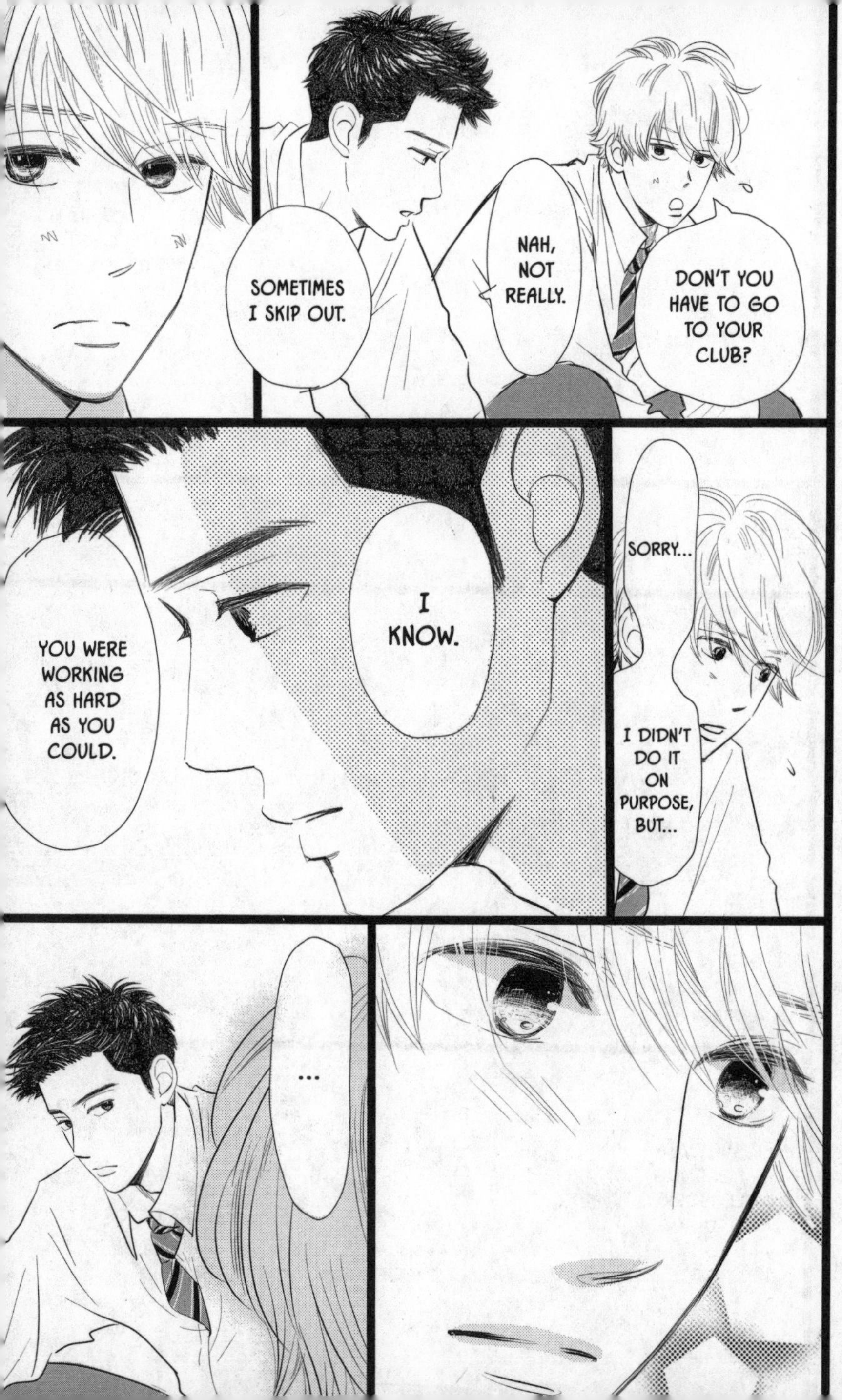
DON'T YOU HAVE TO GO TO YOUR CLUB?
NAH, NOT REALLY.
SOMETIMES I SKIP OUT.
SORRY...
I DIDN'T DO IT ON PURPOSE, BUT...
I KNOW.
YOU WERE WORKING AS HARD AS YOU COULD.
...

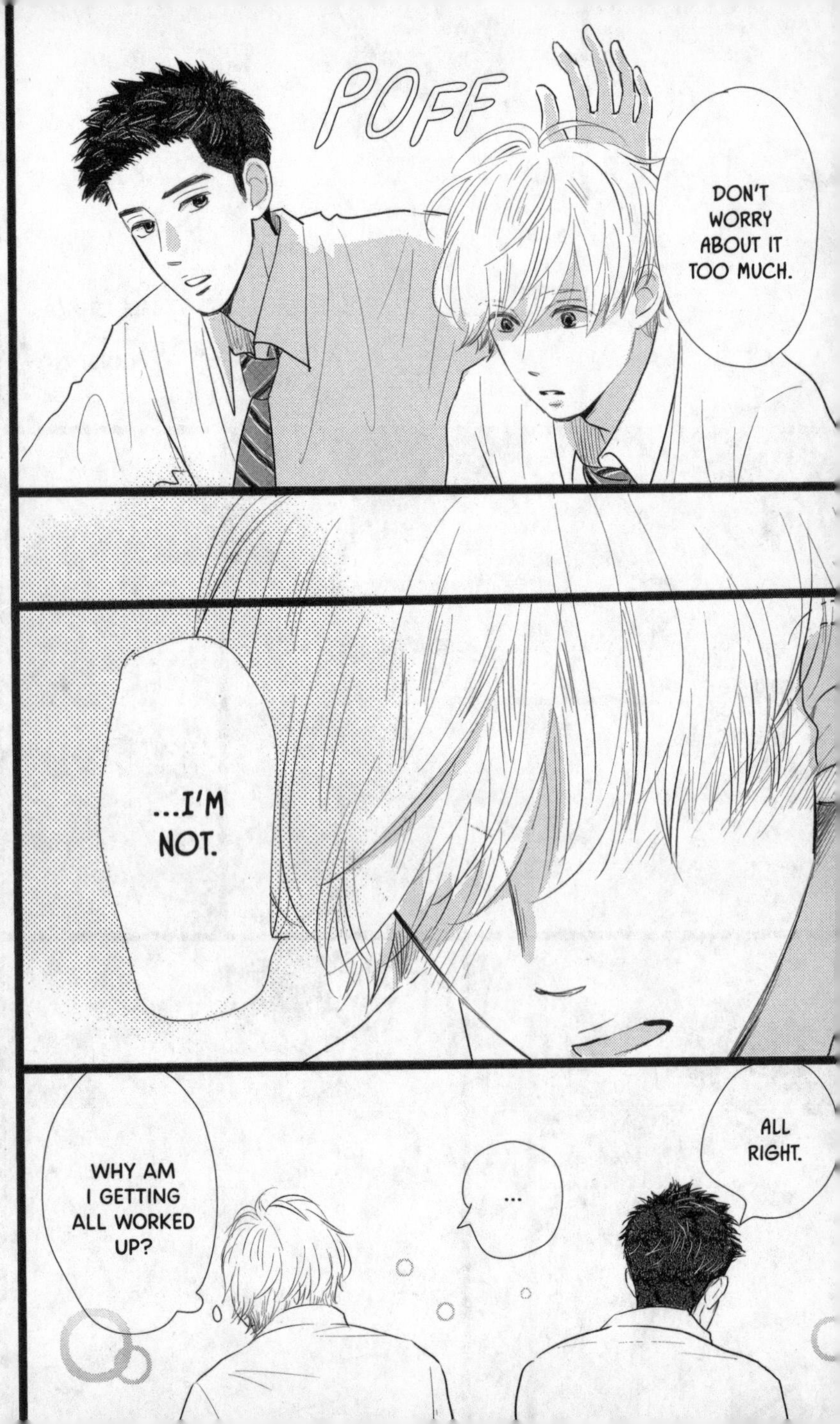

POFF
DON'T WORRY ABOUT IT TOO MUCH.
...I'M NOT.
ALL RIGHT.
...
WHY AM I GETTING ALL WORKED UP?

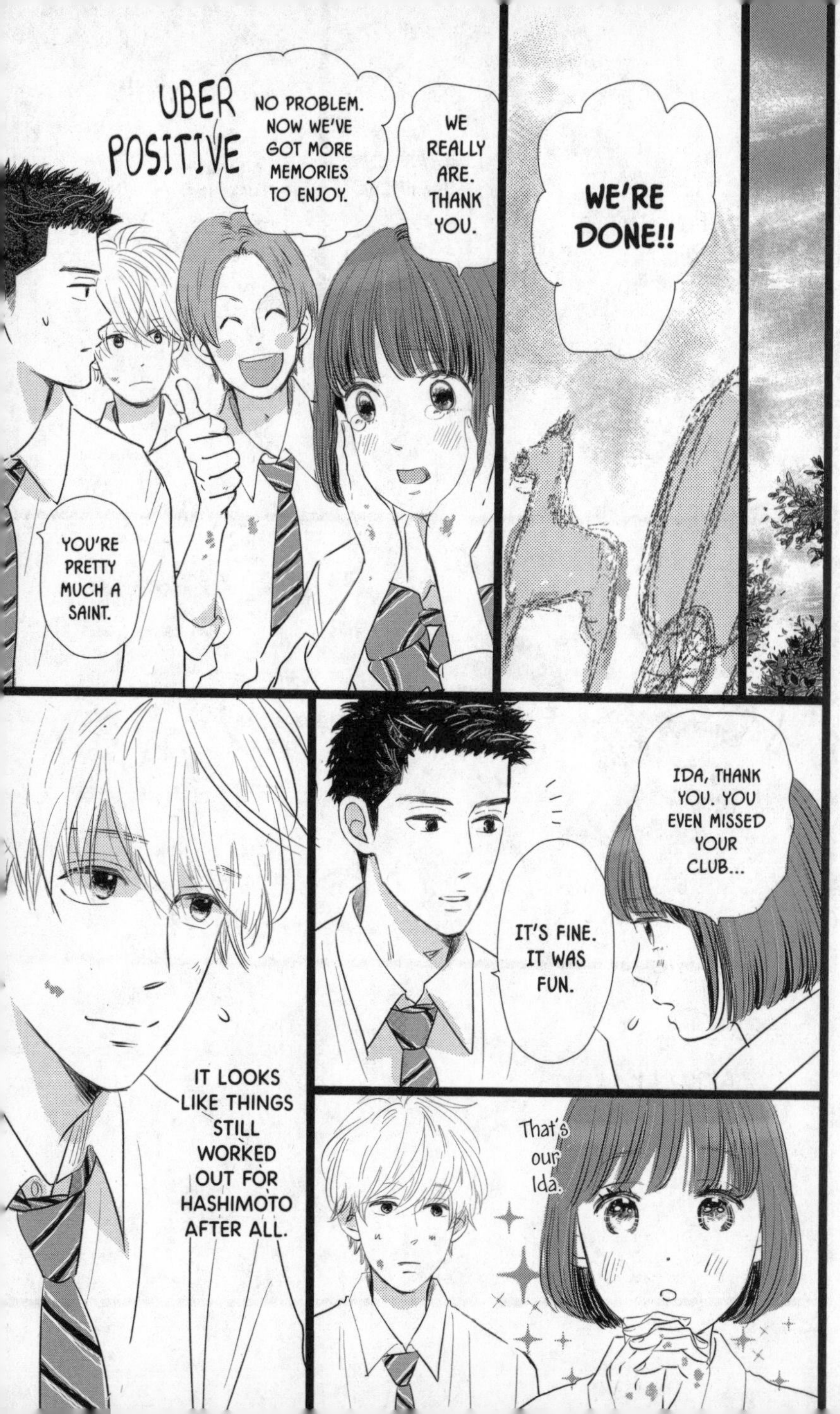
WE'RE DONE!!
WE REALLY ARE. THANK YOU.
NO PROBLEM. NOW WE'VE GOT MORE MEMORIES TO ENJOY.
UBER POSITIVE
YOU'RE PRETTY MUCH A SAINT.
IDA, THANK YOU. YOU EVEN MISSED YOUR CLUB...
IT'S FINE. IT WAS FUN.
That's our Ida.
IT LOOKS LIKE THINGS STILL WORKED OUT FOR HASHIMOTO AFTER ALL.

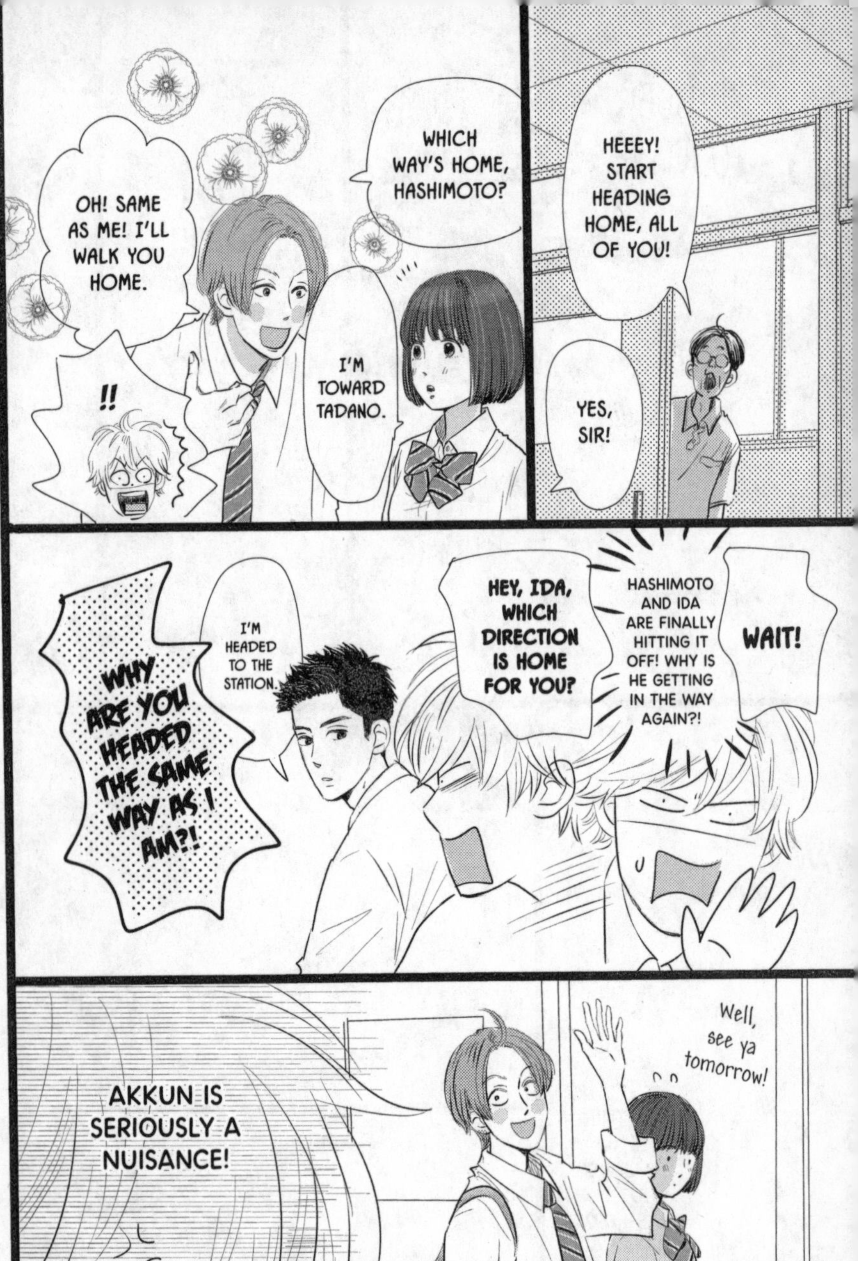
HEEEY! START HEADING HOME, ALL OF YOU!
YES, SIR!
WHICH WAY'S HOME, HASHIMOTO?
I'M TOWARD TADANO.
OH! SAME AS ME! I'LL WALK YOU HOME.
!!
WAIT!
HASHIMOTO AND IDA ARE FINALLY HITTING IT OFF! WHY IS HE GETTING IN THE WAY AGAIN?!
HEY, IDA, WHICH DIRECTION IS HOME FOR YOU?
I'M HEADED TO THE STATION.
WHY ARE YOU HEADED THE SAME WAY AS I AM?!
Well, see ya tomorrow!
AKKUN IS SERIOUSLY A NUISANCE!

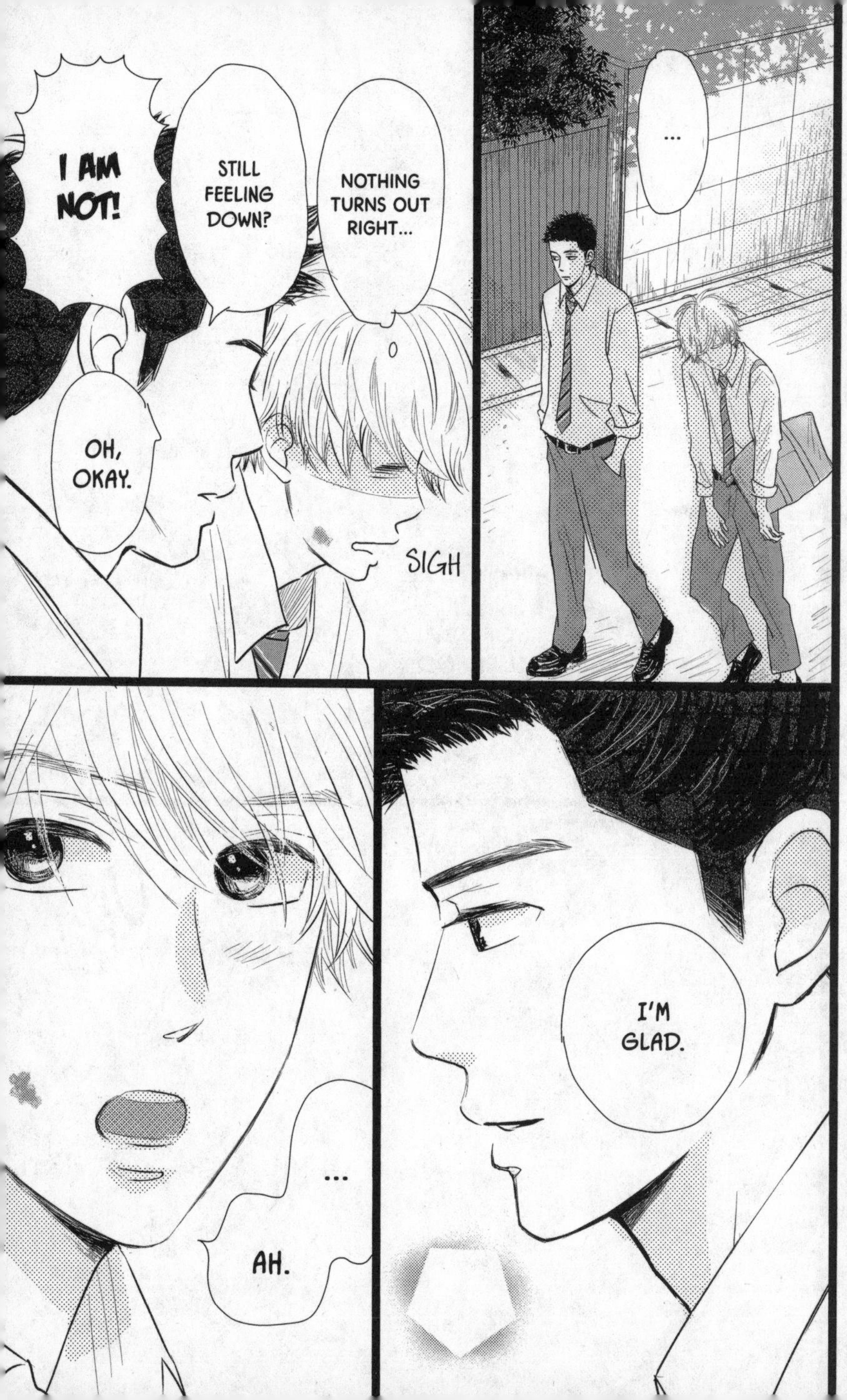
...
NOTHING TURNS OUT RIGHT...
STILL FEELING DOWN?
I AM NOT!
OH, OKAY.
SIGH
I'M GLAD.
...
AH.

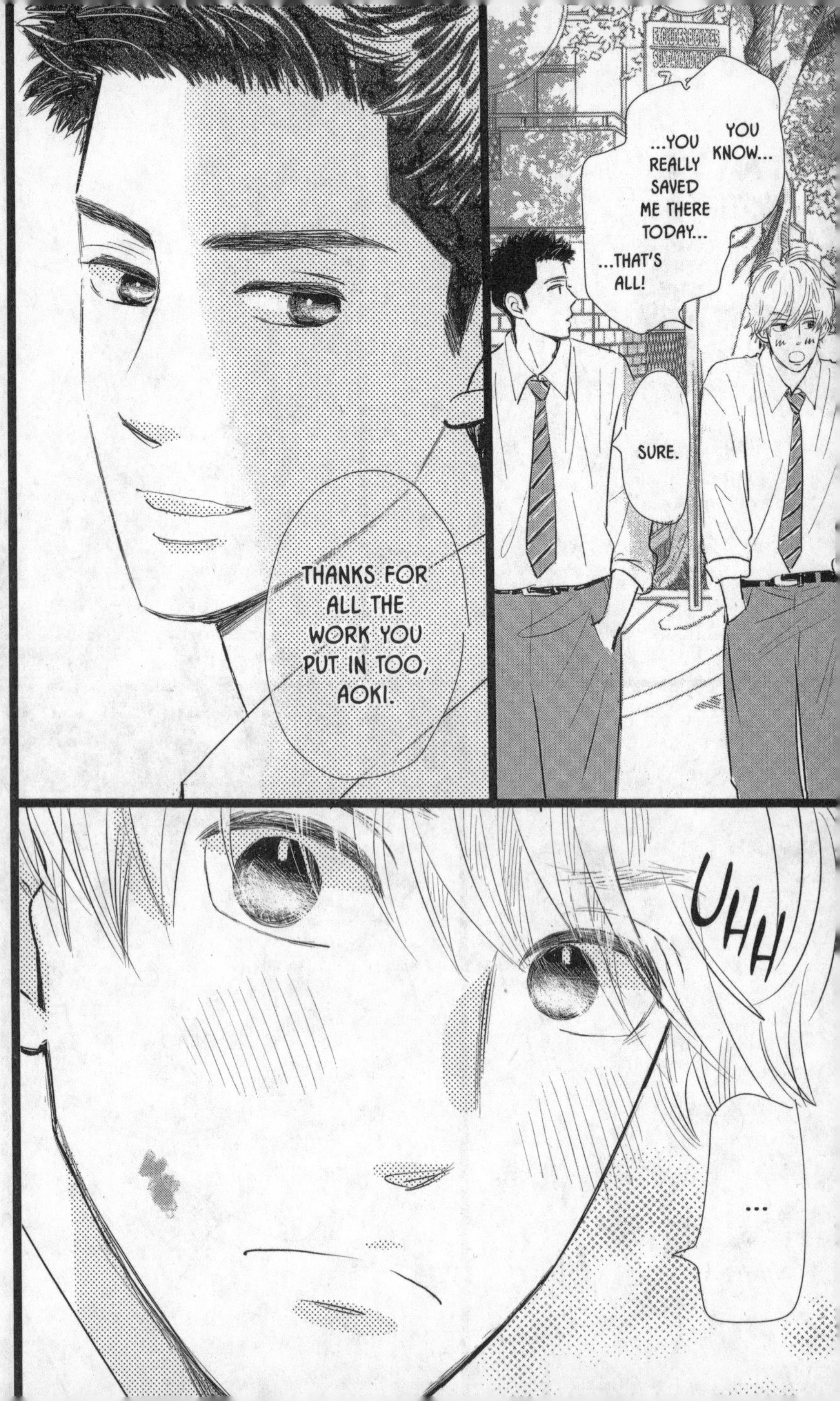
YOU KNOW... ...YOU REALLY SAVED ME THERE TODAY... ...THAT'S ALL!
SURE.
THANKS FOR ALL THE WORK YOU PUT IN TOO, AOKI.
UHH
...

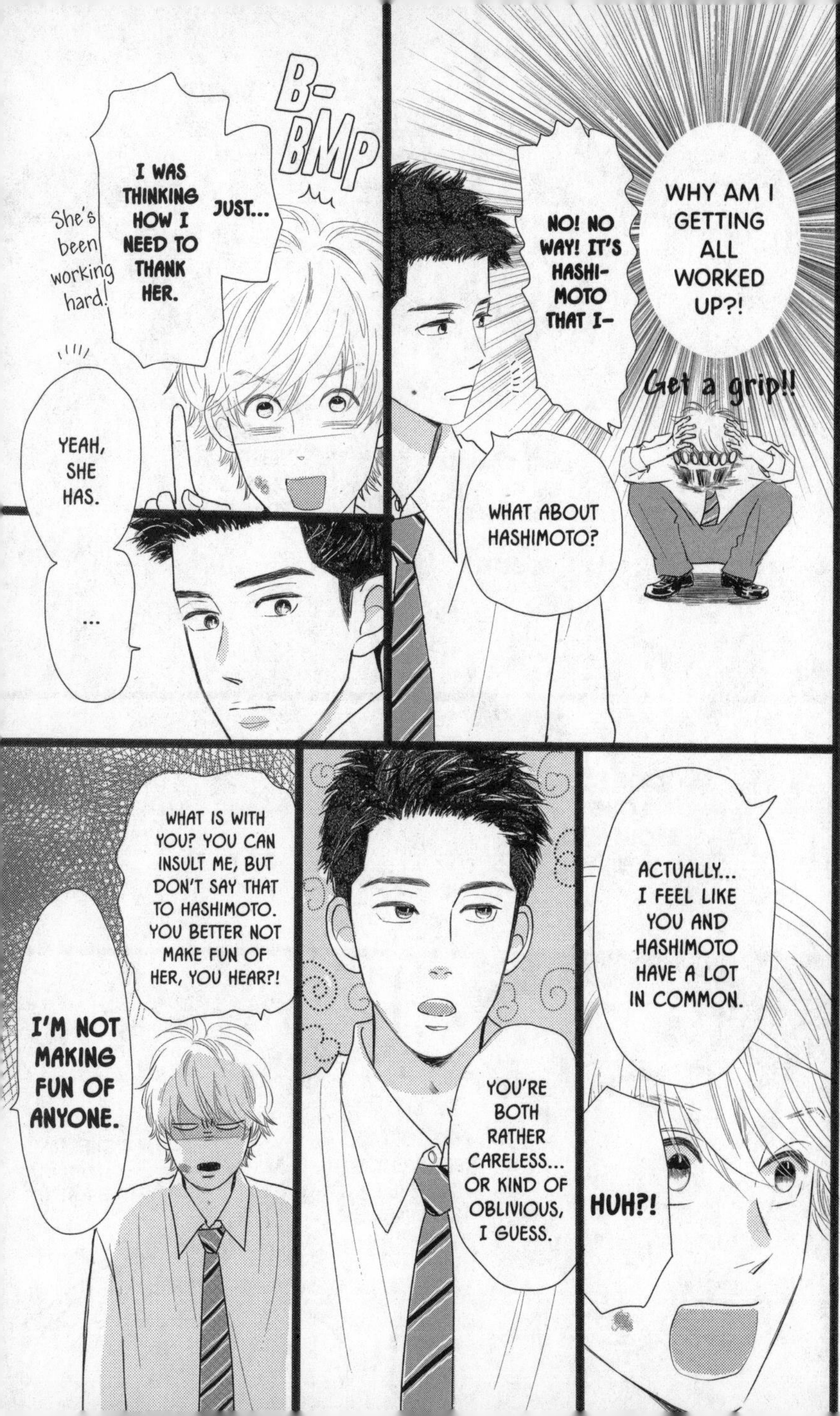
WHY AM I GETTING ALL WORKED UP?!
NO! NO WAY! IT'S HASHIMOTO THAT I-
Get a grip!!
WHAT ABOUT HASHIMOTO?
B-BMP
JUST...
I WAS THINKING HOW I NEED TO THANK HER.
She's been working hard!
YEAH, SHE HAS.
...
ACTUALLY... I FEEL LIKE YOU AND HASHIMOTO HAVE A LOT IN COMMON.
HUH?!
YOU'RE BOTH RATHER CARELESS... OR KIND OF OBLIVIOUS, I GUESS.
WHAT IS WITH YOU? YOU CAN INSULT ME, BUT DON'T SAY THAT TO HASHIMOTO. YOU BETTER NOT MAKE FUN OF HER, YOU HEAR?!
I'M NOT MAKING FUN OF ANYONE.

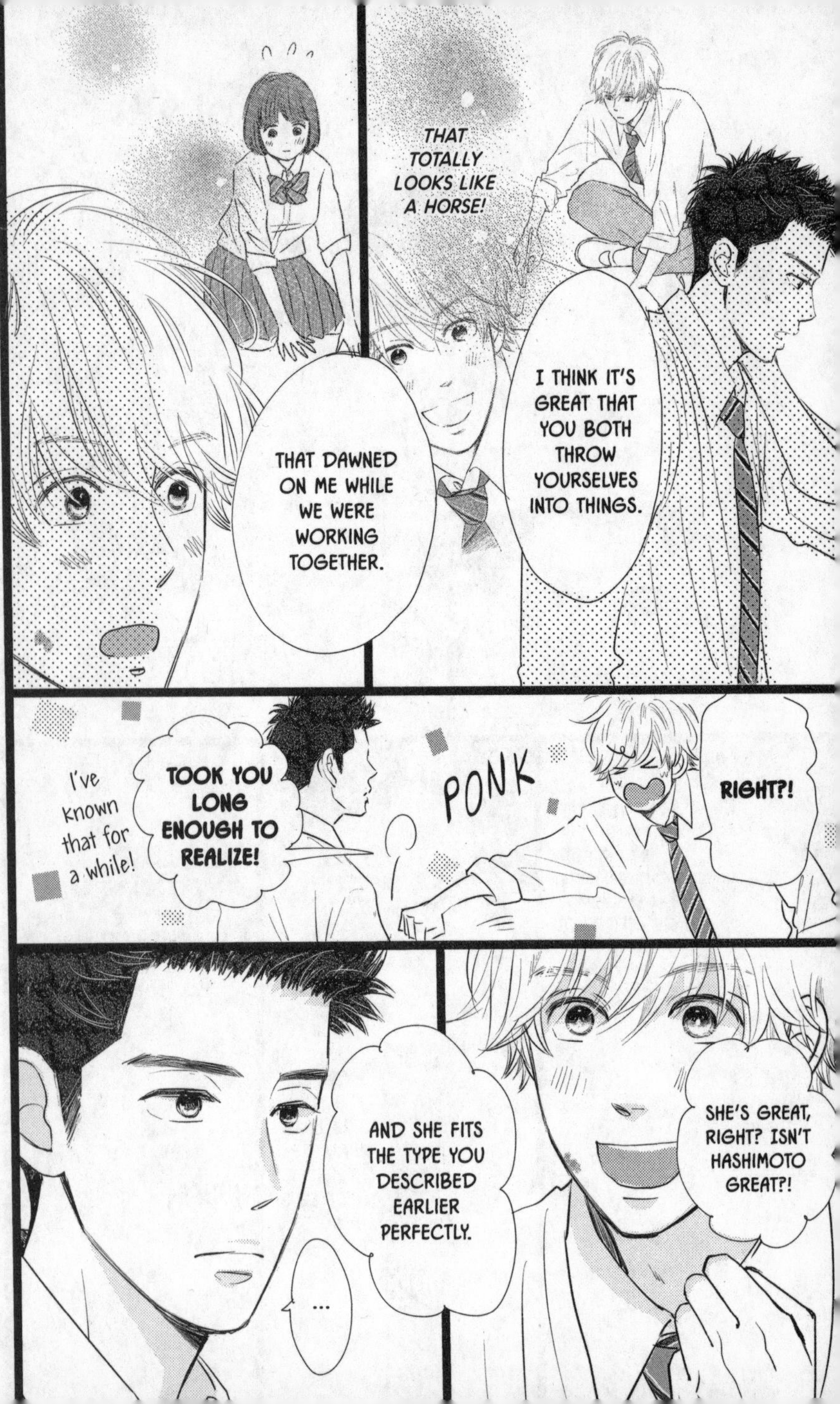
THAT TOTALLY LOOKS LIKE A HORSE!
I THINK IT'S GREAT THAT YOU BOTH THROW YOURSELVES INTO THINGS.
THAT DAWNED ON ME WHILE WE WERE WORKING TOGETHER.
RIGHT?!
PONK
TOOK YOU LONG ENOUGH TO REALIZE!
I've known that for a while!
SHE'S GREAT, RIGHT? ISN'T HASHIMOTO GREAT?!
AND SHE FITS THE TYPE YOU DESCRIBED EARLIER PERFECTLY.
...

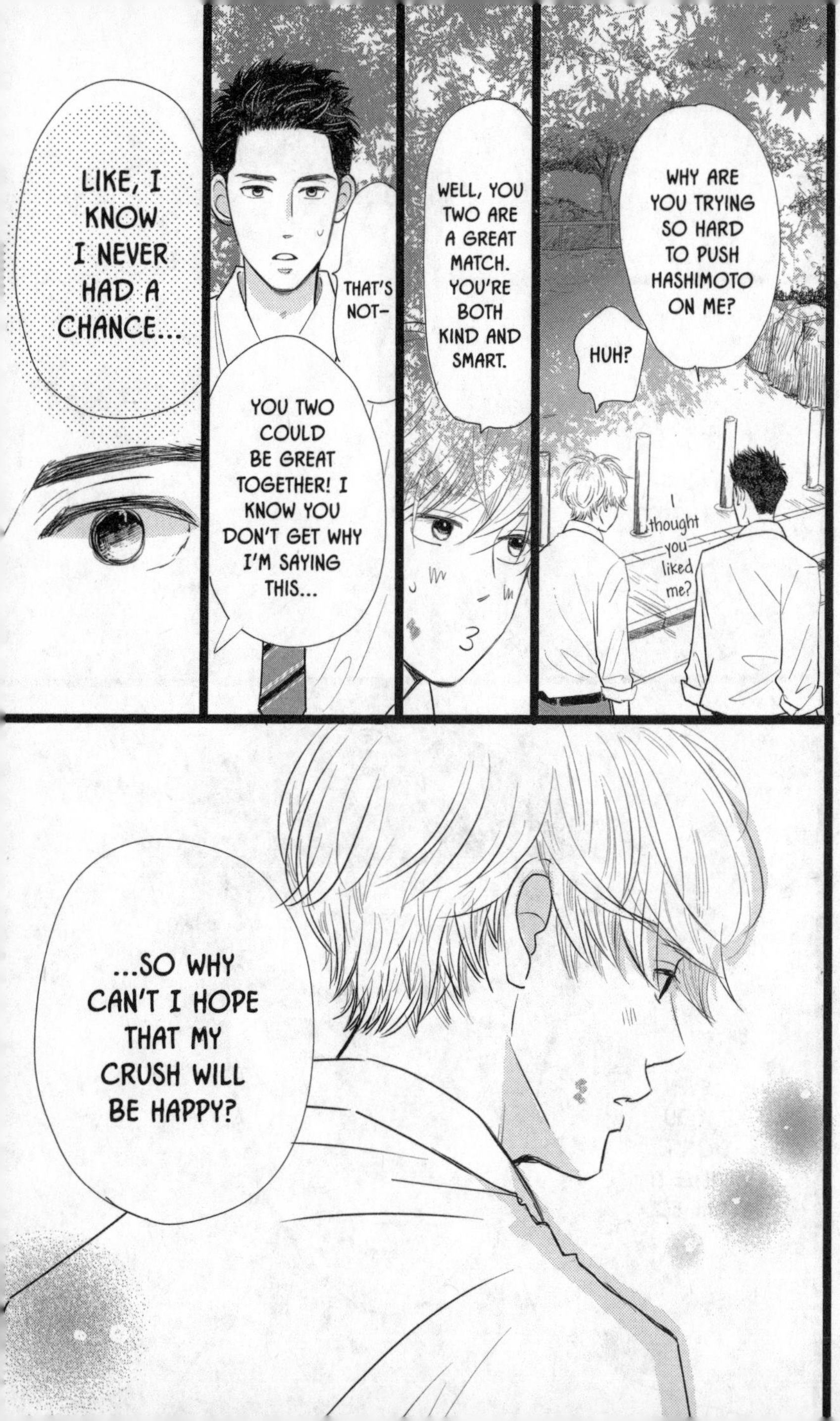
WHY ARE YOU TRYING SO HARD TO PUSH HASHIMOTO ON ME?
HUH?
I thought you liked me?
WELL, YOU TWO ARE A GREAT MATCH. YOU'RE BOTH KIND AND SMART.
THAT'S NOT-
YOU TWO COULD BE GREAT TOGETHER! I KNOW YOU DON'T GET WHY I'M SAYING THIS...
LIKE, I KNOW I NEVER HAD A CHANCE...
...SO WHY CAN'T I HOPE THAT MY CRUSH WILL BE HAPPY?

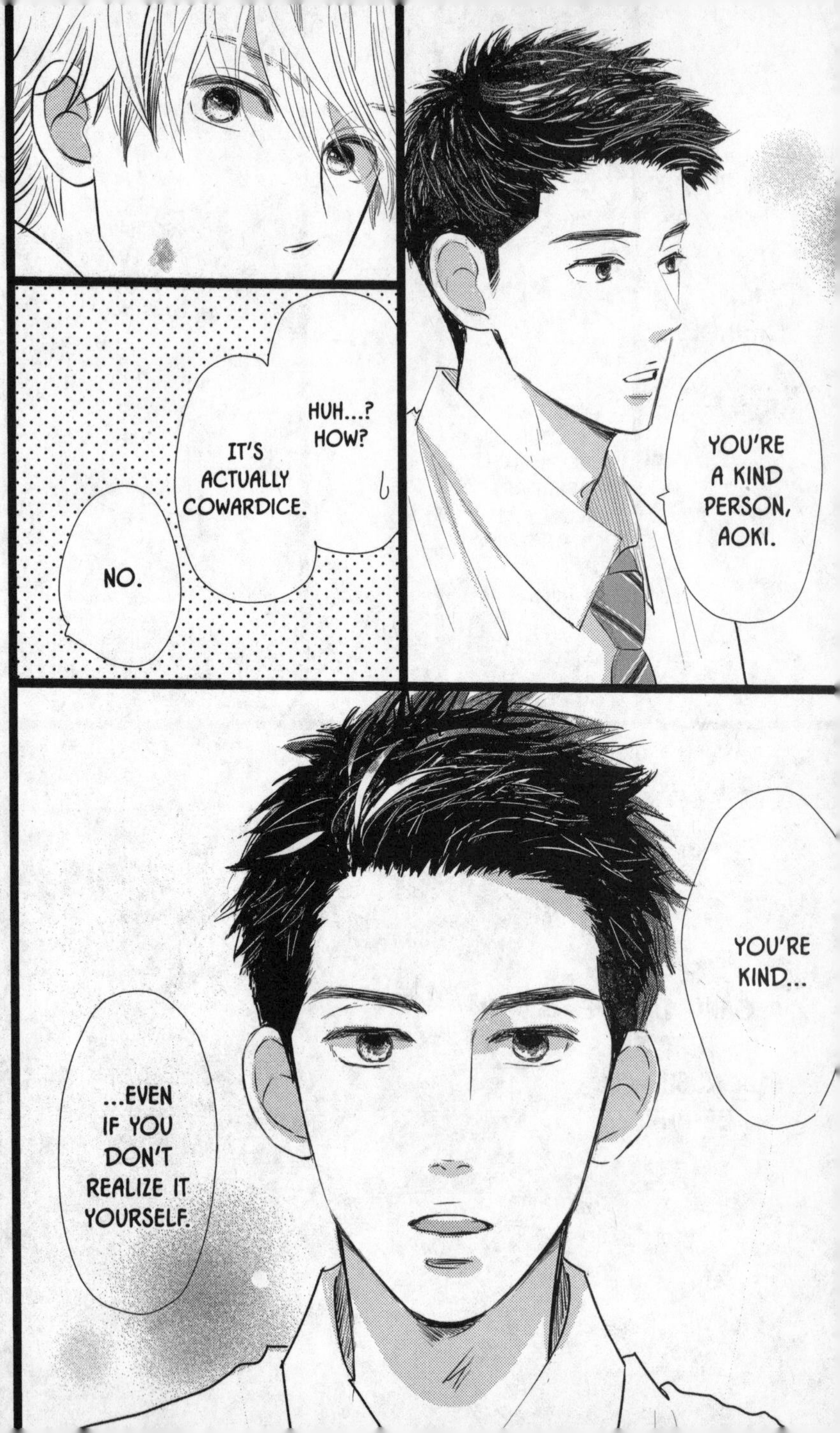
YOU'RE A KIND PERSON, AOKI.
HUH...? HOW?
IT'S ACTUALLY COWARDICE.
NO.
YOU'RE KIND...
...EVEN IF YOU DON'T REALIZE IT YOURSELF.

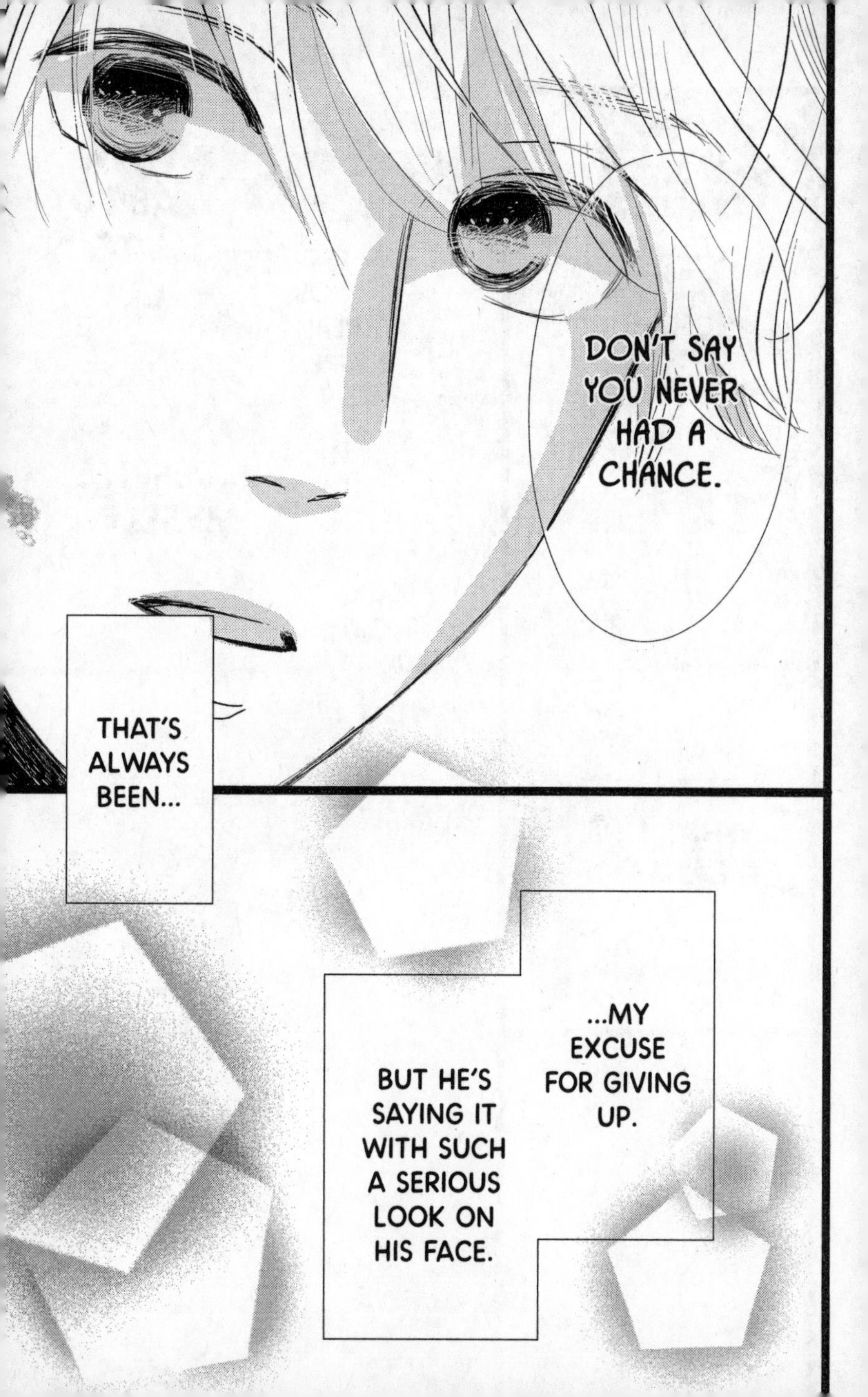
DON'T SAY YOU NEVER HAD A CHANCE.
THAT'S ALWAYS BEEN...
...MY EXCUSE FOR GIVING UP.
BUT HE'S SAYING IT WITH SUCH A SERIOUS LOOK ON HIS FACE.

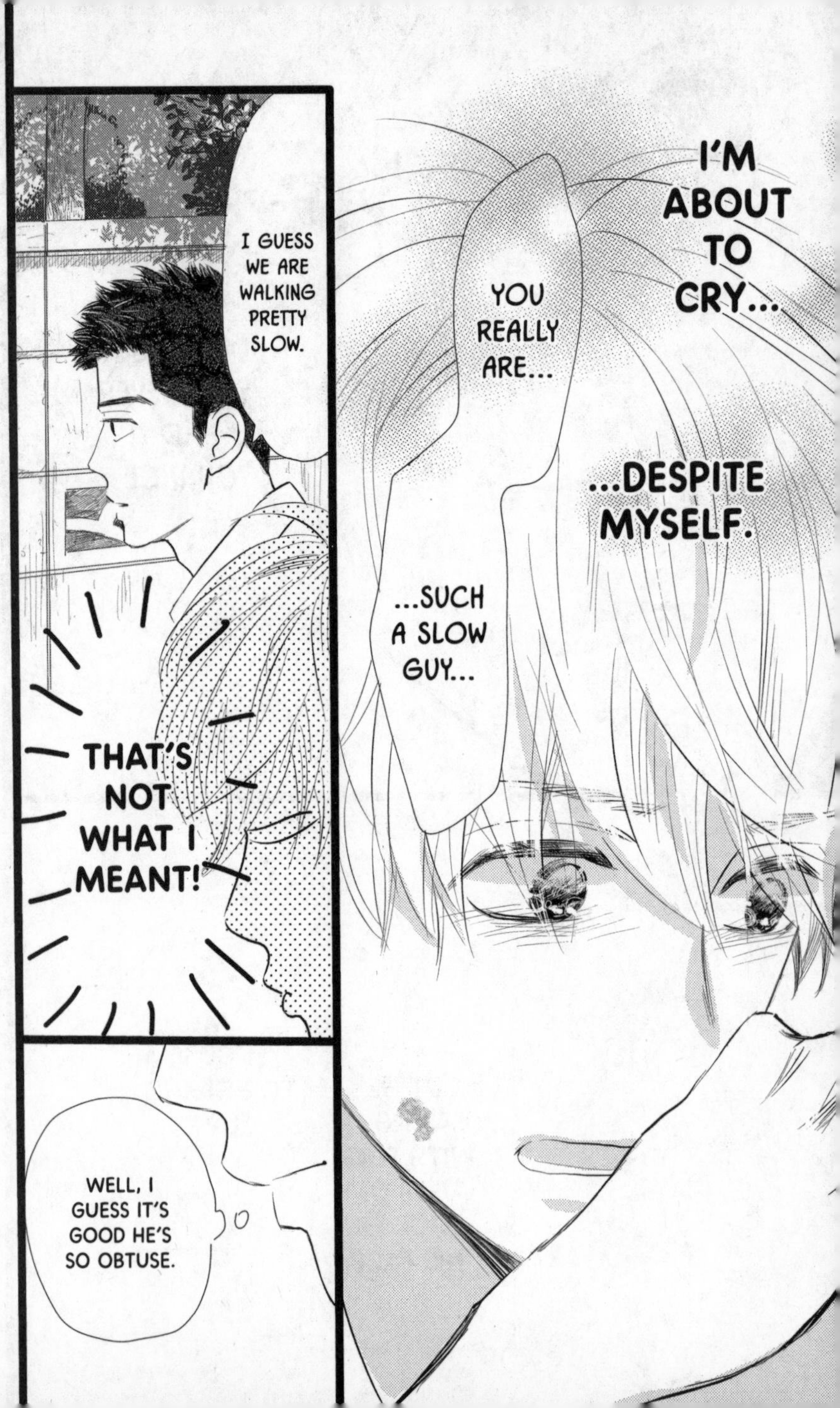
I'M ABOUT TO CRY...
...DESPITE MYSELF.
YOU REALLY ARE... ...SUCH A SLOW GUY...
I GUESS WE ARE WALKING PRETTY SLOW.
THAT'S NOT WHAT I MEANT!
WELL, I GUESS IT'S GOOD HE'S SO OBTUSE.

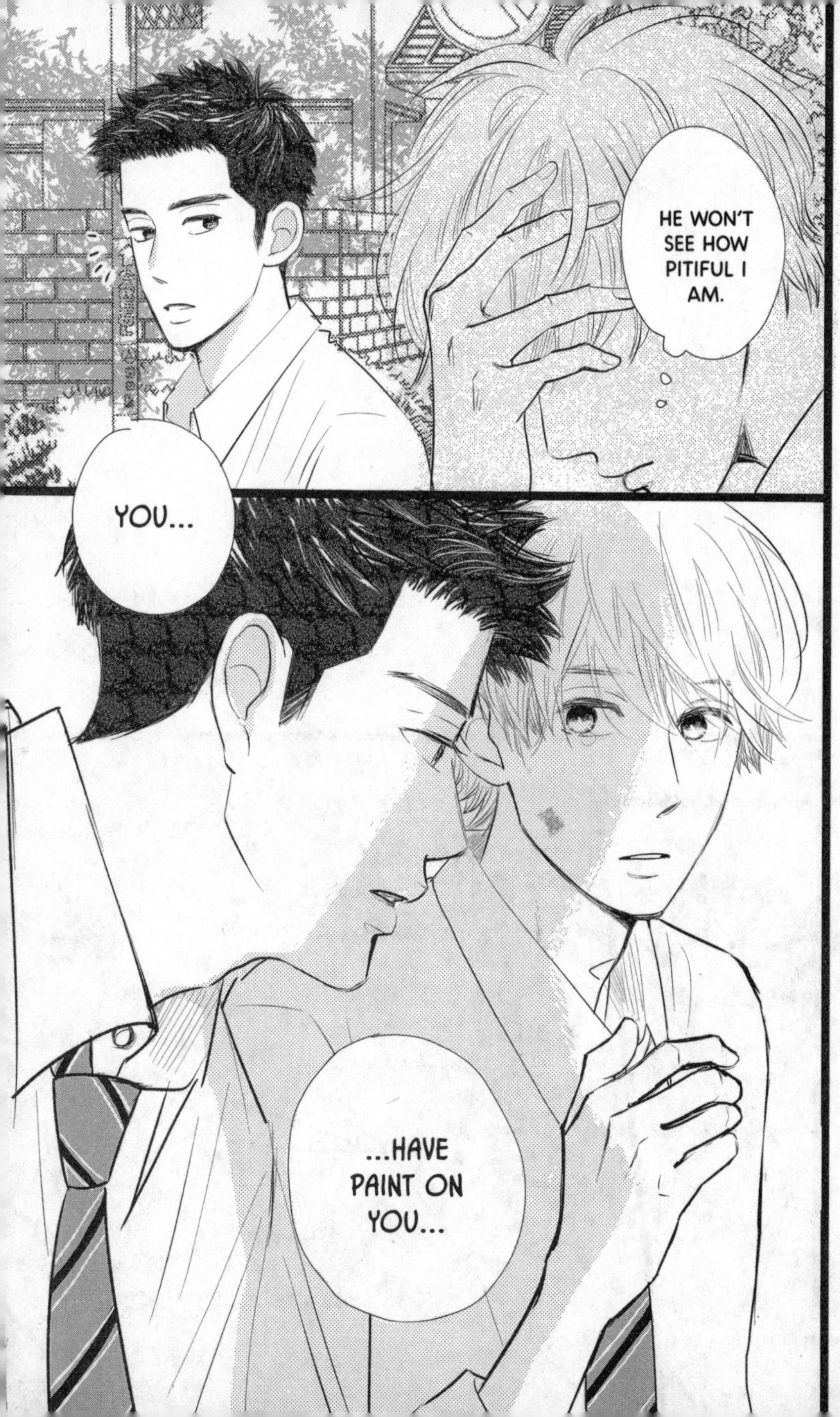
HE WON'T SEE HOW PITIFUL I AM.
YOU...
...HAVE PAINT ON YOU...

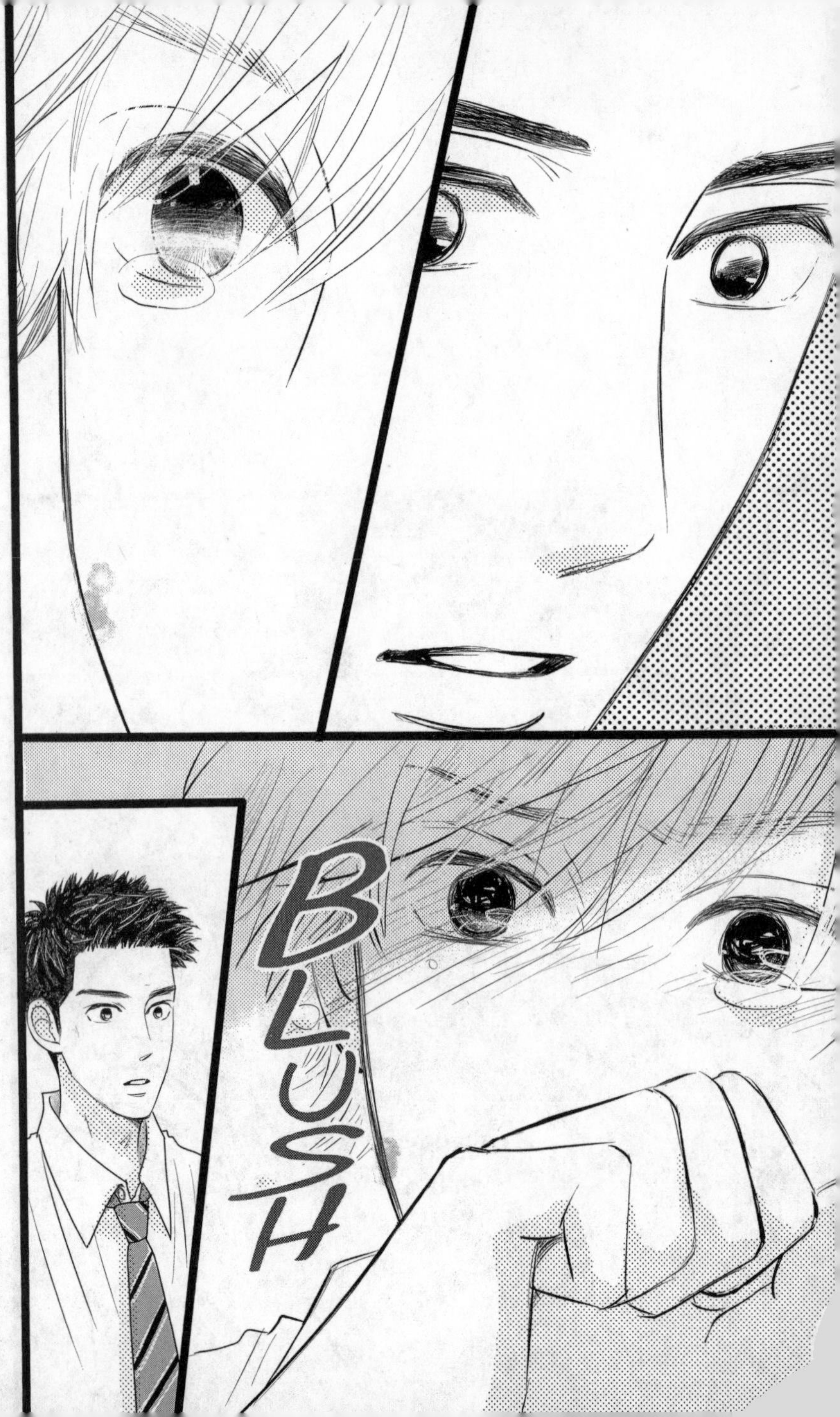
BLUSH

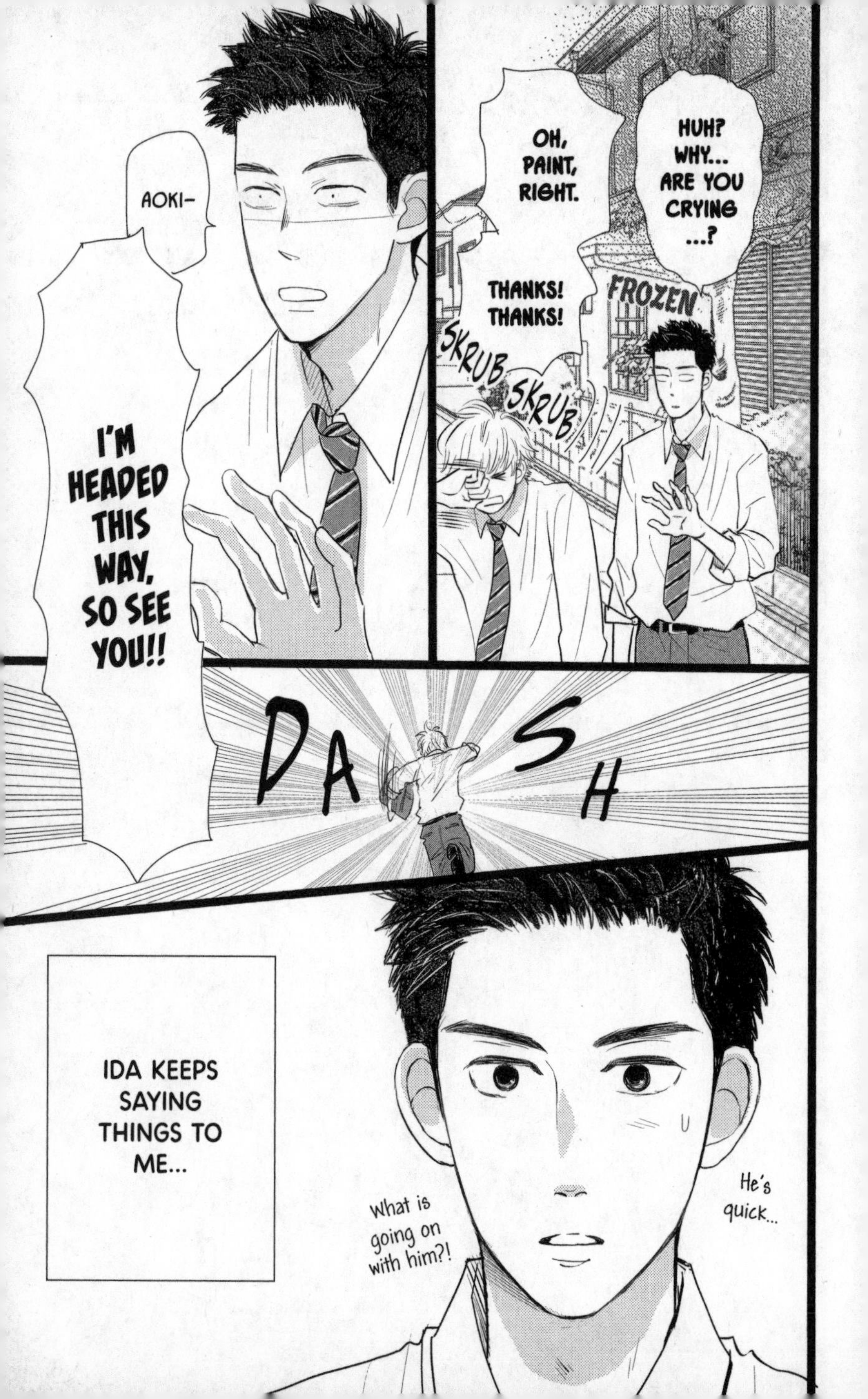
HUH? WHY... ARE YOU CRYING ...?
OH, PAINT, RIGHT.
FROZEN
THANKS! THANKS!
SKRUB
SKRUB
AOKI-
I'M HEADED THIS WAY, SO SEE YOU!!
DASH
He's quick...
What is going on with him?!
IDA KEEPS SAYING THINGS TO ME...

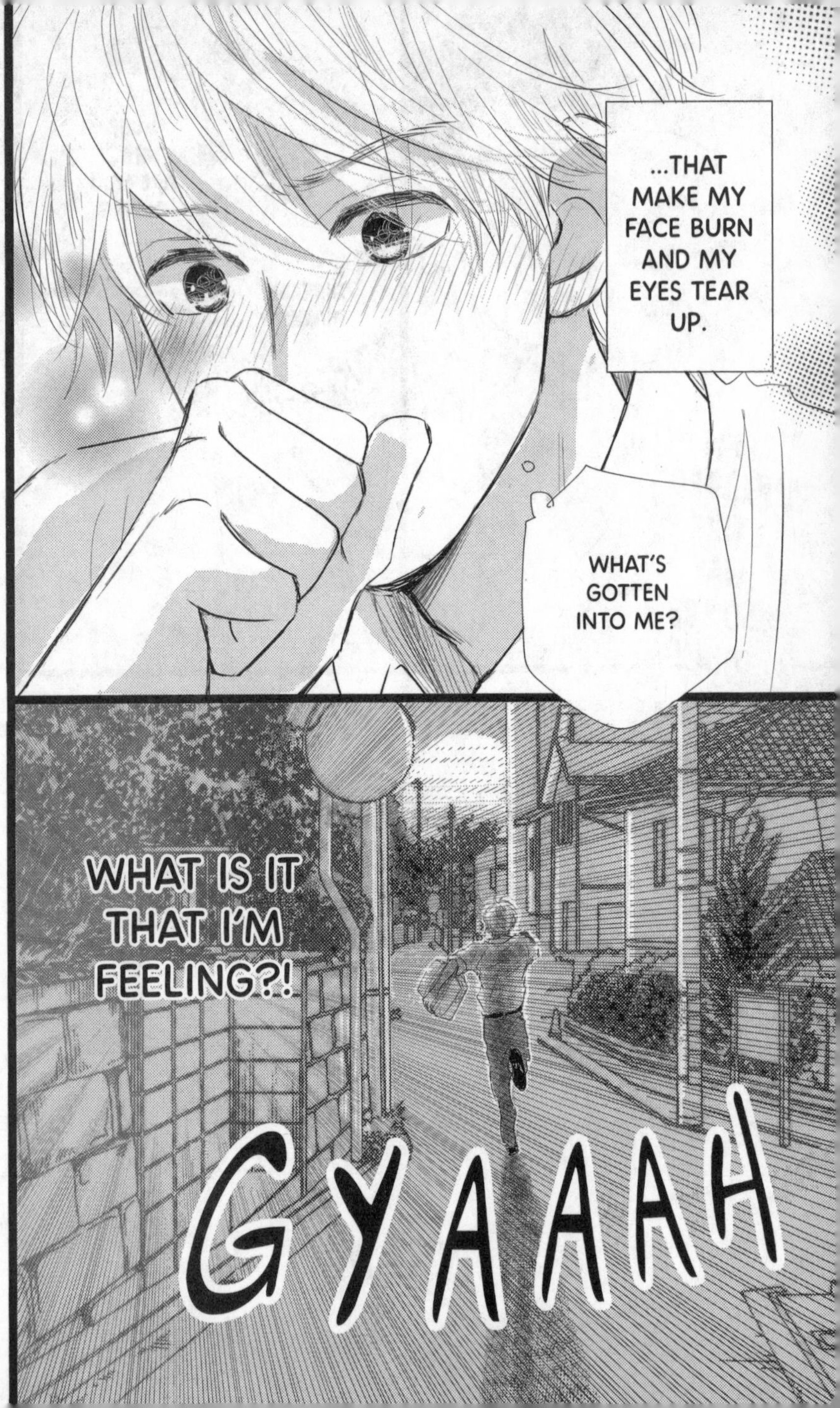
...THAT MAKE MY FACE BURN AND MY EYES TEAR UP.
WHAT'S GOTTEN INTO ME?
WHAT IS IT THAT I'M FEELING?!
GYAAAH

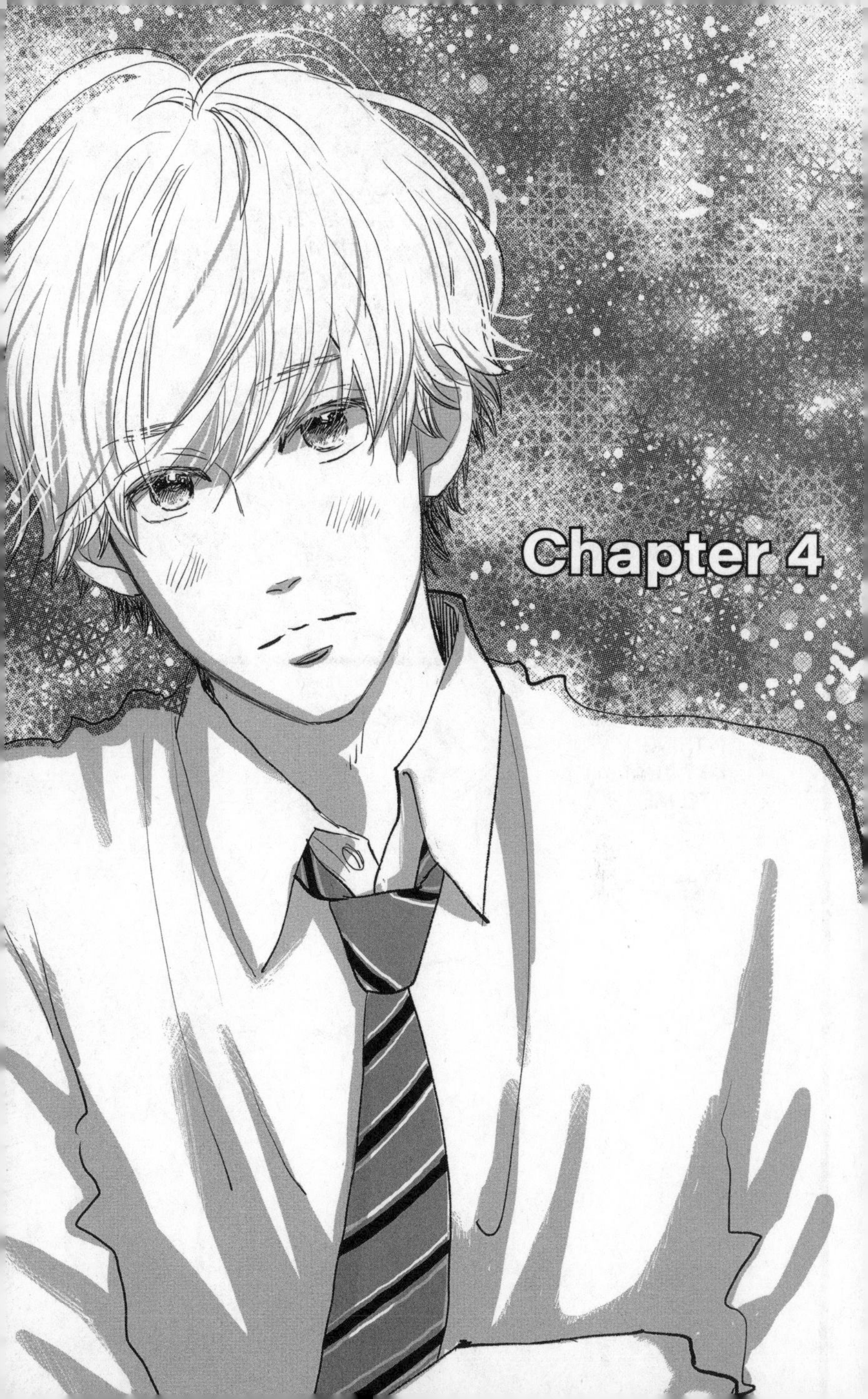
Chapter 4

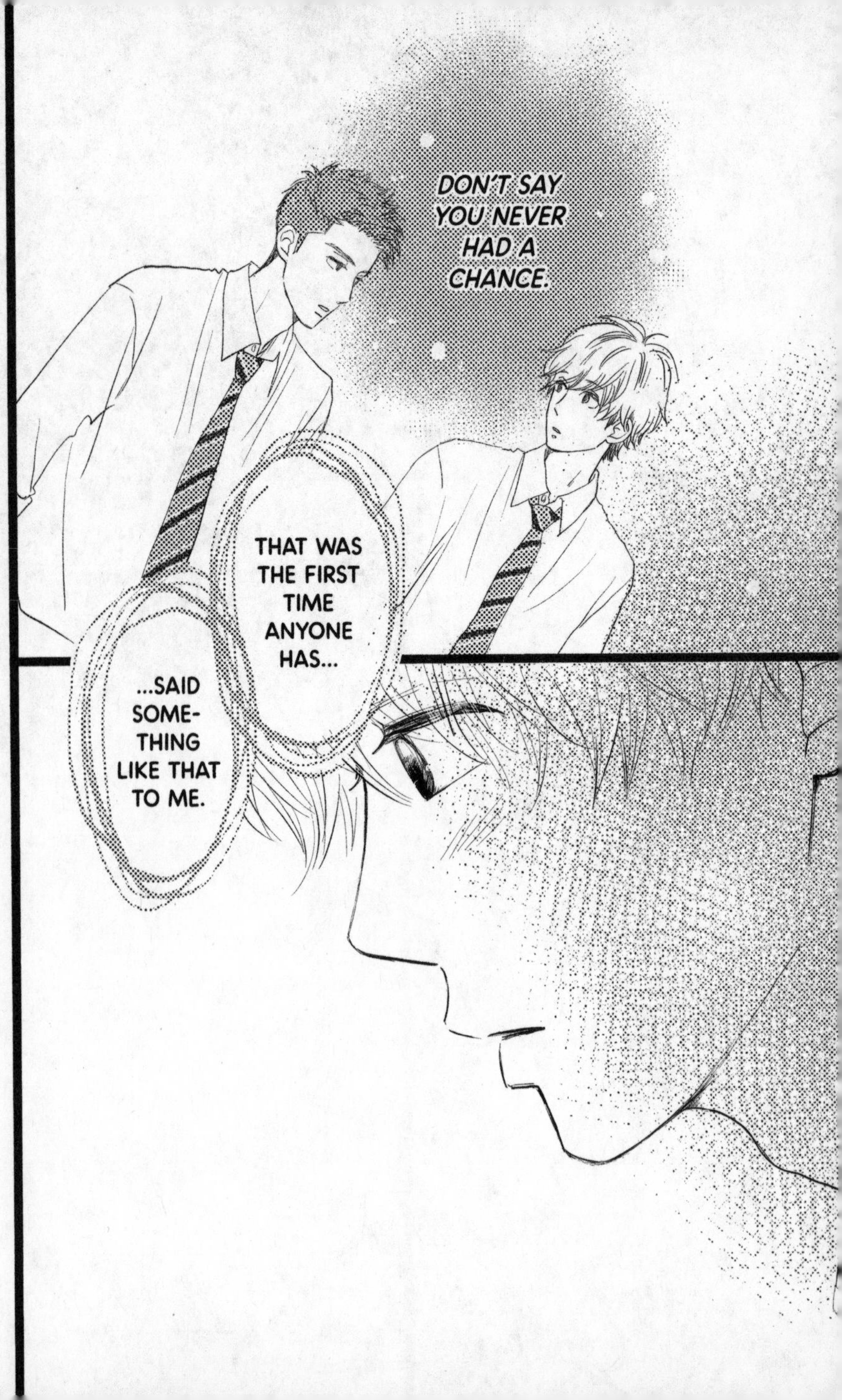
DON'T SAY YOU NEVER HAD A CHANCE.
THAT WAS THE FIRST TIME ANYONE HAS...
...SAID SOME-THING LIKE THAT TO ME.

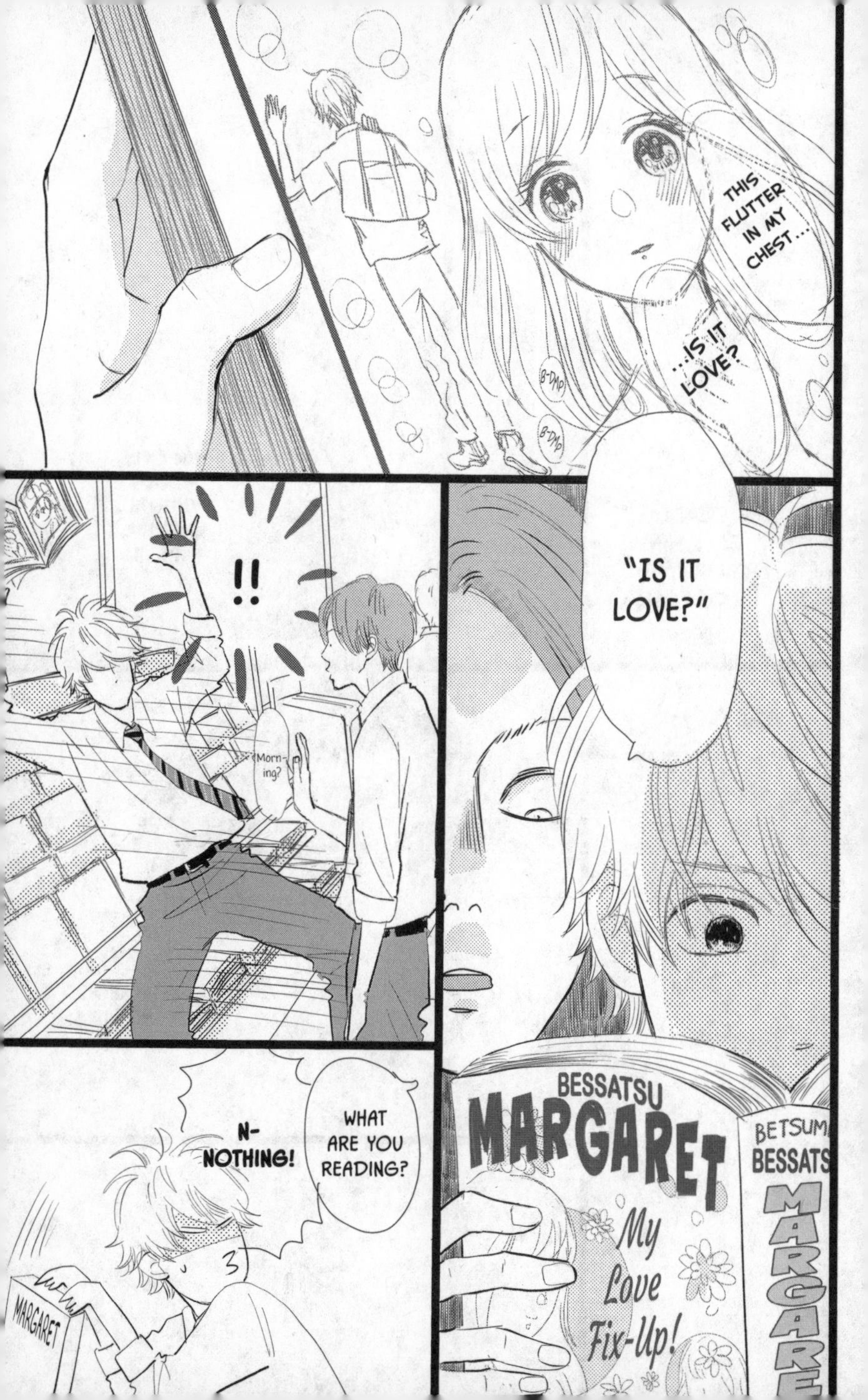
THIS FLUTTER IN MY CHEST...
B-DMP
B-DMP
...IS IT LOVE?
"IS IT LOVE?"
BESSATSU MARGARET
My Love Fix-Up!
!!
Morning?
WHAT ARE YOU READING?
N- NOTHING!
MARGARET

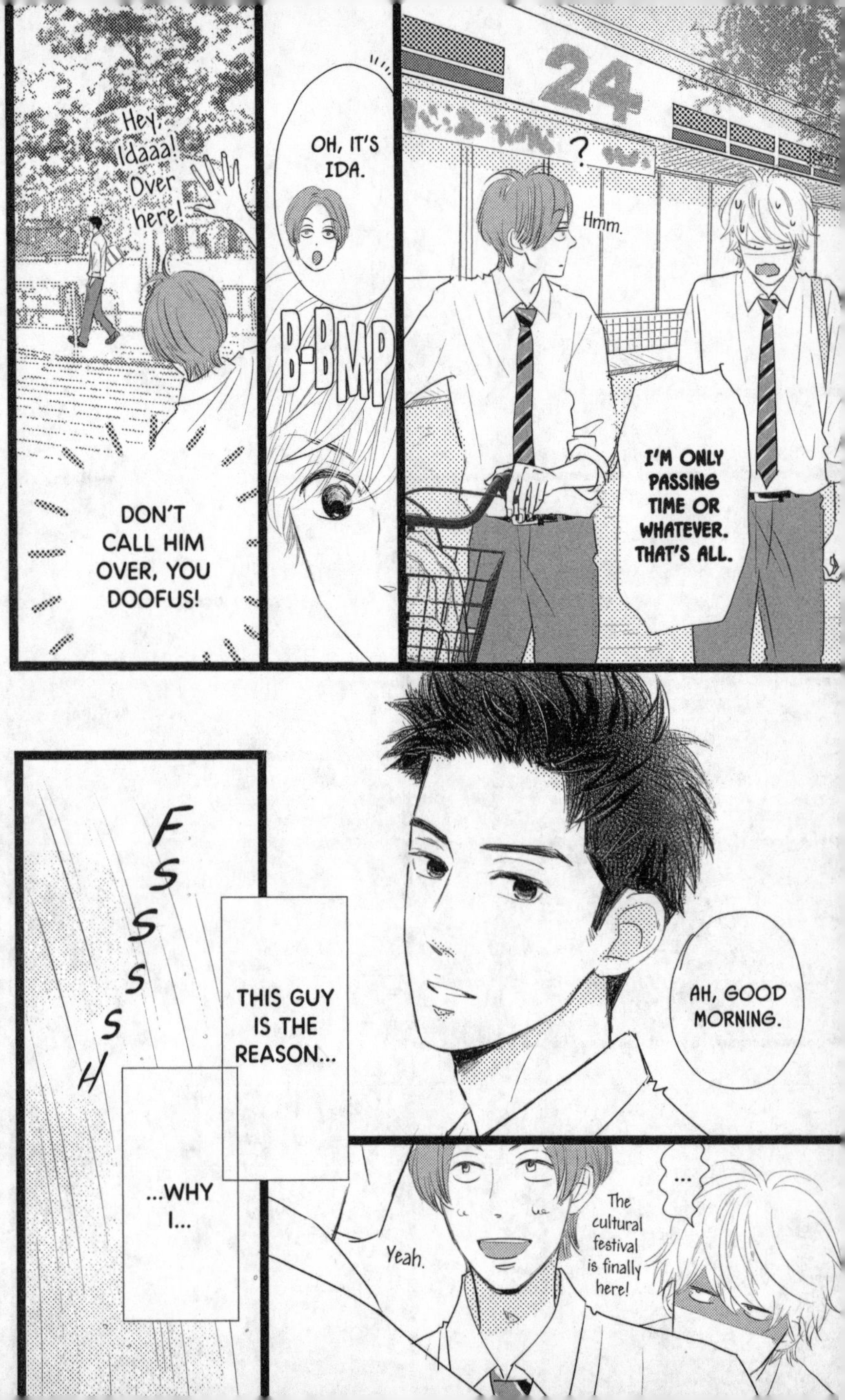
?
Hmm.
I'M ONLY PASSING TIME OR WHATEVER. THAT'S ALL.
OH, IT'S IDA.
B-BMP
Hey, Idaaa! Over here!
DON'T CALL HIM OVER, YOU DOOFUS!
AH, GOOD MORNING.
...
The cultural festival is finally here!
Yeah.
FSSSSH
THIS GUY IS THE REASON...
...WHY I...

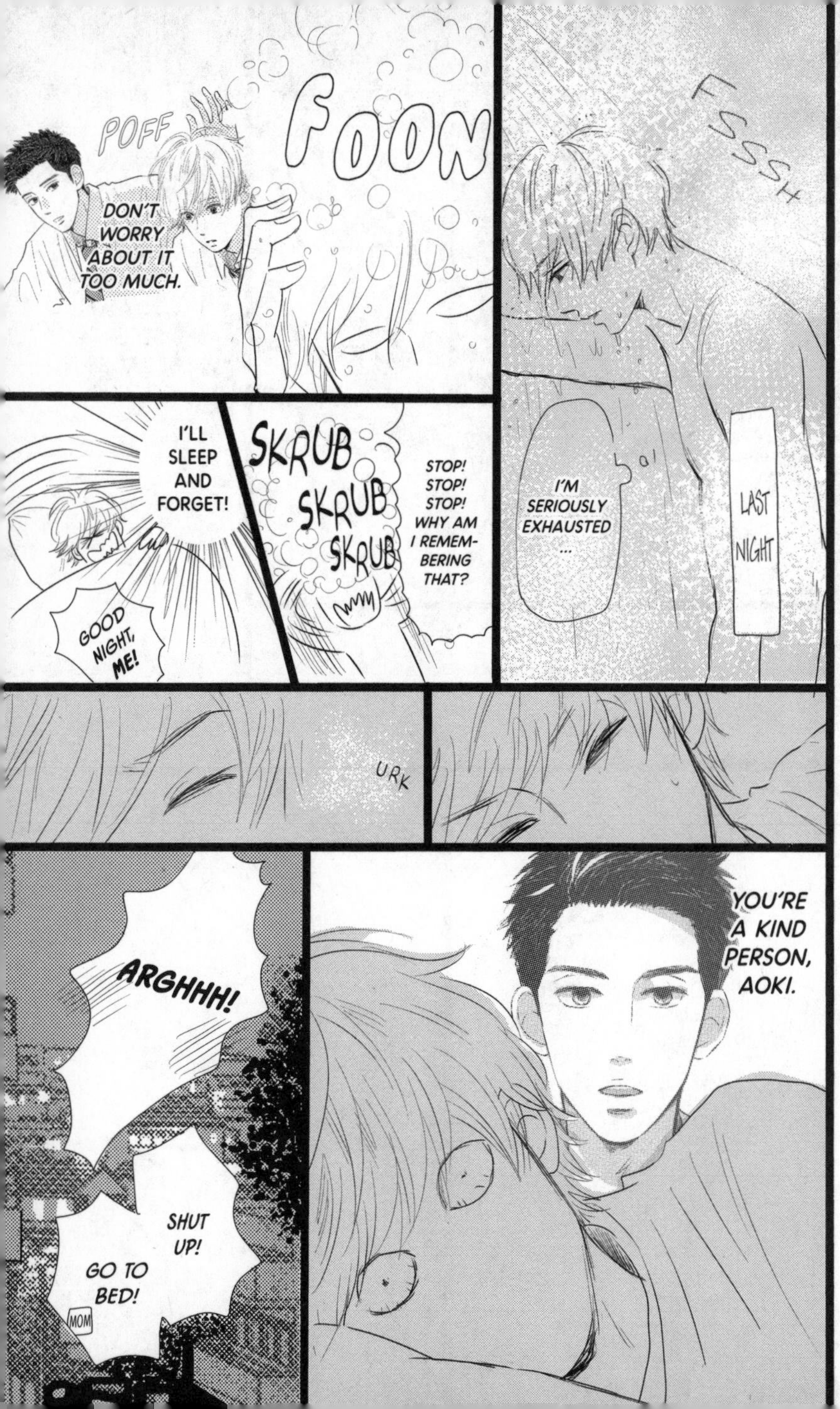
FSSSH
LAST NIGHT
I'M SERIOUSLY EXHAUSTED ...
FOON
POFF
DON'T WORRY ABOUT IT TOO MUCH.
STOP! STOP! STOP! WHY AM I REMEMBERING THAT?
SKRUB SKRUB SKRUB
I'LL SLEEP AND FORGET!
GOOD NIGHT, ME!
URK
YOU'RE A KIND PERSON, AOKI.
ARGHHH!
SHUT UP!
GO TO BED!
MOM

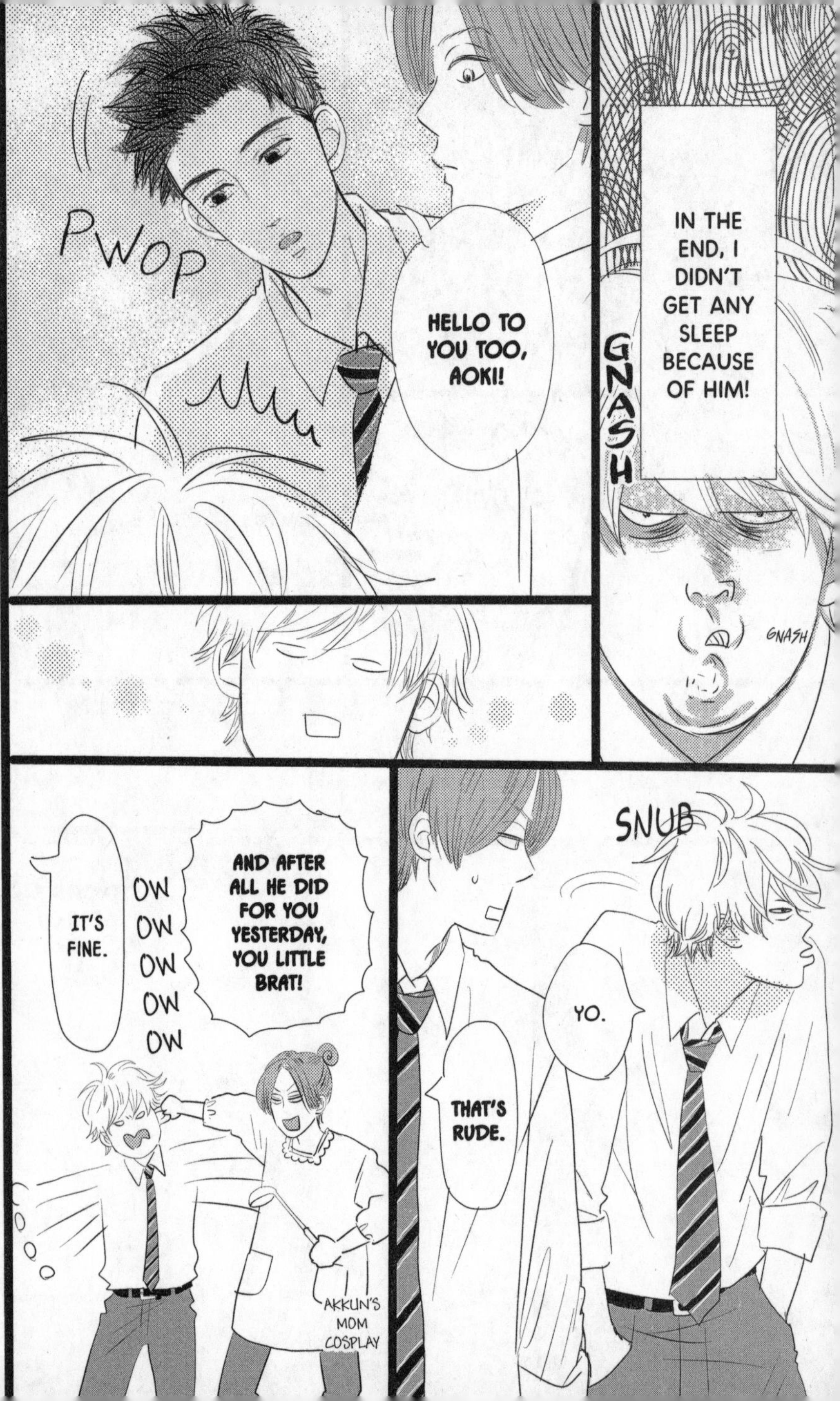
IN THE END, I DIDN'T GET ANY SLEEP BECAUSE OF HIM!
GNASH
GNASH
PWOP
HELLO TO YOU TOO, AOKI!
SNUB
YO.
THAT'S RUDE.
AND AFTER ALL HE DID FOR YOU YESTERDAY, YOU LITTLE BRAT!
OW OW OW OW OW
IT'S FINE.
AKKUN'S MOM COSPLAY

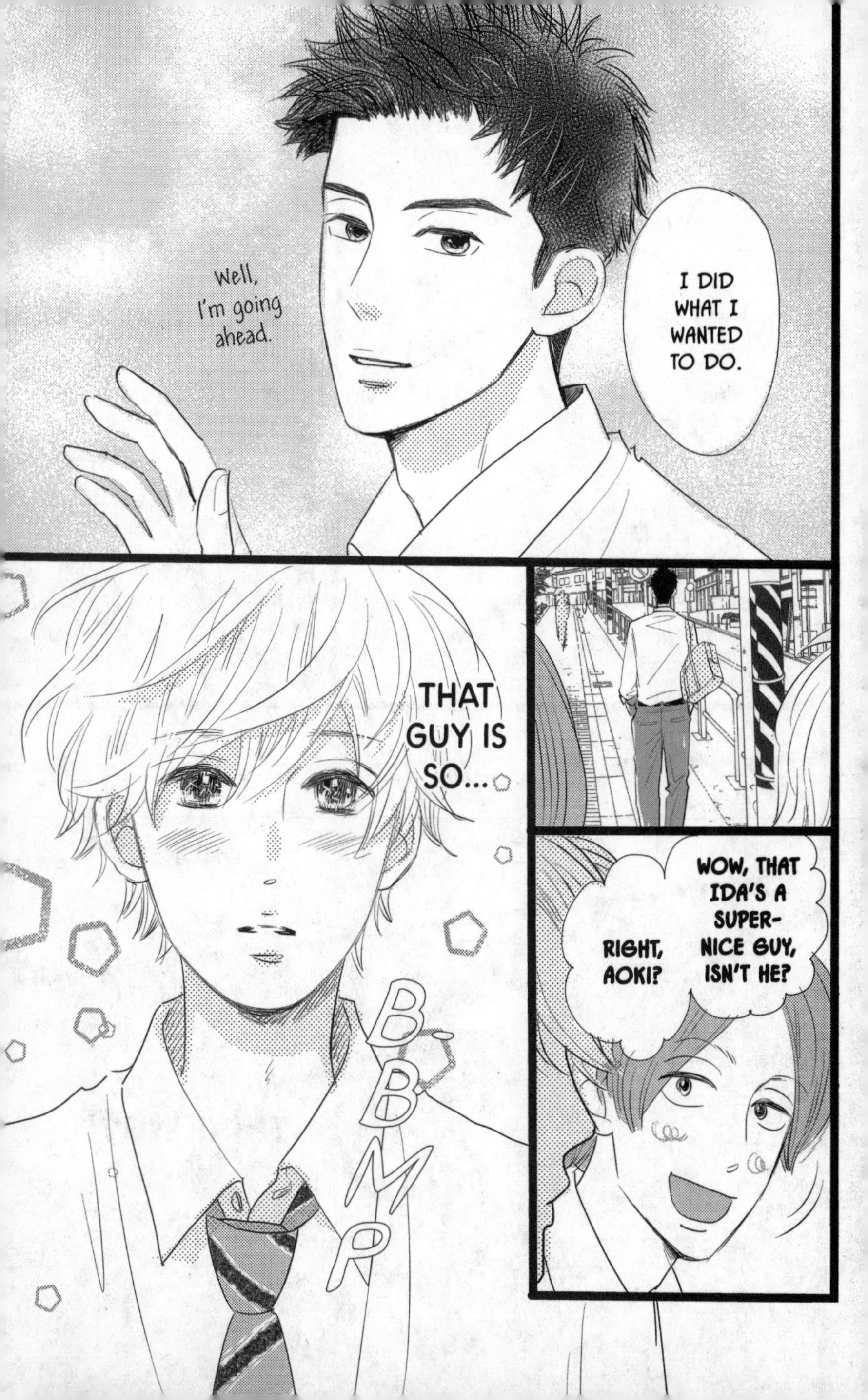
I DID WHAT I WANTED TO DO.
Well, I'm going ahead.
WOW, THAT IDA'S A SUPER-NICE GUY, ISN'T HE?
RIGHT, AOKI?
THAT GUY IS SO...
B-BMP

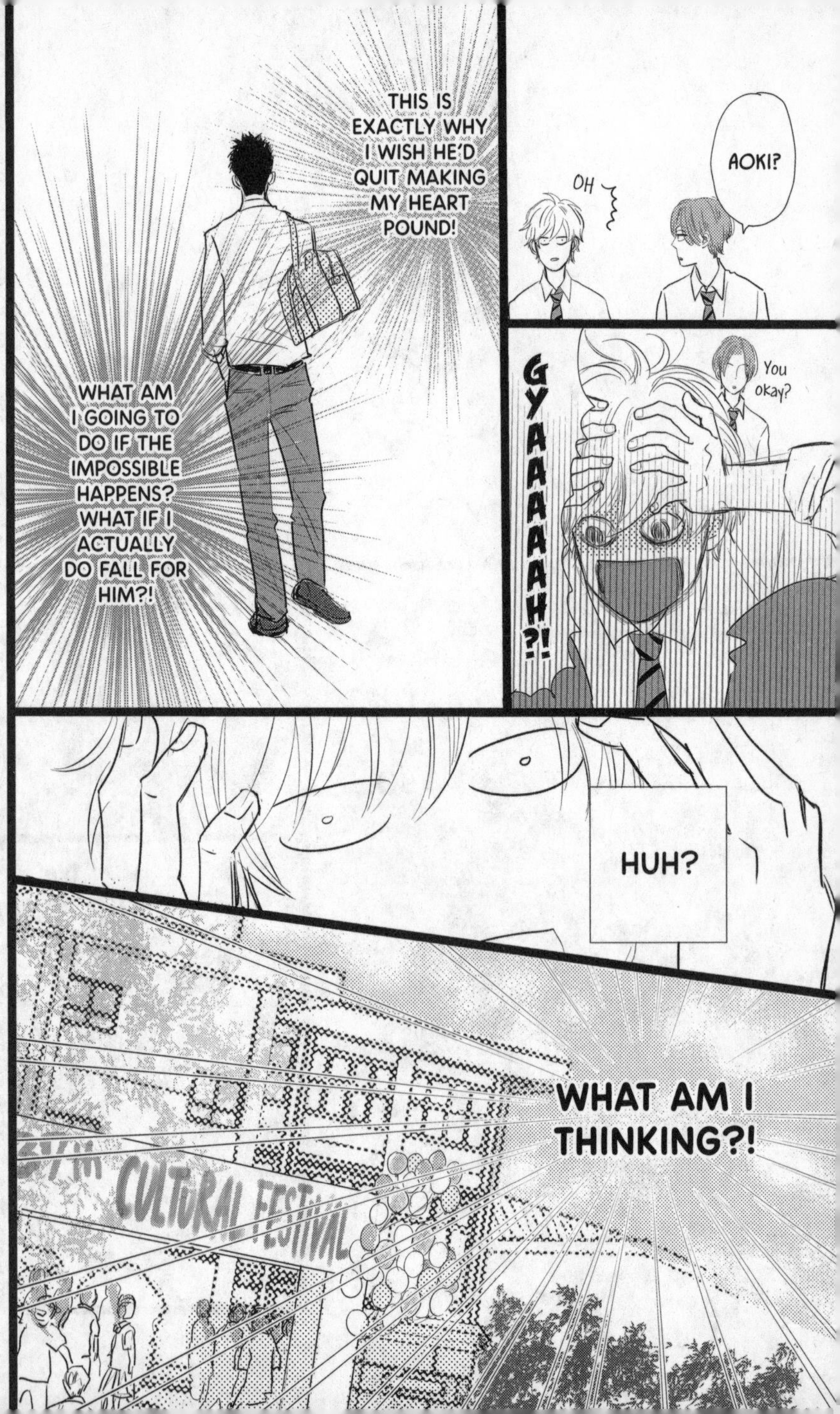
AOKI?
OH
You okay?
GYAAAAAAAH?!
THIS IS EXACTLY WHY I WISH HE'D QUIT MAKING MY HEART POUND!
WHAT AM I GOING TO DO IF THE IMPOSSIBLE HAPPENS? WHAT IF I ACTUALLY DO FALL FOR HIM?!
HUH?
WHAT AM I THINKING?!
CULTURAL FESTIVAL

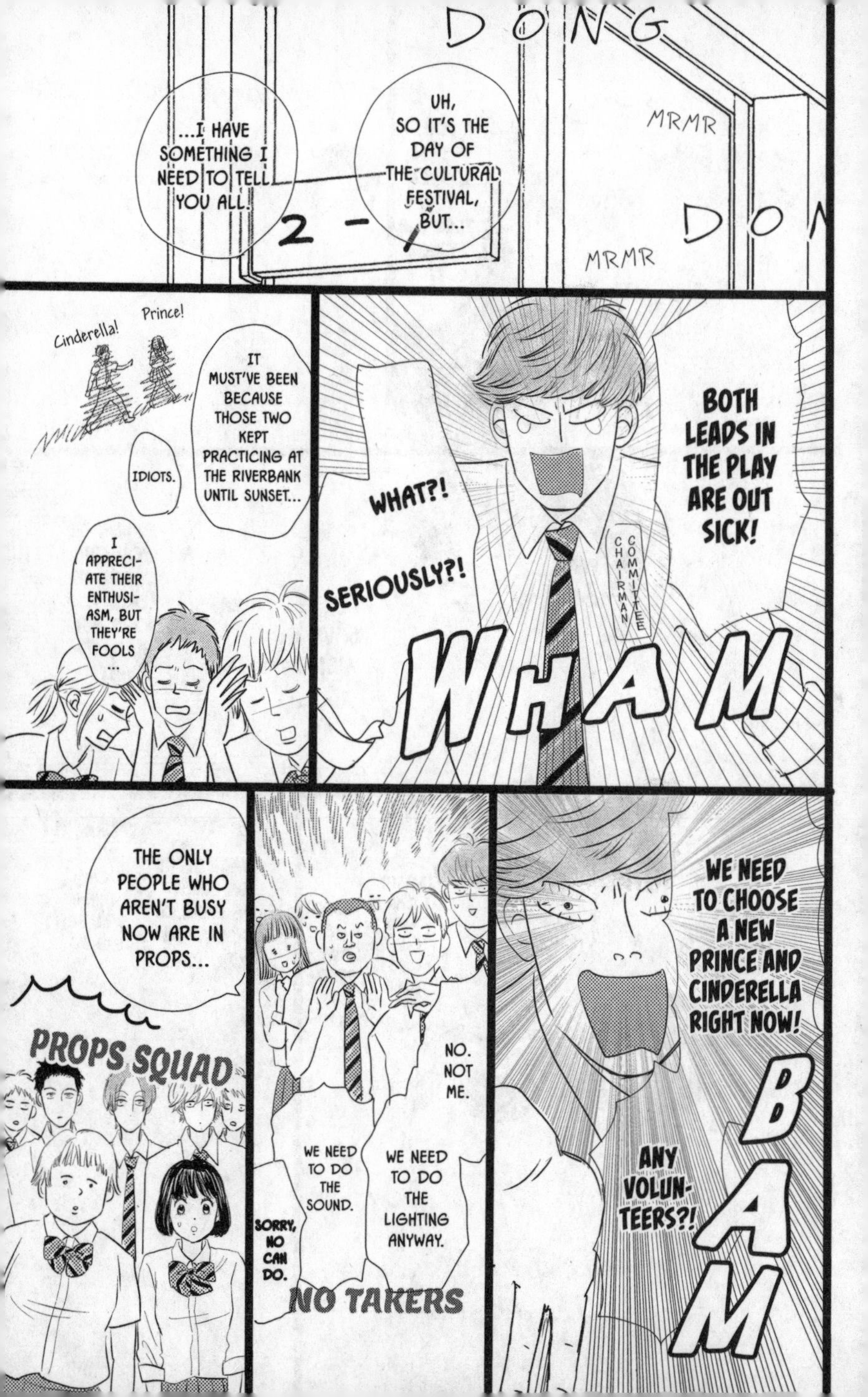
DONG
MRMR
UH, SO IT'S THE DAY OF THE CULTURAL FESTIVAL, BUT...
...I HAVE SOMETHING I NEED TO TELL YOU ALL!
DON
2-1
MRMR
BOTH LEADS IN THE PLAY ARE OUT SICK!
COMMITTEE CHAIRMAN
WHAT?!
SERIOUSLY?!
WHAM
Prince!
Cinderella!
IT MUST'VE BEEN BECAUSE THOSE TWO KEPT PRACTICING AT THE RIVERBANK UNTIL SUNSET...
IDIOTS.
I APPRECIATE THEIR ENTHUSIASM, BUT THEY'RE FOOLS...
WE NEED TO CHOOSE A NEW PRINCE AND CINDERELLA RIGHT NOW!
BAM
ANY VOLUNTEERS?!
NO. NOT ME.
WE NEED TO DO THE LIGHTING ANYWAY.
WE NEED TO DO THE SOUND.
SORRY, NO CAN DO.
NO TAKERS
THE ONLY PEOPLE WHO AREN'T BUSY NOW ARE IN PROPS...
PROPS SQUAD

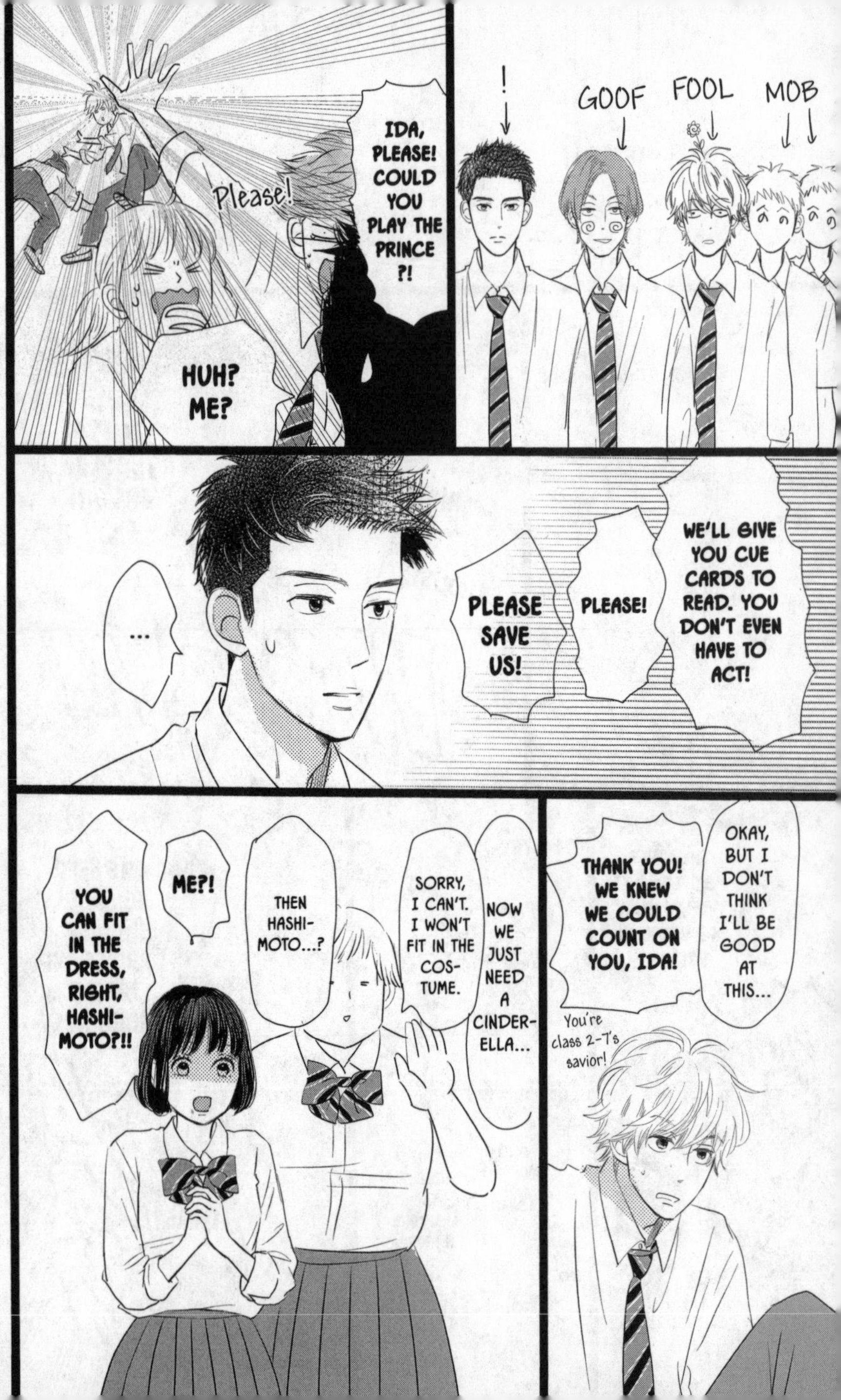
MOB
FOOL
GOOF
!
IDA, PLEASE! COULD YOU PLAY THE PRINCE?!
Please!
HUH? ME?
WE'LL GIVE YOU CUE CARDS TO READ. YOU DON'T EVEN HAVE TO ACT!
PLEASE!
PLEASE SAVE US!
...
OKAY, BUT I DON'T THINK I'LL BE GOOD AT THIS...
THANK YOU! WE KNEW WE COULD COUNT ON YOU, IDA!
You're class 2-7's savior!
NOW WE JUST NEED A CINDERELLA...
SORRY, I CAN'T. I WON'T FIT IN THE COSTUME.
THEN HASHIMOTO...?
ME?!
YOU CAN FIT IN THE DRESS, RIGHT, HASHIMOTO?!!

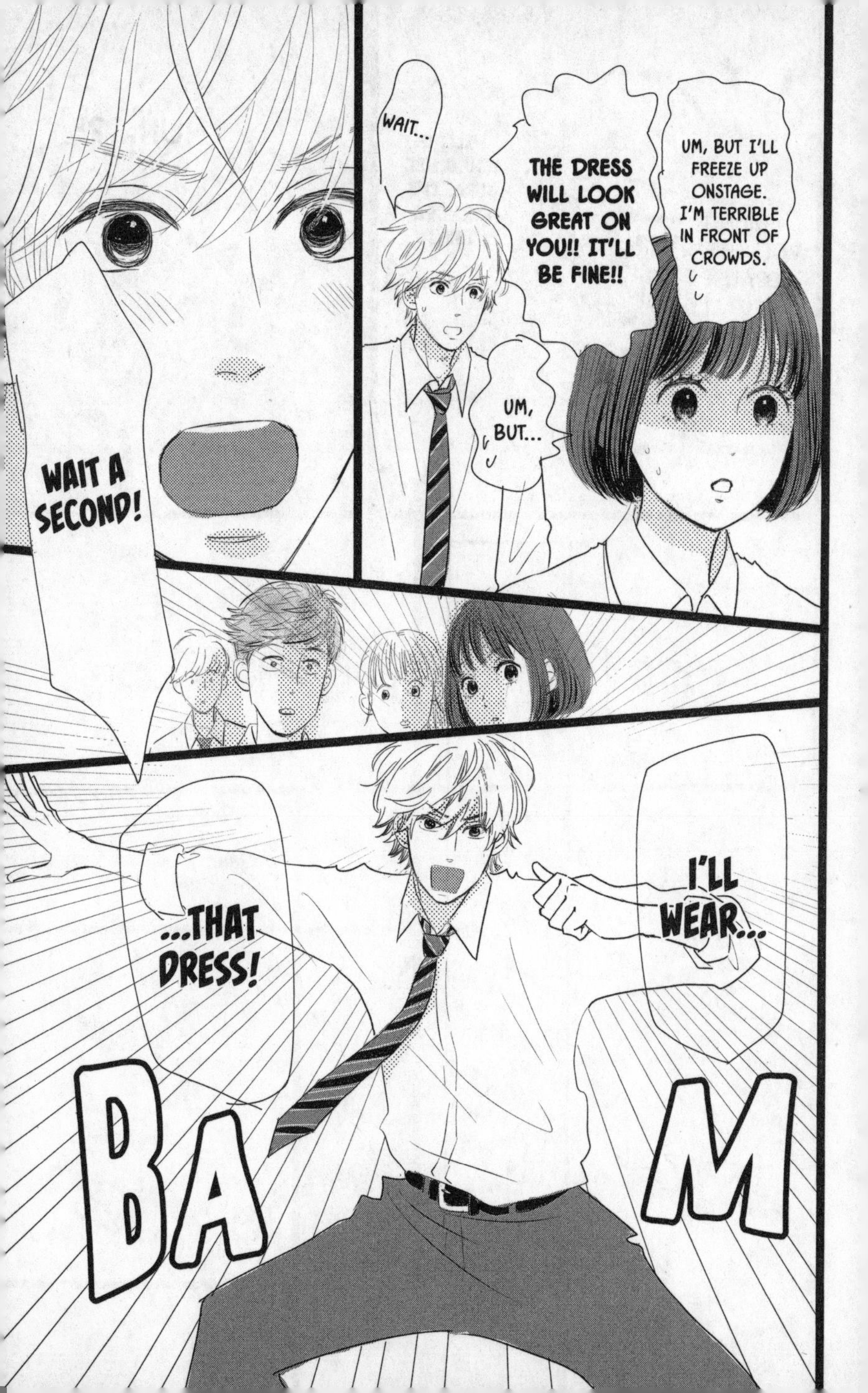

UM, BUT...
THE DRESS WILL LOOK GREAT ON YOU!! IT'LL BE FINE!!
UM, BUT I'LL FREEZE UP ONSTAGE. I'M TERRIBLE IN FRONT OF CROWDS.
WAIT...
WAIT A SECOND!
I'LL WEAR...
...THAT DRESS!
BAM

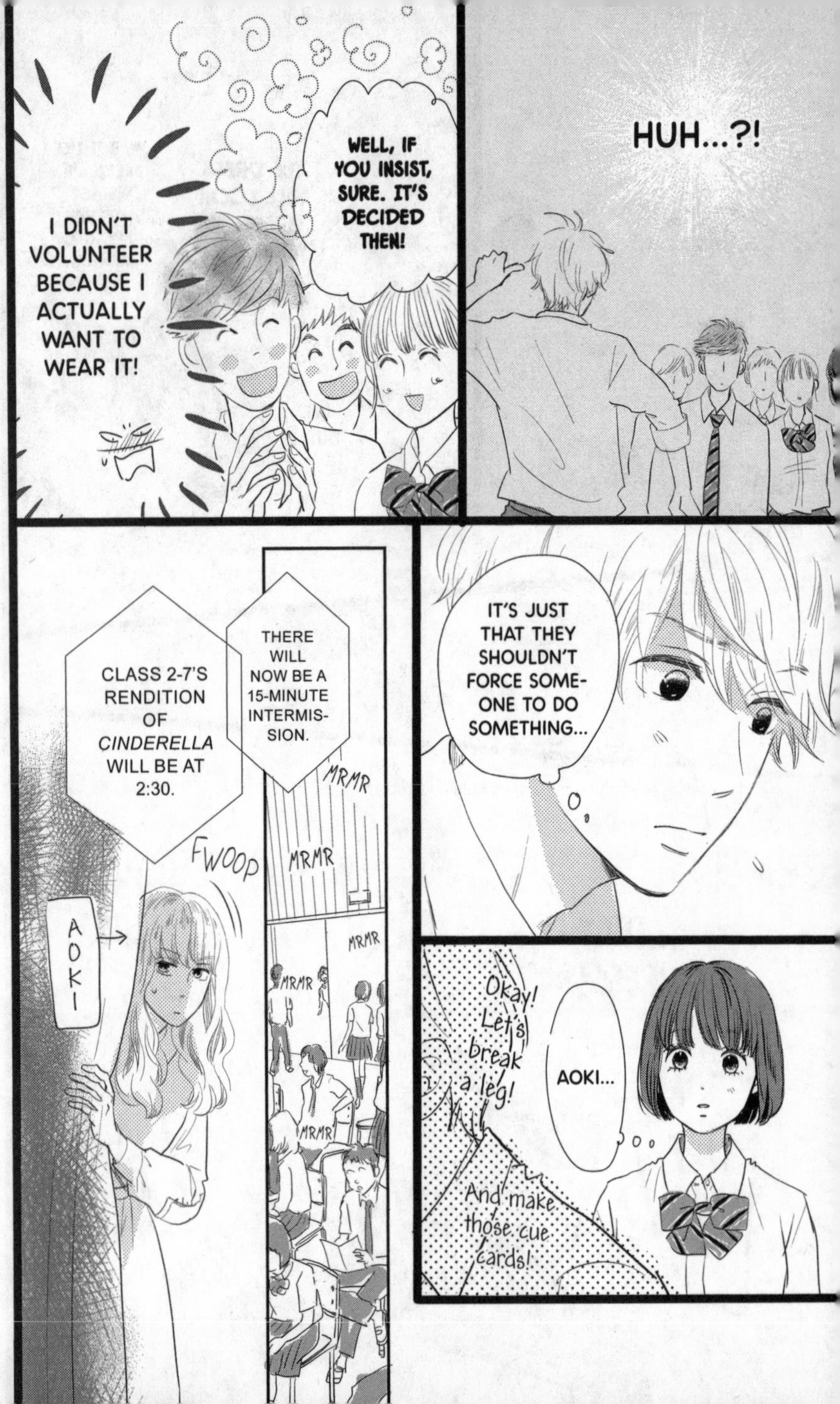
HUH...?!
WELL, IF YOU INSIST, SURE. IT'S DECIDED THEN!
I DIDN'T VOLUNTEER BECAUSE I ACTUALLY WANT TO WEAR IT!
IT'S JUST THAT THEY SHOULDN'T FORCE SOME-ONE TO DO SOMETHING...
AOKI...
Okay! Let's break a leg!
And make those cue cards!
THERE WILL NOW BE A 15-MINUTE INTERMIS-SION.
MRMR
MRMR
MRMR
MRMR
MRMR
CLASS 2-7'S RENDITION OF *CINDERELLA* WILL BE AT 2:30.
FWOOP
AOKI

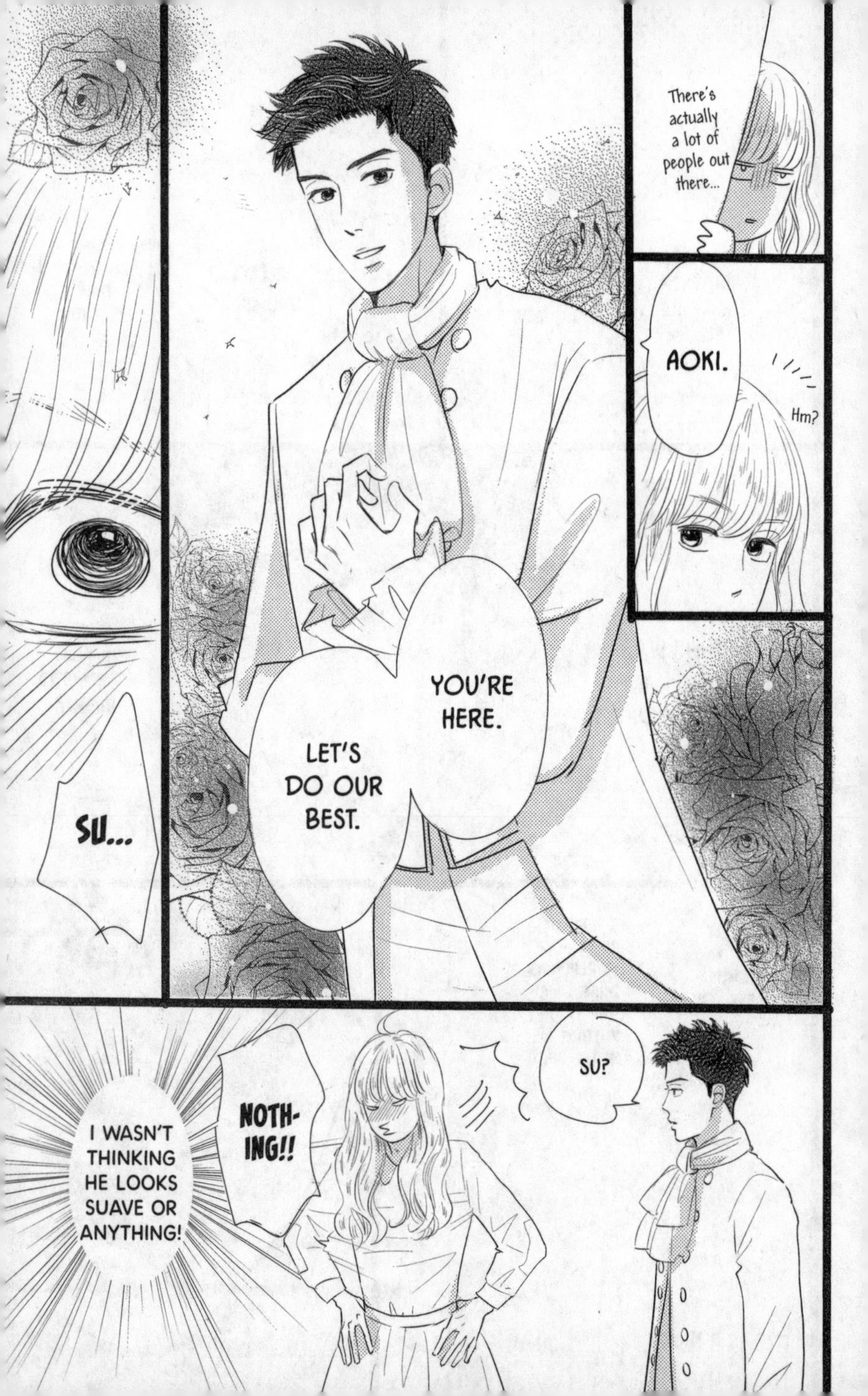
There's actually a lot of people out there...
AOKI.
Hm?
YOU'RE HERE.
LET'S DO OUR BEST.
SU...
SU?
NOTH-ING!!
I WASN'T THINKING HE LOOKS SUAVE OR ANYTHING!

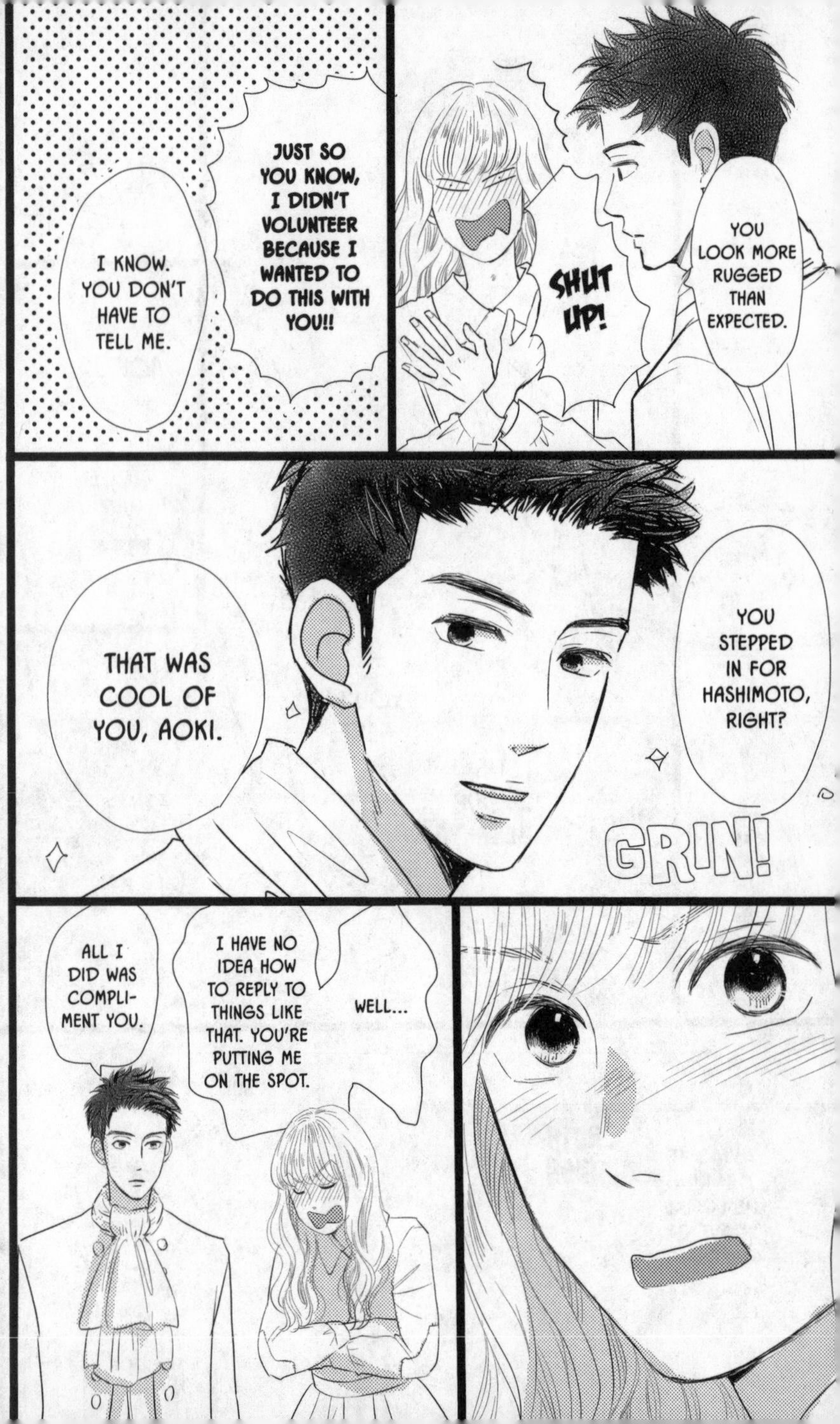
YOU LOOK MORE RUGGED THAN EXPECTED.
SHUT UP!
JUST SO YOU KNOW, I DIDN'T VOLUNTEER BECAUSE I WANTED TO DO THIS WITH YOU!!
I KNOW. YOU DON'T HAVE TO TELL ME.
YOU STEPPED IN FOR HASHIMOTO, RIGHT?
GRIN!
THAT WAS COOL OF YOU, AOKI.
WELL...
I HAVE NO IDEA HOW TO REPLY TO THINGS LIKE THAT. YOU'RE PUTTING ME ON THE SPOT.
ALL I DID WAS COMPLIMENT YOU.

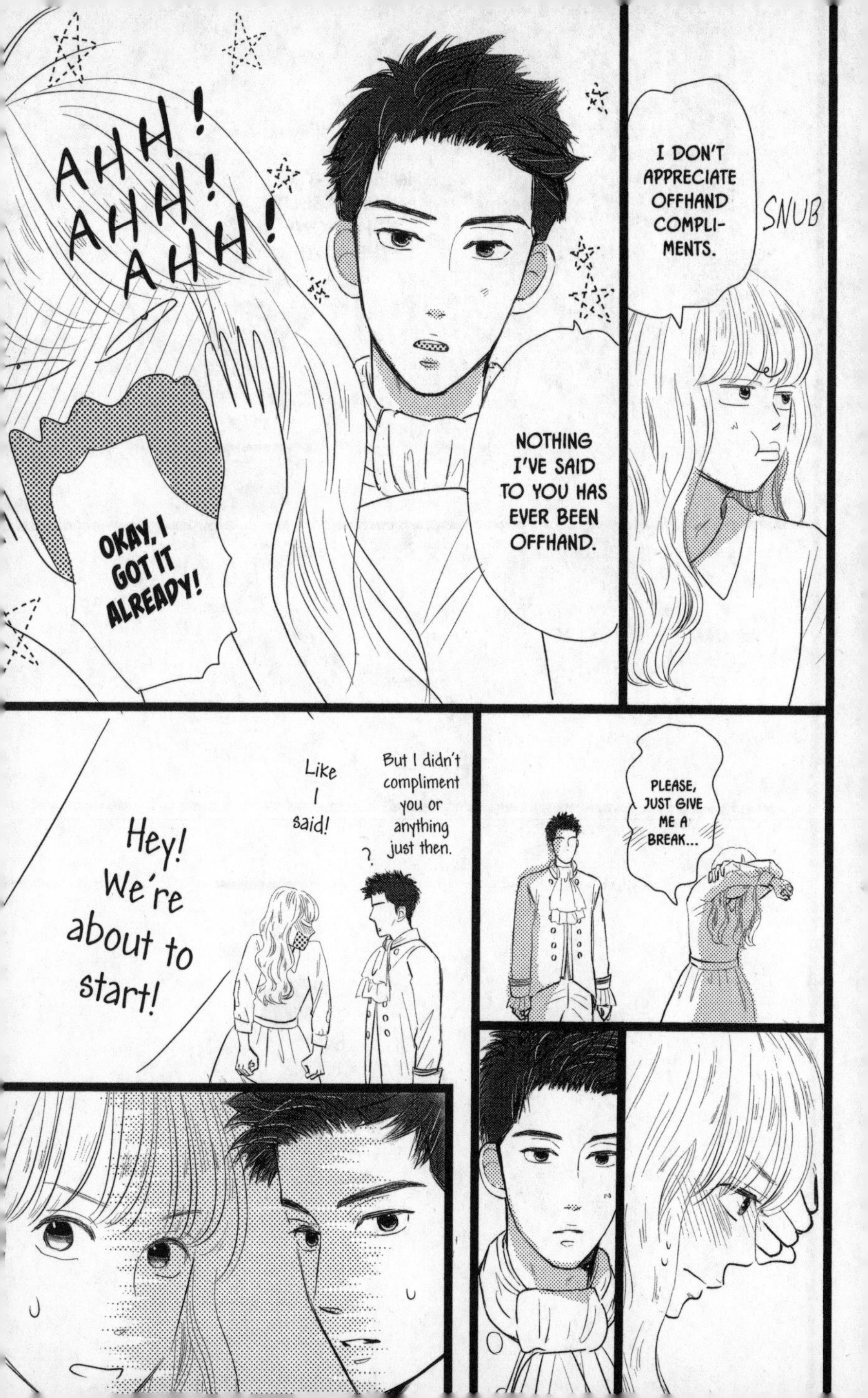
I DON'T APPRECIATE OFFHAND COMPLIMENTS.
SNUB
NOTHING I'VE SAID TO YOU HAS EVER BEEN OFFHAND.
AHH! AHH! AHH!
OKAY, I GOT IT ALREADY!
PLEASE, JUST GIVE ME A BREAK...
But I didn't compliment you or anything just then.
Like I said!
?
Hey! We're about to start!

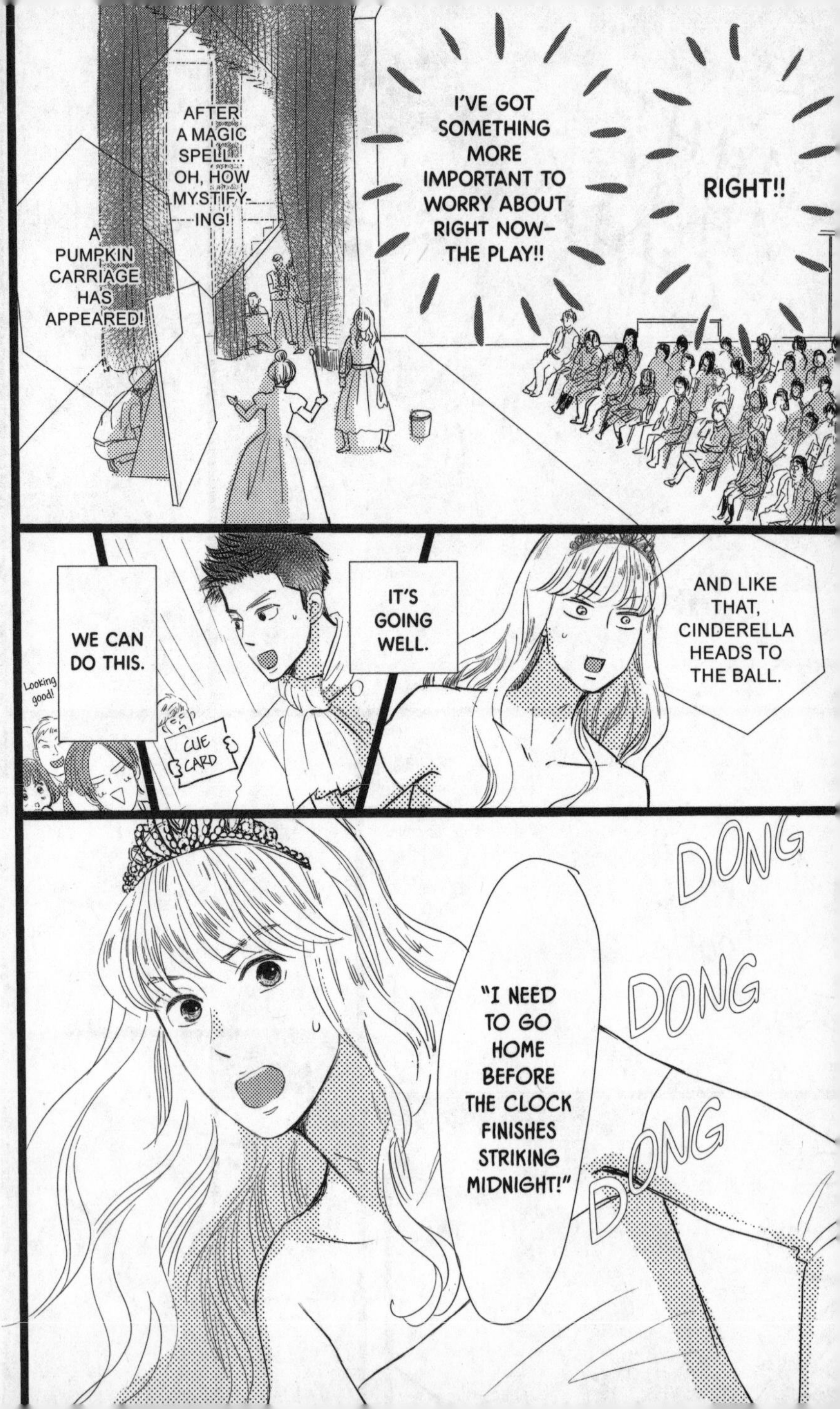
I'VE GOT SOMETHING MORE IMPORTANT TO WORRY ABOUT RIGHT NOW—THE PLAY!!
RIGHT!!
AFTER A MAGIC SPELL... OH, HOW MYSTIFY-ING!
A PUMPKIN CARRIAGE HAS APPEARED!
AND LIKE THAT, CINDERELLA HEADS TO THE BALL.
IT'S GOING WELL.
WE CAN DO THIS.
CUE CARD
Looking good!
"I NEED TO GO HOME BEFORE THE CLOCK FINISHES STRIKING MIDNIGHT!"
DONG
DONG
DONG

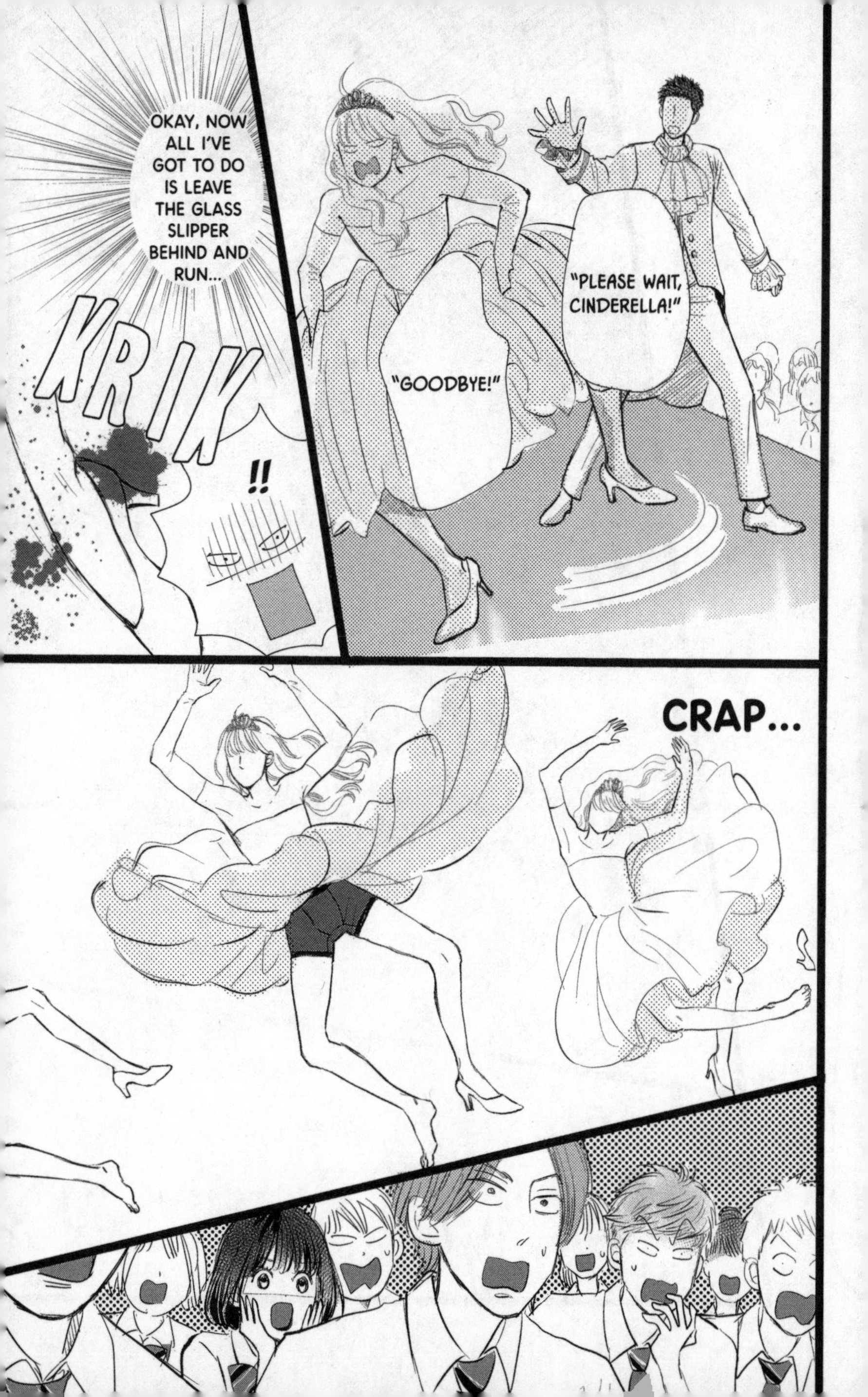
"PLEASE WAIT, CINDERELLA!"
"GOODBYE!"
OKAY, NOW ALL I'VE GOT TO DO IS LEAVE THE GLASS SLIPPER BEHIND AND RUN...
KRIK
!!
CRAP...

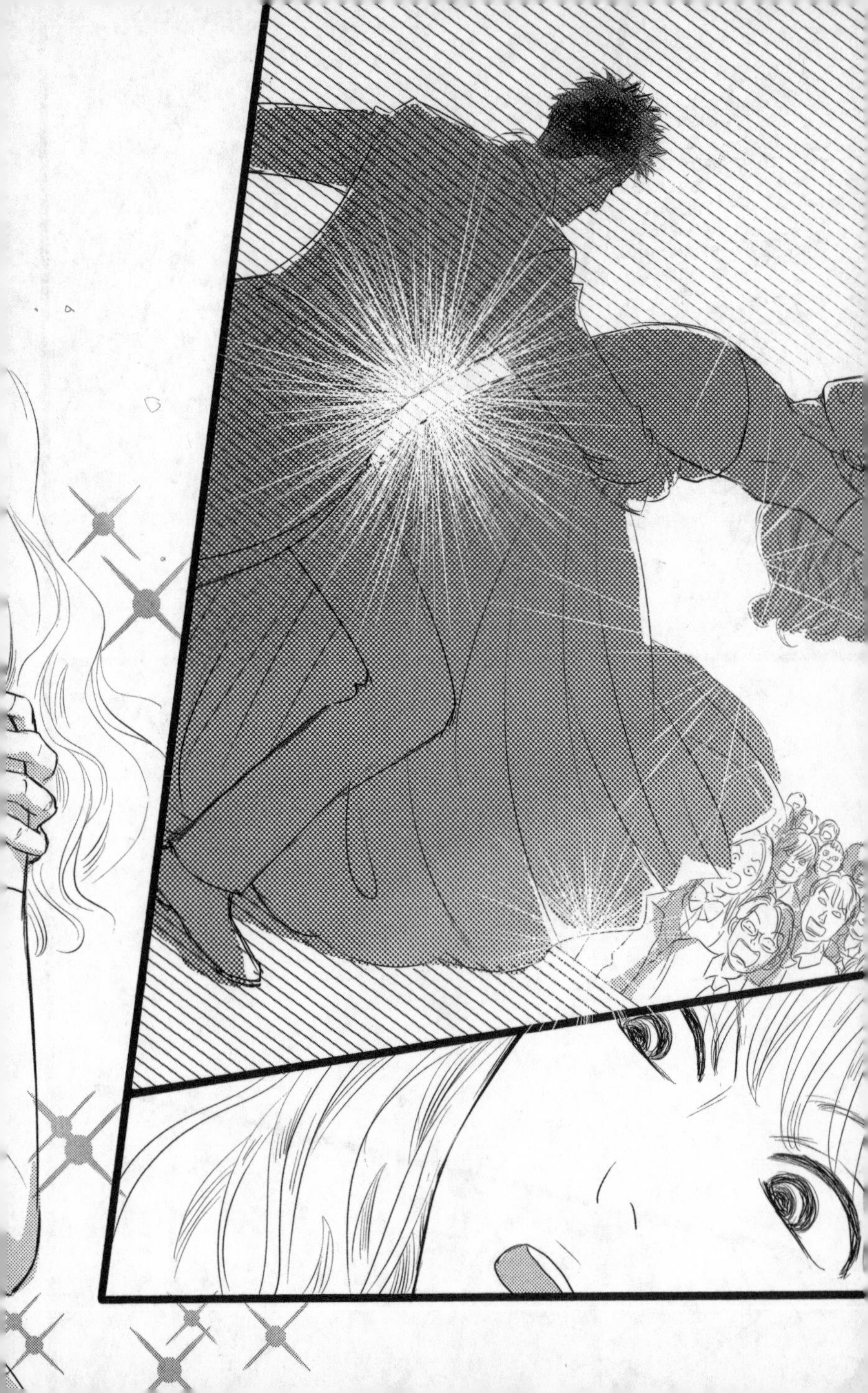

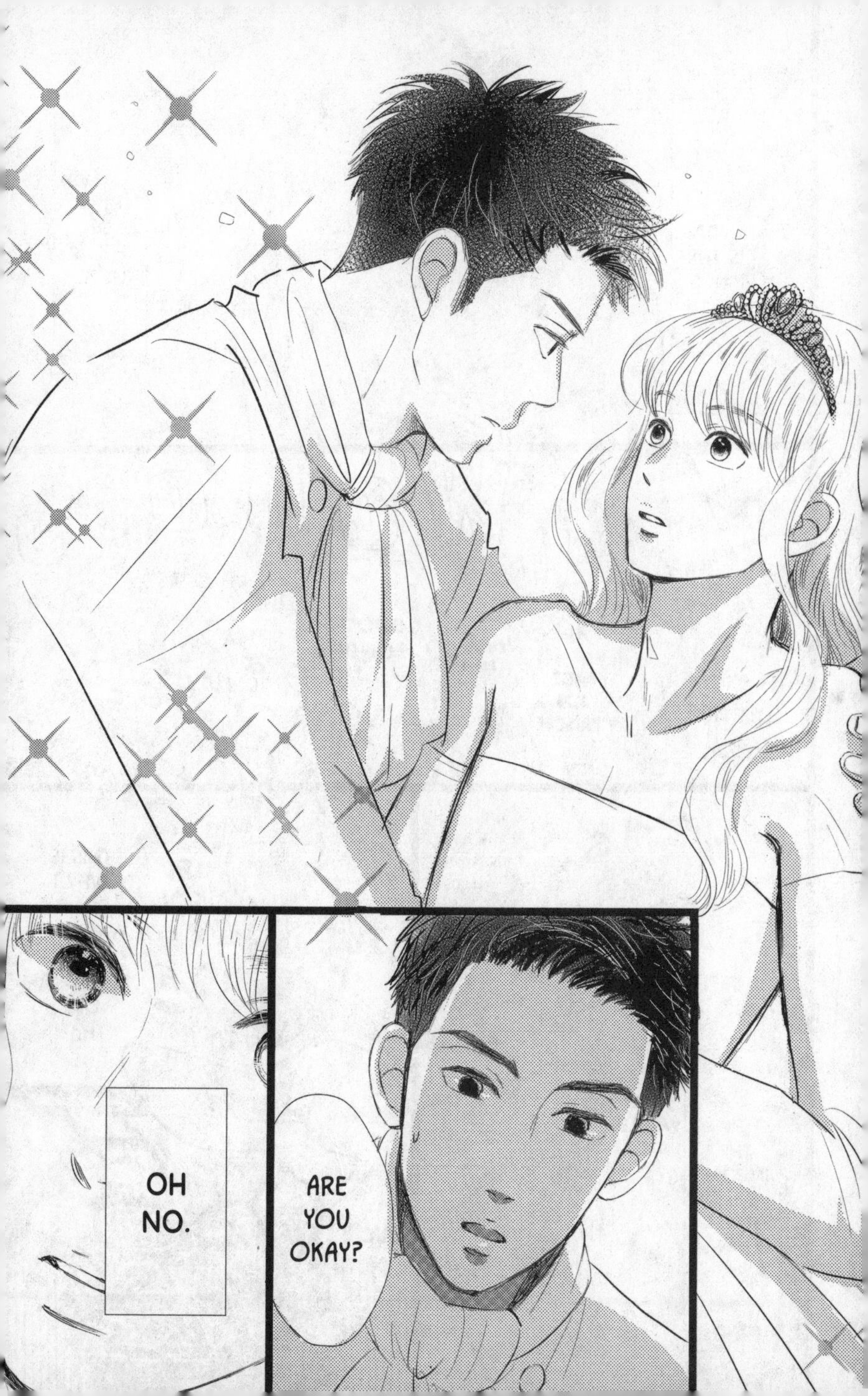
ARE YOU OKAY?
OH NO.

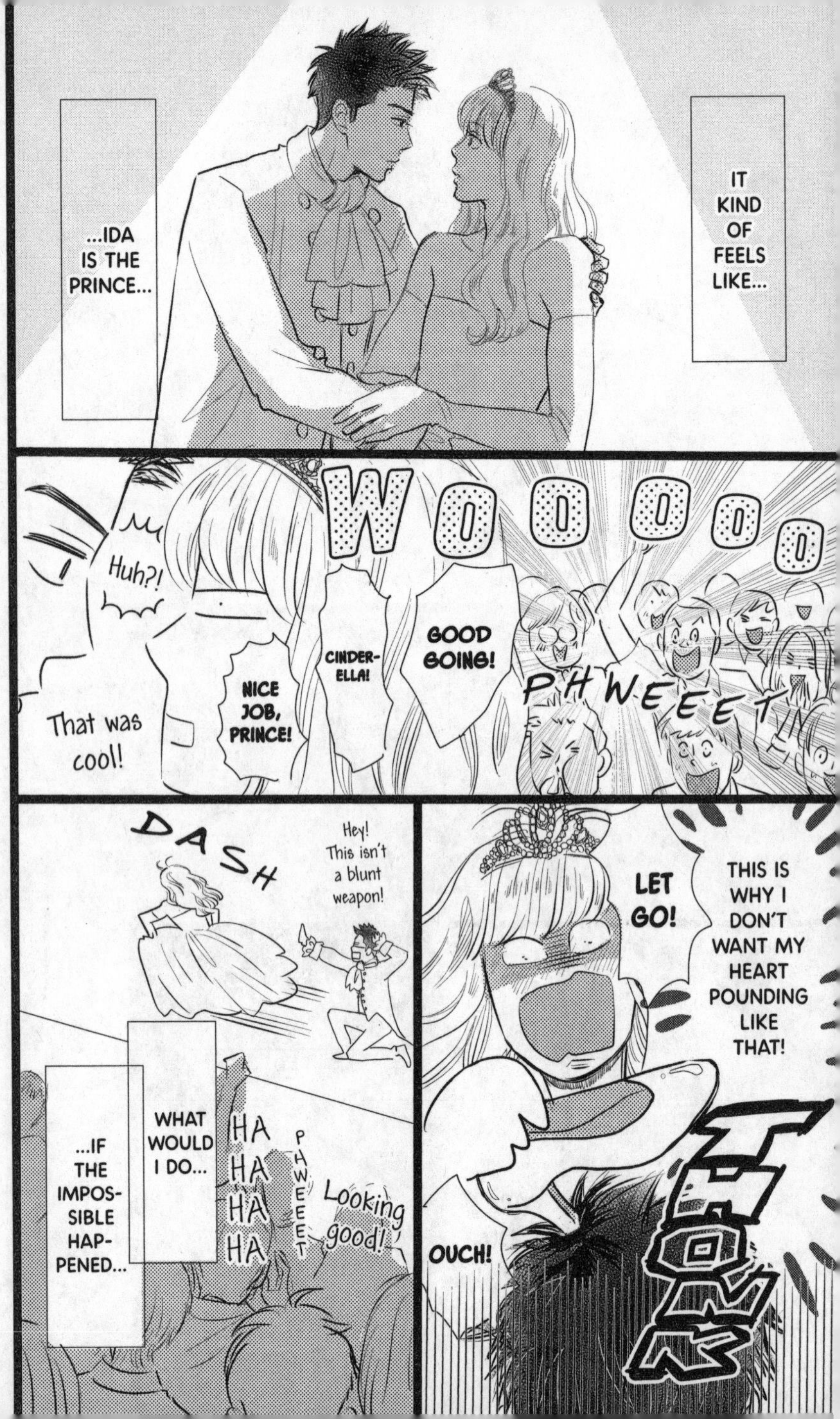

IT KIND OF FEELS LIKE...
...IDA IS THE PRINCE...
WOOOOOO
GOOD GOING!
CINDER-ELLA!
PHWEEET
NICE JOB, PRINCE!
Huh?!
That was cool!
THIS IS WHY I DON'T WANT MY HEART POUNDING LIKE THAT!
LET GO!
THONK
OUCH!
Hey! This isn't a blunt weapon!
DASH
WHAT WOULD I DO...
...IF THE IMPOS-SIBLE HAP-PENED...
Looking good!
PHWEEET
HA HA HA HA

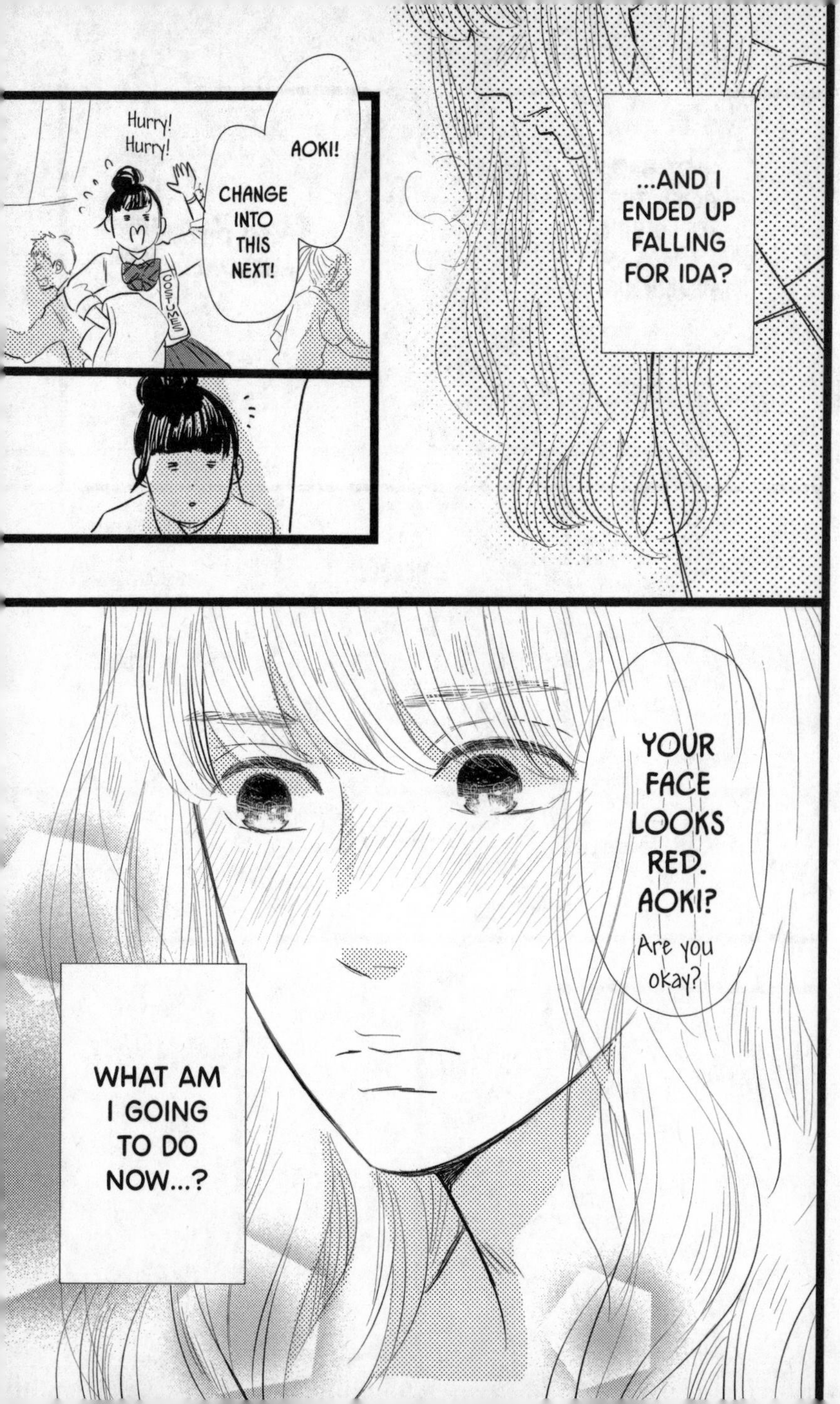
...AND I ENDED UP FALLING FOR IDA?
AOKI! CHANGE INTO THIS NEXT!
Hurry! Hurry!
COSTUMES
YOUR FACE LOOKS RED. AOKI?
Are you okay?
WHAT AM I GOING TO DO NOW...?

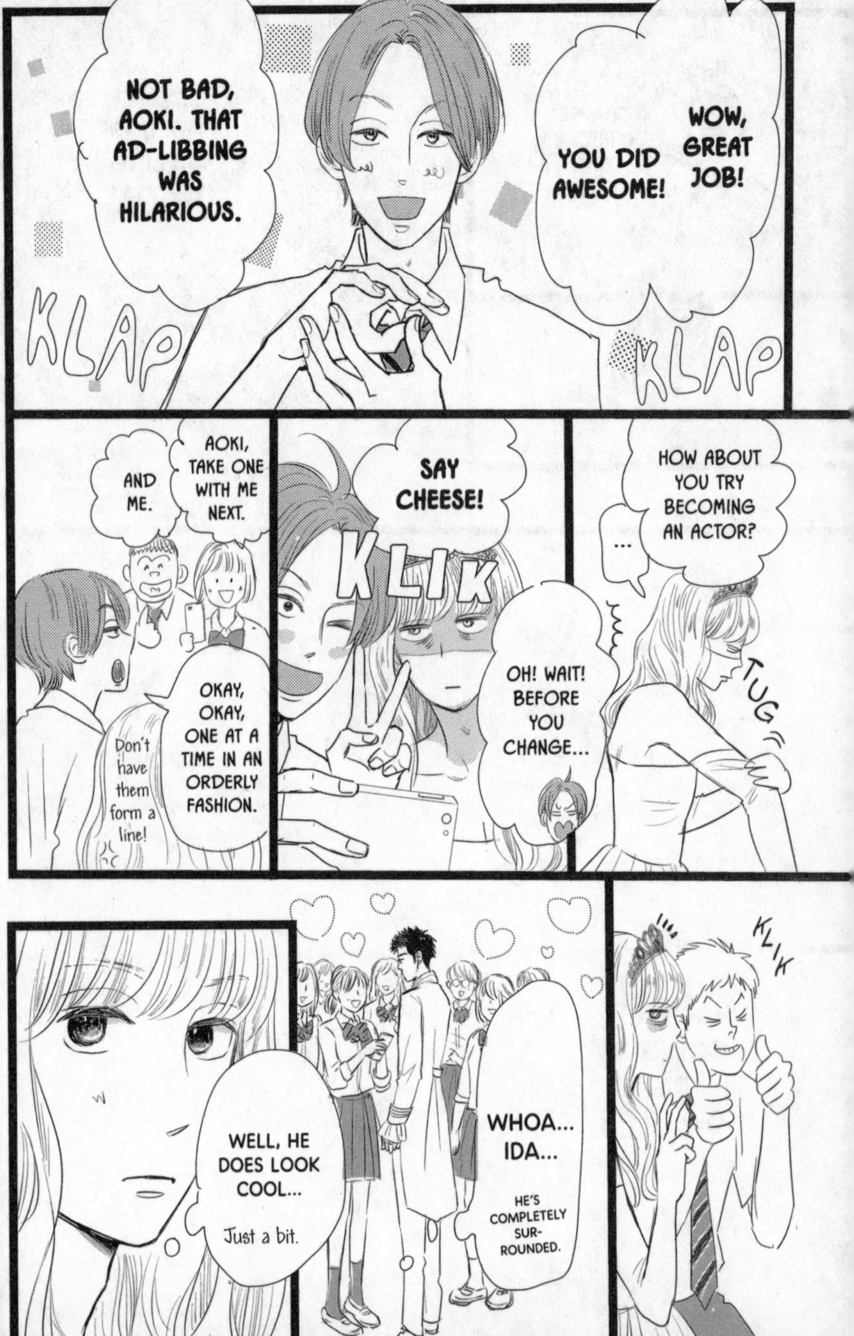
WOW, GREAT JOB!
YOU DID AWESOME!
NOT BAD, AOKI. THAT AD-LIBBING WAS HILARIOUS.
KLAP
KLAP
HOW ABOUT YOU TRY BECOMING AN ACTOR?
...
TUG
SAY CHEESE!
KLIK
OH! WAIT! BEFORE YOU CHANGE...
AOKI, TAKE ONE WITH ME NEXT.
AND ME.
OKAY, OKAY, ONE AT A TIME IN AN ORDERLY FASHION.
Don't have them form a line!
KLIK
WHOA... IDA...
HE'S COMPLETELY SUR-ROUNDED.
WELL, HE DOES LOOK COOL...
Just a bit.

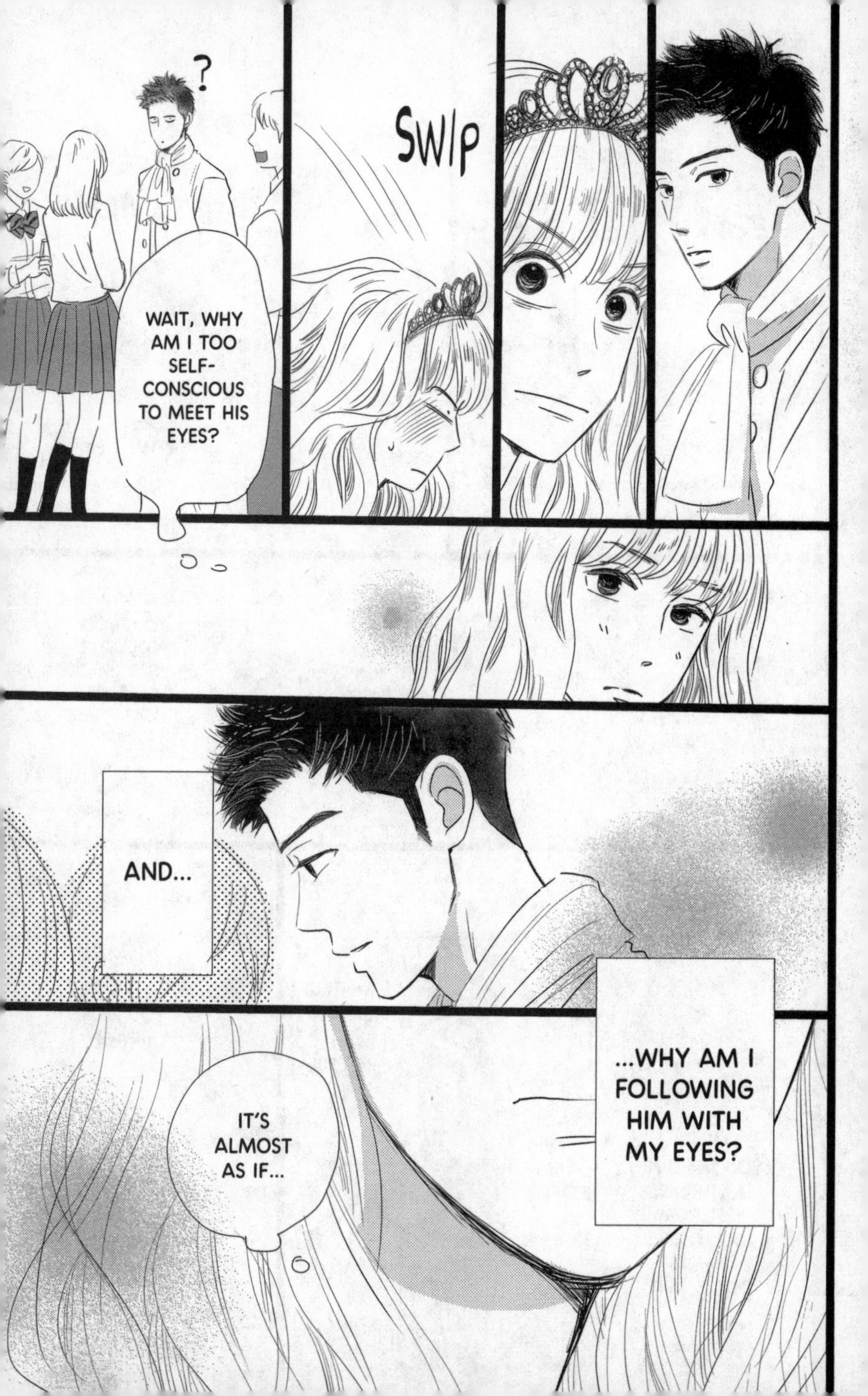
SWIP
?
WAIT, WHY AM I TOO SELF-CONSCIOUS TO MEET HIS EYES?
AND...
...WHY AM I FOLLOWING HIM WITH MY EYES?
IT'S ALMOST AS IF...

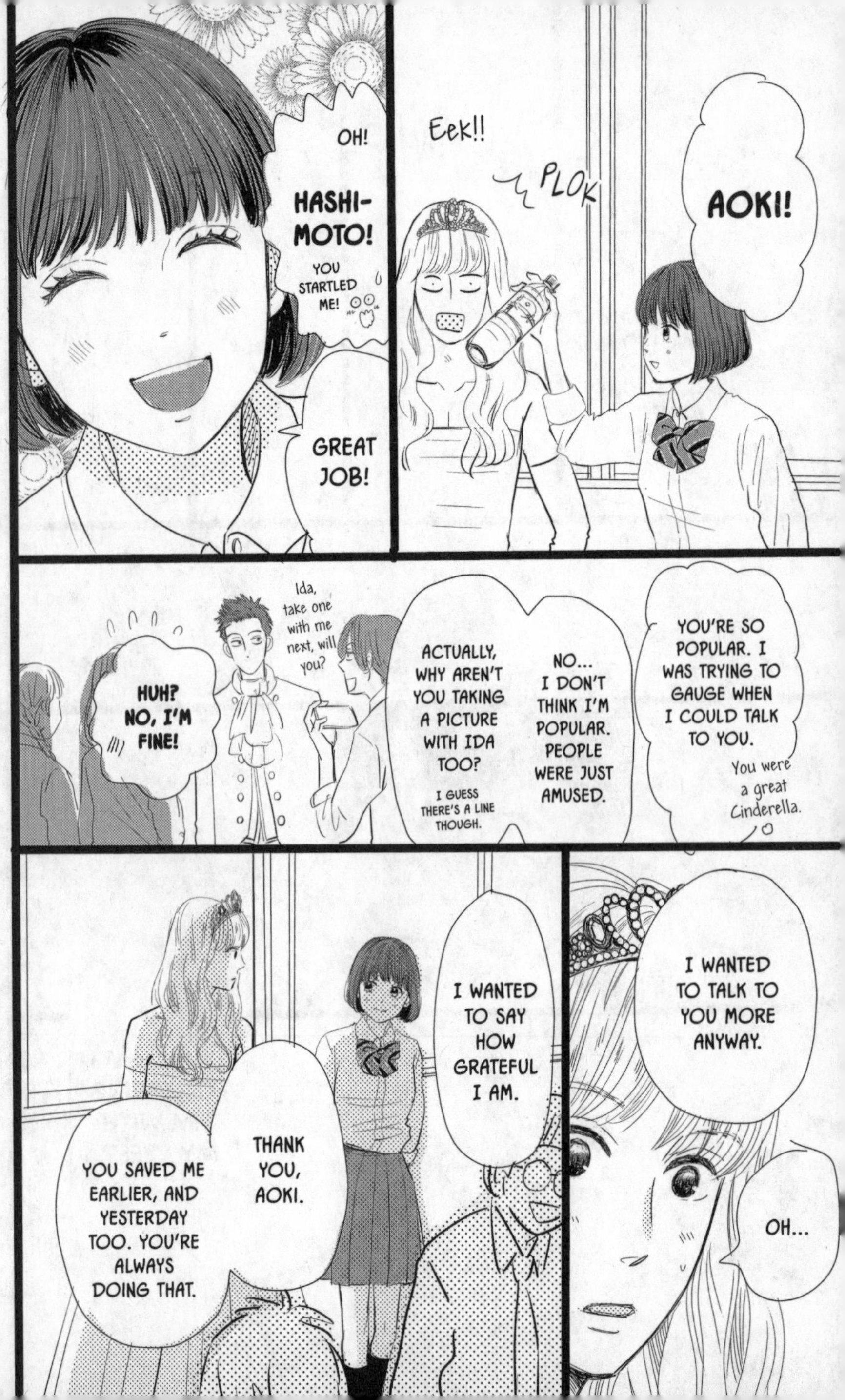
AOKI!
Eek!!
PLOK
OH!
HASHIMOTO!
YOU STARTLED ME!
GREAT JOB!
YOU'RE SO POPULAR. I WAS TRYING TO GAUGE WHEN I COULD TALK TO YOU.
You were a great Cinderella.
NO... I DON'T THINK I'M POPULAR. PEOPLE WERE JUST AMUSED.
ACTUALLY, WHY AREN'T YOU TAKING A PICTURE WITH IDA TOO?
I GUESS THERE'S A LINE THOUGH.
Ida, take one with me next, will you?
HUH? NO, I'M FINE!
I WANTED TO TALK TO YOU MORE ANYWAY.
OH...
I WANTED TO SAY HOW GRATEFUL I AM.
THANK YOU, AOKI.
YOU SAVED ME EARLIER, AND YESTERDAY TOO. YOU'RE ALWAYS DOING THAT.

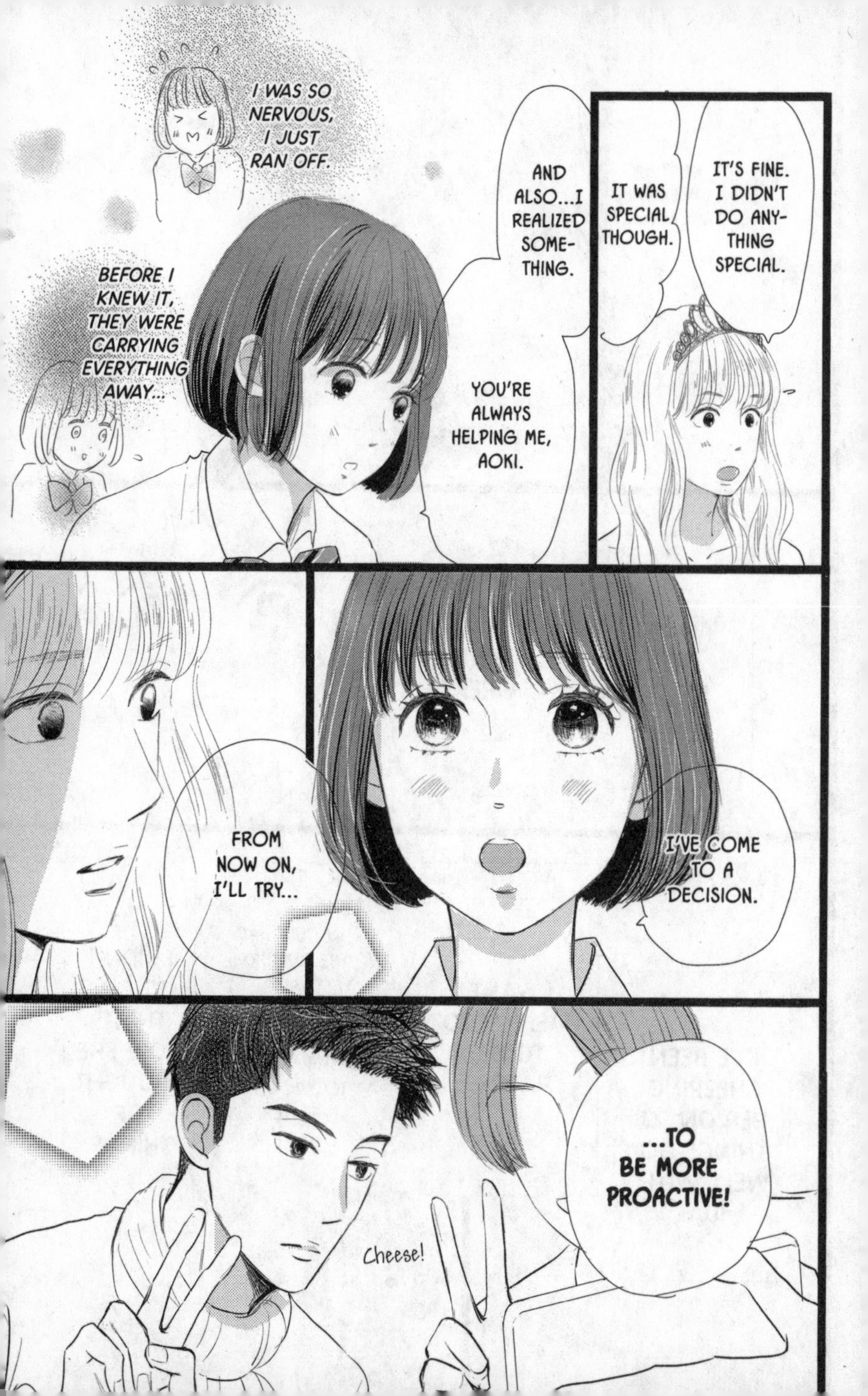
IT'S FINE. I DIDN'T DO ANYTHING SPECIAL.
IT WAS SPECIAL THOUGH.
YOU'RE ALWAYS HELPING ME, AOKI.
I WAS SO NERVOUS, I JUST RAN OFF.
BEFORE I KNEW IT, THEY WERE CARRYING EVERYTHING AWAY...
AND ALSO...I REALIZED SOMETHING.
I'VE COME TO A DECISION.
FROM NOW ON, I'LL TRY...
...TO BE MORE PROACTIVE!
Cheese!

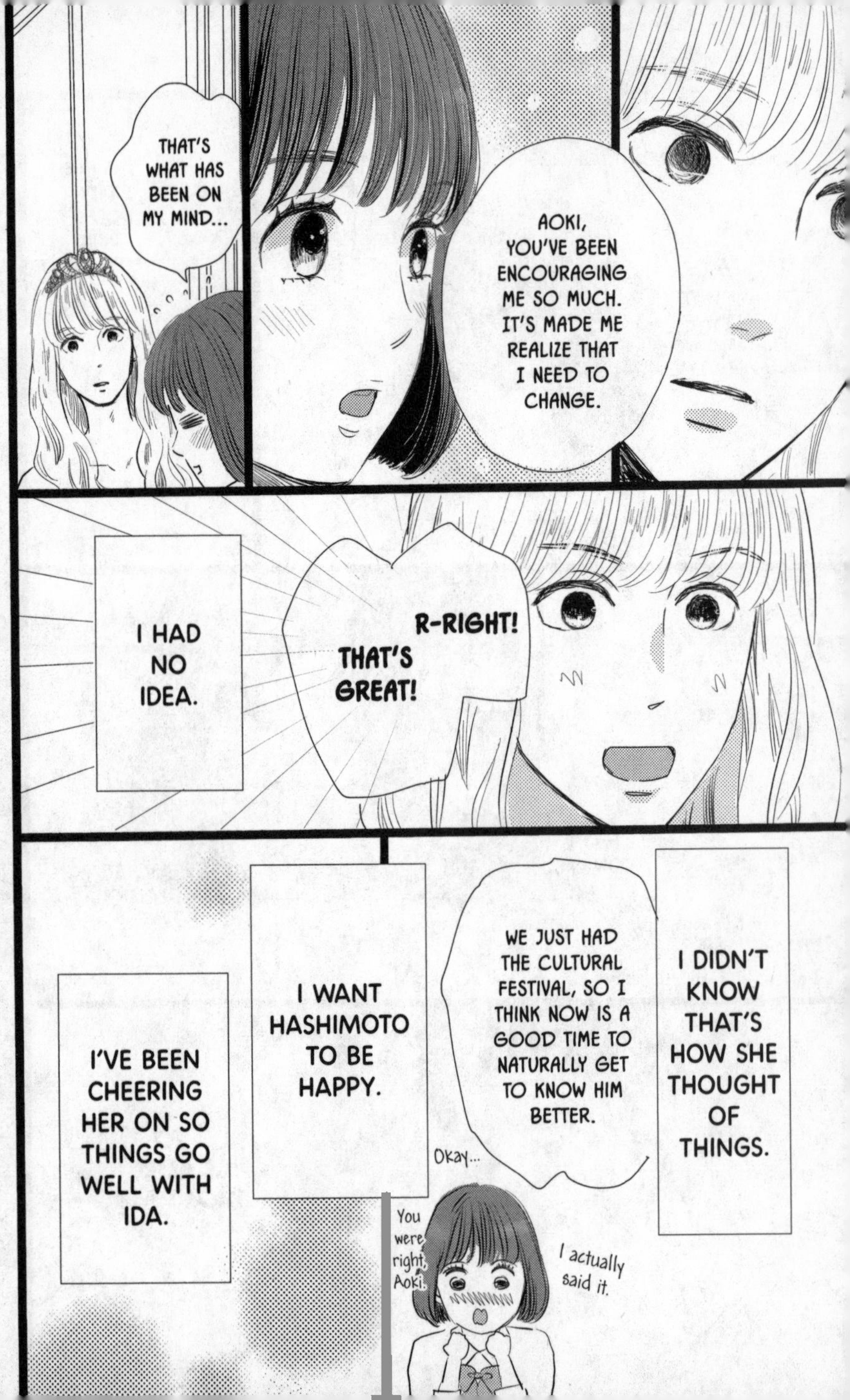
AOKI, YOU'VE BEEN ENCOURAGING ME SO MUCH. IT'S MADE ME REALIZE THAT I NEED TO CHANGE.
THAT'S WHAT HAS BEEN ON MY MIND...
R-RIGHT! THAT'S GREAT!
I HAD NO IDEA.
I DIDN'T KNOW THAT'S HOW SHE THOUGHT OF THINGS.
WE JUST HAD THE CULTURAL FESTIVAL, SO I THINK NOW IS A GOOD TIME TO NATURALLY GET TO KNOW HIM BETTER.
I actually said it.
Okay...
You were right, Aoki.
I WANT HASHIMOTO TO BE HAPPY.
I'VE BEEN CHEERING HER ON SO THINGS GO WELL WITH IDA.

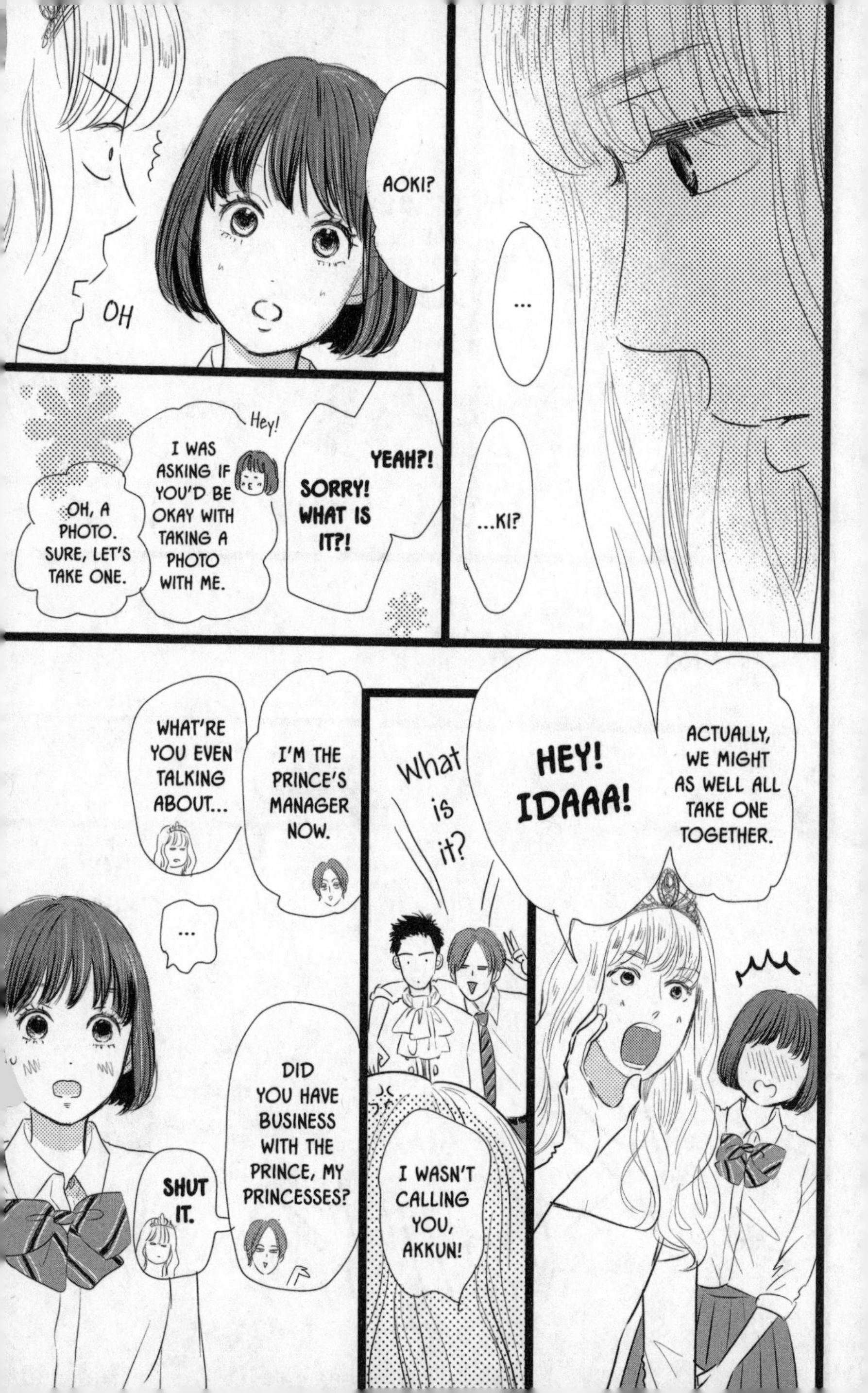
...
...KI?
AOKI?
OH
YEAH?!
SORRY! WHAT IS IT?!
Hey!
I WAS ASKING IF YOU'D BE OKAY WITH TAKING A PHOTO WITH ME.
OH, A PHOTO. SURE, LET'S TAKE ONE.
ACTUALLY, WE MIGHT AS WELL ALL TAKE ONE TOGETHER.
HEY! IDAAA!
What is it?
I WASN'T CALLING YOU, AKKUN!
I'M THE PRINCE'S MANAGER NOW.
WHAT'RE YOU EVEN TALKING ABOUT...
...
DID YOU HAVE BUSINESS WITH THE PRINCE, MY PRINCESSES?
SHUT IT.

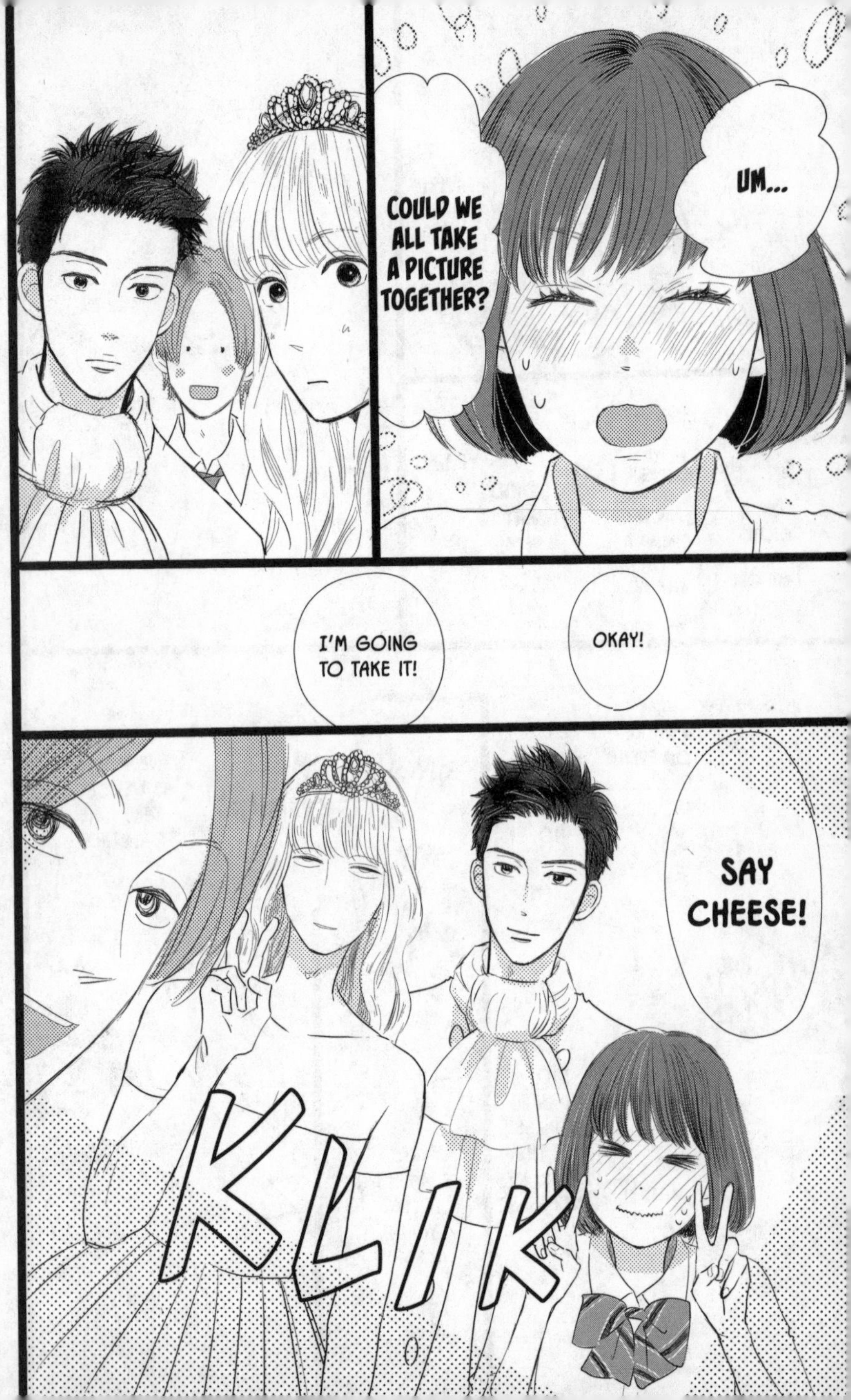
UM...
COULD WE ALL TAKE A PICTURE TOGETHER?
OKAY!
I'M GOING TO TAKE IT!
SAY CHEESE!
KLIK

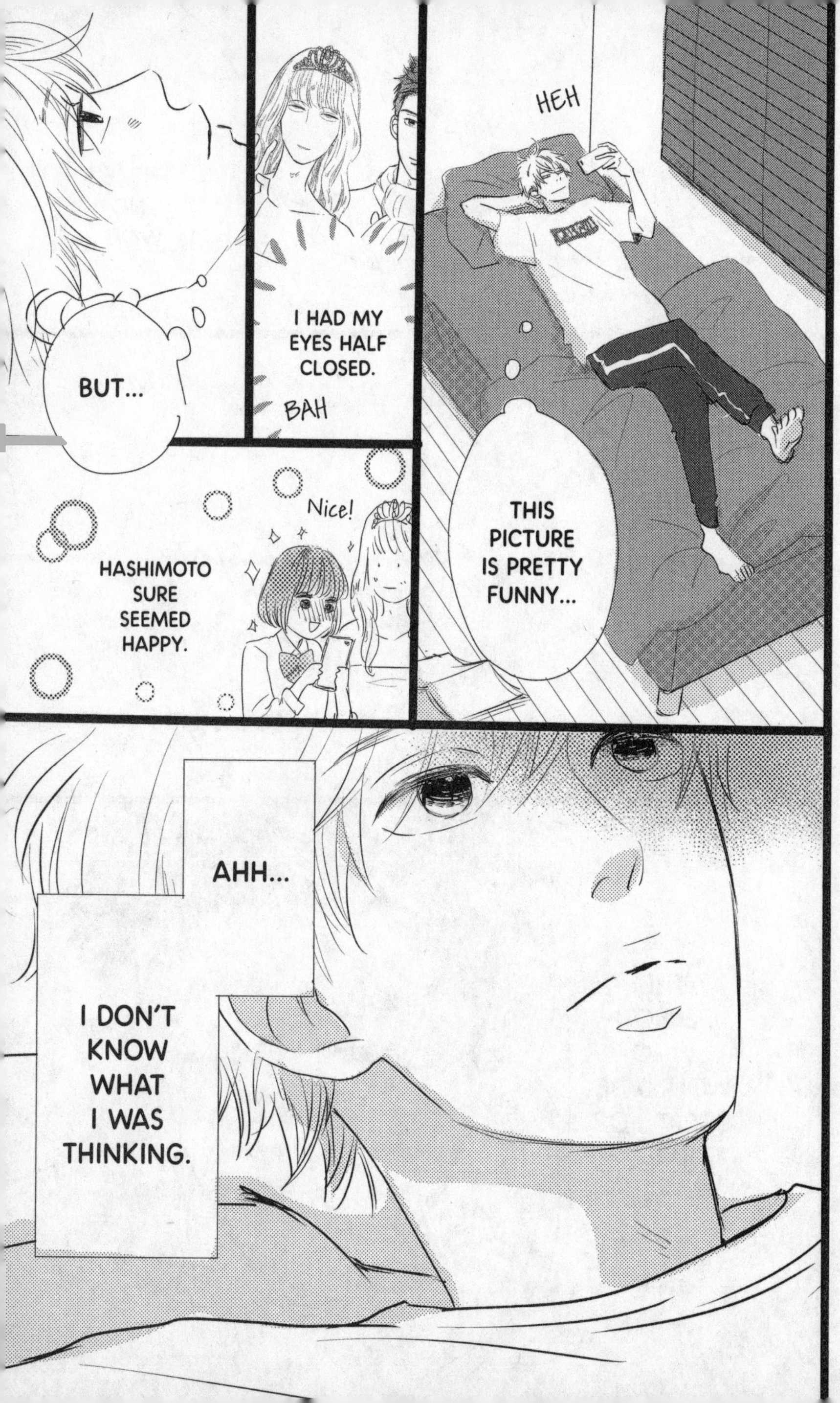
HEH
THIS PICTURE IS PRETTY FUNNY...
I HAD MY EYES HALF CLOSED.
BAH
BUT...
Nice!
HASHIMOTO SURE SEEMED HAPPY.
AHH...
I DON'T KNOW WHAT I WAS THINKING.

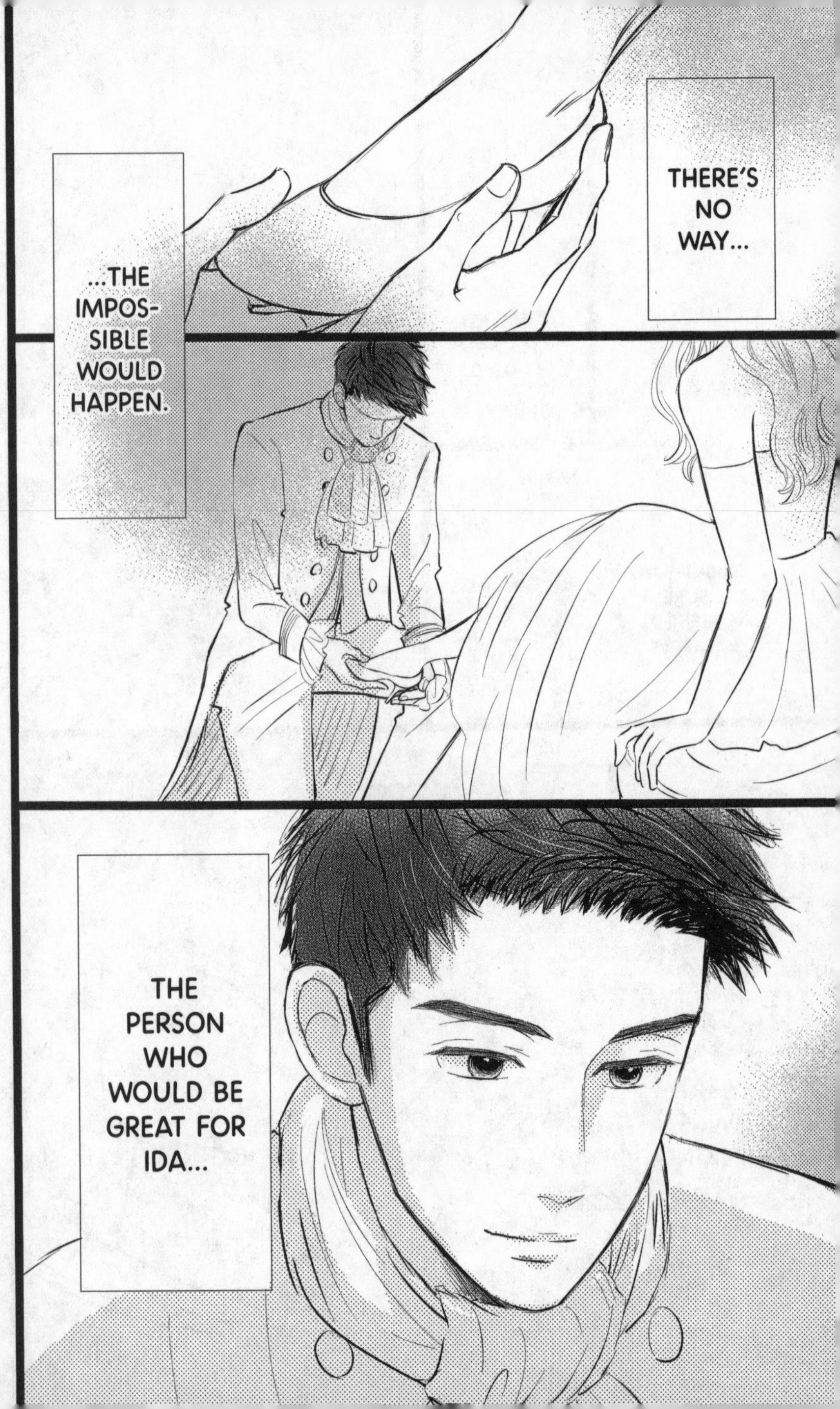
THERE'S NO WAY...
...THE IMPOSSIBLE WOULD HAPPEN.
THE PERSON WHO WOULD BE GREAT FOR IDA...

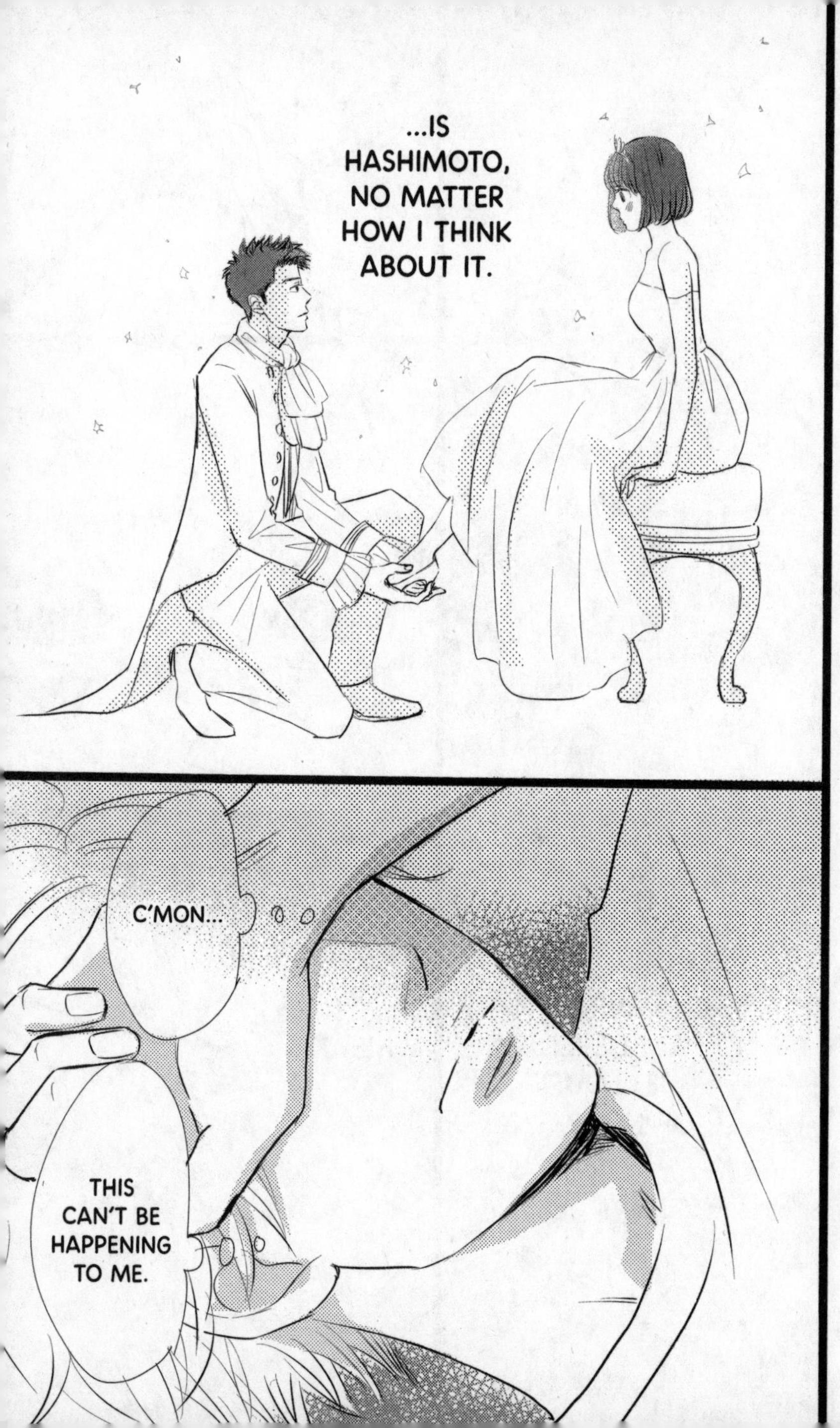
...IS HASHIMOTO, NO MATTER HOW I THINK ABOUT IT.
C'MON...
THIS CAN'T BE HAPPENING TO ME.

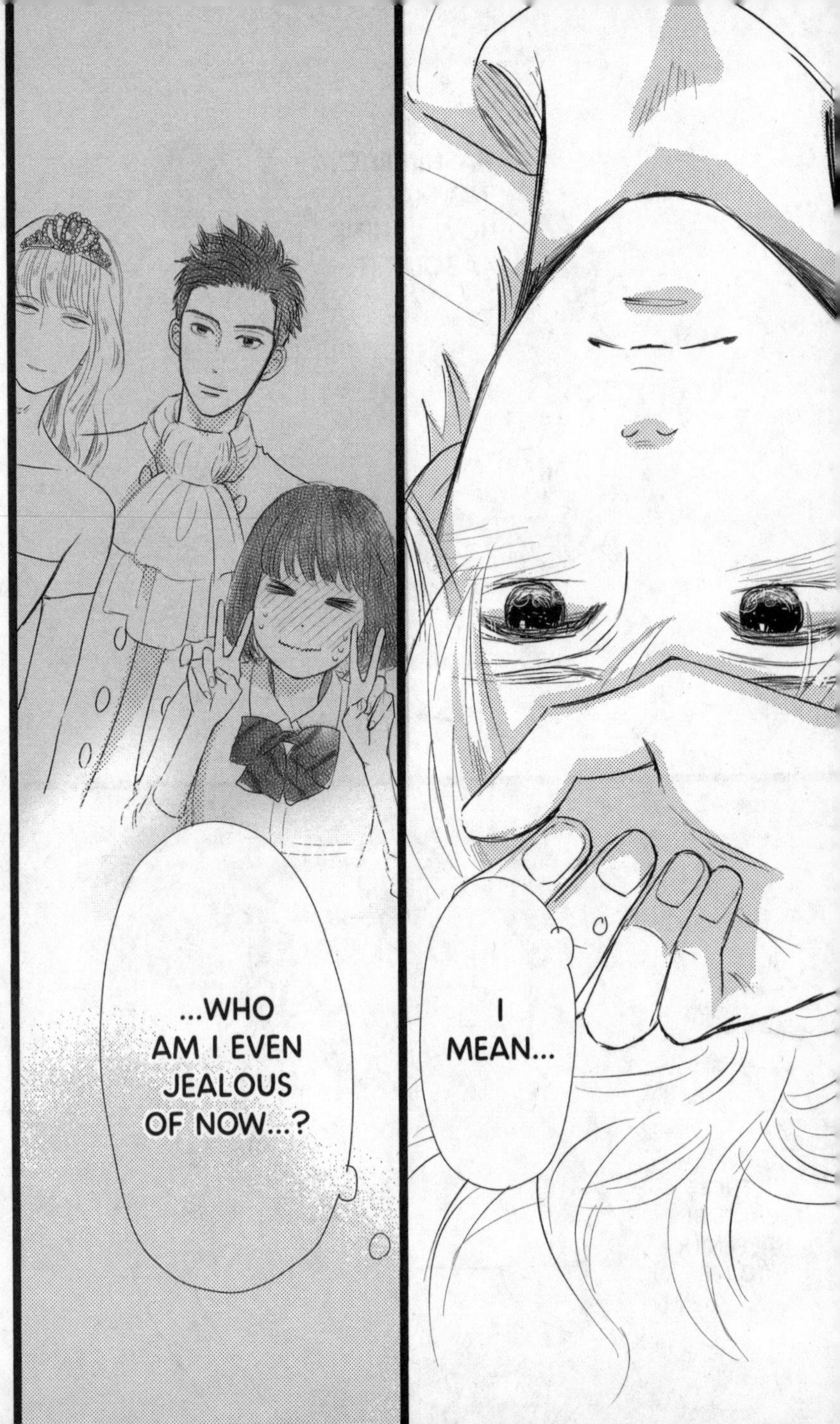
I MEAN...
...WHO AM I EVEN JEALOUS OF NOW...?

Chapter 5

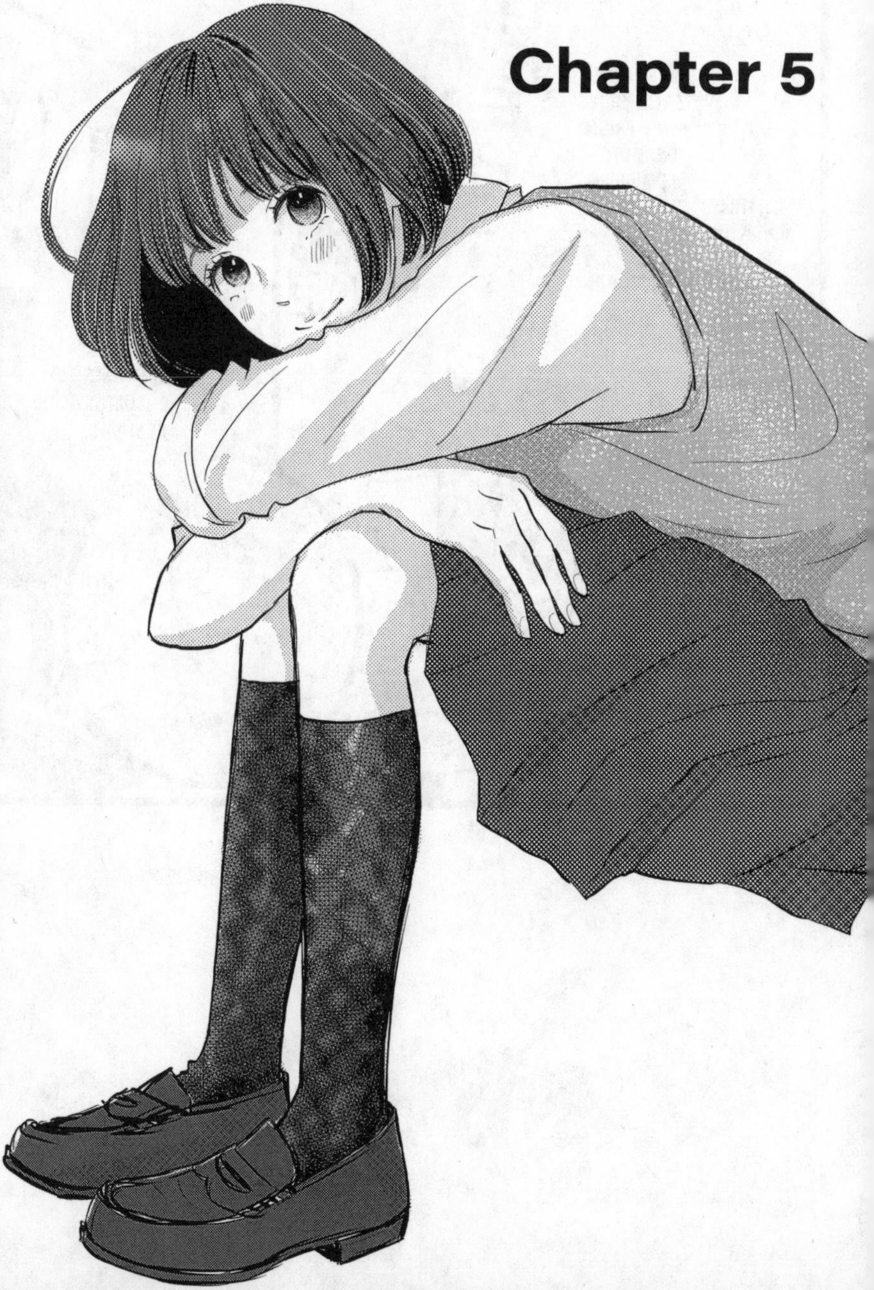

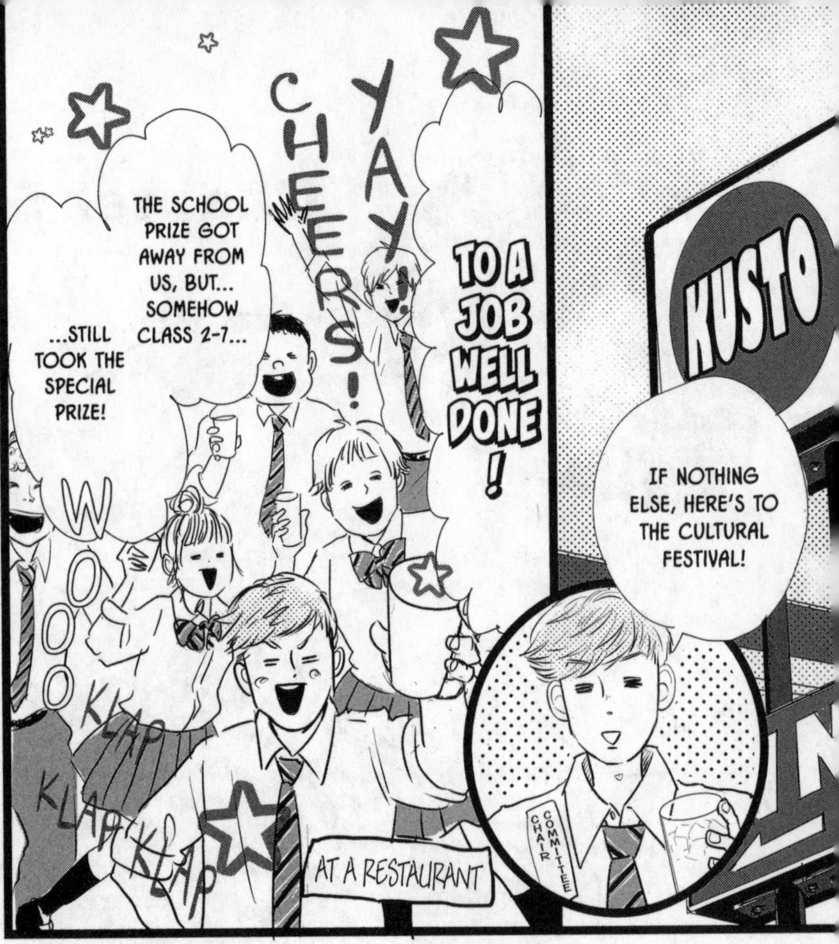
KUSTO
IF NOTHING ELSE, HERE'S TO THE CULTURAL FESTIVAL!
COMMITTEE CHAIR
TO A JOB WELL DONE!
YAY
CHEERS!
THE SCHOOL PRIZE GOT AWAY FROM US, BUT... SOMEHOW CLASS 2-7...
...STILL TOOK THE SPECIAL PRIZE!
WOOOO
KLAP KLAP KLAP KLAP KLAP
AT A RESTAURANT

My Love Mix-Up!

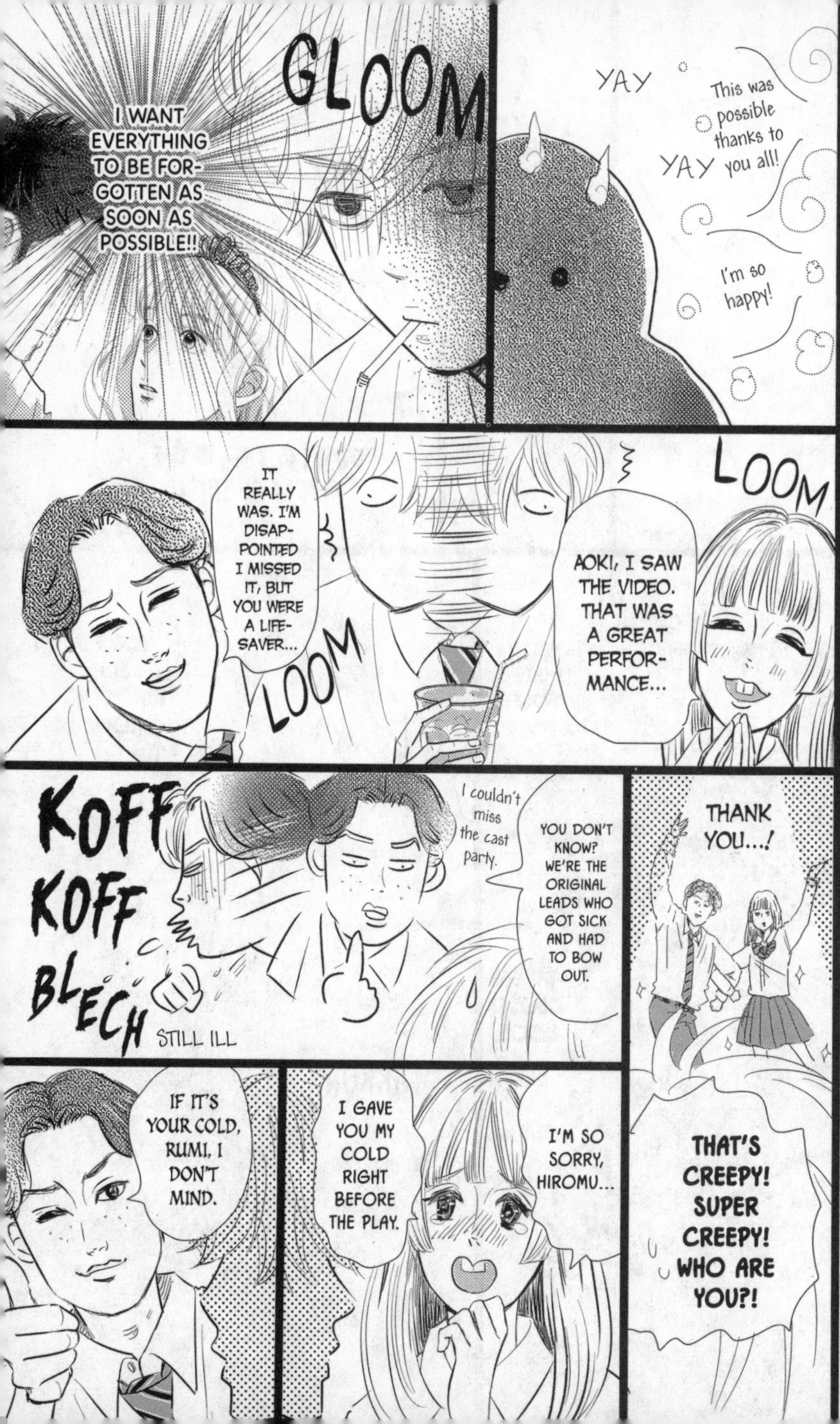
YAY
This was possible thanks to you all!
YAY
I'm so happy!
GLOOM
I WANT EVERYTHING TO BE FORGOTTEN AS SOON AS POSSIBLE!!
LOOM
AOKI, I SAW THE VIDEO. THAT WAS A GREAT PERFORMANCE...
LOOM
IT REALLY WAS. I'M DISAPPOINTED I MISSED IT, BUT YOU WERE A LIFESAVER...
THANK YOU...!
THAT'S CREEPY! SUPER CREEPY! WHO ARE YOU?!
YOU DON'T KNOW? WE'RE THE ORIGINAL LEADS WHO GOT SICK AND HAD TO BOW OUT.
I couldn't miss the cast party.
KOFF
KOFF
BLECH
STILL ILL
I'M SO SORRY, HIROMU...
I GAVE YOU MY COLD RIGHT BEFORE THE PLAY.
IF IT'S YOUR COLD, RUMI, I DON'T MIND.

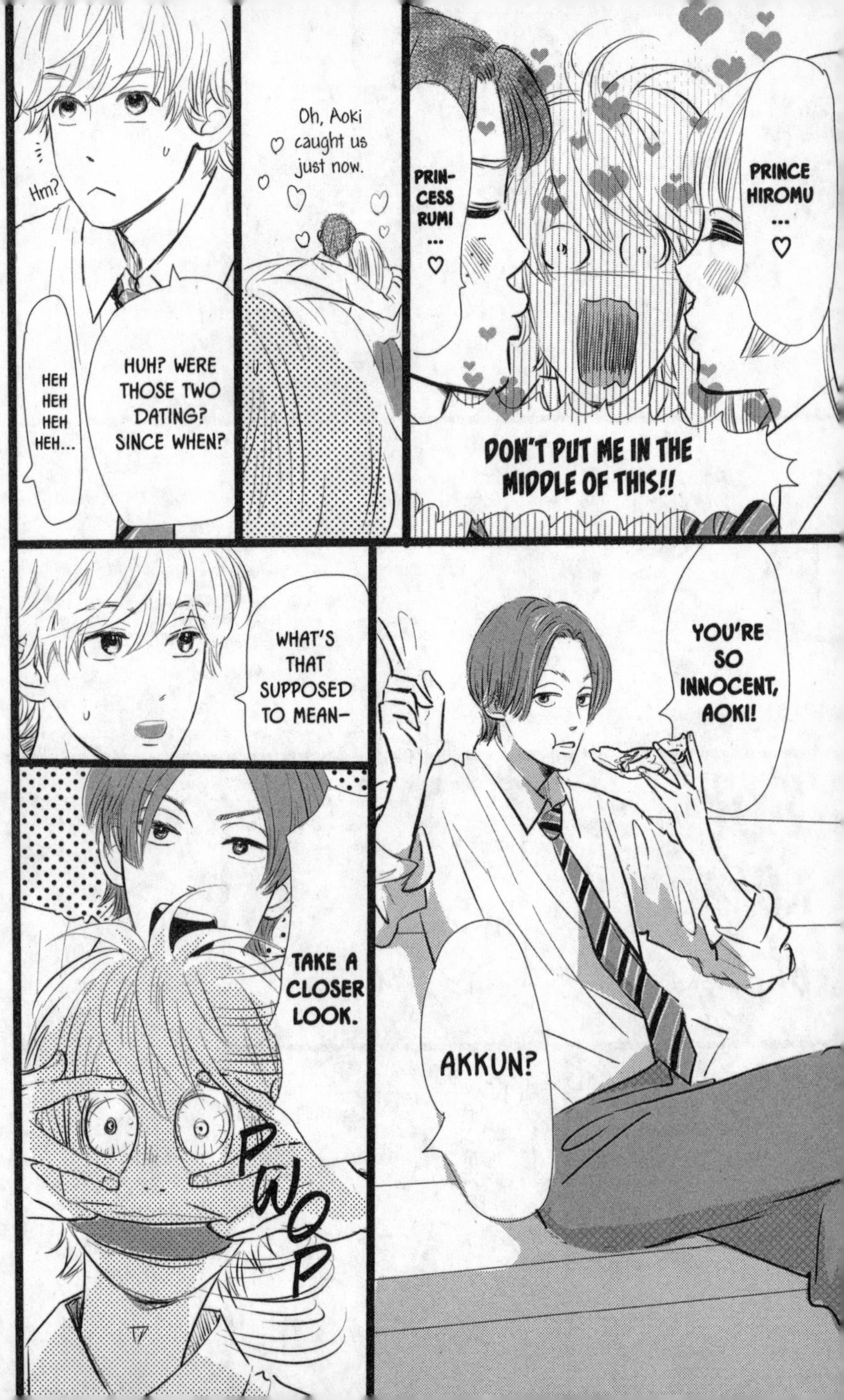
PRINCE HIROMU ... ♡
PRIN-CESS RUMI ... ♡
DON'T PUT ME IN THE MIDDLE OF THIS!!
Oh, Aoki ♡ caught us just now.
Hm?
HUH? WERE THOSE TWO DATING? SINCE WHEN?
HEH HEH HEH HEH...
YOU'RE SO INNOCENT, AOKI!
AKKUN?
WHAT'S THAT SUPPOSED TO MEAN-
TAKE A CLOSER LOOK.
PWOP

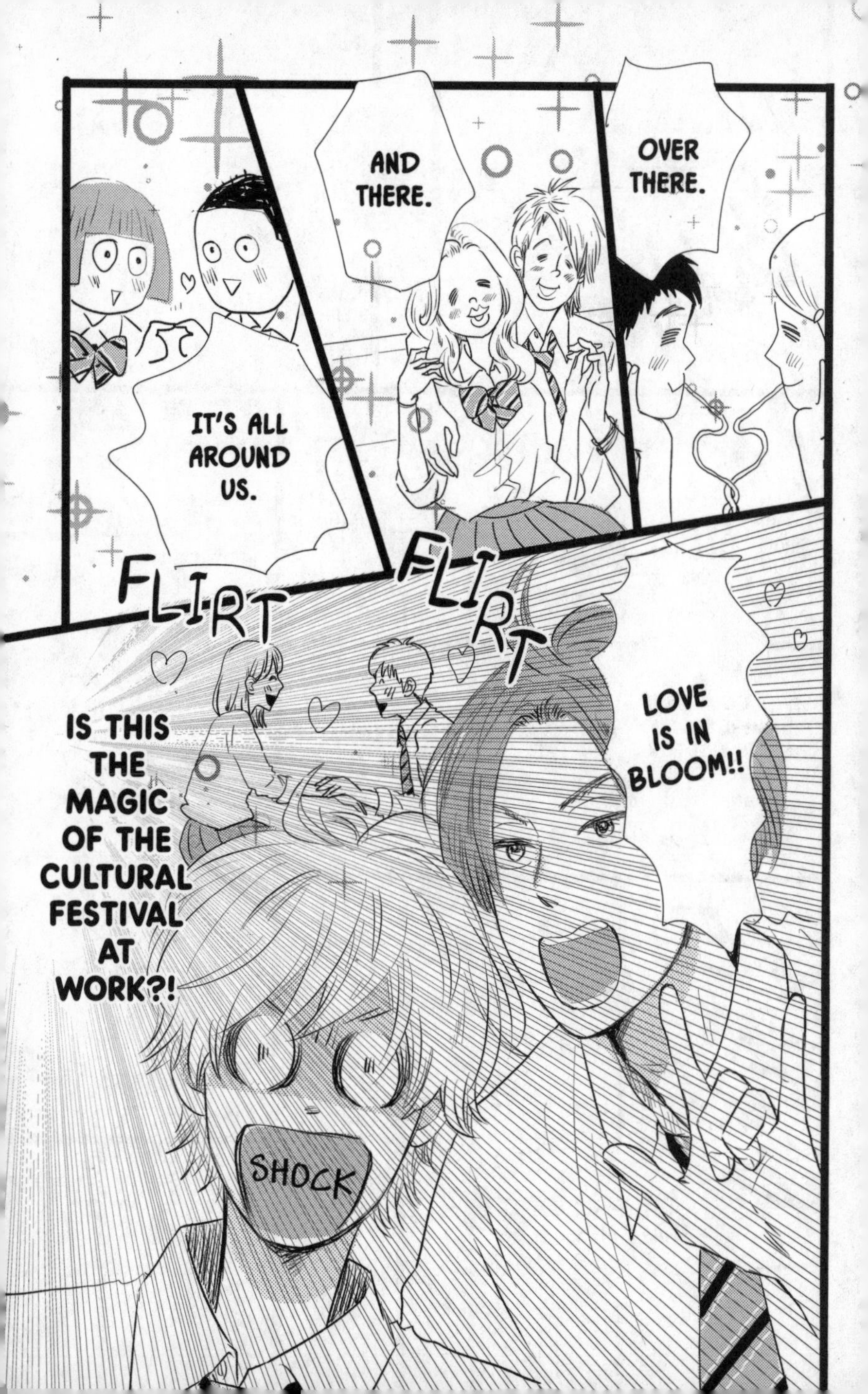
OVER THERE.
AND THERE.
IT'S ALL AROUND US.
FLIRT
FLIRT
LOVE IS IN BLOOM!!
IS THIS THE MAGIC OF THE CULTURAL FESTIVAL AT WORK?!
SHOCK

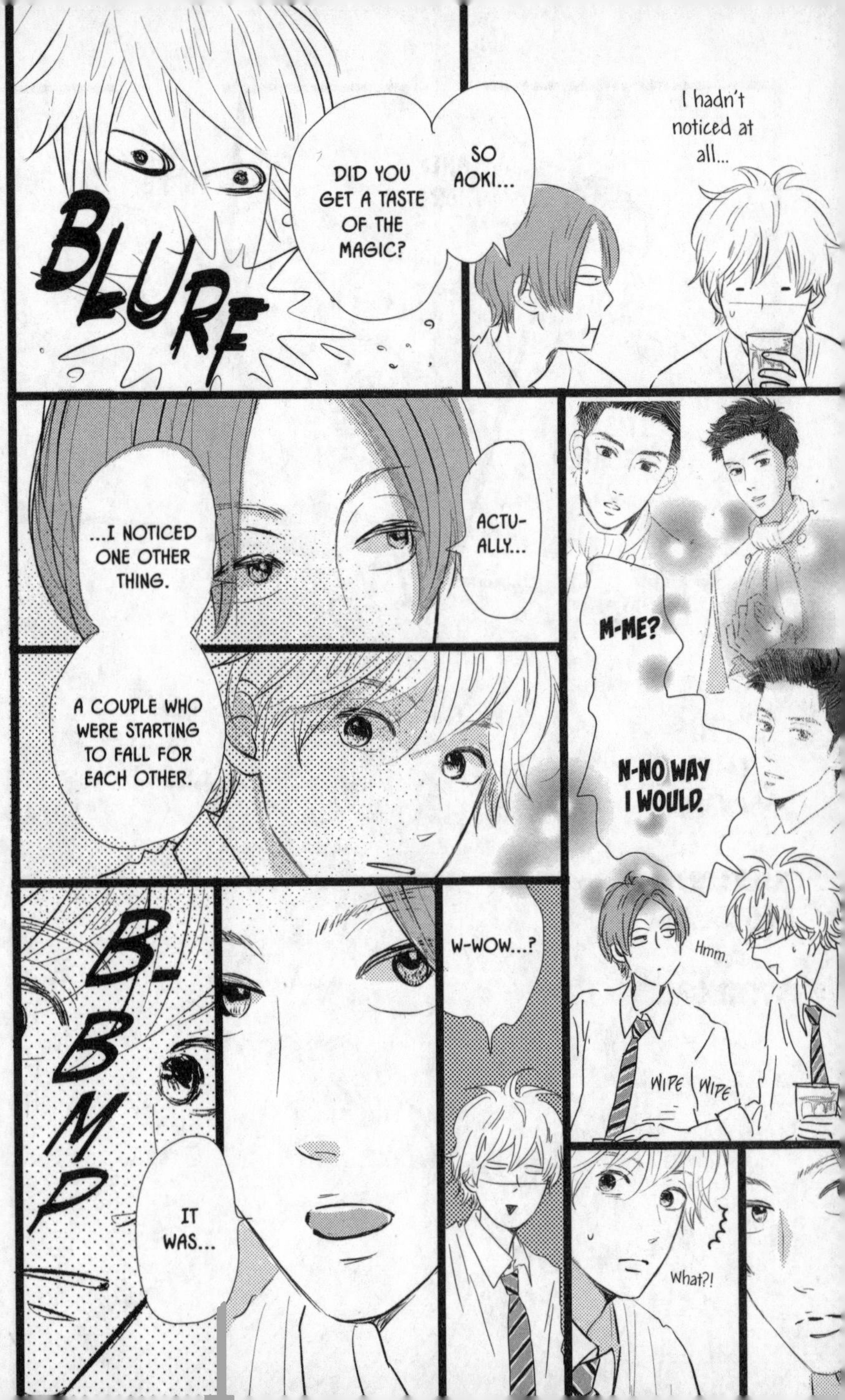
I hadn't noticed at all...
SO AOKI...
DID YOU GET A TASTE OF THE MAGIC?
BLURF
M-ME?
N-NO WAY I WOULD.
Hmm.
WIPE WIPE
ACTU-ALLY...
...I NOTICED ONE OTHER THING.
A COUPLE WHO WERE STARTING TO FALL FOR EACH OTHER.
What?!
W-WOW...?
IT WAS...
B-BMP

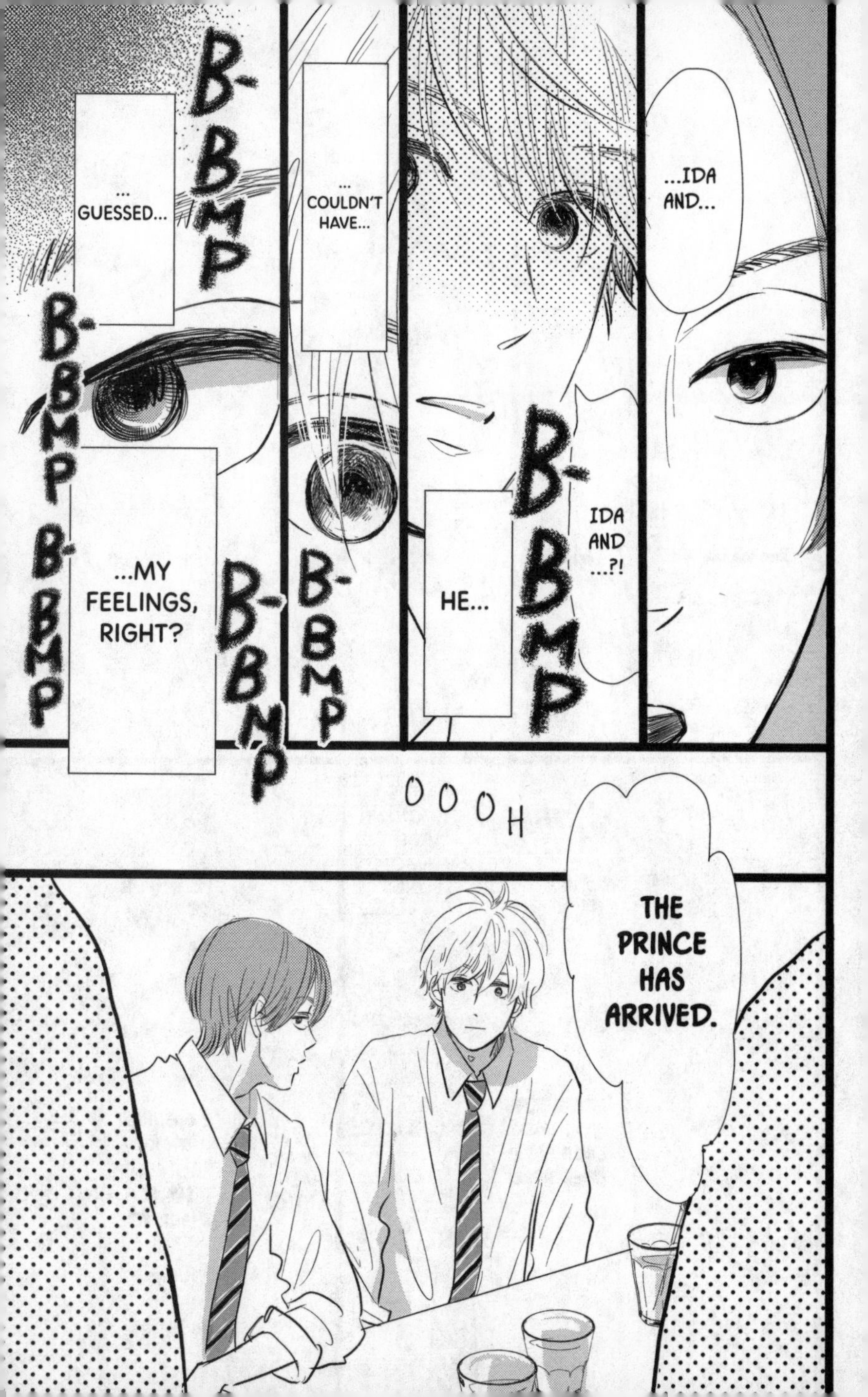
...IDA AND...
IDA AND ...?!
B-BMP
HE...
B-BMP
... COULDN'T HAVE...
B-BMP
B-BMP
... GUESSED...
B-BMP
B-BMP
B-BMP
...MY FEELINGS, RIGHT?
THE PRINCE HAS ARRIVED.
OOOH

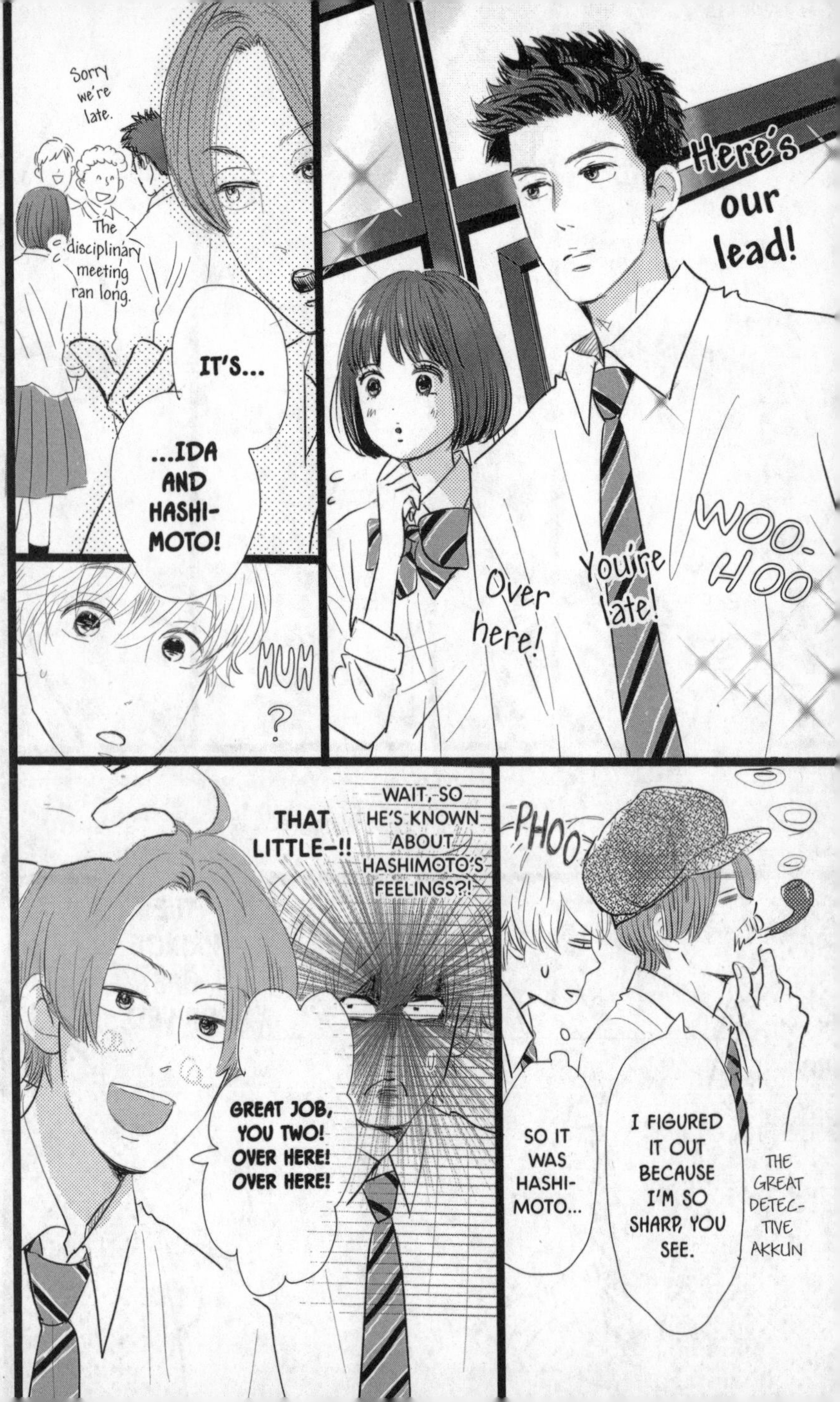
Here's our lead!
WOO-HOO
You're late!
Over here!
Sorry we're late.
The disciplinary meeting ran long.
IT'S...
...IDA AND HASHIMOTO!
HUH
?
PHOO
THE GREAT DETECTIVE AKKUN
I FIGURED IT OUT BECAUSE I'M SO SHARP, YOU SEE.
SO IT WAS HASHIMOTO...
WAIT, SO HE'S KNOWN ABOUT HASHIMOTO'S FEELINGS?!
THAT LITTLE-!!
GREAT JOB, YOU TWO! OVER HERE! OVER HERE!

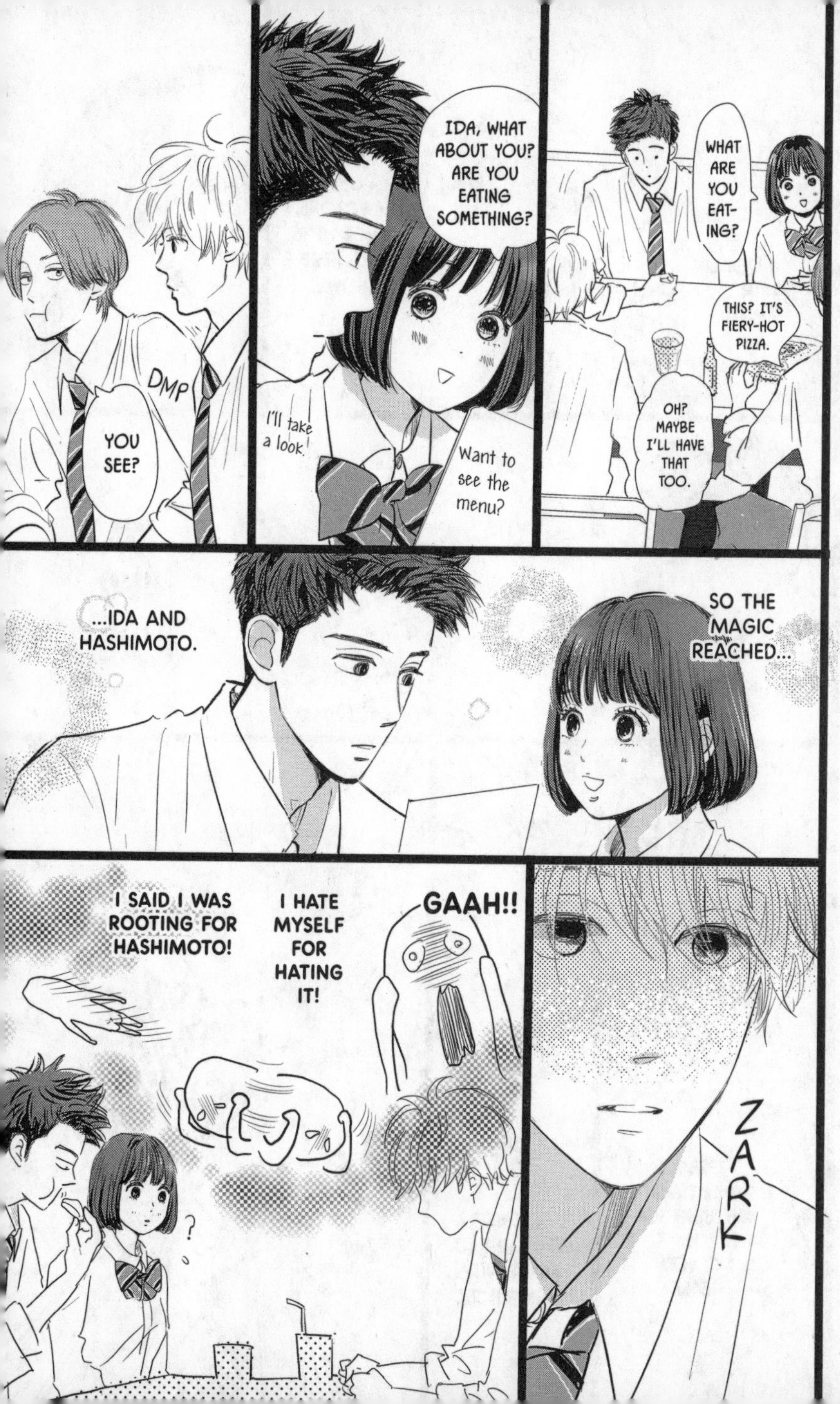
WHAT ARE YOU EATING?
THIS? IT'S FIERY-HOT PIZZA.
OH? MAYBE I'LL HAVE THAT TOO.
IDA, WHAT ABOUT YOU? ARE YOU EATING SOMETHING?
Want to see the menu?
I'll take a look.
DMP
YOU SEE?
SO THE MAGIC REACHED...
...IDA AND HASHIMOTO.
ZARK
GAAH!!
I HATE MYSELF FOR HATING IT!
I SAID I WAS ROOTING FOR HASHIMOTO!
?

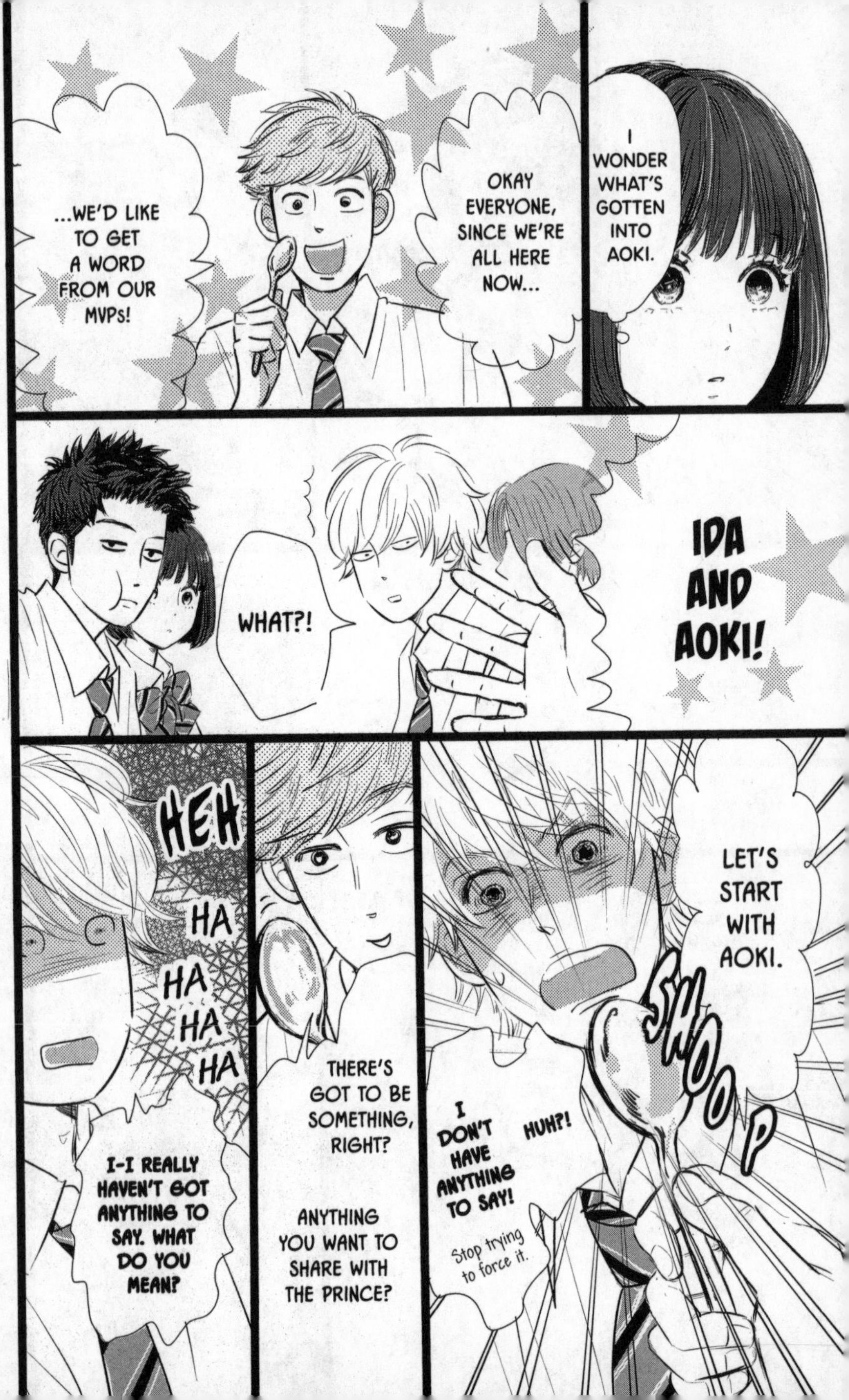
I WONDER WHAT'S GOTTEN INTO AOKI.
OKAY EVERYONE, SINCE WE'RE ALL HERE NOW...
...WE'D LIKE TO GET A WORD FROM OUR MVPs!
IDA AND AOKI!
WHAT?!
LET'S START WITH AOKI.
SHOOOP
HUH?!
I DON'T HAVE ANYTHING TO SAY!
Stop trying to force it.
THERE'S GOT TO BE SOMETHING, RIGHT?
ANYTHING YOU WANT TO SHARE WITH THE PRINCE?
HEH
HA HA HA HA
I-I REALLY HAVEN'T GOT ANYTHING TO SAY. WHAT DO YOU MEAN?

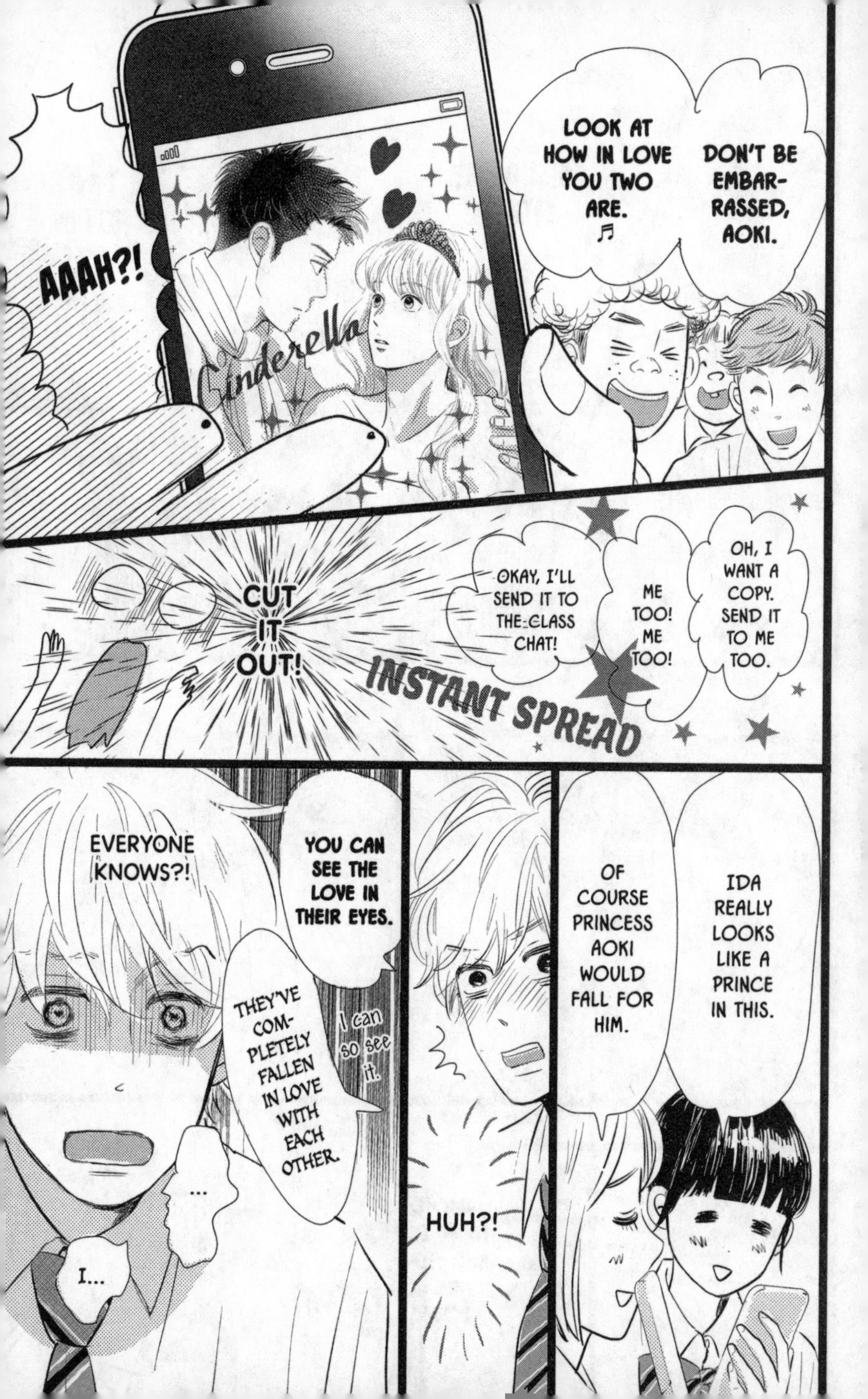
DON'T BE EMBARRASSED, AOKI.
LOOK AT HOW IN LOVE YOU TWO ARE. ♬
AAAH?!
Cinderella
OH, I WANT A COPY. SEND IT TO ME TOO.
ME TOO! ME TOO!
OKAY, I'LL SEND IT TO THE CLASS CHAT!
INSTANT SPREAD
CUT IT OUT!
IDA REALLY LOOKS LIKE A PRINCE IN THIS.
OF COURSE PRINCESS AOKI WOULD FALL FOR HIM.
HUH?!
YOU CAN SEE THE LOVE IN THEIR EYES.
EVERYONE KNOWS?!
I can so see it.
THEY'VE COMPLETELY FALLEN IN LOVE WITH EACH OTHER.
...
I...

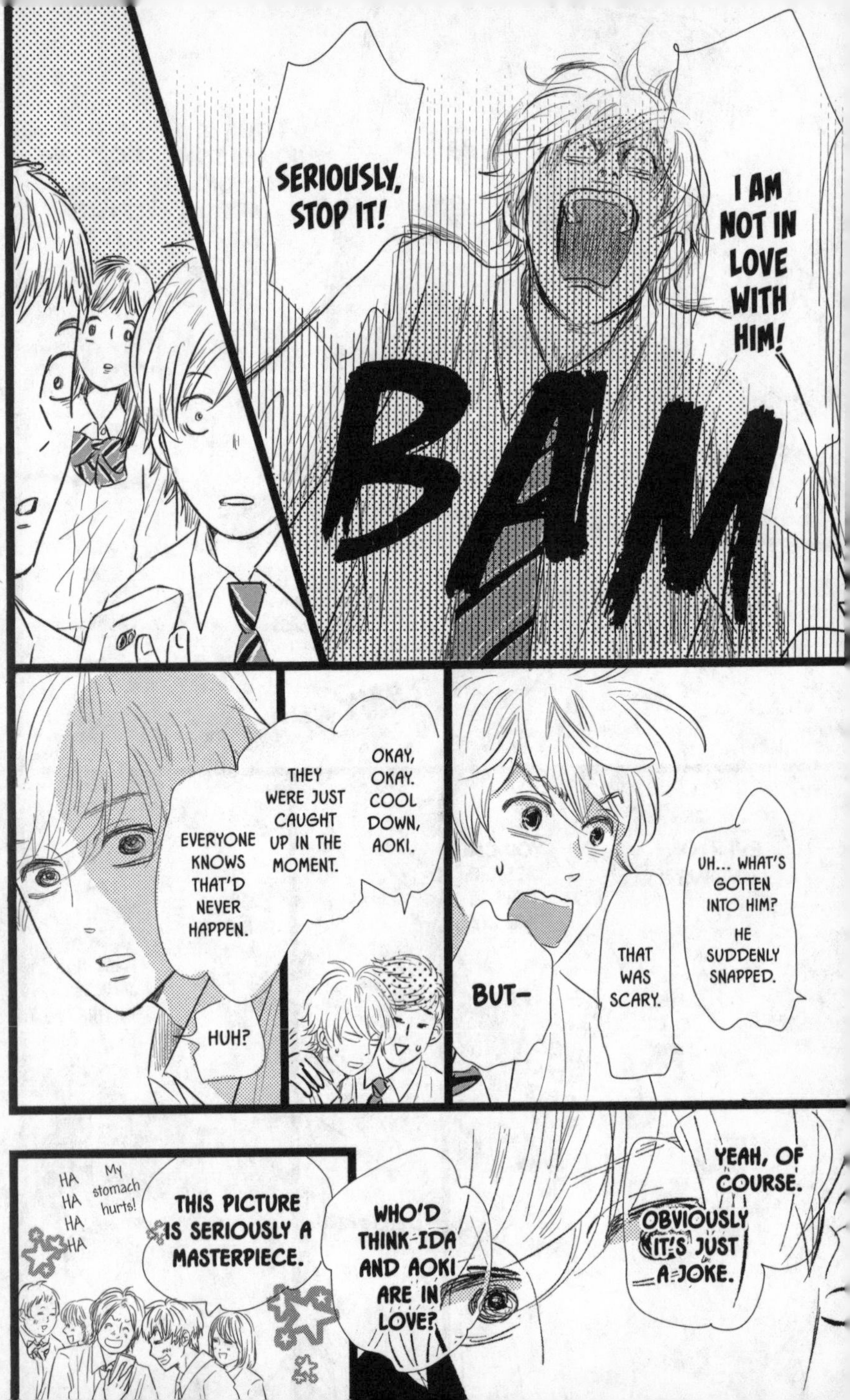
I AM NOT IN LOVE WITH HIM!
SERIOUSLY, STOP IT!
BAM
UH... WHAT'S GOTTEN INTO HIM?
HE SUDDENLY SNAPPED.
THAT WAS SCARY.
BUT-
OKAY, OKAY. COOL DOWN, AOKI.
THEY WERE JUST CAUGHT UP IN THE MOMENT.
EVERYONE KNOWS THAT'D NEVER HAPPEN.
HUH?
YEAH, OF COURSE.
OBVIOUSLY IT'S JUST A JOKE.
WHO'D THINK IDA AND AOKI ARE IN LOVE?
THIS PICTURE IS SERIOUSLY A MASTERPIECE.
My stomach hurts!
HA HA HA HA

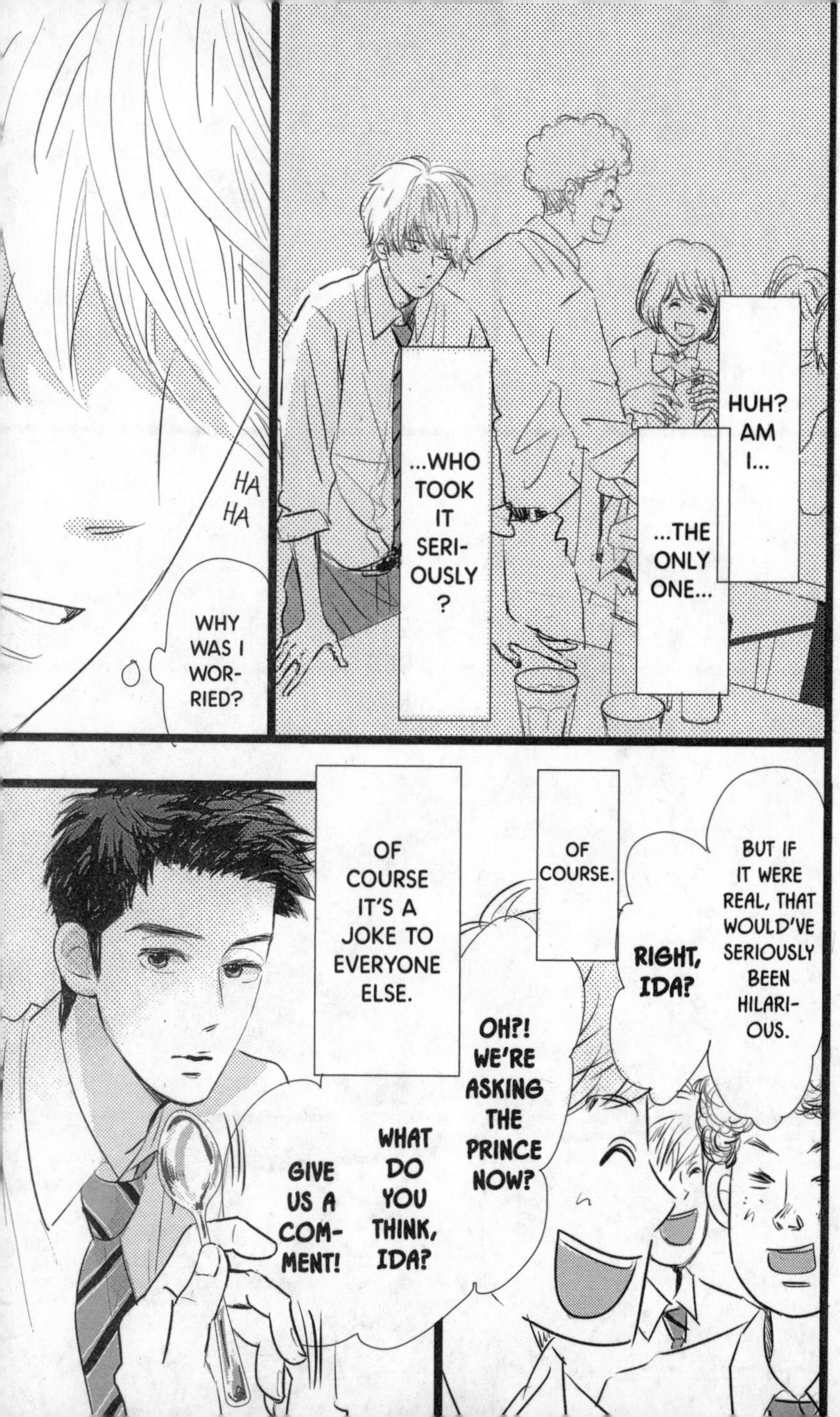
HUH? AM I...
...THE ONLY ONE...
...WHO TOOK IT SERIOUSLY?
HA HA
WHY WAS I WORRIED?
BUT IF IT WERE REAL, THAT WOULD'VE SERIOUSLY BEEN HILARIOUS.
RIGHT, IDA?
OF COURSE.
OF COURSE IT'S A JOKE TO EVERYONE ELSE.
OH?! WE'RE ASKING THE PRINCE NOW?
WHAT DO YOU THINK, IDA?
GIVE US A COMMENT!

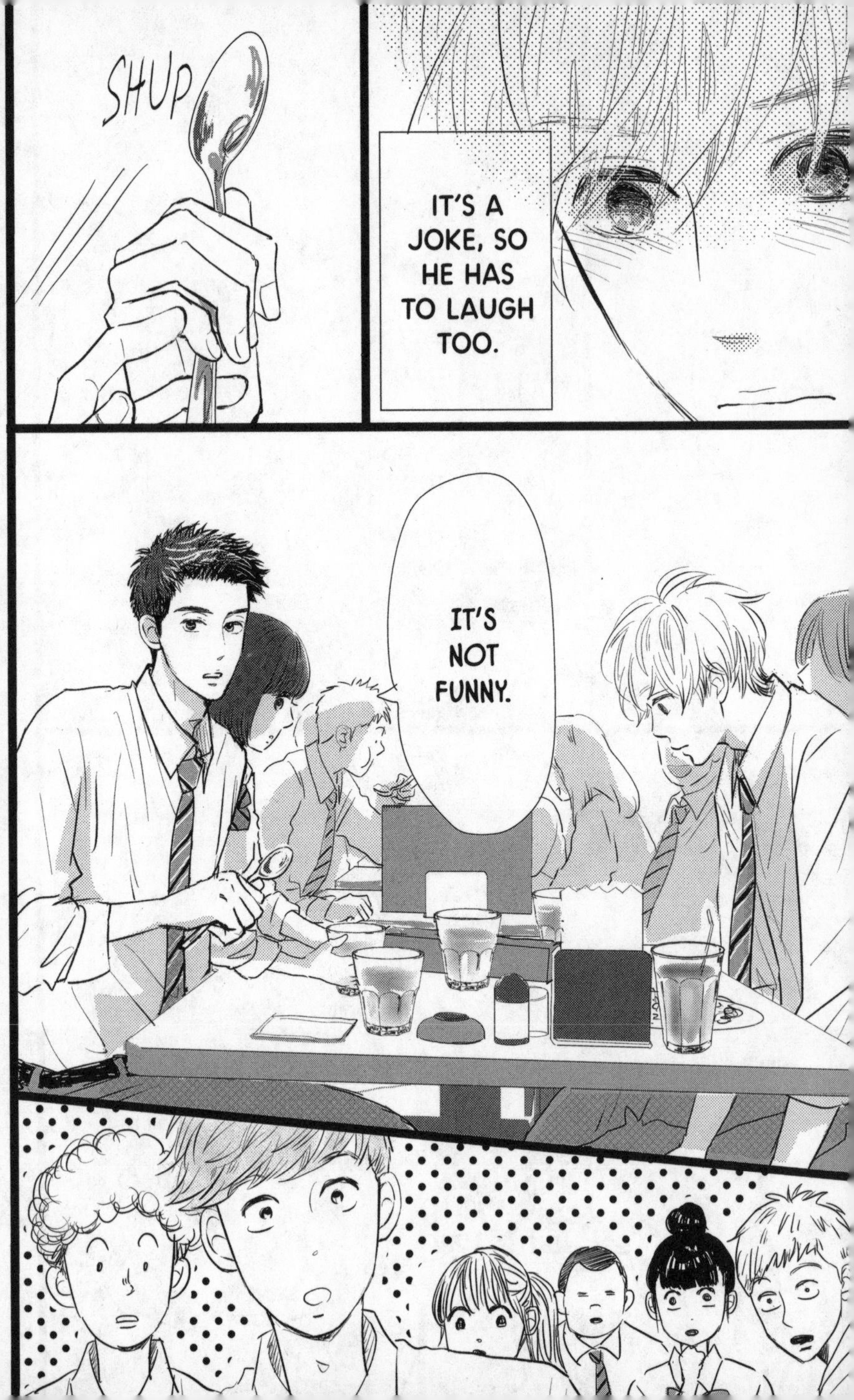
IT'S A JOKE, SO HE HAS TO LAUGH TOO.
SHUP
IT'S NOT FUNNY.

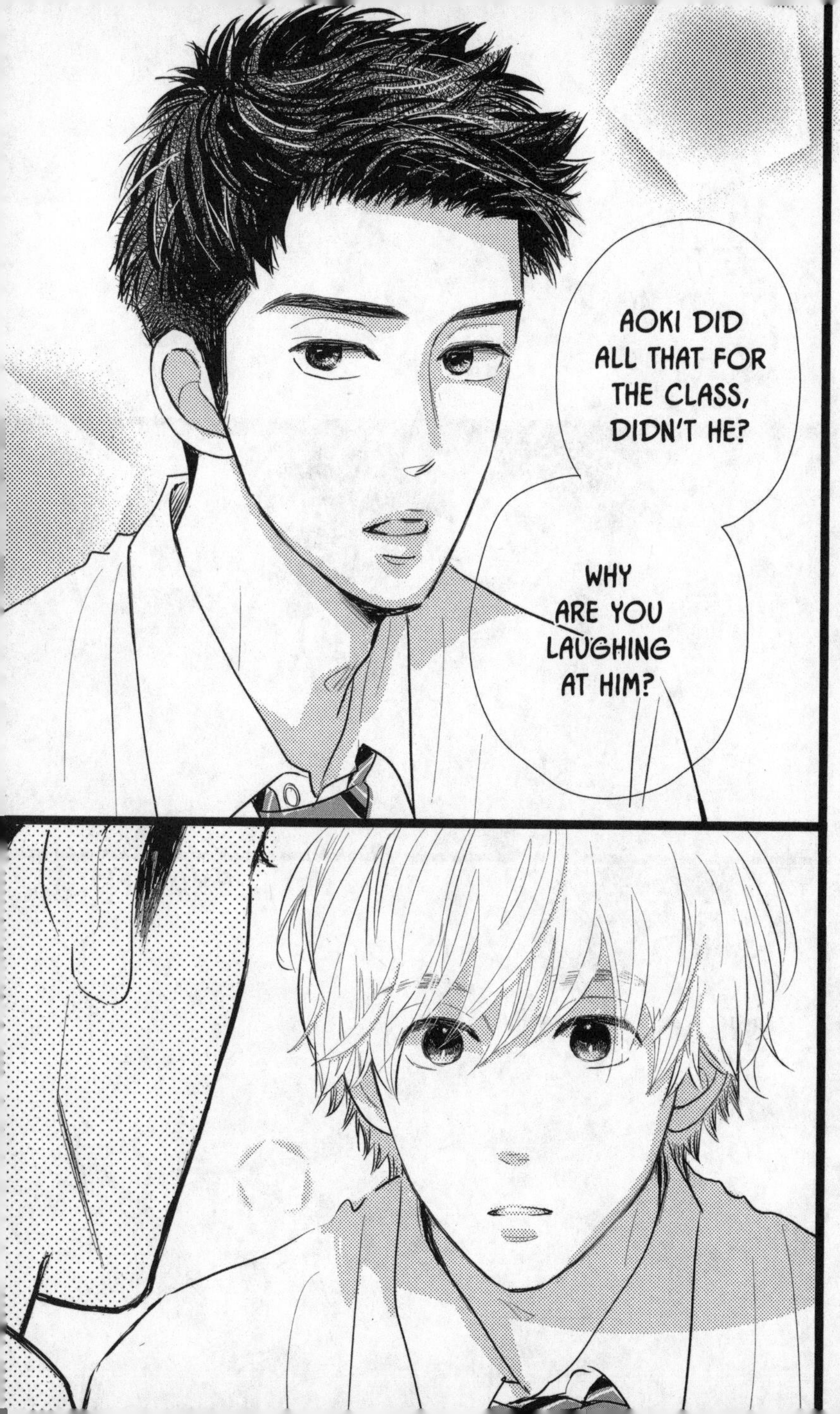
AOKI DID ALL THAT FOR THE CLASS, DIDN'T HE?
WHY ARE YOU LAUGHING AT HIM?

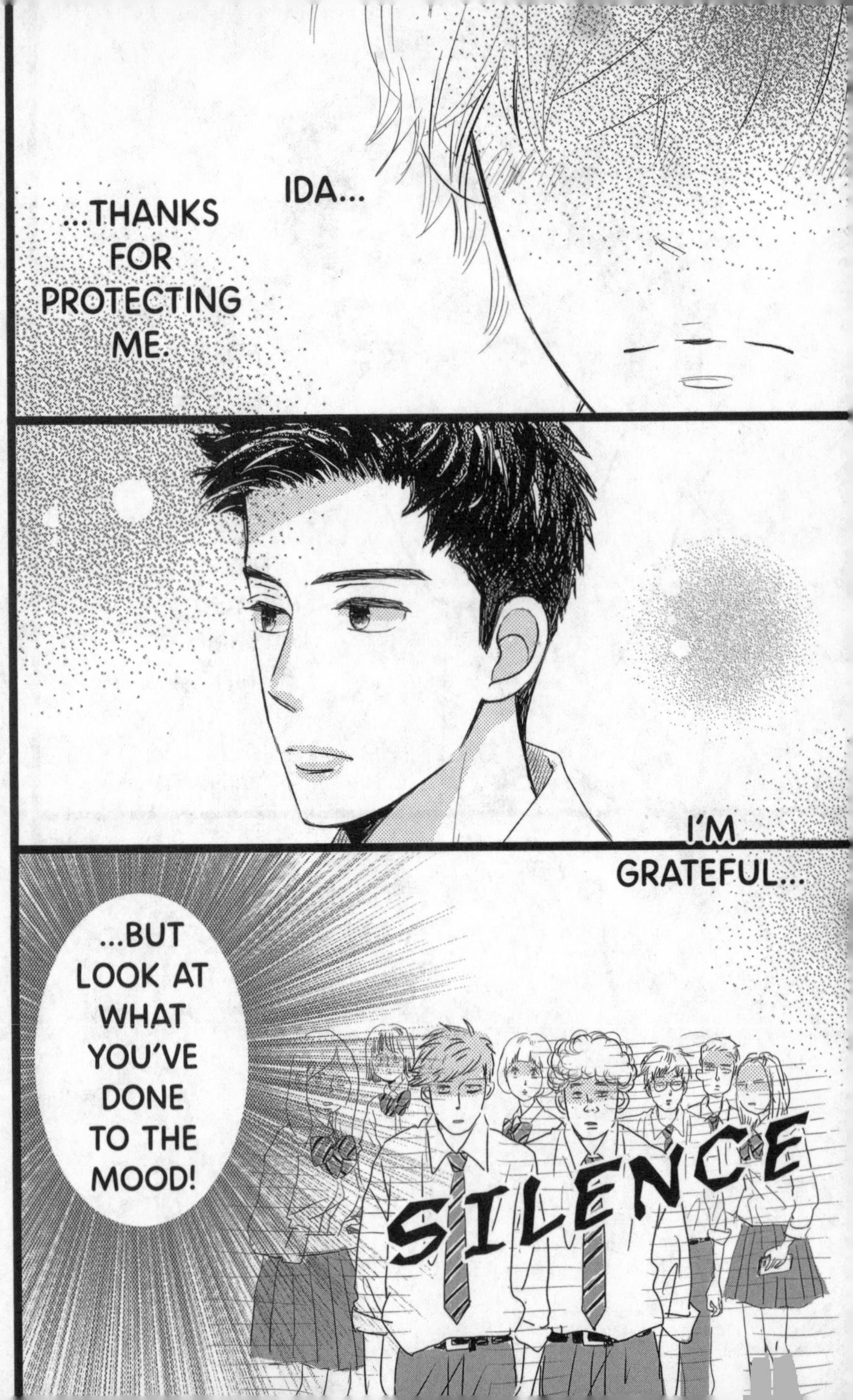
IDA...
...THANKS FOR PROTECTING ME.
I'M GRATEFUL...
...BUT LOOK AT WHAT YOU'VE DONE TO THE MOOD!
SILENCE

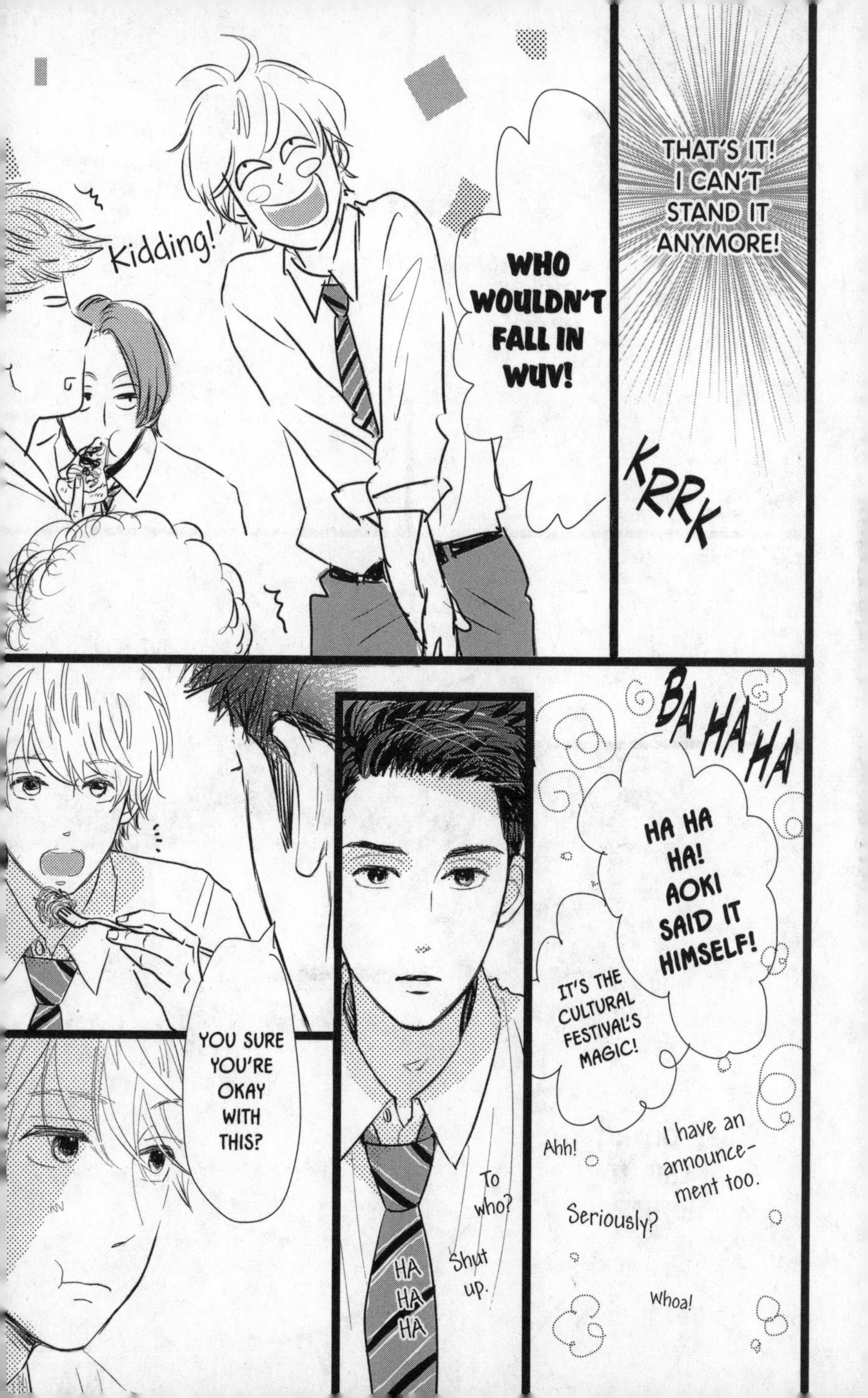
THAT'S IT! I CAN'T STAND IT ANYMORE!
KRRK
WHO WOULDN'T FALL IN WUV!
Kidding!
BA HA HA
HA HA HA! AOKI SAID IT HIMSELF!
IT'S THE CULTURAL FESTIVAL'S MAGIC!
I have an announcement too.
Ahh!
Seriously?
Whoa!
To who?
Shut up.
HA HA HA
YOU SURE YOU'RE OKAY WITH THIS?

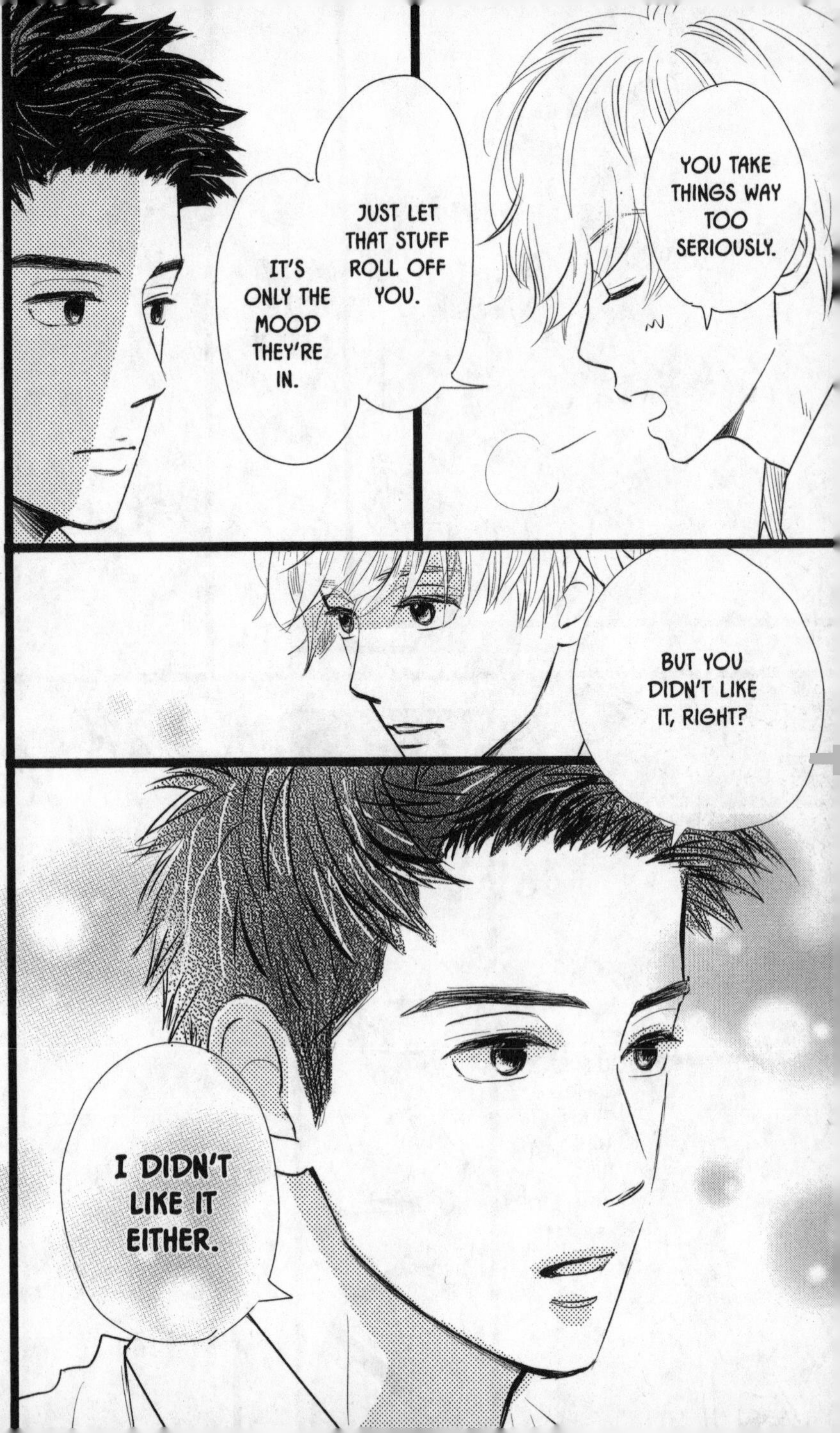
YOU TAKE THINGS WAY TOO SERIOUSLY.
JUST LET THAT STUFF ROLL OFF YOU.
IT'S ONLY THE MOOD THEY'RE IN.
BUT YOU DIDN'T LIKE IT, RIGHT?
I DIDN'T LIKE IT EITHER.

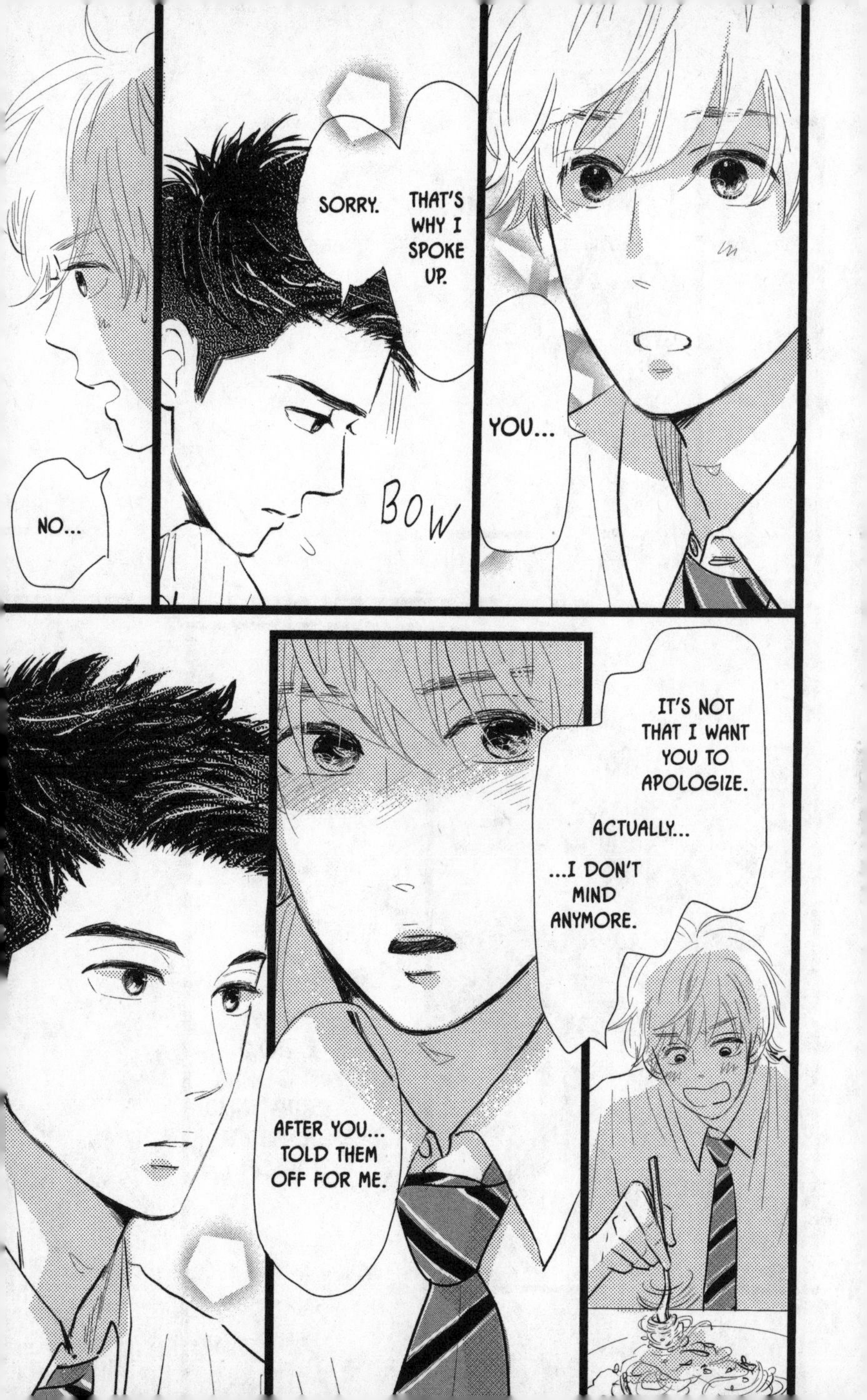
YOU...
THAT'S WHY I SPOKE UP.
SORRY.
BOW
NO...
IT'S NOT THAT I WANT YOU TO APOLOGIZE.
ACTUALLY...
...I DON'T MIND ANYMORE.
AFTER YOU... TOLD THEM OFF FOR ME.

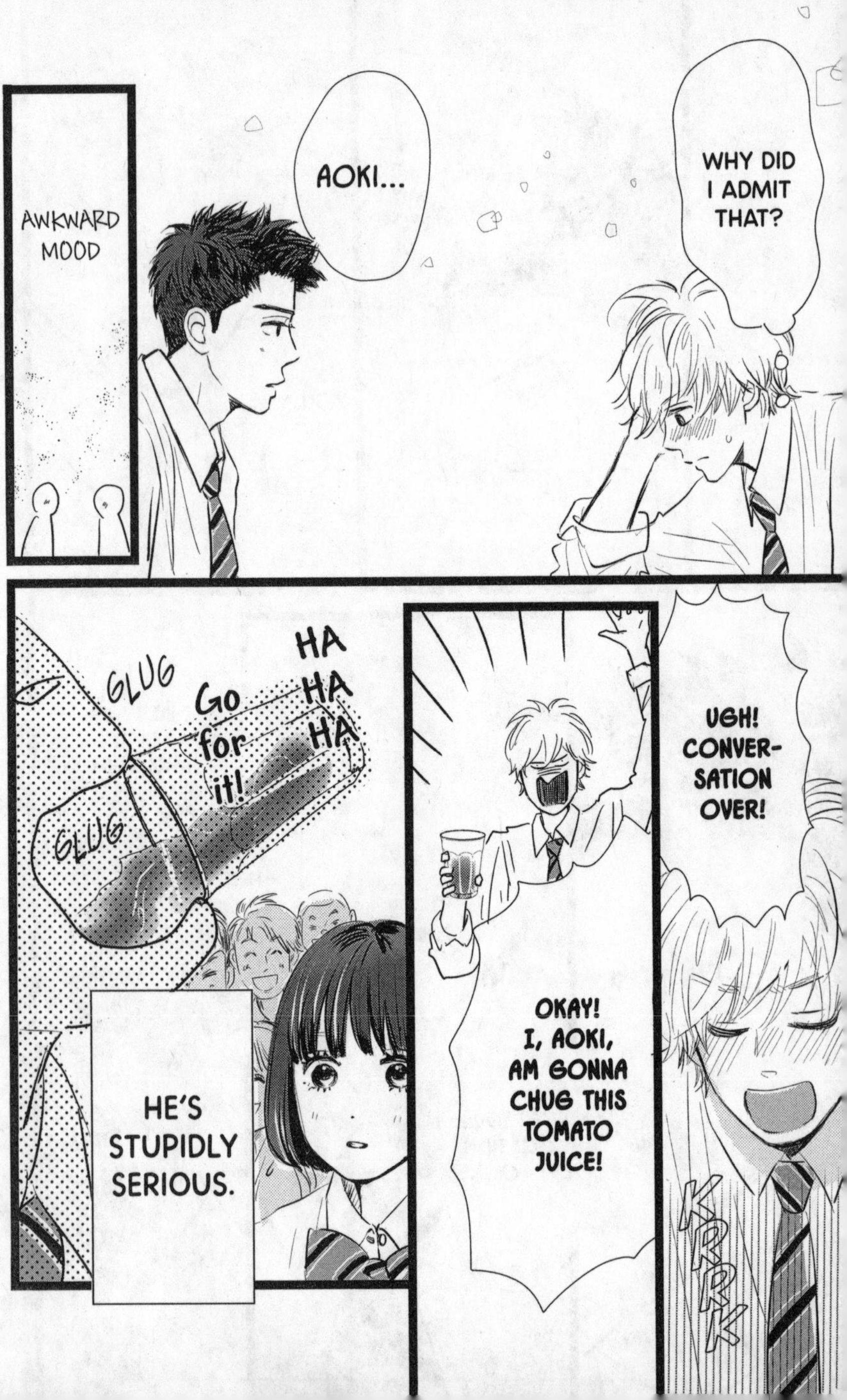
WHY DID I ADMIT THAT?
AOKI...
AWKWARD MOOD
UGH! CONVER-SATION OVER!
KRRK
OKAY! I, AOKI, AM GONNA CHUG THIS TOMATO JUICE!
HA HA HA
GLUG
Go for it!
GLUG
HE'S STUPIDLY SERIOUS.

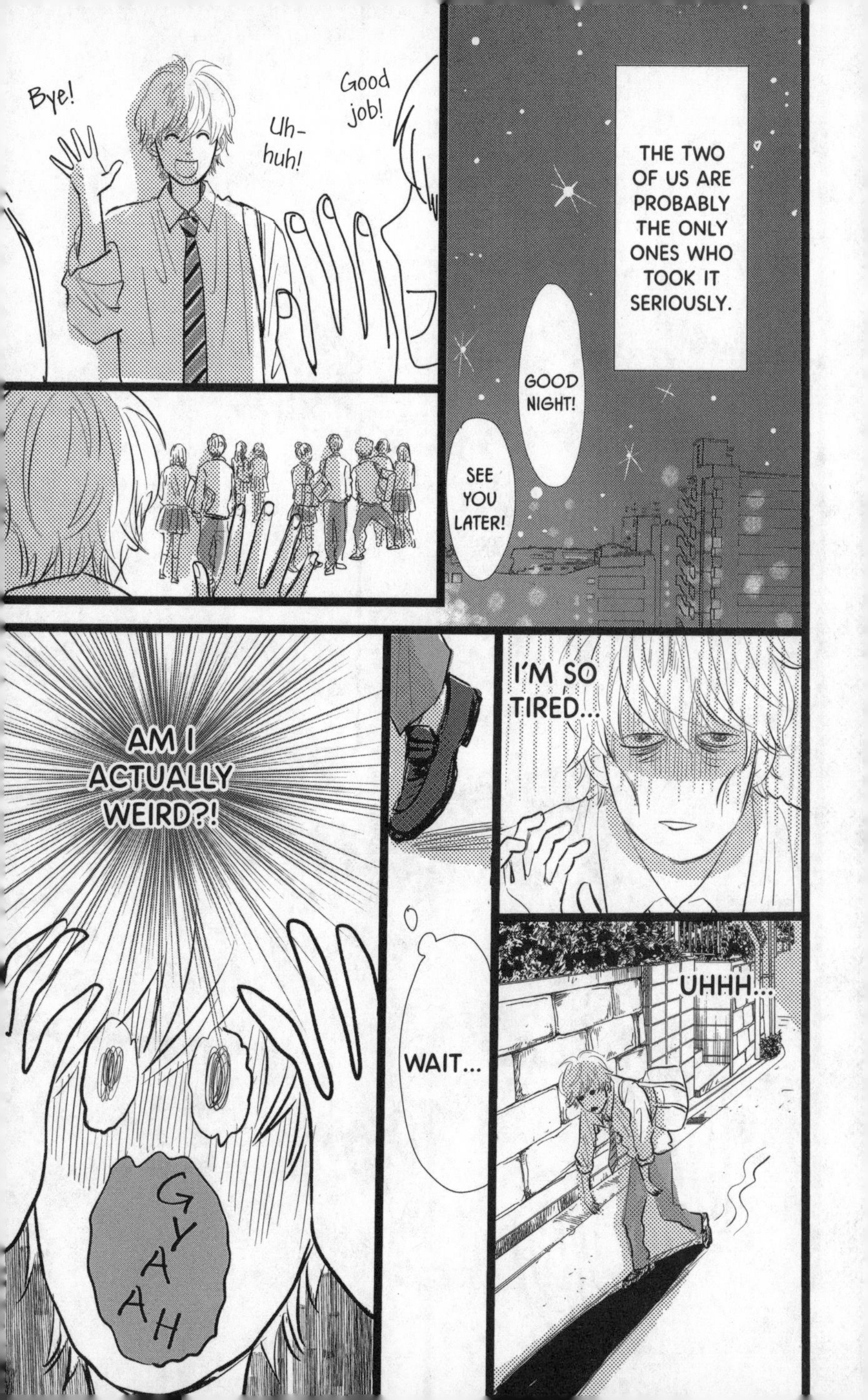
THE TWO OF US ARE PROBABLY THE ONLY ONES WHO TOOK IT SERIOUSLY.
GOOD NIGHT!
SEE YOU LATER!
Good job!
Uh-huh!
Bye!
I'M SO TIRED...
UHHH...
WAIT...
AM I ACTUALLY WEIRD?!
GYAAH

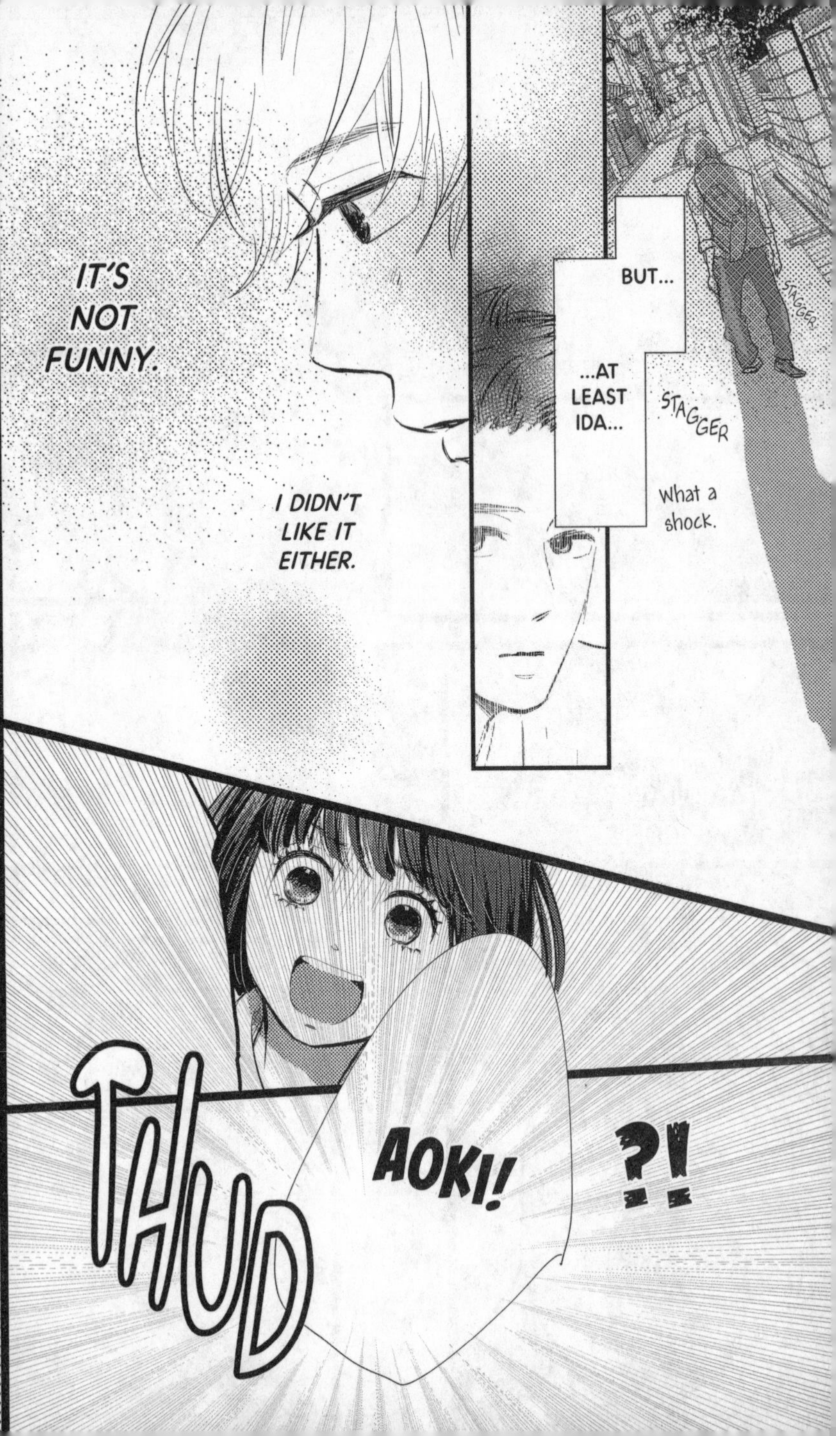
STAGGER
STAGGER
What a shock.
BUT...
...AT LEAST IDA...
IT'S NOT FUNNY.
I DIDN'T LIKE IT EITHER.
?!
AOKI!
THUD

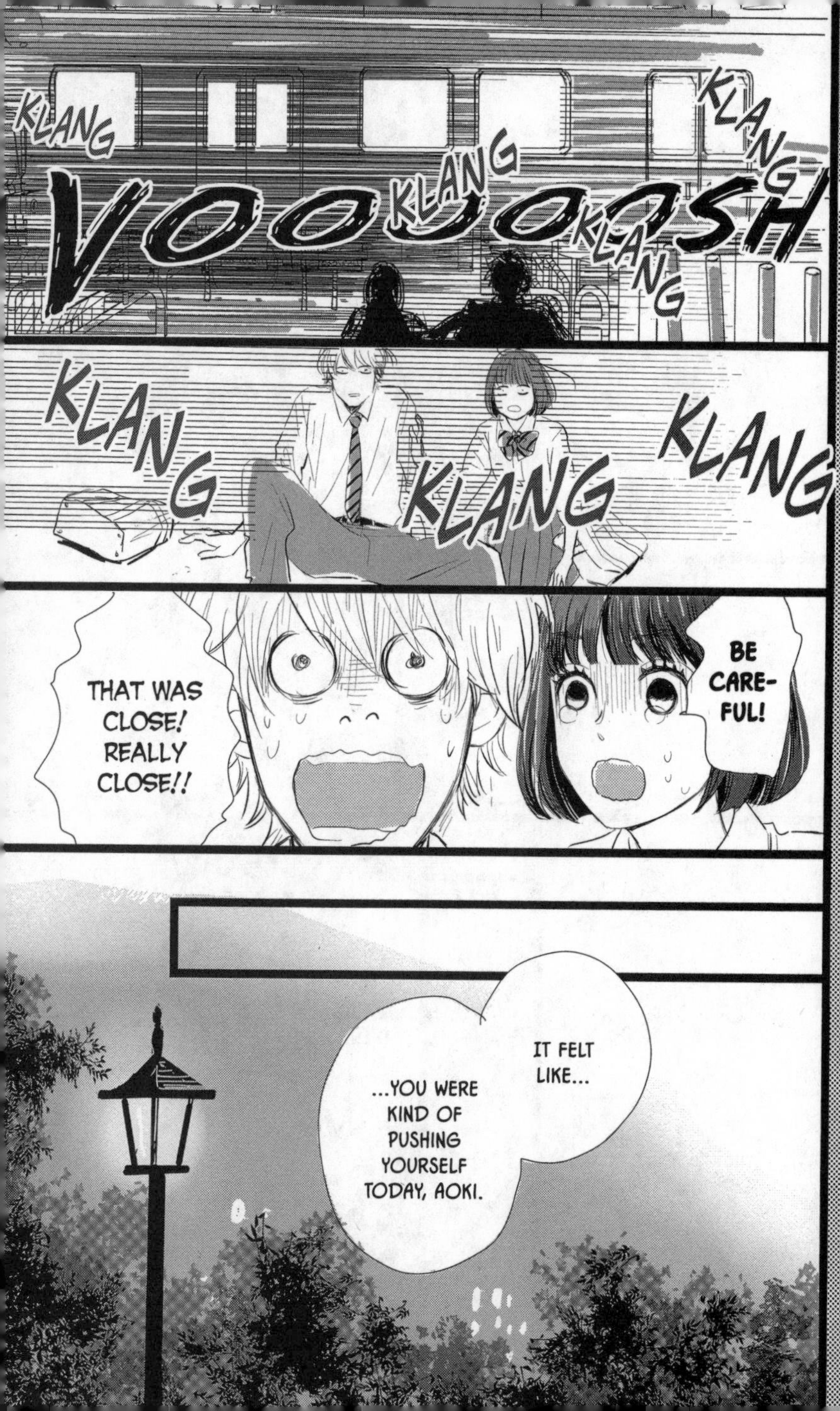
KLANG
KLANG
KLANG
VOOOOOSH
KLANG
KLANG
KLANG
KLANG
KLANG
BE CAREFUL!
THAT WAS CLOSE! REALLY CLOSE!!
IT FELT LIKE...
...YOU WERE KIND OF PUSHING YOURSELF TODAY, AOKI.

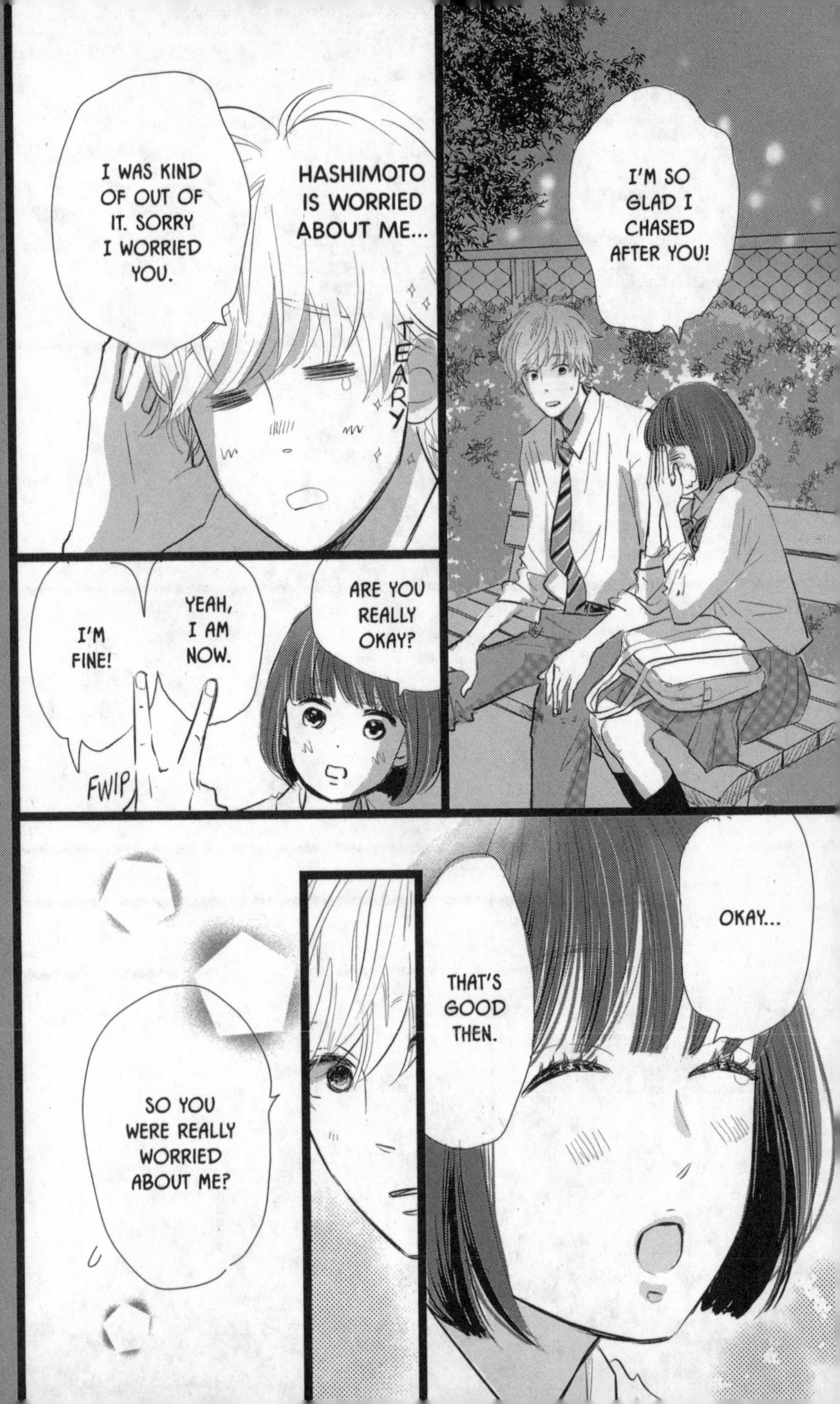
I'M SO GLAD I CHASED AFTER YOU!
HASHIMOTO IS WORRIED ABOUT ME...
TEARY
I WAS KIND OF OUT OF IT. SORRY I WORRIED YOU.
ARE YOU REALLY OKAY?
YEAH, I AM NOW.
I'M FINE!
FWIP
OKAY...
THAT'S GOOD THEN.
SO YOU WERE REALLY WORRIED ABOUT ME?

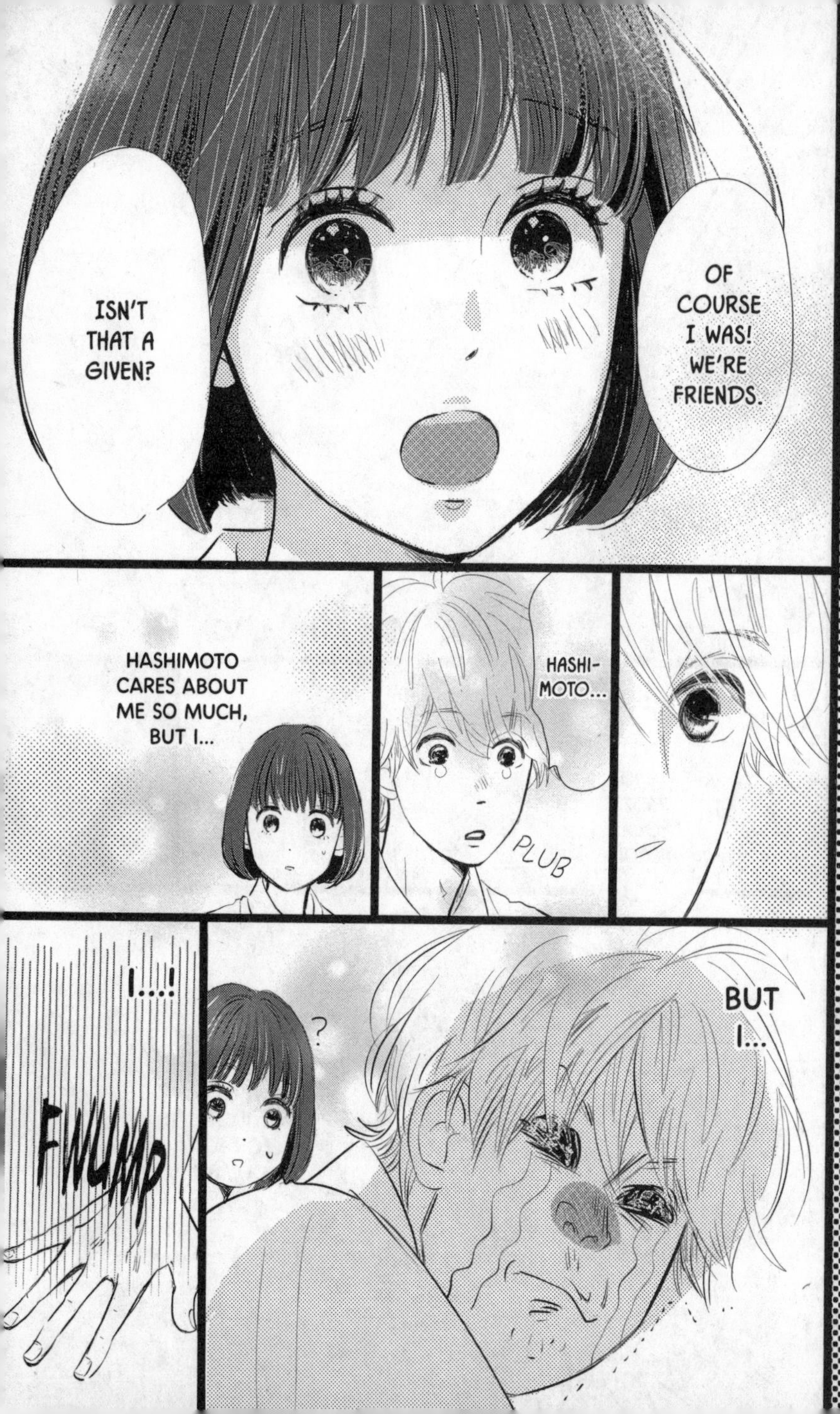
OF COURSE I WAS! WE'RE FRIENDS.
ISN'T THAT A GIVEN?
HASHI-MOTO...
PLUB
HASHIMOTO CARES ABOUT ME SO MUCH, BUT I...
BUT I...
?
I...!
FWUMP

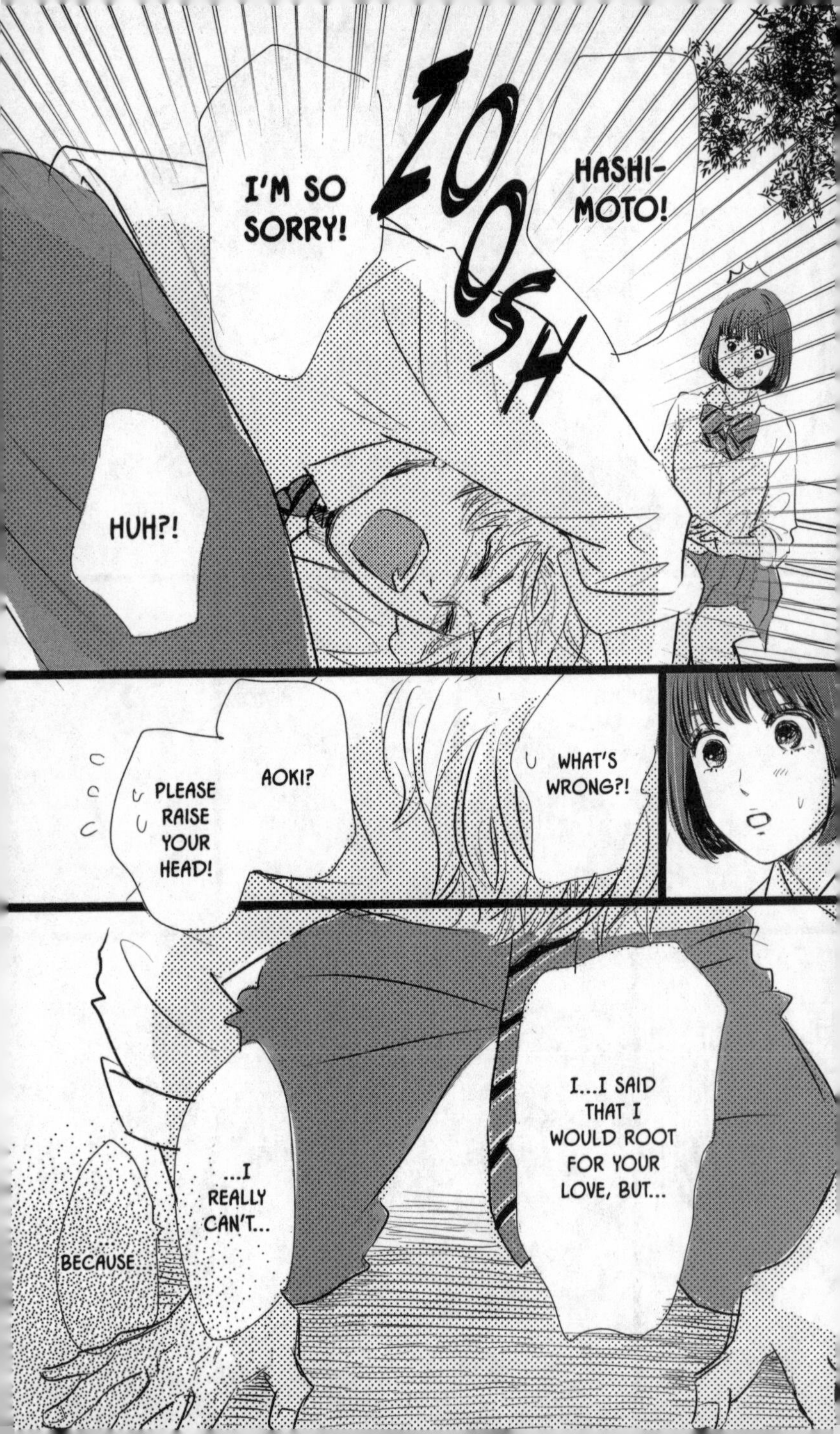
HASHI-MOTO!
ZOOSH
I'M SO SORRY!
HUH?!
WHAT'S WRONG?!
AOKI?
PLEASE RAISE YOUR HEAD!
I...I SAID THAT I WOULD ROOT FOR YOUR LOVE, BUT...
...I REALLY CAN'T...
...BECAUSE...

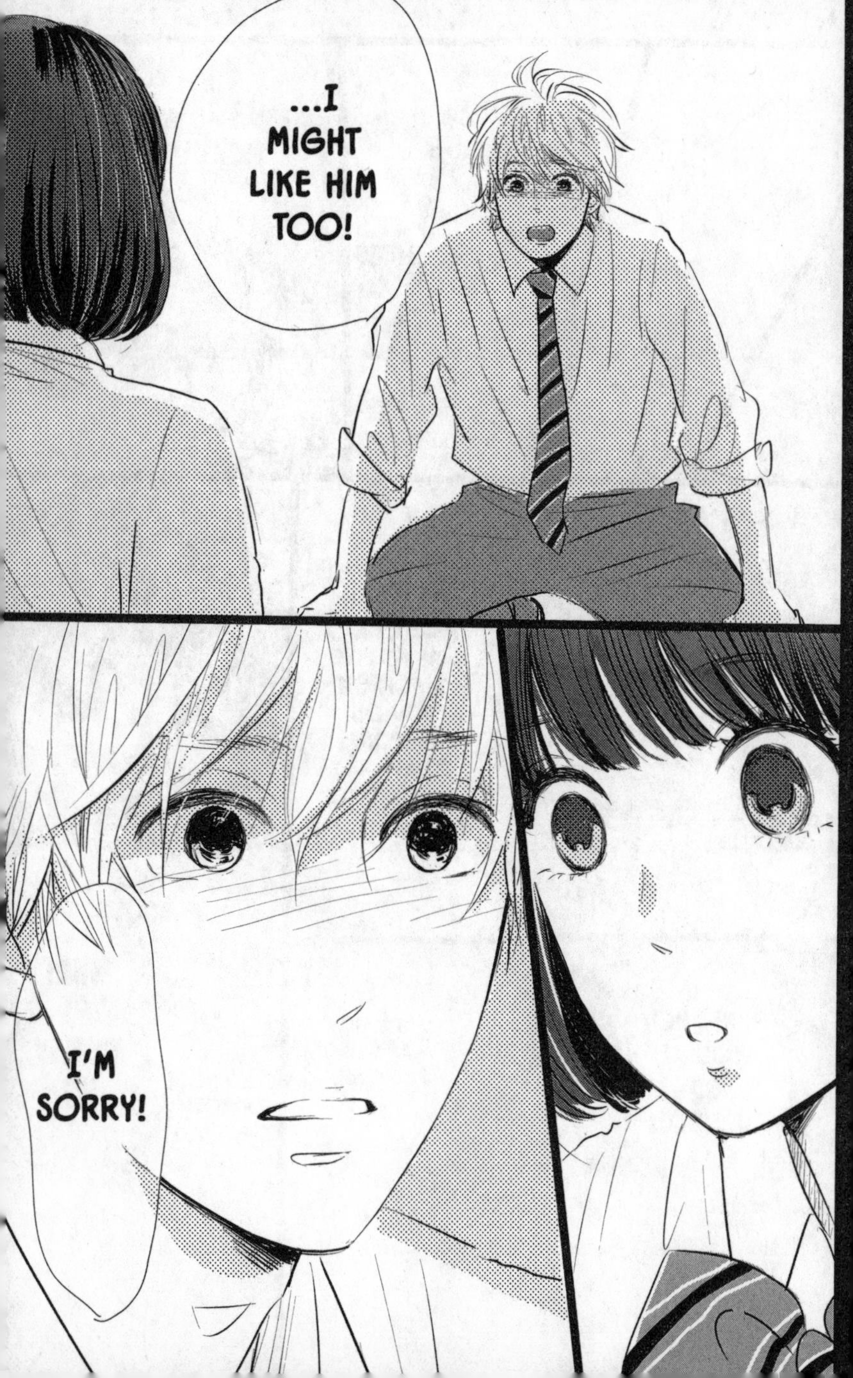
...I MIGHT LIKE HIM TOO!
I'M SORRY!

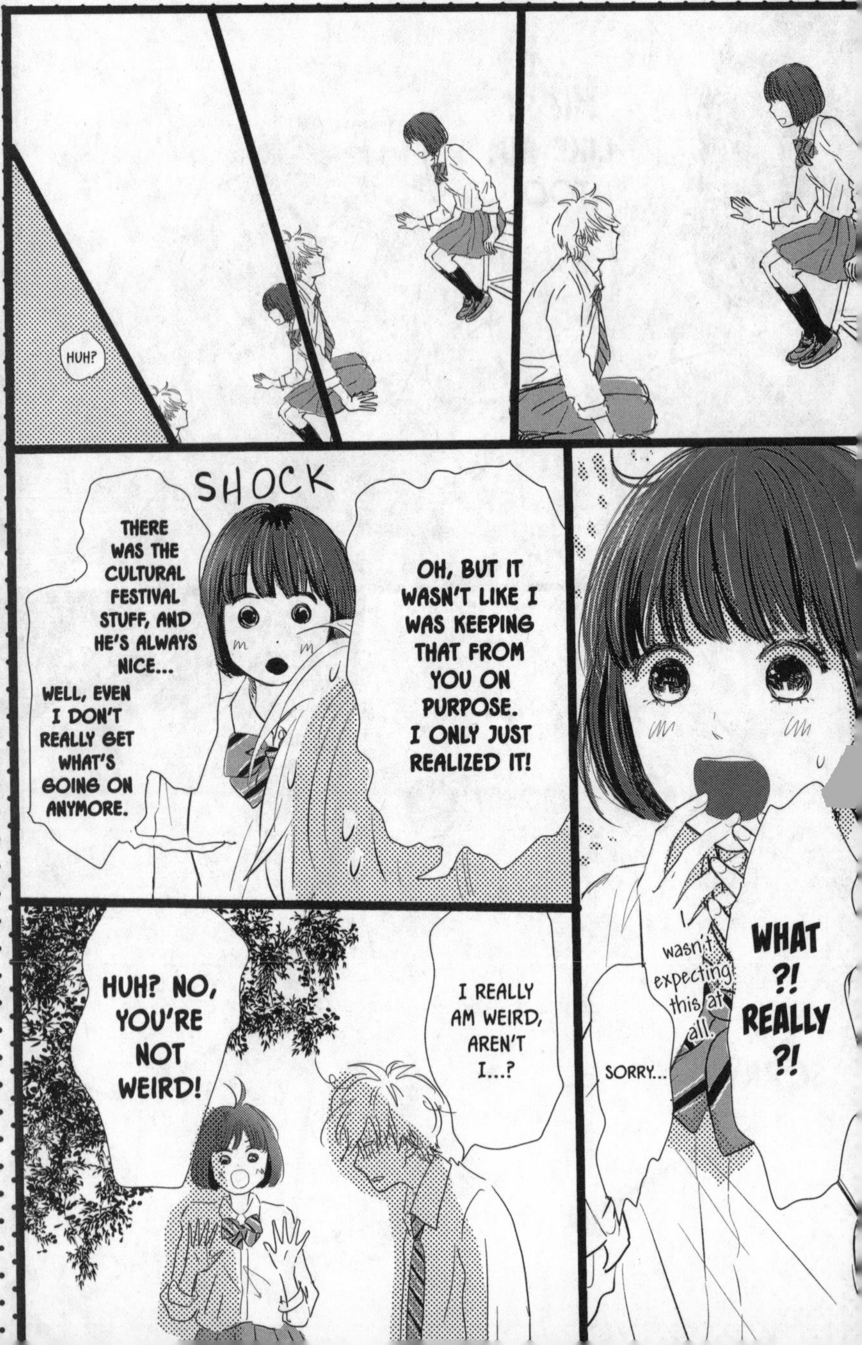
HUH?
WHAT?! REALLY?!
I wasn't expecting this at all.
SORRY...
SHOCK
OH, BUT IT WASN'T LIKE I WAS KEEPING THAT FROM YOU ON PURPOSE. I ONLY JUST REALIZED IT!
THERE WAS THE CULTURAL FESTIVAL STUFF, AND HE'S ALWAYS NICE...
WELL, EVEN I DON'T REALLY GET WHAT'S GOING ON ANYMORE.
I REALLY AM WEIRD, AREN'T I...?
HUH? NO, YOU'RE NOT WEIRD!

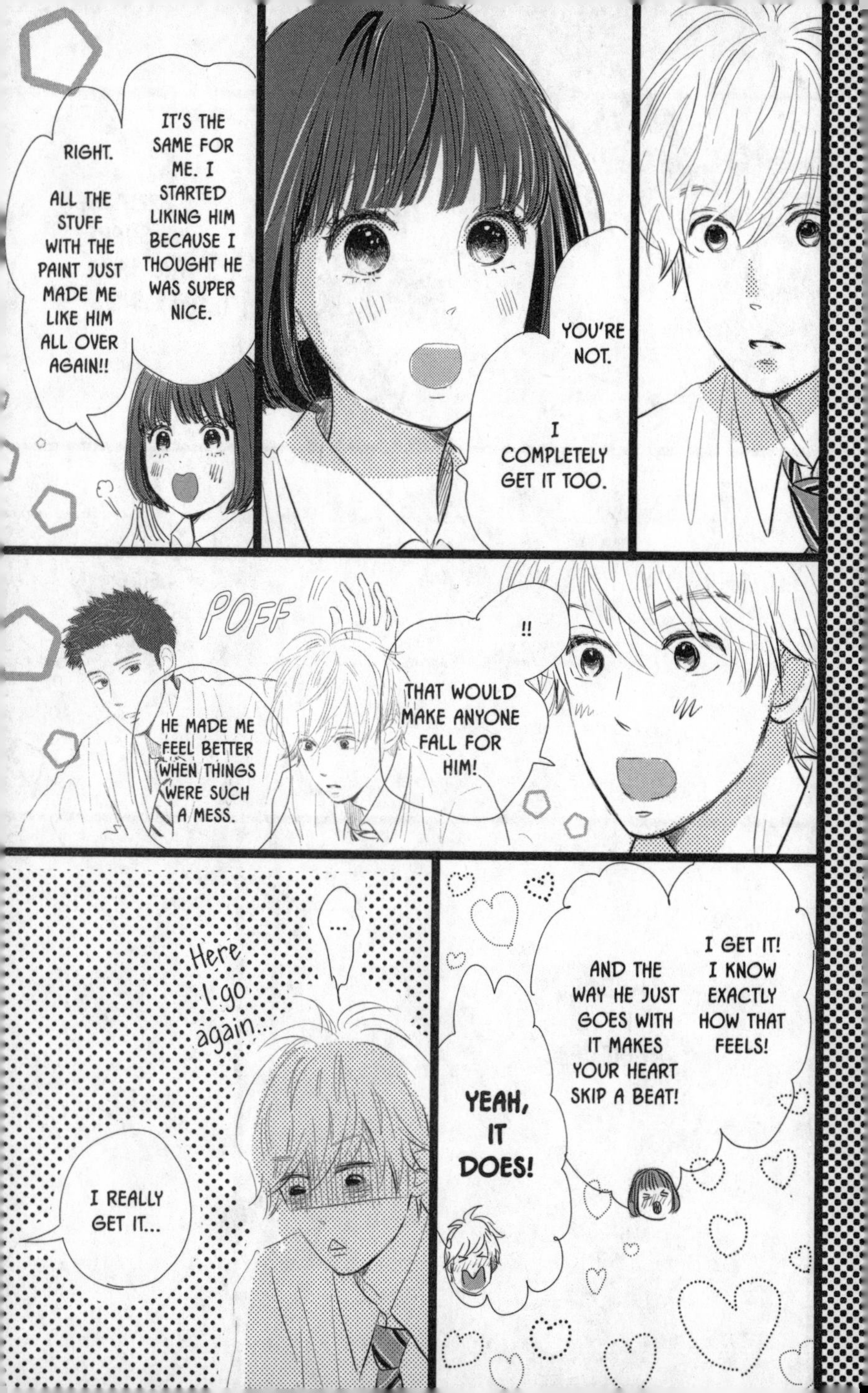
YOU'RE NOT.
I COMPLETELY GET IT TOO.
IT'S THE SAME FOR ME. I STARTED LIKING HIM BECAUSE I THOUGHT HE WAS SUPER NICE.
RIGHT.
ALL THE STUFF WITH THE PAINT JUST MADE ME LIKE HIM ALL OVER AGAIN!!
!!
THAT WOULD MAKE ANYONE FALL FOR HIM!
POFF
HE MADE ME FEEL BETTER WHEN THINGS WERE SUCH A MESS.
I GET IT! I KNOW EXACTLY HOW THAT FEELS!
AND THE WAY HE JUST GOES WITH IT MAKES YOUR HEART SKIP A BEAT!
YEAH, IT DOES!
...
Here I go again...
I REALLY GET IT...

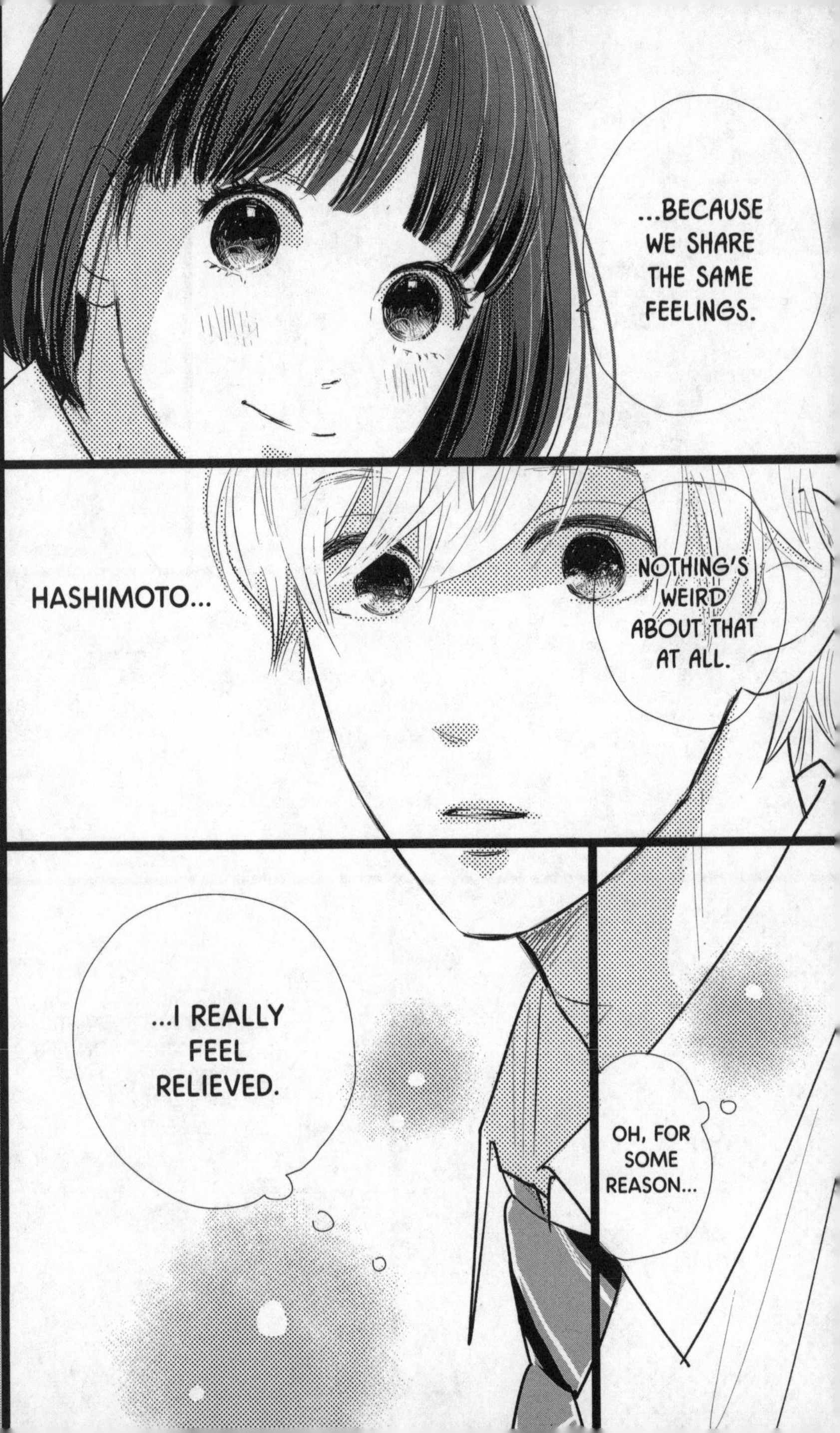
...BECAUSE WE SHARE THE SAME FEELINGS.
NOTHING'S WEIRD ABOUT THAT AT ALL.
HASHIMOTO...
OH, FOR SOME REASON...
...I REALLY FEEL RELIEVED.

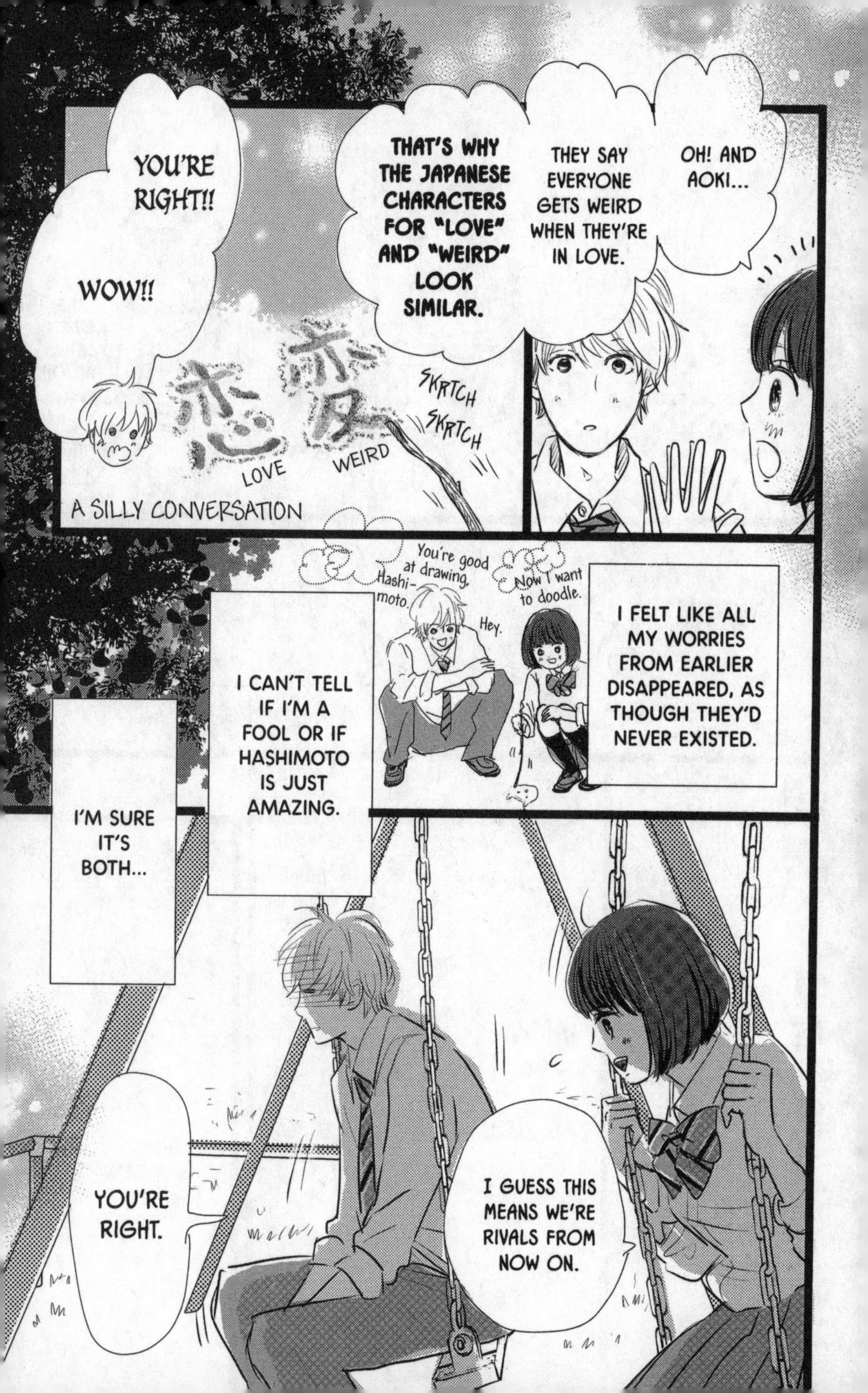

OH! AND AOKI...
THEY SAY EVERYONE GETS WEIRD WHEN THEY'RE IN LOVE.
THAT'S WHY THE JAPANESE CHARACTERS FOR "LOVE" AND "WEIRD" LOOK SIMILAR.
SKRTCH SKRTCH
YOU'RE RIGHT!!
WOW!!
恋 LOVE
変 WEIRD
A SILLY CONVERSATION
I FELT LIKE ALL MY WORRIES FROM EARLIER DISAPPEARED, AS THOUGH THEY'D NEVER EXISTED.
Now I want to doodle.
You're good at drawing, Hashimoto.
Hey.
I CAN'T TELL IF I'M A FOOL OR IF HASHIMOTO IS JUST AMAZING.
I'M SURE IT'S BOTH...
I GUESS THIS MEANS WE'RE RIVALS FROM NOW ON.
YOU'RE RIGHT.

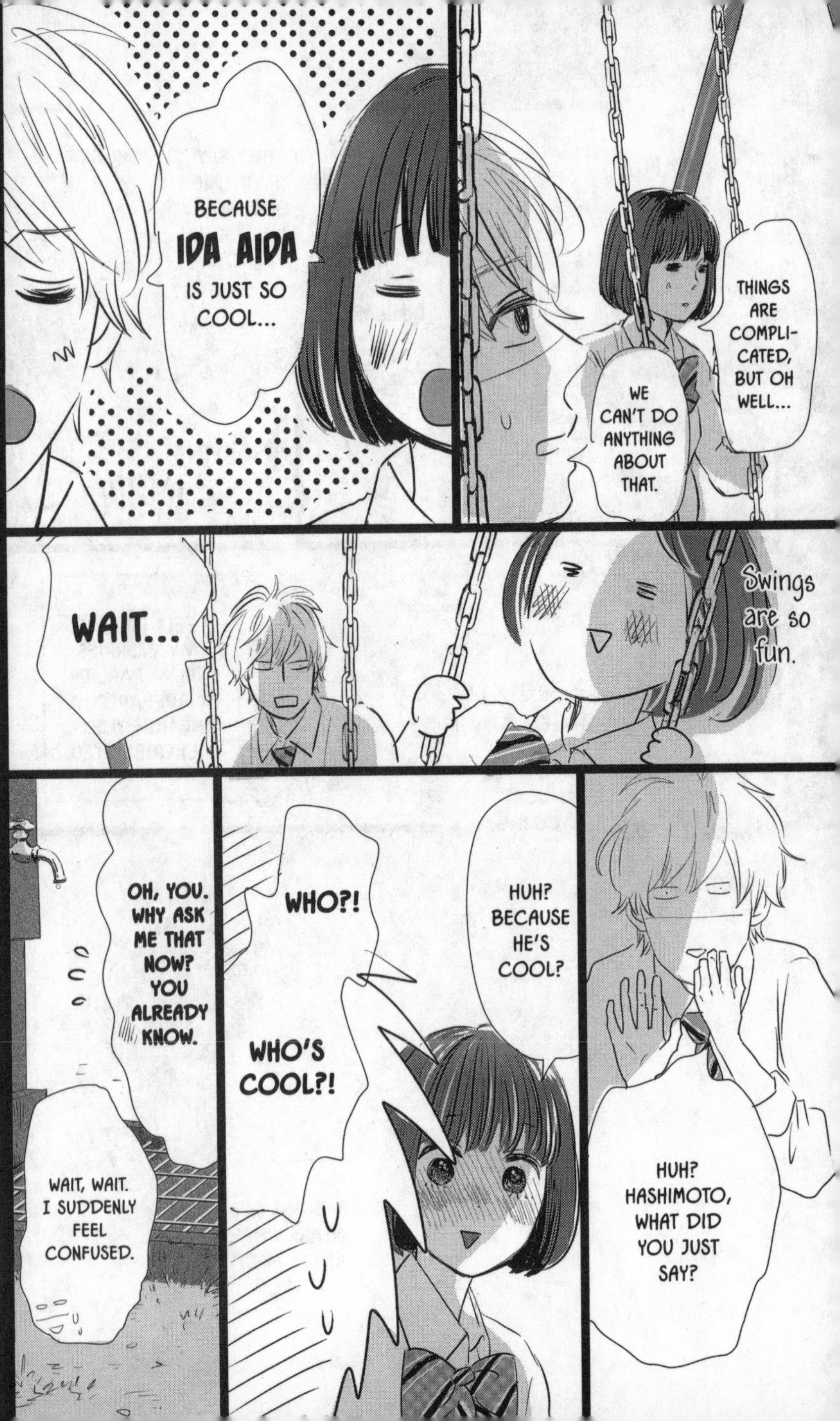
THINGS ARE COMPLICATED, BUT OH WELL...
WE CAN'T DO ANYTHING ABOUT THAT.
BECAUSE IDA AIDA IS JUST SO COOL...
Swings are so fun.
WAIT...
HUH? HASHIMOTO, WHAT DID YOU JUST SAY?
HUH? BECAUSE HE'S COOL?
WHO?!
WHO'S COOL?!
OH, YOU. WHY ASK ME THAT NOW? YOU ALREADY KNOW.
WAIT, WAIT. I SUDDENLY FEEL CONFUSED.

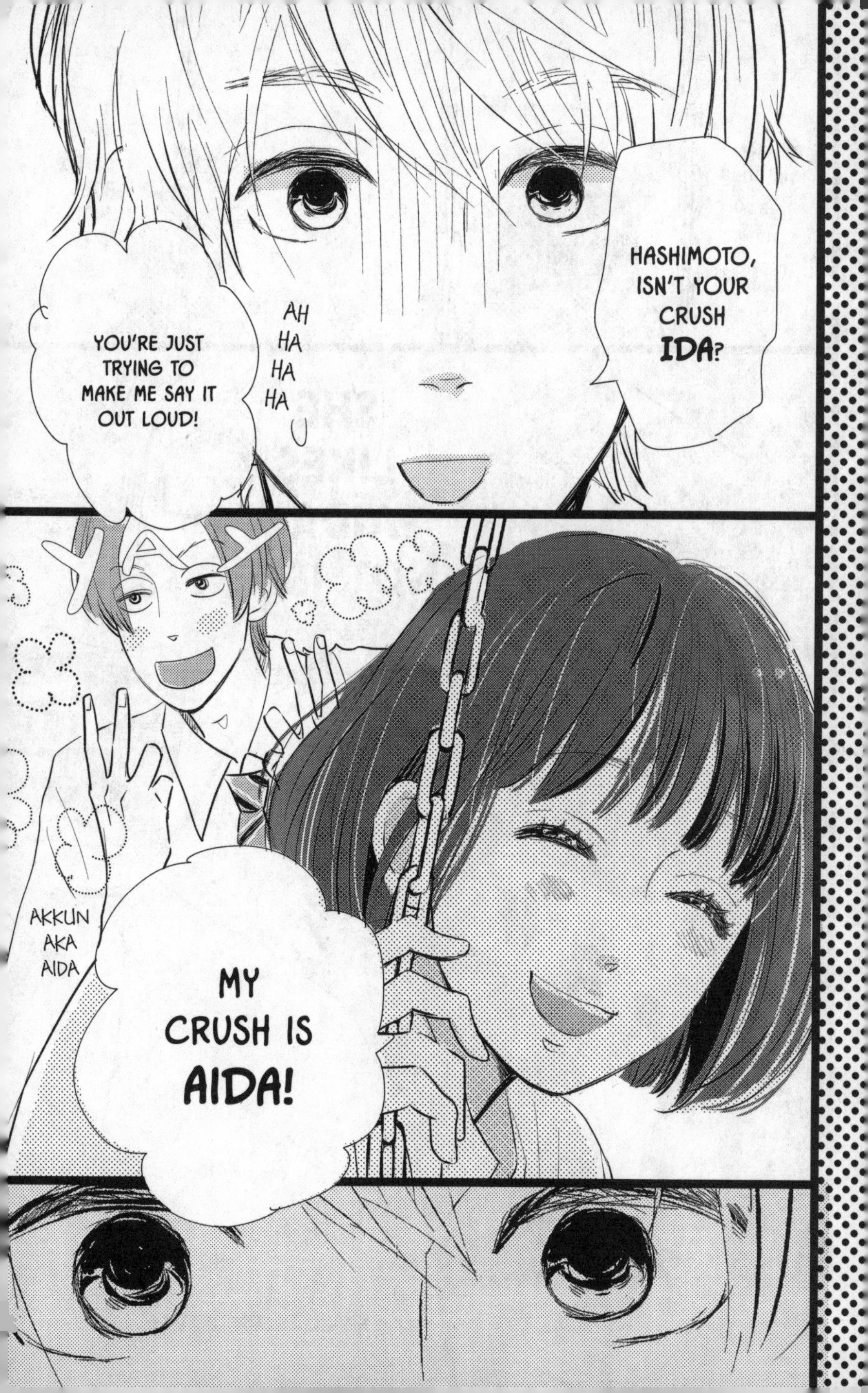
HASHIMOTO, ISN'T YOUR CRUSH IDA?
AH HA HA HA
YOU'RE JUST TRYING TO MAKE ME SAY IT OUT LOUD!
YAY
MY CRUSH IS AIDA!
AKKUN AKA AIDA

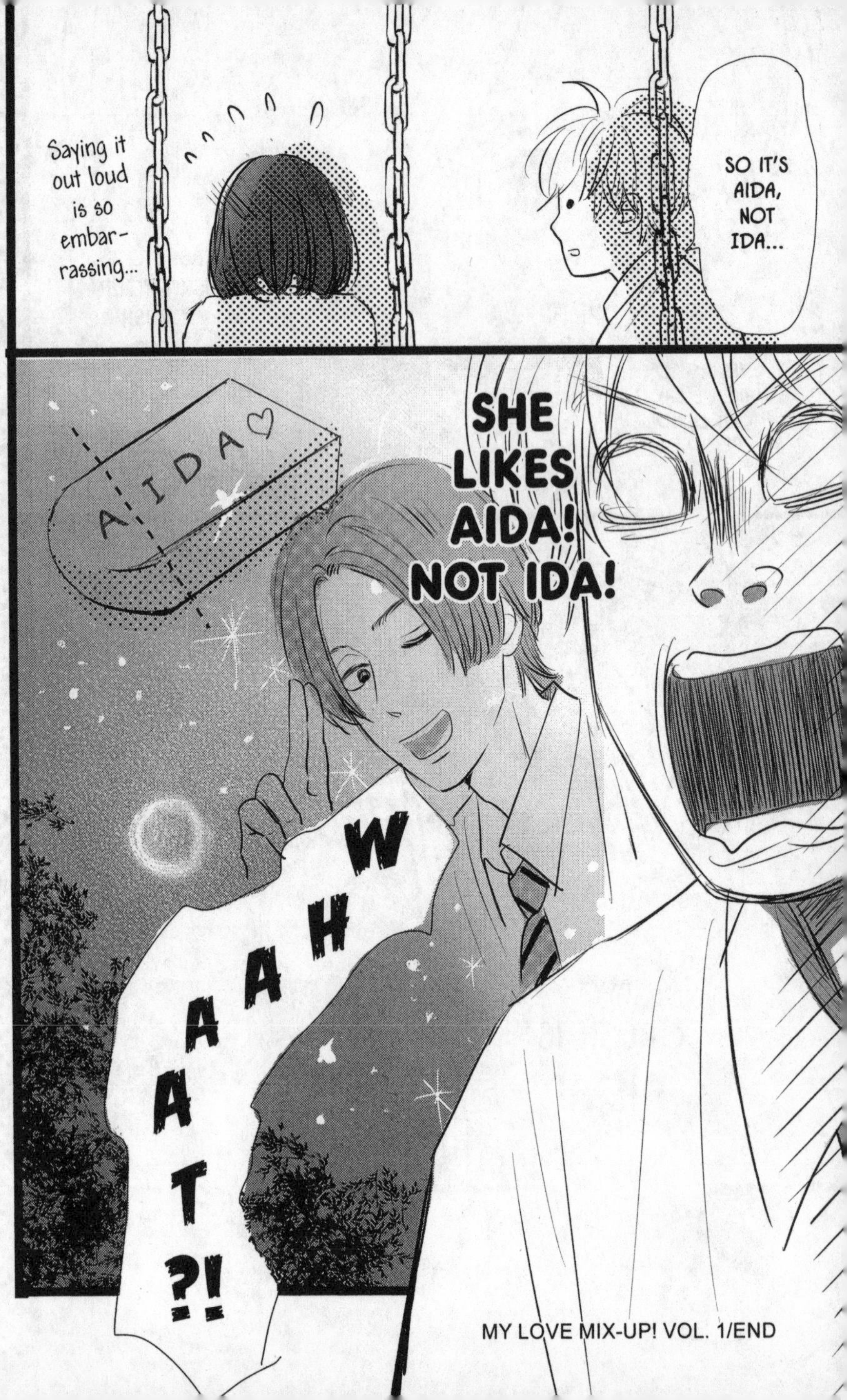
SO IT'S AIDA, NOT IDA...
Saying it out loud is so embarrassing...
AIDA
SHE LIKES AIDA! NOT IDA!
WHAAAT?!

MY LOVE MIX-UP! VOL. 1/END

Hello!

Nice to meet you for the first(?) time. I'm the artist, Aruko. Thank you for picking up volume 1 of *My Love Mix-Up!* I feel like I'm an auntie in the family watching over which way the love between the characters will go with heart-pounding anticipation. I hope you'll watch over them with me. I'll do my very best with my limited abilities to make the adorable characters that Hinekure gave birth to beloved!!

Thanks for your support!!

November 2019

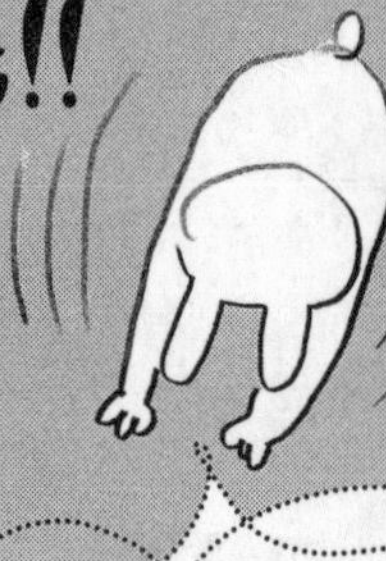

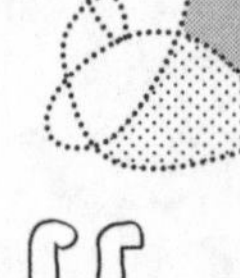

I'm super grateful to my editor Sawada ♡ and my assistant Asai. ♡

Thank you so very much for reading volume 1.

I apologize for abruptly inserting myself here. I'm Wataru, and I've been given the honor of writing the story. I was given the opportunity to work on this manga with Aruko, who I am a huge fan of. I feel deeply moved. Even now, each day I still keep thinking to myself, "This isn't a dream...?" I am truly grateful to Aruko, who has forged such a precious bond with me, and to the editorial departments at *Margaret* and LINE manga!!!

This isn't really an inside scoop, but I met Aruko the other day. I wrote thorough notes about what I wanted to talk about, but the moment I actually met Aruko, I was so nervous, I forgot all about them. By the time I realized, I was on the bullet train home. I was flabbergasted. Aruko was really so wonderful and kind. I'll live with this bittersweet memory in my heart for the rest of my life. Thank you so much.

Wataru Hinekure

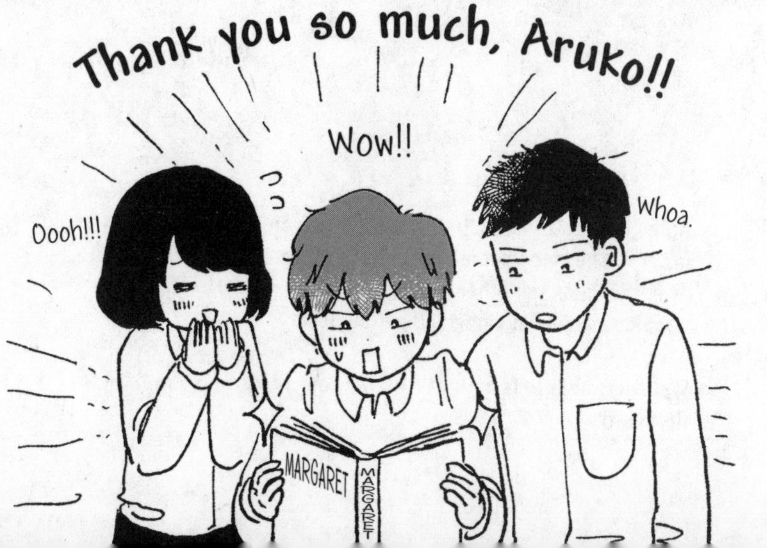
Thank you so much, Aruko!!
Wow!!
Whoa.
Oooh!!!
MARGARET
MARGARET

There are people who claim they start humming subconsciously while walking, which I thought couldn't possibly be something someone could do without being aware of it. However, once the first volume of *My Love Mix-Up!* went on sale, I was thrilled—so thrilled that I almost started subconsciously dancing.

Aruko

I'm thankful volume 1 is out! It would make me so happy if you enjoy it. Personally I really like Hashimoto's face when she's embarrassed.

Wataru Hinekure

Aruko is from Ishikawa Prefecture in Japan and was born on July 26 (a Leo!). She made her manga debut with *Ame Nochi Hare* (Clear After the Rain). Her other works include *Yasuko to Kenji*, and her hobbies include laughing and getting lost.

Wataru Hinekure is a night owl. *My Love Mix-Up!* is Hinekure's first work.

My Love Mix-Up!

Vol. 1
Shojo Beat Edition

STORY BY
Wataru Hinekure

ART BY
Aruko

Translation & Adaptation/Jan Cash
Touch-Up Art & Lettering/Inori Fukuda Trant
Design/Yukiko Whitley
Editor/Nancy Thistlethwaite

KIETA HATSUKOI © 2019 by Wataru Hinekure, Aruko
All rights reserved.
First published in Japan in 2019 by SHUEISHA Inc., Tokyo.
English translation rights arranged by SHUEISHA Inc.

The stories, characters, and incidents mentioned in this
publication are entirely fictional.

Printed in the U.S.A.

Published by VIZ Media, LLC
P.O. Box 77010
San Francisco, CA 94107

10 9 8 7 6 5 4 3 2
First printing, October 2021
Second printing, November 2021

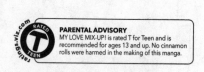

viz.com   shojobeat.com

Stop!
You may be reading the wrong way.

In keeping with the original Japanese comic format, this book reads from right to left—so action, sound effects, and word balloons are completely reversed to preserve the orientation of the original artwork. Check out the diagram shown here to get the hang of things, and then turn to the other side of the book to get started!

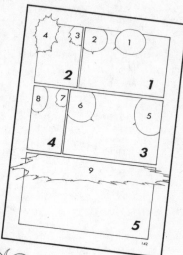